Dallas '63

CONTENTS

INTRODUCTION

I

We the people seem to have the freest book trade in the world. Certainly we have the biggest. Cruise the mighty Amazon, and you will see so many books for sale in the United States today as would require more than four hundred miles of shelving to display them—a bookshelf that would stretch from Boston's Old North Church to Fort McHenry in South Baltimore.

Surely that huge catalog is proof of our extraordinary freedom of expression: The US government does not ban books, because the First Amendment won't allow it. While books are widely banned in states like China and Iran, *no* book may be forbidden by the US government *at any level* (although the CIA censors books by former officers). Where books *are* banned in the United States, the censors tend to be private organizations—church groups, school boards, and other local (busy)bodies roused to purify the public schools or libraries nearby.

Despite such local prohibitions, we can surely find any book we want. After all, it's easy to locate those hot works that once *were* banned by the government as too "obscene" to sell, or mail, until the courts ruled otherwise on First Amendment grounds—*Fanny Hill, Howl, Naked Lunch*. We also have no trouble finding books banned here and there as "antifamily," "Satanic," "racist," and/or "filthy," from *Huckleberry Finn* to *Heather Has Two Mommies* to the Harry Potter series, just to name a few.

II

And yet, the fact that those bold books are all in print, and widely read, does *not* mean that we have the freest book trade in the world. On the contrary: For over half a century, America's vast literary culture has been disparately policed, and imperceptibly contained, by state and corporate entities well placed and perfectly equipped to wipe out wayward writings. Their ad hoc suppressions through the years have been far more effectual than those quixotic bans imposed on classics like *The Catcher in the Rye* and *Fahrenheit 451*. For every one of those bestsellers scandalously purged from some provincial school curriculum, there are many others (we can't know how many) that have been so thoroughly erased that few of us, if any, can remember them, or have ever heard of them.

How have all those books (to quote George Orwell) "dropped into the memory hole" in these United States? As America does *not* ban books, other means—less evident, and so less controversial—have been deployed to vaporize them. Some almost never made it into print, as publishers were privately warned off them from on high, either on the grounds of "national security" or with blunt threats of endless corporate litigation. Other books were signed enthusiastically—then "dumped," as their own publishers mysteriously failed to market them, or even properly distribute them. But it has mainly been the press that stamps out inconvenient books, either by ignoring them, or—most often— laughing them off as "conspiracy theory," despite their soundness (or because of it).

Once out of print, those books are gone. Even if some few of us have not forgotten them, and one might find used copies here and there, these books have disappeared. Missing from the shelves and never mentioned in the press (and seldom mentioned even in our schools), each book thus neutralized might just as well have been destroyed en masse—or never written in the first place, for all their contribution to the public good.

III

The purpose of this series is to bring such vanished books to life— first life for those that never saw the light of day, or barely did, and second life for those that got some notice, or even made a splash, then slipped too quickly out of print, and out of mind.

These books, by and large, were made to disappear, or were hastily forgotten, not because they were too lewd, heretical, or unpatriotic for some touchy group of citizens. *These* books sank without a trace, or faded fast, because they tell the sort of truths that Madison and Jefferson believed our Constitution should pro- tect—truths that the people have the right to know, and needs to know, about our government and other powers that keep us in the dark.

Thus the works on our Forbidden Bookshelf shed new light— for most of us, it's *still* new light—on the most troubling trends and episodes in US history, especially since World War II: America's broad use of former Nazis and ex-Fascists in the Cold War; the Kennedy assassinations, and the murders of Martin Luther King Jr., Orlando Letelier, George Polk, and Paul Wellstone; Ronald Rea- gan's Mafia connections, Richard Nixon's close relationship with Jimmy Hoffa, and the mob's grip on the NFL; America's terroris- tic Phoenix Program in Vietnam, US support for South America's most brutal tyrannies, and CIA involvement in the Middle East; the secret histories of DuPont, ITT, and other giant US corpora- tions; and the long war waged by Wall Street and its allies in real estate on New York City's poor and middle class.

The many vanished books on these forbidden subjects (among others) altogether constitute a shadow history of America—a his- tory that We the People need to know at last, our country having now become a land with billionaires in charge, and millions not allowed to vote, and everybody under full surveillance. Through this series, we intend to pull that necessary history from the shadows at long last—to shed some light on how America got here, and how we might now take it somewhere else.

Mark Crispin Miller

FOREWORD

"They [the FBI] would like to have us fold up and quit." So said the Warren Commission's Chief Counsel J. Lee Rankin in a once-secret session of the Warren Commission.[1] The same quote might be applied to the American public, encouraged by the country's leadership not to look too closely at the implausible story of how their President was gunned down in public, at the height of the Cold War, supposedly by a lone malcontent.

Among the uniquely American citizen army who didn't fold up and quit, but instead took up the investigation that the government had only pretended to conduct, Peter Dale Scott stands out (and not only because he is Canadian). At 86, he has pursued the questions arising from Dallas, on and off, for longer than almost anyone alive. Far more important than longevity has been the amazing breadth and depth of insight and analysis he has brought to the matter.

Readers of his *Deep Politics and the Death of JFK*[2] were treated to a perspective far different from most books on the assassination, typically focused tightly on forensics or anomalies in the Warren Report. His wide-ranging but detailed analysis of the relationships between the individuals and organizations involved in the case was an eye opener for many, and provided a needed broader perspective on the case.

As one small example among many, only someone with Peter Scott's breadth of knowledge would pick up on clues in the Warren Commission's mistranslation of its interview with Oswald's killer Jack Ruby, which when read properly points to a more politically-connected Ruby than the "second lone nut" the Commission tried to paint him as. Ruby had tried to engage Chief Justice Warren by dropping the name of an oil-connected Dallas lawyer named Alfred McLane. Warren knew very well what Ruby was talking about, acknowledging "Alfred was killed in a taxi in New York." But the Commission Hearings managed to mis-spell every instance of McLane's name, in three different ways, seemingly determined to render the transcript meaningless to readers. It was to most, but not to Peter Dale Scott, who knew to whom Ruby and Warren had referred despite the garbled transcription.[3]

More generally, Peter Dale Scott has written cogently on the Commission's portrait of Ruby as a hapless "police buff", which was demolished by the House Assassinations Committee. But he also pointed out that the Committee's depiction of the Jewish Ruby as a figure in the Italian mafia was almost as false. He noted that Ruby's contacts were more frequently with Teamsters-related individuals than "La Cosa Nostra," which put Ruby into the milieu where organized crime and politics blend together.

A second work, *Deep Politics II*, now renamed *Oswald, Mexico, and Deep Politics*,[4] was written early in the period during the 1990s when an avalanche of declassified records were released following the outcry over Oliver Stone's film *JFK*. The book remains a decade later a crucial guide to the mysteries surrounding Lee Harvey Oswald's alleged contacts with Cuban and Soviet embassies in Mexico City just weeks before Kennedy's assassination in Dallas.

The electrifying effect these purported contacts had on the federal response to the assassination is now indisputable; the Warren Commission was formed in large part to combat them. In one now publicly available taped phone call, President Johnson told his old Senate mentor Richard Russell "we've got to take this out of the arena where they're testifying that Khrushchev and Castro did this and did that and kick us into a war that can kill 40 million Americans in an hour . . ."[5]

In an earlier phone call, FBI Director J. Edgar Hoover had informed Johnson that Oswald had been impersonated in Mexico City, an idea that puts a whole new light on the allegations of Communist conspiracy emanating from the visit. This recording, made less than 24 hours after Kennedy's death, would later be erased.[6]

Deep Politics II covered far more ground than just these matters, examining with great patience and insight the maddening conflicts in the CIA records on the Mexico City affair. The book extends beyond Mexico City as well; one important chapter entitled "The Kennedy-CIA Divergence Over Cuba" explored the divergence in goals between the President and the CIA over Cuba, that hottest of hotspots during the Kennedy presidency.

The present work has something in common with both of these earlier books, and extends its vision beyond both. As has been Peter Scott's approach on this and other topics on which he has written, from the Vietnam War to Iran-Contra to 9/11, he focuses closely on details missed by other observers, and then connects them to a far wider perspective.

The first chapters are in some ways a continuation of *Deep Politics II*, with their focus on Oswald, Mexico, and the CIA. Chapter 3 explores the idea that Oswald's government files, chock full of weird contradictions, misinformation, and misspellings, were in reality part of a "marked card" operation as part of the CIA's famed "molehunt." In such an intelligence game, variations in the same information would be placed in different files, as a so-called "barium meal" to see which version (isotope) of the radioactive data would pop up in enemy hands.

The CIA has been a perennial focus of writing on the Kennedy assassination. But Oswald was a Marine after all, and his curious discharge and seemingly abetted defection to the Soviet Union raises questions about Oswald's possible ties to military intelligence agencies. Chapter 4 alerts readers to the gaping hole in relevant records that might shed light on this matter. Peter Scott's focus here is primarily on Marine G-2 records. Readers may also be interested in the lack of Office of Naval Intelligence files and researcher Bill Kelly's discussion of the Assassination Records Review Board's failure to obtain them.[7]

The shift in focus from CIA records to military records pres-
ages the central chapters of this book, which illuminate important
aspects of the hatred of Kennedy that existed in right-wing circles,
both outside and within the U.S. military. Due primarily to Kennedy's perceived "weakness" on foreign policy related to Cuba,
Vietnam, and the Soviet Union, people in the John Birch Society
and other right-wing groups were also inflamed by Kennedy's
approach to civil rights and other domestic matters, in a manner not dissimilar to the paranoid and overwrought perception of
Barack Obama that is felt in some conservative groups today.

The current work focuses on some of the people in these groups
as well as the larger context. Some names are familiar, like that of
Dallas-based former General Edwin Walker. It was Ruby himself
in his jail-cell meeting with Earl Warren who said ". . . if it takes my
life at this moment to say it . . . there is a John Birch Society right
now in activity, and Edwin Walker is one of the top men of this
organization—take it for what it is worth, Chief Justice Warren."[8]

Another familiar name is Joseph Milteer, an organizer for the
right-wing Constitution Party who was taped in early November
1963 predicting that Kennedy would be killed "from an office
building with a high-powered rifle." But as usual Peter Scott has
much more to say than most observers, and brings in less familiar
names such as a Constitution party leading thinker and former
Marine General named Pedro del Valle.

Here the book broaches the topic of coup d'état, and those in
the U.S. and abroad who discussed not only the desire for it but
also the means to bring it about. And an important part of this
discussion is the notion of "false flag" operations, which include
in their planning the pinning of blame on some other person or
group. This notion was hardly unknown—the few handwritten
records left behind by CIA assassinations program head Bill Harvey included the phrase "Cover: planning should include provi-
sion for blaming Sovs. or Czechs in case of blow"[9]

A more prominent example of planning for false-flag operations within the U.S. government is Operation Northwoods, the
once-secret 1962 plans for faking Cuban attacks on U.S. interests in
order to provide the necessary provocation for an invasion. Peter

Scott points out the almost insurrectionary nature of these proposals, which Kennedy immediately rejected. But he places them
in a larger context of such false-flag operations both within the
US—the "discovered" cache of supposed Cuban arms in Venezuela in November 1963 was almost certainly such an operation, and
one not of Kennedy's devising—and outside the U.S. His discussion of the possible meetings between U.S. military planners and
Italians involved in the documented false-flag reign of terror in
that country, if true, is highly troubling.

These central chapters raise the chilling specter of coup d'état,
and connect to the earlier chapters, where the author alerts readers
to the false information planted in pre-assassination government
files connecting Oswald to Cuba. Of particular note is the cable on
the afternoon of the assassination from U.S. Army intelligence in
Texas to the U.S. Strike Command in Florida, saying falsely that
Oswald had "defected to Cuba," something repeated in altered
form by FBI Director Hoover to Robert Kennedy the same day.[10]
According to FBI Agency James Hosty, sources told him that fully
armed warplanes had been sent toward Cuba that afternoon, and
called back.

Was this all perhaps part of a false-flag operation to kill two
birds with one stone—Kennedy and Castro's Cuba? What if
Oswald had not been arrested in Dallas, but instead, as confessed
plot participant John Martino said, was supposed to be killed outside the country (plausibly, in Mexico, on the way to Cuba). With
the "Communist killer" dead, who then would have determined
that the voice on tapped telephone lines in Mexico City was not
that of the now-dead Oswald?

James Galbraith, son of Kennedy's Ambassador to India John
Kenneth Galbraith, recently wrote publicly what he had previously told myself and others privately. Galbraith said that Bill Moy-
ers, who rode Air Force One back from Dallas to Washington on
11/22, sat down next to a forlorn LBJ at one point on the flight, and
Johnson had looked up and said "I wonder if the missiles are flying" (meaning U.S. missiles).[11] What is unknown is whether this
question occurred before or after what we now know was a frantic
attempt to establish the whereabouts of Air Force General Curtis

LeMay, the man in charge of SAC bombers.[12] LeMay was prominent among those military officers chafing under Kennedy—during the Cuban Missile Crisis, LeMay was furious over the blockade plan and told Kennedy "this is almost as bad as the appeasement at Munich."[13]

A fascinating transitional chapter weaves together discussion of Watergate, the too-often ignored figure of William Pawley, and the enigma of Robert Kennedy's silence. In earlier works Peter Scott showed how a "phase one" depiction of Oswald as a Communist killer was systematically morphed into a politically safer "phase two" portrait of a disaffected Marxist loner. In the present work, the author explores the genesis of a "phase three" story that JFK was killed by Cubans connected directly to Robert Kennedy. The origins of this false but powerful story, a "political H bomb in the words of columnist Drew Pearson," can perhaps be traced to events before the assassination, and then later re-emerged during calls for a re-investigation of JFK's murder in 1967. This story may very well have been the key to ensuring the Attorney General's silence on his own brother's murder.

The final chapters of the present book widen the focus even further, beyond discussion of a possible coup d'état among disgruntled military and non-military right-wingers. And the topics under discussion widen beyond the Kennedy assassination to other "anomalous events" from Watergate to the October Surprise to 9/11, and factors they have in common. Here Peter Scott swings back around to discussions of deep politics and the "deep state", and his overarching thesis regarding the American political system, that the overt political system is part of a larger system, and that this larger system uses violence when the mechanisms of the overt state are not sufficient.

With such a grand scope, it may be easy for naysayers to dismiss Peter Scott, to say that too much of what is presented is incomplete or speculative. Such is the nature of the territory in which his work dwells, and of course caution is warranted. The author himself, despite asking very big questions, is careful to distinguish what is proven, what is likely, and what is simply a possibility.

I would say to skeptics that Peter Dale Scott has been very right before, when working with little data, and therefore is someone well worth paying attention to. A prime example of this is Kennedy's Vietnam policy. Back in the 1970s when every historian simply knew that Johnson had just continued Kennedy's policies with respect to Vietnam, Peter Scott's was a voice in the wilderness. Before even the publication of the text of the now-famous NSAM-273, the one policy statement whose drafting encompassed both administrations, Peter Scott pored over the few available tea leaves and discerned the troubling indications that policy had subtly but markedly changed under Johnson. Decades later, with the declassification of formerly-secret 1963 plans for the complete withdrawal from Vietnam,[14] the memoirs of Robert McNamara, and much more, we have a far more complete picture. And while ultimate questions of intent are difficult and according to the author himself a waste of time, history has vindicated his voice in the wilderness, and mainstream history has largely swung around in the face of overwhelming documentary evidence. Kennedy was in the process of executing a withdrawal from Vietnam at the moment of his death, and this withdrawal was quietly discontinued.

Peter Dale Scott is indeed well worth listening to. This book is the culmination of his earlier work on the Kennedy assassination, and its connections to the larger political forces at work. If you want to see where the evidence has led one very informed person who has studied these matters for longer than almost anyone, read on.

Rex Bradford

PREFACE

Peter's book is a terrific read. If you are fascinated by politics, it's like chicken soup for the psyche. Nonetheless, I can hear a few dissenting voices asking, "How do you put your arms around all the different aspects of his inquiry?"

The first chapter is an overview that sets the stage. Peter discusses the tension between detente and hegemony. When you look at the world of the sixties and seventies in that light, events take new significance.

The second chapter describes how the CIA, the DFS and drug trafficking networks have been exempt from the rule of law, and how this exemption has resulted in suppression of much of the rich evidence surrounding the JFK assassination.

The third chapter, "Oswald and the Hunt for Popov's Mole," is my favorite chapter. When I read an earlier version of this chapter in 2009, Peter's explanation of how Oswald's file was used for molehunts during the last four years of his life was the inspiration for my book *State Secret*.

Chapter 4 is not for the timid. Peter analyzes the actions of naval intelligence, marine intelligence, the Office of Special Investigations, and the State Department, among others. At the end, he puts forward the hypothesis that the State Department and military intelligence were at loggerheads about the Oswald case—again, throughout the last four years of his life. At this point, Peter is setting up the parameters of the deep state and how its factions compete with each other.

Chapter 5 is the heart of the book. Peter describes our present governance as a "dyadic deep state" as Wall Street on one side and the radical right on the other. It's much like what Carl Oglesby described as the Yankee-Cowboy War. The difference is that Peter sees these forces as dependent on one another even as they tug at each other for dominance in various spheres. Peter suggests that these two forces may have revolted against JFK and brought him down.

Chapter 6 is about William Pawley. A cold, distant figure becomes very alive in these pages. He may have been the first American to suggest to Eisenhower that Castro should be assassinated. How did someone often described as a "former ambassador" of the fifties have his fingers in so many public and private schemes right up until the rise of Reagan?

Chapter 7 is what I call the story of Continuity of Government (COG). In my mind, the COG network at some point dedicated itself to becoming a power base all its own. Peter discusses several deep events in US history—Dallas, Watergate, the October Surprise of 1980, Iran-Contra, and 9/11—and looks at how the COG network repeatedly gained more power for itself.

In the final chapter, the discussion turns to how JFK, LBJ, Nixon, Ford and Carter were all brought down by the deep state. By 1980, the turnover in power from the presidency to these forces was largely complete.

What I remain most struck by is how the COG network—specifically its aspect as the White House Communications Agency (WHCA)—was right in the thick of the story of JFK's assassination. I'm always most interested in documents, and tapes in particular. What happened to the records of the WHCA transmissions during the hours after Kennedy's death, and the Secret Service communications in the hours before and after his death? Mostly they went into a deep dark hole.

That deep dark hole represents much of the history of the United States. Peter guides us into and through the darkness.

Peter says that he is wrapping up his work on JFK and other subjects so he can devote himself to poetry. I get it. Consider this book as another form of poetry.

Bill Simpich

AUTHOR'S NOTE

Previous Versions of These Chapters

A version of Chapter 2 was published as "Overview: The CIA, the Drug Traffic, and Oswald in Mexico, History-Matters.com, December 2000, www.history-matters.com/pds/dp3_overview. htm.

A version of Chapter 3 was first published as "Oswald and the Hunt for Popov's Mole," The Fourth Decade, IV, 3, March 1994.

A version of Chapter 6 was first published as "William Pawley, the Kennedy Assassination, and Watergate: TILT and the "Phase Three" Story of Clare Boothe Luce," GlobalReseearch. ca, November 28, 2012, http://www.globalresearch.ca/william-pawley-the-kennedy-assassination-and-watergate-tilt-and-the-phase-three-story-of-clare-boothe-luce/5313486.

A version of Chapter 7 was first published as "The Hidden Government Group Linking JFK, Watergate, Iran-Contra and 9/11," WhoWhatWhy, October 5, 2014, http://whowhatwhy.com/2014/10/05/the-hidden-government-group-linking-jfk-watergate-iran-contra-and-911/.

A version of Chapter 8 was first published as "The Fates of American Presidents Who Challenged the Deep State (1963–1980)," The Asia-Pacific Journal: Japan Focus, November 2, 2014, http://japan-focus.org/-Peter_Dale-Scott/4206.

Abbreviated Citations

Throughout this book WR, WH, and WCD refer to the Report, Hearings, and unpublished Documents of the Warren Commission (1964); AR and AH refer to the Report and Hearings of the House Select Committee on Assassinations (1979).

NARA #000-00000-00000 refers to a document RIF (reference) number in the National Archives. Nearly all those cited in this book can be seen on line by searching for them by the RIF 13-digit number on the Mary Ferrell Foundation website, http://www.maryferrell.org. At the same website can also be seen all the records in the preceding paragraph, as well as citations to the Watergate Hearings.

Dallas '63

1

Introduction: The JFK Assassination as a Structural Deep Event

Two kinds of power can be discerned at work in the byzantine processes of American politics. In *The American Deep State*, I used two terms from Hannah Arendt (following Thucydides) to describe them: "persuasion through arguments" (πείθειν), versus "coercion" by force and violence (βία)."[15] In another essay, Arendt wrote that only the former was true power: "violence and power [i.e., persuasive power] are not the same. . . . Power and violence are opposites; where the one rules absolutely, the other is absent."[16] One can add that a persuasive politics is one of openness, whereas a violent politics is usually shrouded in exclusion and secrecy.

The distinction is both extremely important and hard to define precisely; a number of other opposing terms can be used, that are roughly but not exactly coterminous. Arendt herself also writes of "top down" and "bottom up" power, others of egalitarian or democratic versus oppressive power. It is clear that top-down power is not always violent, just as democratic power is not always non-violent. However the terms "persuasive," "bottom-up," and "democratic," even if not synonymous or exactly coterminous, help us to focus on a Socratic ideal of influence by persuasion that has, though the centuries, been a lodestar of western civilization. By contrast their opposites—"violence," "top-down," "repressive"—epitomize what I believe civilization should be moving away from.

These dyadic alternatives represent not just alternative ideologies and life-styles, but also divisions in most large-scale societies and bureaucracies. Here we find agencies, like the U.S. State Department, whose stated aim is diplomatic persuasion, and other agencies, like the Pentagon, whose business, ultimately, is violence. In America always, but particularly in the Kennedy era, we have seen occasional confrontations between the two tendencies on both the bureaucratic and also the popular levels: witness the wrangles over the meaning and application of the Second Amendment.

In this book I would also like to paraphrase Arendt's contrast between power and violence by using two common terms with a common Greek origin: true power unites consolidates a society through *dialogue*; violence divides a society through the *dialectics* inherent in violence. For whereas power tends to resolve and reduce social tensions through persuasion, violence tends to perpetuate them by creating resentment and opposition.

As authors from Aeschylus to Jacques Ellul have written, "violence creates violence."[17] The dialectical response may be delayed for centuries, as in pre-revolutionary France or Tsarist Russia, but violence can create social divisions that are very difficult to resolve or dissipate. America is an outstanding exemplar of both forces: the product of a revolution proclaiming equality, it is still living with the violent consequences of slavery.

In foreign policy Since World War Two, American foreign policy has witnessed the interplay of two opposing strategies towards the Soviet Union: coexistence through persuasive diplomacy at the United Nations, versus military dominance disguised by the code phrase "Peace Through Strength." The title of a policy book by statesman-financier Bernard Baruch in 1952, "Peace Through Strength" was a slogan used by Ronald Reagan (and by Republican platforms since) to describe an overt strategy of global domination and American hegemony. It was used to proclaim the official end of an earlier U.S. foreign policy, dating from the end of Eisenhower administration to the beginning of Jimmy Carter's—a policy of détente.

But the Pax Americana in the post-Reagan era of U.S. hegemony has not been peaceful at all, quite the reverse. As former U.S. Army officer Andrew Bacevich has commented, "belief in the efficacy of military power almost inevitably breeds the temptation to put that power to work. 'Peace through strength' easily enough becomes 'peace through war.'"[18] In my last chapter I compare the last years of the Pax Americana today to the last years of the Pax Britannica in the late 19th Century, when hubristic over-reaching led dialectically to a series of minor conflicts, followed by a World War.

The tension between the two American policies, détente versus hegemony, has been acute since the fall of the Berlin Wall. Jack Matlock, former U.S. ambassador to Moscow and an adviser on Russian affairs to Reagan and G.H.W. Bush, has said more than once that when Gorbachev, after negotiations the West, agreed in 1990 to pull back Soviet troops in Eastern Europe, the West in return gave a "clear commitment" not to expand.[19]

Yet the American response was in fact quite different. As Matlock wrote recently in the *Washington Post*,

> President Bill Clinton supported . . . the expansion of NATO to include former Warsaw Pact countries. Those moves seemed to violate the understanding that the United States would not take advantage of the Soviet retreat from Eastern Europe. . . . [To Putin] President George W. Bush . . . delivered the diplomatic equivalent of swift kicks to the groin: further expansion of NATO in the Baltics and the Balkans, and plans for American bases there.[20]

On one level it is possible to view American foreign policy of the last half century as one of a shifting ebb and flow between the two policies, détente versus hegemony. But on another level there has been an unchecked and significant structural change between the agencies advocating them. Since World War Two there has been a visible loss of power by those U.S. agencies advocating détente (most notably the State Department) to the agencies advocating expansion and hegemony (the Department of Defense, and its post-war ally in intervention, the CIA).

The massive projection of U.S. wealth and power abroad has produced a massive increase of covert unchecked power in

Washington, to the extent that we now have what the journalists
Dana Priest and William Arkin have called

> two governments: the one its citizens were familiar with,
> operated more or less in the open: the other a parallel top
> secret government whose parts had mushroomed in less
> than a decade into a gigantic, sprawling universe of its own,
> visible to only a carefully vetted cadre—and its entirety . . .
> visible only to God.[21]

The latter has become so powerful that some of us have come to
call it the "deep state."[22]

Mike Lofgren has described the visible public state as "the tip
of the iceberg," and the covert deep state as "the subsurface part of
the iceberg."[23] But this metaphor, though spatially useful, misses
an important difference between the two levels. The public state
that we see is a defined structure; the deep state, in contrast, passes
through covert agencies into an undefined system, as difficult to
define, but also as real and powerful, as a weather system. More
specifically, it interacts not only with the public state but also with
higher sources of its power: most significantly with the financial
institutions of Wall Street that were responsible for forcing a CIA
on a reluctant President Truman in the first place.[24]

Because of this interaction, I find myself sometimes using
"deep state" in an inclusive sense, to refer to all those forces outside
the public state with the power to influence its policies, and more
often using "deep state" in a restrictive sense, meaning those active
covert agencies in and around Washington, that sometimes take
guidance in their policies, not from the White House, but from the
deep state as a whole. This ambiguity in language may sometimes
be confusing, but reflects the ambiguity and diffuseness of deep
power itself.

For example, we must also take into account the private consulting firms, like Booz Allen Hamilton, to which 70 percent of
America's huge intelligence budget is now outsourced.[25] And they
in turn work with the huge international oil firms and other mul-
tinational corporations that project a U.S. presence throughout the

world.[26] These corporations, and oil companies in particular, desire U.S. hegemony as a guarantee to their overseas investments, and as an inducement to governments in remote places like Kazakhstan to be open to influence from America, not just from their immediate neighbors Russia and Iran.

The power of the public state is based on the constitution and periodic elections, and is thus limited by checks and balances. The power of the covert deep state, in contrast, is unchecked; and has expanded as the global U.S. presence has expanded. The two kinds of power were destined to come into conflict. The public state aims at openness and persuasion. The deep state represents the opposite, intervention by secrecy and violence.

This is a book about the assassination of President John F. Kennedy, who after the brush with nuclear war in the Cuban Missile Crisis took initial steps to reduce the role of hegemonic violence in American foreign policy. But on another level this is also a book tracing, especially in its last chapter, how the forces of hegemonic violence in America came to be prevalent over the once pre-dominant forces in America calling for containment, parity, and coexistence.

It is a central proposition of this book that the road to U.S. hegemony must be understood as in part a consequence of a series of structural deep events. And this series began with the assassination in 1963 of a president who was moving to change U.S. policies with respect to Cuba, Vietnam, and above all the Soviet Union.

By "structural deep events" I mean events that are never fully understood, arise out of ongoing covert processes, have political consequences that enlarge covert government, and are subsequently covered up by demonstrable omissions and falsifications in historic records. Here the assassination in Dallas can be compared to later structural deep events, notably Watergate and 9/11.[27]

I cannot say often enough that I am not attributing all these deep events to any single agency or "secret team." Nor is the purpose of this book to identify the president's killers. But in Chapter 2 I will show how alleged evidence about Lee Harvey Oswald in Mexico was manipulated and altered by elements in the CIA and their Mexican clients, the Dirección Federal de Seguridad (DFS).

In other words, elements in the U.S. Government (not limited to the CIA) were involved in the assassination cover-up.

In Chapter 3 we will see that Oswald, far from being a neglected "lone nut," had generated government files that were being manipulated and altered from at least the time of his alleged defection to the Soviet Union in 1959. In Chapter 4, we will see how these manipulated files became the subject of extended disagreement between the State Department, on the one hand, and military intelligence agencies, on the other—at a time when State and Pentagon were also divided on the issue of coexistence with Cuba and the Soviet Union, or alternatively the rollback of communism by invading Cuba.

Glenview, Illinois, the home of Marine Intelligence files on Oswald, had also hosted a meeting in 1960 of the Christian Anti-Communist Crusade (CACC) that attacked Eisenhower's growing rapprochement with Moscow. The CACC was part of a well-funded interlocking right-wing complex of anti-détente organizations that also included the John Birch Society and the American Security Council.

I deal with the assassination itself in Chapter 5, and show how some elements in this Birchite right-wing complex exploited the assassination for political purposes. This paralleled the manipulation of the U.S. official investigation of the assassination, in a brief vain attempt to implicate a Cuban, Paulino Sierra Martinez. (Sierra had been working, at the request of Robert Kennedy, to move out of the United States Cuban exile groups who had been attacking Soviet ships in Havana harbor.) Some in the Birchite complex may even have had prior knowledge of the assassination.

In Chapter 6 I look at the mysterious movements of a wealthy right-wing industrialist, William Pawley, a man with Birch Society connections who also had the ear of Republican presidents Eisenhower and Nixon. In particular we shall look at how a mysterious raid into Cuba the summer before the assassination, the so-called Bayo-Pawley mission (involving at least two of the future Watergate burglars), may have been planned precisely to ensure that the CIA, *Life,* President Nixon, and perhaps even the Kennedy family, would later be coerced into an assassination cover-up.

In moving from a focus on Oswald's files to a focus on the assassination itself, this book will survey many different aspects of the American deep state, from those forces underpinning the power of the Kennedy White House to those opposed to the Kennedy White House. In my last two chapters I will argue that a showdown in the 1960s and 1970s between those two opposing attitudes to power—the open forces of democratic persuasion (the public state) versus the exclusive and covert forces of violence and dominance (the deep state), led to a series of structural deep events: Dallas, Watergate, and the so-called October Surprise of 1980. All three terminated the careers of presidents who had attempted to cut back the growing power of the CIA.

In Chapter 7 I will argue that these structural deep events (even though not the work of a single mastermind or secret team) were nonetheless all inter-connected, arising from a common milieu and with certain recurring characteristics.

In Chapter 8 I shall argue also that in the same two decades embracing the Vietnam War (1960–1980), the growing unchecked power of the deep state contested and repeatedly overcame the democratically elected authority of the White House. Three presidents in this period —Kennedy, Nixon, and Carter—took steps to challenge the growing power of the CIA; and in diverse ways all three saw their political careers terminated by structural deep events: assassination, Watergate, and the so-called October Surprise. (Less dramatically, the careers of Johnson and Ford were also ended.)

But in this unfortunate and very conflicted period in U.S. presidential history, the first of these shocks to White House power came from the gunshots in Dallas in 1963.

2

The CIA, the Drug Traffic, and Oswald in Mexico

Overview: The Mexican CIA-Mob Nexus

Those who have spent years trying to assess the role of the Kennedy assassination in US history are accustomed to the debate between structuralists and conspiratorialists. In the first camp are those who argue, in the spirit of Marx and Weber, that the history of a major power is determined by large social forces; thus the accident of an assassination, even if conspiratorial, is not an event altering history. (On this point Noam Chomsky and Alex Cockburn agree with the mainstream US media they normally criticize.)

At the other end of the spectrum are those who talk of an Invisible Government or Secret Team, who believe that surface events and institutions are continuously manipulated by unseen forces. For these people the assassination exemplifies the operation of fundamental historical forces, not a disruption of them.

For years I have attempted to formulate a third or middle position. To do so I have relied on distinctions formulated partly in neologisms or invented terms. Over forty years ago I postulated that our overt political processes were at times seriously contaminated by manipulative covert politics or *parapolitics*, which I then defined as "a system or practice of politics in which accountability is consciously diminished."[28] In *Deep Politics and the Death of JFK*, I moved towards a less conspiratorial middle alternative. I discussed instead the interactions of what I called deep political processes, emanating from plural power sources and all only occasionally visible, all usually repressed rather than recognized. In contrast to parapolitical processes, those of deep politics are open-ended, not securely within anyone's power or intentions.

In 1995 I brought out *Deep Politics II* (since reissued as *Oswald, Mexico, and Deep Politics*),[29] which I thought of at the time as a case study in deep politics: how secret U.S. government reports on Oswald in Mexico became a reason to cover up the facts about the assassination of JFK. But it was also a specialized study, since in this case most of the repressed records of events, now declassified, occurred within the workings of the CIA, FBI, military intelligence, or their zones of influence. It was hence largely a study in parapolitics. It verged into true deep politics only near the end, when it described how a collaborating Mexican agency, the DFS (Dirección Federal de Seguridad) was deeply involved in the international drug traffic. *Deep Politics*, in contrast, looked continuously at the interaction between government and other social forces, such as the drug traffic.

Both books represented an alternative kind of history, or what I call deep history. Deep history differs from history in two respects. First, it is an account of suppressed events, at odds with the publicly accepted history of this country. (One might say that history is the record of politics; deep history, the record of deep politics.) Second, deep history is often restored from records which were themselves once repressed. In short, deep history is a reconstructed account of events denied by the public records from which history is normally composed.[30]

A key example concerns a tape of someone calling himself "Lee Oswald," discussing in a phone call to the Soviet Embassy about having met a consul there by the name of Kostikov, a KGB agent. As we shall see, this tape should have been preserved and investigated as a prime piece of evidence to frame Oswald as an assassin. We have documentary evidence, initially suppressed, that one day after the President's murder this tape was listened to by FBI agents in Dallas, who determined that the speaker was in fact not Lee Harvey Oswald. Yet almost immediately this event was denied by other reports, including cables claiming—falsely—that the tape had already been destroyed before the assassination.

A brief but important digression here about history. Most people assume that "history" simply refers to what has happened but is now gone. In fact the dictionary reminds us that the first meaning of the word (cognate to the word "story") is to a narrative or *record* of events, and only after that to "the *events* forming the subject matter of history."[31] What of events whose records are destroyed or falsified? These dictionary definitions seem to assume that what is true is also what is recorded.

There is thus a latent bias in the evolution of the word "history" that is related to the structuralist, rationalist assumptions referred to in my first paragraph. History (or at least what I like to call archival history) has always been the way a culture chooses to record and remember itself; and it tends to treat official records with a respect they do not always deserve.

It is reasonable to talk about the CIA records in this book as suppressed, as so many of them were never allowed to reach even the Warren Commission, let alone the public, until up to three decades later with the Assassination Records Review Board (ARRB). Thus neither the Commission nor the American public were allowed to hear about allegations that Oswald had had sexual relations with two employees of the Cuban Embassy in Mexico City, that at least one of these liaisons (with Silvia Durán) had been part of an international Communist plot against Kennedy, and that Durán had admitted this (albeit under torture) in response to questions from the Mexican DFS or secret police.

More importantly, the CIA and FBI suppressed a major clue to the existence of a pre-assassination conspiracy. This was that an unknown person had falsely presented himself as Lee Oswald in a phone call to the Soviet Embassy in Mexico City. The FBI initially reported that the person making the recorded call "was not Lee Harvey Oswald."[32] Later the FBI and CIA conspired, swiftly and clumsily, to conceal both the falsity of the impersonation and the fact that

FBI agents had exposed the falsehood by listening to the tape. The Warren Commission learned nothing about these two facts.

It is important to understand that this suppression was entirely consistent with intelligence priorities of the period. This important clue had been planted in the midst of one of the most sensitive CIA operations in the 1960s: its largest intercept operation against the telephones of an important Soviet base. One can assume that this clue was planted by conspirators who knew that the CIA response, possibly approved by higher authority, would be to suppress the truth. The CIA was protecting its sources and methods (in accordance with the responsibilities enumerated in its enabling statute). The result was obstruction of justice in a crime of the highest political significance.

As we shall see in the following pages, one of the important sources of covert agencies' power is their ability to falsify their own records, without fear of outside correction. Does this ability to rewrite their own history empower them to affect, if not control, the history of the rest of society? I believe the evidence in this book will justify a limited answer to this question: covert agencies, and the CIA in particular, were powerful enough to control and defuse a possible crisis in U.S. political legitimacy. They did so by reinforcing an unsustainable claim: Oswald killed the President, and he acted alone.

The CIA and the International Drug Traffic

But the power of the CIA to influence history became even greater when, as we shall see, they acted in concert with forces allied to the powerful international drug traffic. Most people are unaware of the size of this unrecorded drug economy. In 2008 the United Nations Office on Drugs and Crime estimated the profits from the global drug trade to be $352 billion; and reported that the funds from laundering illicit drugs, now often estimated to be third largest commodity in international trade, "became an important factor" in preventing a number of major banks from collapsing during the 2008 economic meltdown.[33]

While estimates of the unrecorded drug traffic remain

questionable, it is obvious that this traffic is large enough to be a major factor in both the economic and political considerations of government, *even while it does not form part of recorded economic statistics.* The unrecorded, illicit, but nonetheless important shadow economy is so large, and so powerful, that often governments have no choice but to plan to manage it, even before attempting to suppress it.[34]

There is a third factor contributing to the invisible alliance of the CIA, the independently wealthy, and the banks that cater to them. Informed observers of American politics have more than once commented to me that most of the hundred wealthiest people in the US know each other, and in addition often have connections to both the CIA and to organized crime. There is no shortage of anecdotal examples: James Angleton of CIA Counterintelligence delivering the sole eulogy at the small private funeral of Howard Hughes, or Joseph Kennedy Sr. being a point-holder in the same casino (the Cal-Neva) as Chicago mob figure Sam Giancana.[35] Perhaps more relevant to the milieu of the JFK assassination is the example of Clint Murchison, Sr. Murchison paid for the horse-racing holidays of FBI Director J. Edgar Hoover at the same time as he sold stakes in his investments to mob figures like Jerry Catena, and enjoyed political influence in Mexico.[36]

These connections are no accident. More often than not, as we shall see in examining the career of William Pawley, the extremely wealthy acquired their resources by ignoring or bending the rules of society, not by observing them. In corrupting politicians, or in bypassing them to secure unauthorized foreign intercessions, both the mob and the CIA can be useful allies. In addition drug profits need to be laundered, and banks can derive a significant percentage of their profits by laundering them, or otherwise bending or breaking the rules of their host countries.[37] Citibank came under Congressional investigation after having secretly moved $80 million to $100 million for Raúl Salinas de Gortari, brother of former Mexican president Carlos Salinas.[38]

As a rule the power of the biggest drug traffickers is not autonomous, but depends on their government connections; and the top trafficker in any country is usually the one with the best government connections. This means not just that the government is protecting certain drug traffickers, but also that these drug traffickers will have an interest in protecting the government. I believe that an example of this is the collaboration we shall examine in Mexico, between the CIA and the corrupt DFS, to influence history by presenting false stories about Oswald. But it would be very wrong to think of the CIA-DFS collaboration as a simple alliance.

One of the most crime-ridden CIA assets we know of is the Mexican DFS, which the US helped to create. From its foundation in the 1940s, the DFS, like other intelligence agencies in Latin America, was deeply involved with international drug-traffickers.[39] By the 1980s possession of a DFS card was recognized by DEA agents as a "license to traffic;" DFS agents rode security for drug truck convoys, and used their police radios to check of signs of American police surveillance.[40] Eventually the DFS became so identified with the criminal drug-trafficking organizations it managed and protected, that in the 1980s the DFS was (at least officially) closed down.[41] Thus the CIA-DFS alliance was at best an uneasy one, with conflicting goals. The CIA's concern was to manage and limit the drug traffic, while the DFS sought to manage and expand it.

Management of the drug traffic takes a variety of forms: from *denial* of this important power source to competing powers (the first and most vital priority), to *exploitation* of it to strengthen the existing state. There now exists abundant documentation that, at least since World War II, the US Government has *exploited* the drug traffic to finance and staff covert operations abroad. Perhaps the most conspicuous example is the massive paramilitary army organized and equipped by the CIA in Laos in the 1960s, for which drugs were the chief source of support. This alliance between the CIA and drug-financed forces has since been repeated in Afghanistan (1979), Central America (1982–87), and most recently Kosovo (1998).

It is now fairly common, even in mainstream books, to describe this CIA exploitation of the drug world as collaboration against a common enemy. For example Elaine Shannon, in a book written with DEA assistance, speaks as follows of the CIA-DFS alliance:

DFS officials worked closely with the Mexico City station
of the US Central Intelligence Agency and the attaché of
the Federal Bureau of Investigation. The DFS passed along
photographs and wiretapped conversations of suspected
intelligence officers and provocateurs stationed in the large
Soviet and Cuban missions in Mexico City. . . . The DFS
also helped the CIA track Central American leftists who
passed through the Mexican capital.[42]

But it is important to remember that such alliances were often first
formed in order to deny drug assets to the enemy. In Mexico as in
Asia, just as in the US "Operation Underworld" on the docks of
New York City, the US Government first began its drug collabora-
tions out of fear that drug networks, if not given USG protection,
would fall under that of some other foreign power.

"Operation Underworld," like its Mexican equivalent, began
after signs that the Sicilian Mafia in New York, like the Latin drug
networks of Central and South America, were being exploited
by Axis intelligence services. The crash program of assistance to
Kuomintang (KMT) drug networks in post-war Southeast Asia
was motivated in part by a similar fear, that these networks would
come under the sphere of mainland Chinese influence.

Thus it would be wrong to portray the CIA-drug alliance,
particularly in Mexico, as one between like-minded allies. The
cooperation was grounded in an original, deeper suspicion; and,
especially because dealing with criminals, the fear of betrayal was
never absent. This was particularly true of the DFS when guided
by Luis Echeverría, a nationalist who in the late 1960s (despite
being a CIA asset, with the cryptonym LITEMPO-8) developed
stronger relations between Mexico and Cuba. Some have questioned whether the increased Cuban-Mexican relations under his
presidency (1970–76) were grounded partly in the drug traffic,
overseen by his brother-in-law.[43]

Even in 1963 the fear of offending Mexico's (and Echeverría's)
sensibilities led the CIA to cancel physical surveillance of a Soviet
suspect (Valeriy Kostikov); the CIA feared detection by the DFS,
who also had Kostikov under surveillance.[44] By the 1970s there

were allegations that the CIA and/or FBI were using the drug traffic to introduce guns into Mexico, in order to destabilize the left-leaning Echeverría government.[45]

This is perhaps the moment to point out another special feature of the US-DFS relationship in Mexico. Both the CIA and FBI (as Shannon noted, and as we shall see) had their separate connections to the DFS and its intercept program. The US effort to wrest the drug traffic from the Nazi competition dated back to World War II, when the FBI still had responsibility for foreign intelligence operations in Latin America. Winston Scott, the CIA Station Chief in Mexico City, was a veteran of this wartime overseas FBI network; and he may still have had an allegiance to Hoover while nominally working for the CIA.[46] We shall see that on a key policy matter, the proposed torture of Oswald's contact Silvia Durán, Scott allied himself with the FBI Legal Attache and the Ambassador, against the expressed disapproval of CIA Headquarters.

What is particularly arresting about this CIA-mob nexus that produced false Oswald stories, is its suggestive overlay with those responsible for CIA-mob assassination plots. Key figures in the latter group, such as William Harvey and David Morales, did not conceal their passionate hatred for the Kennedys. It is time to focus on the CIA-mob connection in Mexico as a milieu which will help explain, not just the assassination cover-up, but the assassination itself.

The Exemption of the CIA from the Rule of Law

From other sources, we learn more about the autonomy of the CIA. It was almost by accident that the public learned of a secret agreement, in violation of a Congressional statute, whereby the CIA was exempted from reporting crimes of which it was aware to the Justice Department. This agreement was so secret that for almost two decades successive Attorneys General were unaware of it.[47] (My understanding is that the agreement arose from a "flap" in Thailand, where a CIA/OSO officer who was about to report on the local drug traffic was murdered by another from the OPC, who was working with it.)[48]

Although this agreement was temporarily ended under the Ford Administration, a new secret Memo of Understanding under Reagan again lifted the obligation to report the criminal acts of CIA assets who were drug-traffickers. I have argued elsewhere that these covert agreements have been significant factors in augmenting the flows of heroin and cocaine into this country.

Obviously a memo from the Reagan Administration is of little relevance to the Kennedy assassination. But it is of extreme relevance that a prior agreement was in force from the mid-1950s to the mid-1970s, exempting the CIA from a statutory requirement to report any criminal activity by any of its employees or assets. This agreement, drawn up under Eisenhower and eventually rescinded under Gerald Ford, was so secret that the Attorneys General under JFK and LBJ (including Robert Kennedy) were never informed of it.[49] We can assume however that the agreement was known to those CIA officers who suppressed an important clue that would have led to their Soviet intercept program, and thereby obstructed a proper investigation of President Kennedy's murder.

This exemption from a statutory obligation might be considered anomalous, except that in one form or another the CIA has enjoyed such exemptions for most of its history.

Oswald, Russia, and Cuba: How the Managed Oswald Stories Led to the Warren Commission

As noted earlier, the DFS played a central role, along with the CIA, in the management of conspiratorial stories about Oswald in Mexico, including the false Oswald-Soviet intercept. The key to this procedure, as I argued in *Deep Politics*, was a two-fold process. "Phase One" put forward the phantom of an international plot, linking Oswald to the USSR, to Cuba, or to both countries together. This phantom was used to invoke the danger of a possible nuclear confrontation, which induced Chief Justice Earl Warren and other political notables to accept "Phase Two," the equally false (but less dangerous) hypothesis that Oswald killed the President all by himself.

This book affords a close-up look of the genesis of the Phase-One story, and how it was first promoted and then defused by the CIA.

Michael Beschloss has revealed that, at 9:20 AM on the morning of November 23, CIA Director John McCone briefed the new President. In Beschloss' words: "The CIA had information on foreign connections to the alleged assassin, Lee Harvey Oswald, which suggested to LBJ that Kennedy may have been murdered by an international conspiracy."[50] (It is not certain whether the conspiracy McCone referred to on November 23 involved Cuba or the Soviet Union.)

Beschloss's account implies that McCone's "information" concerned Oswald's alleged visit in September 1963 to the Soviet Embassy in Mexico City:

> A CIA memo written that day reported that Oswald had visited Mexico City in September and talked to a Soviet vice consul whom the CIA knew as a KGB expert in assassination and sabotage. The memo warned that if Oswald had indeed been part of a foreign conspiracy, he might be killed before he could reveal it to U.S. authorities.[51]

An internal CIA memo of November 23, asserting the claim Oswald talked to Kostikov, bases it on an alleged phone intercept that, I shall argue, was almost certainly falsified.[52]

President Johnson appears to have had this information in mind when, a few minutes after the McCone interview, he asked FBI Director J. Edgar Hoover if the FBI "knew any more about the visit to the Soviet embassy."[53]

But widely scattered clues suggest that the US Government was thinking of a Cuban connection to Oswald even before the Soviet one. Already on November 22 the FBI was reporting a claim never mentioned in CIA records: that the false Oswald-Soviet phone call was made by Oswald while telephoning "from the Cuban Embassy."[54]

FBI Agent James Hosty, who handled the Oswald file in Dallas, has written that he learned later from two independent sources that at the time of Oswald's arrest, "fully armed warplanes were sent screaming toward Cuba. Just before they entered Cuban airspace, they were hastily called back. With the launching of airplanes, the entire U.S. military went on alert."[55]

These planes would have been launched from the U.S. Strike Command (USSTRICOM) at McDill Air Force Base in Florida. We have a cable from U.S. Army Intelligence in Texas, dated November 22, 1963, transmitting a false report to the Strike Command that Oswald had defected to Cuba in 1959 and was "a card-carrying member of the Communist Party."[56] As discussed below, these allegations are incompatible with the present "Phase-Two" account of Oswald's life, but were corroborated at the time. At 4:00 PM on the afternoon of November 22, Hoover told Bobby Kennedy that Oswald "went to Cuba on several occasions, but would not tell us what he went to Cuba for."[57] (There is nothing in current FBI files on Oswald, as released to the public, to suggest either that Oswald had visited Cuba, or that he had been interrogated about such visits by the FBI.)

We know from other sources that Bobby Kennedy, on the afternoon of November 22, was fearful of a Cuban involvement in the assassination. Jack Anderson, the recipient of much secret CIA information, suggests that this concern may have been planted in Bobby's head by CIA Director McCone.

> When CIA chief John McCone learned of the assassination, he rushed to Robert Kennedy's home in McLean, Virginia, and stayed with him for three hours. No one else was admitted. Even Bobby's priest was turned away. McCone told me he gave the attorney general a routine briefing on CIA business and swore that Castro's name never came up. . . . Sources would later tell me that McCone anguished with Bobby over the terrible possibility that the assassination plots sanctioned by the president's own brother may have backfired. Then the following day, McCone briefed President Lyndon Johnson and his National Security Advisor McGeorge Bundy. Afterward McCone told subordinates—who later filled me in—what happened at that meeting. The grim McCone shared with Johnson and Bundy a dispatch from the U.S. embassy in Mexico City, strongly suggesting that Castro was behind the assassination.[58]

Such dispatches did emanate from the Mexico City embassy, although we know of none as early as November 23. Three days later the Ambassador, Thomas Mann, the CIA Station Chief, Winston Scott, and the FBI Legal Attache, Clark Anderson, enthusiastically promoted wild allegations that Oswald's act had been plotted and paid for inside the Cuban Embassy.[59] We know that McCone was wedded to this story, and continued to share it confidentially even after its narrator, the Nicaraguan double agent Gilberto Alvarado, recanted it on November 30.

The Early Oswald-Cuba Information Gap

The publicly released CIA record shows no trace of any linkage between Oswald and Cuba from Mexico until late November 23, long *after* McCone saw the President. But as we shall see this absence is itself suspicious, indeed hard to believe. There are too many loose clues that CIA Headquarters already had heard more about Oswald and Cuba than the purportedly complete record of CIA cables would account for. This would suggest that the record has been smoothed over to efface any "Phase-One" trace of a credible Cuban implication.

For example, one of the CIA officers in Mexico City who worked on the pre-assassination Oswald file "was certain that a second cable reporting Oswald's contacts with the Cuban Embassy had been sent to Headquarters prior to the assassination."[60] But there is no surviving CIA trace of any reason on November 22 to link Oswald, or the assassination, to Cuba, or possibly covert action against Cuba.

The FBI, in contrast, has now released a November 22 memo that already linked Oswald to the Cuban Embassy in Mexico:

> By Secret teletype dated 10/10/63 CIA advised . . . that a sensitive source on 10-1-63 had reported that Lee Oswald contacted the Soviet Embassy . . . inquiring whether the Embassy had received any news concerning a telegram. . . . (The Legal Attache in Mexico advised 11-22-63 that this was a telephone call made from the Cuban Embassy to the Soviet Embassy and a transcript thereof is being forwarded.)"[61]

There is no known corroboration for the Legal Attache's claim on November 22 that the call was made from the Cuban Embassy. However this early mention of the Cuban Embassy suggests that the FBI in Mexico City may indeed have had its own sources of information, including both intercepts and informants. (It is now officially admitted that the CIA had penetration agents inside the Cuban Embassy, and the FBI may have as well.)[62]

Perhaps the strongest indication of deeper FBI knowledge is a CIA memo of December 11; this argued against the public release of the first FBI report on the case, "because the Soviets would see that the FBI had advance information on the reason for Oswald's visit to the Soviet Embassy."[63] *Advance* information???

It is commonplace now to attribute the cover-up to early reports about Oswald and Cuba. For example, Jack Anderson suggests that a cover-up was ordered by Johnson himself, on the basis of what McCone told him on November 23 about Mexico City. According to Anderson, McCone argued that

> Nikita Khrushchev was on the ropes inside the Kremlin, humiliated over backing down . . . during the Cuban missile crisis. [This was indeed true, as his ouster in 1964 would show.] If Castro were to be accused of the Kennedy assassination, Americans would demand revenge against Cuba, and Khrushchev would face another Cuban crisis. . . . This time he might do something reckless and provoke a nuclear war, which would cost forty million lives. It was a staggering figure that the new president repeated to others.[64]

Telephone transcripts in the LBJ Library confirm that LBJ used this argument to coerce Senator Richard Russell into serving on the Commission.[65] Chief Justice Earl Warren told William Manchester that Johnson persuaded him to lead the Warren Commission by raising the same threat of war against Castro and Khrushchev: "Why, if Khrushchev moved on us, he could kill 39 million in an hour."[66]

The Manipulation or Management of the Mexico Oswald Stories

Whatever the details, we see how important were CIA stories about Oswald's foreign involvements in securing a Commission committed from the outset to the finding that Oswald acted alone. The CIA's role might be defensible if the information were objective and well-grounded. But as this book will show, the stories of Oswald's Cuban involvements were virtually worthless. The two main sources for them, Silvia Durán and Gilberto Alvarado, both changed their stories repeatedly, under the threat or actual application of torture by the Mexican secret police. Alvarado actually recanted his story, as the Warren Commission was informed; however the Warren Commission did not learn that Alvarado claimed to have been told that, if he did not recant, he would be hung by his testicles.[67] And the supposed objective record of intercepted phone calls by Oswald is, as we shall see, just as seriously flawed.

In the days after the murders in Dallas, the U.S. was flooded with dubious stories, most of them swiftly discredited, linking Oswald to either a Cuban or Soviet conspiracy. Those which most preoccupied the FBI and CIA all came out of Mexico. These stories exhibited certain common characteristics.

1) They all came either directly from an intelligence source, or from someone in the hands of an intelligence agency. Nearly always, the agency involved was the Mexican DFS or secret police. The DFS, along with the Nicaraguan intelligence service, which was also a source, were under CIA tutelage.

2) The stories changed over time, to support either a pro-conspiratorial hypothesis ("Phase One"), or a rebuttal of this ("Phase Two").

3) The Warren Commission was led to believe that the "Phase-One" stories were without basis. In fact a number of unresolved anomalies suggest that behind them was some deeper truth, still not revealed.

4) As just noted, the two main sources, Silvia Durán and Gilberto Alvarado, gave varying stories while detained by the DFS. Of the two, Durán was actually tortured, and Alvarado reportedly threatened with torture. Far from regretting this use of

torture, the Ambassador, Thomas Mann, the CIA Station Chief, Winston Scott, and the FBI Legal Attache, Clark Anderson, argued strenuously, in the face of Washington's expressed disapproval, for Durán's arrest and rearrest by the DFS, and that DFS torture be used again.[68]

In retrospect, these stories should not have been taken seriously. In fact the CIA was able to rely on them, not as a source of truth, but as a source of coercive influence over the rest of government. It will help us to understand what was going on if we refer to the stories, not as "information" or even as "allegations," but as **managed stories**. To say this leaves open the question of who were the ultimate managers—the DFS, U.S. officers in Mexico, or higher authorities in Washington.

The full history is complex and confused, with many unanswered questions. But nearly all of these managed stories, along with others outside Mexico to be discussed later, resolve into this simple pattern of a Phase One/Phase Two evolution.

1) Silvia Durán's managed story:

Luis Echeverría, the Mexican Minister of Gobernación (which directed the DFS), told Winston Scott on November 23 that Silvia Durán had given a "written statement attesting to two visits by Oswald."[69] According to the sequence of documents in Oswald's 201 file, no written statement from Durán's DFS interview reached CIA Headquarters until November 28, after Langley had asked for it on November 27.

There is however evidence that the CIA HQ received a written Durán statement, not in the Oswald 201 file, from a back channel.[70] Already on November 24 we find a cable from "John Scelso" (John Whitten) at Headquarters, who has already read it: "After analyzing all the [cable] traffic and reading the statement of Silvia Duran, one important question still puzzles us."[71] Even earlier, on November 23, the CIA opined in a Headquarters memo to the FBI that Oswald probably wanted a Soviet visa first, then a Cuban transit visa while waiting for it. The memo added that "This is also the conclusion reached by Silvia Duran, the Mexican national employee of the Cuban Embassy who dealt with OSWALD."[72] Durán could indeed easily have voiced this opinion, but there is nothing in the Oswald 201 file that indicates how CIA HQ could have known this.

It seems likely that the 10-page written Durán statement sent on November 27 was designed to replace an earlier, suppressed statement referred to in the CIA cable of November 23. Summarizing the contents of this first statement, the cable repeated the "Phase-One" allegation that Oswald said he was a "Communist and admirer of Castro."[73] But what the CIA found worthy of reporting on November 23 (that Oswald said he was a Communist) has disappeared from the November 26 10-page written statement, as later from two subsequent differing versions of Durán's November 23 interview, all of them "Phase Two".

None of the "Phase-One" or "Phase-Two" versions mention what Silvia told the Cuban Ambassador after her release: that the DFS asked her "if she had personal relations and even if she had intimate [i.e. sexual] relations with him." (In his phone call reporting this to the Cuban President, overheard by the CIA, the Ambassador also commented on the bruises inflicted on Durán during the interview.)[74]

From whatever source, rumors of a Durán-Oswald sexual relationship were soon floating through the US Embassy in Mexico City in the first week after the assassination, when they were heard by an FBI agent, Larry Keenan, who had been sent down by Washington.[75] A Cuban exile who was also a CIA agent, Salvador Diaz Verson, claimed to have heard in the offices of the Mexico City newspaper *Excelsior*, on November 25, that the DFS had learned from Durán that Oswald "had contacted DURAN, and had stayed in her home in Mexico City."[76] (Silvia Durán herself testified that the DFS had given the results of her first interrogation to *Excelsior*, where a version of them was published.)[77]

As late as 1967 Durán reportedly told a CIA agent, LIRING-3, that in her November 23 interrogation she had been "interviewed thoroughly and beaten until she admitted that she had an affair with Oswald."[78] CIA Station Chief Win Scott later reported on this "Phase-One" allegation as a fact, "the fact that Silvia Durán had sexual intercourse with Lee Harvey Oswald on several occasions when the latter was in Mexico City."[79]

A decade later Durán confirmed to the House Assassinations Committee staff that she had been questioned about sexual relations with Oswald, which she linked to the claim that "we were Communists and that we were planning the Revolution."[80]

> all the time they tell me that I was a Communist . . . and they insisted that I was a very important person for . . . the Cuban Government and that I was the link for the International Communists—the Cuban Communists, the Mexican Communists and the American Communists, and that we were going to kill Kennedy, and I was the link. For them I was very important.[81]

We shall see that the theory of an international Communist assassination conspiracy, with the Oswald-Durán relationship at its center, was one propounded by Durán's cousin-in-law, Elena Garro de Paz, who was already in DFS custody. Durán blamed her "cousin" [i.e. Garro] for her arrest by the DFS.[82]

Whatever the details, there is a conspicuous contrast between the "Phase-One" accounts of this November 23 interview, beginning with the missing "written statement" of November 24, and the extant "Phase-Two" accounts. None of the extant versions mention either a conspiracy or a sexual relationship. Yet a State Department officer later told Secretary of State William Rogers that he had heard from the Deputy Chief of the CIA Station (Alan White) that the DFS had indeed interrogated Silvia Durán about the substance of the Garro allegations.[83]

The credibility of the Durán allegations is still further complicated by the hints and rumors, explored in the Lopez report, that Silvia Durán "may have been a source of information for either the CIA or the Mexicans."[84]

2. Gilberto Alvarado's managed story:

Another version of the Garro sexual assassination conspiracy theory was put forward on November 25 by an agent of Nicaraguan dictator Somoza. In brief, Oswald was supposed to have volunteered in the Cuban Embassy to kill President Kennedy; and to have received $6,500 in cash for the job (in front of Alvarado, a stranger). Alvarado's claim also overlapped in vivid particulars with the Garro story, even to such details as Oswald's companions (a tall thin Negro with reddish hair, a blonde-haired hippie with a Canadian passport), and the intimate embrace he received from a girl inside the Embassy.[85]

There was an inherent problem with Alvarado's story, so grave that it raises questions why Alvarado was ever treated with such seriousness by the US Embassy in Mexico. This is that Alvarado claimed to have seen Oswald in the Cuban Embassy on September 18, a date when (as the FBI quickly established) Oswald was still in New Orleans. This problem vanished when Alvarado amended the date to September 28.[86] This happened to be exactly the date on which the CIA (falsely, I shall argue below) placed Oswald in the Cuban Embassy. Given the extent of bad faith misreporting by the CIA about Oswald in the Cuban Embassy, we have to ask if this "correction" of Alvarado's story had not been inspired by his CIA or DFS interrogators.

The "Phase-One" Alvarado story was also soon retracted, and replaced by a "Phase-Two" denial. On November 30 the DFS told the CIA "that Alvarado has signed a statement saying that his story of seeing Oswald inside the Cuban Embassy is completely false." This information was immediately forwarded to CIA headquarters, who in turn forwarded it to the White House.[87] This tied up the "lead being pursued in Mexico," which, as Hoover told LBJ on November 29, had delayed the FBI's hope "to have the investigation wrapped up" by that time.[88]

There is more to the Alvarado story. As we have seen, he had retracted his retraction by December 3, claiming it was obtained under threat of DFS torture. Alvarado subsequently underwent a lie detector test by a technician from Washington, and failed it.[89]

The essential point is that there was both a "Phase-One" and a "Phase-Two" version of the managed Alvarado story, which alternated in close synchrony with the political needs of the moment. As the *Washington Post* has noted, a "Phase-One" version of the Alvarado story reached Lyndon Johnson soon before he coerced Warren into accepting the Chairmanship of the Warren Commission:

Later that afternoon [at 4:30 PM] November 29, Johnson asked Warren to come to the White House. It was around this time that Johnson received a call [at 1:40 PM] from Hoover updating the investigation. The "angle in Mexico is giving us a great deal of trouble," Hoover said. Oswald had not been in Mexico on Sept. 18, as Alvarado had [originally] said, but Alvarado had now changed the date to Sept. 28, a day Oswald was known to have been there.[90]

It is not known if Johnson brought up the Alvarado story when pressuring Warren. Certainly other cables had reached the White House on the same day, which weakened rather than increased the likelihood of Cuban involvement. A CIA cable to the White House at 1:30 PM had notified the White House that the Mexicans interviewing Silvia Durán now believed she had been involved only with visas.[91] A cable at 4:15 told the White House that Alvarado did not recognize a photo of Durán, and the Mexicans now doubted his story.[92] From the CIA's record, it would appear that it was Johnson, rather than the CIA, who selectively screened the data to secure Earl Warren's compliance.

The Alvarado story in its brief and varied career was quintessentially managed, and manageable. Deeply flawed from the outset by an impossible alleged date, it was turned up, and then turned off, to meet the changing needs of his managers. There are indications that the Mexico City Station knew from the outset that the Alvarado story was false, and may indeed have planted it. According to a later report from CIA HQ to the Warren Commission,

Alvarado was known to CIA as a former informant of a Central American security service and to have been used to penetrate communist guerrilla groups. He said that he was in Mexico City still working for his service, trying to get himself accepted by the Cubans as a communist so they would take him to Cuba for guerrilla training.[93]

But in the initial cable to HQ about Alvarado, he was identified only as a Nicaraguan who "claims he awaiting false Mexican documentation prior receiving sabotage training Cuba."[94] The author of this cable, "M.C. Choaden," has been identified as David Phillips, a specialist in disinformation who, as the Lopez Report noted, later lied significantly about his role in the CIA's investigation of the JFK assassination.[95]

In a second cable, "L.F. Barker" (David Phillips' Cuban Operations colleague Robert Shaw) reported that Alvarado had admitted he was a member of the Nicaraguan Secret Service, but saw that as no reason to question his story. On the contrary, "Barker" described Alvarado as a "young, quiet, very serious person, who speaks with conviction."[96] As late as November 27, Ambassador Mann reported that the CIA ("CAS") officer interviewing Alvarado "was impressed by Alvarado."[97] Still later, as noted above, Alvarado modified his story to bring the date of his Oswald observance exactly into line with the date, September 28, when the CIA (wrongly) alleged Oswald to have been there.

It should be understood that the Nicaraguan Secret Service, like other intelligence networks in Mexico and Central America, worked closely with the CIA. It later emerged that the CIA in Managua had already prepared several reports of which Alvarado, while in the Nicaraguan Secret Service, was the ultimate source. Thus the FBI seems to have got it right when in its own reports it described Alvarado as a "source of CIA's" or "CIA source."[98]

A common denominator underlying this CIA connection is that, in Nicaragua exactly as in Mexico, the CIA's intelligence sources were grounded in the drug traffic. It has been known for some time that the CIA's chief asset in Nicaragua was the leadership of the corrupt National Guard, which has been called "one of the most corrupt military establishments in the world.[99]

We now learn that Alvarado, the "CIA source," reported "directly to General Gustavo Montiel, Chief of the Intelligence Service of the Nicaraguan Army."[100] As we shall see, Montiel was later denounced as a principal in a "massive car theft ring" run by Norwin Meneses, described in other CIA cables as "the kingpin of narcotics traffickers in Nicaragua."[101] We shall return to this striking similarity between these CIA assets—Montiel in Nicaragua, Nazar Haro in Mexico—that both were said to be involved in a network or networks dealing simultaneously in massive car smuggling (south) and narcotics smuggling (north).

Given the known ambiguities about Alvarado's double identity as an intelligence agent, one can easily fault the leaders of the US Embassy in Mexico (Ambassador Mann, Station Chief Scott, and FBI Legat Anderson), for claiming that "there appears to be a strong possibility that a down payment was made to Oswald in the Cuban Embassy here."[102] But it is not clear that the management of the Alvarado story was integral to the Kennedy assassination plot. It is clear that the CIA was and is hiding something about Oswald and the Cuban Embassy. The Alvarado story might have been no more than a convenient diversion: a chance to focus attention on a different (and false) narrative.

3. The Elena Garro de Paz managed story.

One reason the Alvarado story could be endorsed vigorously by CIA Station Chief Scott was that it was corroborated in small details by other "Phase-One" stories, also from intelligence sources, and later similarly retracted.[103] One of these corroborative stories was directly attributed to "a CIA man in Dallas," who allegedly told reporter Jerry O'Leary that Oswald returned from Mexico "with $5,000 which he did not have when he went into Mexico." O'Leary telephoned this information to FBI Headquarters.[104] The FBI account of this event commented, "In other words, the CIA man in Dallas leaked information to O'Leary."[105] However a CIA cable the next day reported from Mexico the rumor that Oswald had deposited $5000 in the United States after he got back from Mexico, and attributed the story to "an ODENVY [FBI] man named Clark."[106]

No "Phase-One" allegation corroborated Alvarado more closely than that of the well-known right-wing Mexican writer Elena Garro de Paz. She claimed she had been present at a party where she had heard a Communist discussion of Kennedy, in which "they came to the conclusion that the only solution was to kill him."[107] She had also seen Oswald with the same people at a party given by Rubén Durán, the brother-in-law of Silvia Durán, "who she later learned was Oswald's mistress while he was here." In accounts given to the American Embassy in 1965, she linked Oswald to the same striking companions as did Alvarado: "a Latin

American Negro man with red hair" and someone with "long blond hair."[108]

When I wrote about the Garro allegations in 1993, I discounted them, on the grounds that Alvarado's story of a "Negro with reddish hair" had already been published in September 1964 in the Warren Report.[109] I now think it much more likely that some version of the Garro story had reached the DFS, or been planted by them, in the days following the assassination. No one disputes Garro's story that the DFS took her into protective custody between November 23 and November 30. Her story would explain why on the same day the DFS arrested, not only Silvia, but her husband Horacio, her sister-in-law Lydia Durán, and her brother-in-law Rubén Durán and his wife Betty (all placed by Garro in Oswald's presence at the incriminating party).[110] It would also explain why, on November 23, the DFS was grilling Silvia so aggressively about her sexual affair and Communist plotting with Oswald.[111] Finally it would explain why Silvia on November 23 attributed her arrest to her "cousin" [i.e. Garro] whom she "does not like."[112]

The management of the Garro story was different in one respect from the treatment of Silvia Durán and Alvarado: It was a "Phase-One" story from start to finish; as it never reached Washington through the usual CIA channels, so there was no need to reshape or retract it. The management consisted of keeping her in DFS custody, at a time when FBI personnel should have been interviewing her.[113]

4. The Management of the False Oswald Intercepts—October 1:

It has been customary to contrast the fluid, changing stories about Oswald from human sources with the allegedly "hard," objective reports of Oswald himself talking, or being discussed, in intercepts obtained from a tap on Mexican phone lines into the Soviet Embassy.[114] However this intercept record is deeply flawed, and in part almost certainly falsified. In addition to containing false information, the intercepts share two other features with the managed stories discussed above. They supplied the changing need for first "Phase-One" and then "Phase-Two" stories. And they too reached the CIA via the Mexican DFS, the most likely candidate to have falsified them. (Although it is customary to talk of "CIA intercepts," the initial tapping and taping were handled by the DFS.)

It is helpful to consider the intercepts in the chronological order in which they reached CIA Headquarters. We see then that the intercepts can be divided into two categories: two early "Phase-One" intercepts, hinting that Oswald was part of an international Communist conspiracy, and a host of later "Phase-Two" intercepts, clarifying that Oswald's sole purpose for visiting the Soviet and Cuban Consulates was in connection with obtaining a Cuban visa.

We have already referred to the suggestive "Phase-One" character of the first intercept, the only one forwarded to Washington before the assassination. This linked the name of Lee Oswald to a Soviet Consul, Kostikov, whom the CIA later identified (at least for a time) as a KGB Agent from Department Thirteen, specializing in assassinations. The cable deserves to be quoted verbatim:

> Acc[ording] LIENVOY [the CIA's phone intercept program] 1 Oct 63, American male who spoke broken Russian said his name Lee Oswald (phonetic), stated he at Sovemb on 28 Sept when spoke with Consul whom he believed be Valeriy Vladimirovich Kostikov. Subj asked Sov guard Ivan Obyedkov who answered if there anything new re telegram to Washington. Obyedkov upon checking said nothing received yet, but request had been sent.[115]

Almost certainly this speaker was not the Lee Harvey Oswald who visited the Soviet Union, and spoke relatively fluent Russian.[116] No less an authority than J. Edgar Hoover advised Lyndon Johnson of this by telephone on the morning of November 23: "We have up here the tape and the photograph of the man who was at the Soviet embassy, using Oswald's name. That picture and the tape do not correspond to this man's voice, nor to his appearance."[117] Audio tapes for these LBJ phone calls have been preserved at the LBJ Library. However nothing of this conversation can be heard on the relevant tape; it would appear to have been erased.[118]

Hoover's reasons for saying this were laid out in a Letterhead

Memorandum sent out on the same day to the President and to the Secret Service:

> The Central Intelligence Agency advised that on October 1, 1963, an extremely sensitive source had reported that an individual identified himself as Lee Oswald, who contacted the Soviet Embassy in Mexico City inquiring as to any messages. Special Agents of this Bureau, who have conversed with Oswald in Dallas, Texas, have observed photographs of the individual referred to above and have listened to a recording of his voice. These Special Agents are of the opinion that the above-referred-to individual was not Lee Harvey Oswald."[119]

Other FBI cables and memoranda confirm that the tape was indeed flown up on a US Navy plane from Mexico City to Dallas, where FBI agents confirmed the voice was not Oswald's.

John Newman has shown in detail how this initial candor was obfuscated by subsequent clumsy attempts by the Mexico City CIA to assert, falsely, that the tape, and others like it, had been erased.[120] By noon EST November 23, the Mexico City CIA Station had cabled headquarters to say that "Station unable compare voice as first tape erased prior receipt second call" (on October 1).[121]

This false claim was soon abandoned. A headquarters memo reports that by 7 AM EST November 24, headquarters knew that the first tape *had* been reviewed, and the voice found to be identical with that in the other intercepts.[122] Anne Goodpasture, who handled the intercepts in the Mexico City CIA station, has confirmed that she herself commented on an internal document that the voices on the first and other intercepts had been compared (by "Douglas Feinglass" [Boris Tarasoff], the responsible translator) before the assassination.[123]

Later on the same critical day of November 23, the CIA reverted to a second false cover story: that all the Oswald intercept tapes had been erased by that time, not just the first. The FBI notified its Dallas office that evening that "With regard to the tapes [deletion] referred to herein, CIA has advised that these tapes have been erased and are not available for review."[124] This crucial lie (concealing the existence of evidence which could have led to a conspirator in the assassination) was repeated the next day in a cable from CIA Mexico City to headquarters: "HQ has full transcripts all pertinent calls. Regret complete recheck shows tapes for this period already erased."[125]

However contemporary CIA documents suggest that comparisons of the voices on the tapes *had* been made, including tapes only listened to after November 22.[126] I do not accept this as conclusive evidence of the survival of the pre-assassination tapes, because (as I shall argue shortly), nothing said by the CIA about these alleged Oswald intercepts can be accepted as certain. But in April 1964 two members of the Warren Commission staff, William Coleman and David Slawson, visited the Mexico City CIA Station, and later said they listened to the pre-assassination tape of the man identifying himself as "Lee Oswald."[127] So the tape existed on November 23, when FBI agents are supposed to have listened to it. And the rebuttal that the tapes had been destroyed is false.

In 1976 the staff of the Church Committee discovered the evidence that the October 1 tape had been listened to, revealing the role of an Oswald impersonator; and they reported also the ensuing cover-up. Their staff report, only recently released, noted cogently as follows:

> On November 25, 1963—some two days after Dallas cabled the Bureau that the tapes had been erased—Bureau supervisor Burt Turner cabled legat stating: "If tapes covering any contact subject [Oswald] with Soviet or Cuban embassies available forward to Bureau for laboratory examination. Include tapes previous reviewed Dallas if they were returned to you."[128]

But this explosive staff report was ignored in Book V of the Church Committee's Final Report, which purported to review the performance of the intelligence agencies in the investigation of the assassination of President John. F. Kennedy.[129] In a misleadingly detailed chronology of CIA and FBI behavior on

November 23 and 24, 1963, the central problem of the October 1 tape in Dallas is ignored altogether.[130]

The cover-up was perpetuated, in a more sophisticated manner, by the House Select Committee on Assassinations [HSCA]. Its report stated, no less than three times, that no "recording of Oswald's voice" was ever "received" or "listened to" in the United States.[131] This language is a lawyer's subterfuge: what was received and listened to was precisely *not* a recording of Oswald's voice.[132]

In contrast to other "benign" "Phase-Two" cover-ups of a false Oswald-Soviet link, this cover-up in November 1963 can only be called sinister. The October 8 intercept cable was the strongest single piece of evidence for an illusory Oswald-Soviet assassination conspiracy. By concealing its falsity, the CIA and FBI did not just keep alive the illusion. More importantly, they obstructed the pursuit of the most important available clue at that time of a high-level assassination conspiracy.

Digression: The October 1 Kostikov Intercept and the November 9 "Kostin" Letter

This clue did not stand alone. It dovetailed with a letter, purportedly from Oswald, which was mailed from Irving, Texas on November 12 to the Soviet Embassy in Washington. In this letter, the writer spoke of "my meetings [sic] with comrade Kostin in the Embassy of the Soviet Union, Mexico City." The letter also alluded suggestively to the lack of time there "to complete our business." Even more alarmingly, the author revealed knowledge that the Consul in the Cuban Embassy had been "replaced."[133] (The CIA confirmed later that Consul Azcue "was scheduled to leave in October but did not leave until November 18.")[134] And finally the writer spoke of speaking with Dallas FBI Agent James Hosty on November 1, a claim which would cause considerable post-assassination embarrassment to the FBI at the very highest levels.[135]

The Warren Commission accepted the genuineness of this letter, largely because of corroborating evidence in the form of a rough draft, said to be in Oswald's handwriting, which Ruth Paine allegedly discovered and then after the assassination gave to James

Hosty.[136] The Soviets however considered the letter to be a fake. In a post-assassination analysis they observed that the letter was typed, whereas *all* of Oswald's other correspondence had been in his own handwriting. As the Soviet Ambassador pointed out at the time, the tone was also quite dissimilar to anything Oswald had communicated before; it gave "the impression we had close ties with Oswald and were using him for some purposes of our own."[137]

I myself suspect that neither the letter nor the rough draft were genuine. There is no evidence that Oswald had plural "meetings" with Kostikov; I doubt that he had any. There is only one slight passing reference to the question of Oswald's and Marina's possible return to the Soviet Union, which had been the sole topic of their urgent appeals to the Washington Consulate in July.[138] It is surprising that there is no reference whatsoever to the Consulate's rejection, just one month earlier in October, of Marina's application to return to the Soviet Union.[139]

What is particularly suspect about the November 9 Kostin letter is its timing. After being intercepted by the FBI on its way to the Soviet Embassy in Washington, the letter was summarized and communicated to Dallas, where the news arrived on November 22. Hosty thus only learned of it right after the assassination. Had he learned earlier, Oswald would probably have been put under surveillance; and the assassination story could not have unfolded as it did.

As for the rough draft, I believe that it was composed, as well as discovered, after the assassination: to corroborate, and also neutralize, the dubious Kostin letter. The "draft" pointedly converts the typed letter's ominous "Phase-One" language ("time to complete our business") into an innocuous description of Kostikov's role ("time to assist me").[140]

Quite independently, and for different reasons, the researcher Jerry Rose also argued that "the typed version was generated before the handwritten one," the latter designed "to create proof that Oswald had written the letter."[141] Among other things, Rose pointed out that six words spelt incorrectly in the "final" typed version, are in fact spelt correctly in the "draft"; while there are no misspellings in the "draft" that are corrected in the "final" version.[142] It is worth adding that virtually all the evidence that arrived separately to the authorities from the Paine household—a note about Gen. Edwin Walker, a pristine Mexican bus ticket—is suspect.[143]

The Kostikov intercept, and the supporting Kostin letter, were and remain two of the most incontrovertible clues of a pre-assassination conspiracy. The CIA and FBI conspired together to suppress the known fact that the voice of the intercept was not Oswald's; and the CIA, at least, saw this as an operational matter.[144] The CIA's behavior here was in accordance with its agreement with the Department of Justice. Its priority was to protect its sources and methods—in this case, one of its most secret and important intercept operations. By prior agreement, it put this priority ahead of the pursuit of justice—in this case, the major U.S. political crime of the century.

Whoever did have control of the originating typewriter should be considered a prima facie suspect in the murder conspiracy.[145]

5. The Management of the False Oswald Intercepts—September 28:

The second intercept forwarded to Washington, at 2 PM EST on November 23, must have seemed even more indicative of a mysterious relationship between Oswald, the Cubans, and the Soviets. Keep in mind that at this stage the cables to Washington had not yet indicated that Oswald's visits to the two Embassies were in pursuit of a visa:

On 28 Sep 63 Silvia Duran Cuban Emb called Sov Consul saying Northamerican there who had been Sov Emb and wish speak with Consul. Uniden Northamerican told Sov consul quote "I was in your Emb and spoke to your consul. I was just now at your Emb and they took my address." Sov Consul says, "I know that." Uniden Northamerican speaks Russian "I did not know it then. I went to the Cuban Emb to ask them for my address because they have it" Sov Consul "Why don't you come again and leave your address with us It is not far from the Cuban Emb". Uniden Northamerican "Well, I'll be there right away."[146]

This strange intercept might have appeared credible if the DFS had truly heard from Silvia Durán in her first interview (as alleged by Salvador Diaz Verson) that Oswald "had stayed in her home in Mexico City."[147]

Nevertheless, as discussed below, this alleged intercept is even more improbable than the first. Both the Soviet and the Cuban Embassies were closed to the public on September 28, a Saturday. Durán has subsequently testified that she made only one phone call on Oswald's behalf, on Friday September 27; and that she did not see Oswald again on Saturday (3 AH 49-51). MEXI 7023 notes further that the unidentified Northamerican "spoke terrible, hardly recognizable Russian;" as already noted, Oswald was relatively fluent in Russian.

In 1993 a new witness claimed that, although the Soviet Embassy was closed to the public on Saturday, Oswald was indeed admitted there. This witness was Oleg Nechiporenko, a Soviet KGB official who claimed to taken part in a Saturday morning meeting in the Embassy with Oswald and also Kostikov.[148] However Nechiporenko also denied strenuously, on videotape, that there could have been any phone calls into the Soviet Embassy on September 28; because the switchboard was closed.[149]

The September 28 "address" intercept, is even more than the October 1 "Kostikov" intercept, an important clue as to the perpetrators of the Kennedy assassination. It is possible that on October 1, the Soviet phone and CIA intercept program were exploited by an outsider, about whom we know only that his Russian (and quite possibly his English) was bad.[150]

If Durán and Nechiporenko are correct, however, the alleged "address" intercept of September 28, did not occur at all, at least in its purported form of a phone call to the Soviet Embassy. In this case we would have a strong clue that conspirators to frame Oswald in a "Phase-One" conspiracy existed *within* the LIENVOY intercept process, either in the CIA, or (as I shall suggest) within the DFS.

Let me summarize the arguments that the "address" intercept of September 28 was a fake through and through:

1) Both the Cuban Consulate and the Soviet Consulate were closed on September 28.

2) Silvia Durán has testified repeatedly that on September 28 Oswald was not in the Cuban Consulate, where their voices are alleged to have been overheard (3 AH 49-50).

3) Oleg Nechiporenko of the Soviet Embassy is the chief source supporting the claim that Oswald was in the Soviet Embassy on September 28. Yet he has stated, on video, that the telephone switchboard was closed on September 28, and that there could have been no phone conversations on that day.

4) The voice said to be Oswald's was reportedly that of the first "Kostikov" intercept, and if so not that of the Dallas Lee Harvey Oswald.

Response to the "Phase-One" Intercepts

It was in response to these two intercepts, but especially the second, that the CIA Station Chief moved unilaterally to have the Mexican DFS arrest Silvia Durán:

> Silvia DURAN, the girl who put Oswald in touch with the Soviet Embassy, is a Mexican citizen. It is suggested that she be arrested as soon as possible by the Mexican authorities and held incommunicado until she can be questioned on the matter. She lives at Bahia de Morlaco #74. Her mother lives at Ebro # 12. Her brother [i.e. brother-in-law Rubén Durán] lives at Herodoto #14."[151]

Note that the CIA already had information on both Silvia and Rubén Durán, and may have been responsible for the latter's arrest as well.[152]

Four days later this second intercept was being characterized by Win Scott in "Phase-Two" language:

> A telephone call . . . by Silvia DURAN who puts on an unidentified norteamerican man who tells the Soviet that he was just at their Embassy and wants to give them his address. The Soviet tells him to return to the Embassy with the address.[153]

But the ominous importance attached to it originally is reflected in the tone of the questions the CIA (apparently CIA station chief Scott in Mexico) prepared on November 24 or 25:

> Was the assassination of President Kennedy planned by Fidel CASTRO Ruz; and were the final details worked out inside the Cuban Embassy in Mexico? . . .
>
> Did the Cuban Embassy furnish him a place to stay in Mexico City? It is reliably reported that OSWALD did not know his address in Mexico City, but the Cuban Embassy did know his address in Mexico City. . . .
>
> If CASTRO planned that OSWALD assassinate President Kennedy, did the Soviets have any knowledge of these plans?[154]

That Scott formulated these questions on November 25 suggests that he already contemplated the rearrest and reinterview of Silvia Durán (as he and Ambassador Mann, along with the FBI attache, formally requested one day later).[155] Indeed the ominous questions may have contributed to Durán's rearrest, after they were read on the night of November 25 to the President of Mexico.[156] If so, the apparently fortuitous arrival of Alvarado on November 25 fit into a project already formed in the mind of the Mexico Chief of Station.

The Arrival of the "Phase-Two" "Visa" Intercepts

Meanwhile, late on November 23 (according to Oswald's 201 file), Washington received its first "Phase-Two" version of why Oswald had visited the two Embassies. About five hours after the second "Phase-One" cable arrived, Washington read for the first time additional intercept transcripts suggesting that someone ("probably Oswald") had sought Durán's help in getting a Cuban transit visa in order to go to the Soviet Union.[157] This more benign alternative was soon corroborated by the first detailed report of Durán's statement after being arrested, the so-called "JKB version" (see Chapter 4) which was hand-carried to Washington by a CIA officer on November 27.[158] "JKB", or "JK Benadum," was the pseudonym used by George Munro, an outside CIA officer who was employed in sensitive positions by both the FBI and the CIA in Mexico City.[159]

It is often assumed that the "Phase-Two" "visa" intercepts corroborate the "Phase-Two" testimony from Silvia Durán about Oswald's desire for a visa. In one respect, this is not true. Early reports of Silvia Durán's testimony say that the Soviets said on the phone that Oswald's case "would have to be referred to Moscow."[160] This accords with the language typed on to Oswald's visa application, that the Soviets said "that they had to wait for authority from Moscow."[161]

But the transcript of the alleged Durán phone call at 4:26 PM on September 27 has the "outside man" (i.e. the Soviet official) saying, just as clearly, "we have to await the approval of Washington" ("deben de esperar la contestación de Washington").[162] The reference to Washington here alludes back to, and puts a "Phase-Two" spin on, the reference in the "Phase-One" Kostikov intercept, when Oswald allegedly asked "if there anything new re telegram to Washington."[163] It cannot however be reconciled with the Durán testimony and the visa application. Either the intercept or the testimony (if not both) has to be false.

The belated appearance of these "Phase-Two" intercepts (about a visa) poses some very embarrassing questions about the CIA's performance. Station Chief Win Scott later wrote in his autobiographical manuscript, *Foul Foe*, that

> Lee Harvey Oswald became a person of great interest to us during this 27 September to 2 October, 1963 period . . . [In] the Warren Commission Report [p. 777] the *erroneous statement was made that it was not known until after the assassination that Oswald had visited the Cuban Embassy*! . . . Every piece of information concerning Lee Harvey Oswald was reported immediately after it was received. . . . These reports were made on all his contacts with both the Cuban Consulate and the Soviets.[164]

A CIA memo written in 1975 by CIA Counterintelligence Chief George Kalaris, successor to James Angleton, also reported that "there were several Mexico City cables in October 1963 also concerned with Oswald's . . . visits to the Soviet and Cuban Embassies."[165] (Only one such cable reached the Warren Commission.)

The Lopez Report gathered corroborating reports, principally from the two Russian translators, that Oswald was already of interest to the CIA Station before the October 1 intercept, and that Oswald (as Win Scott wrote elsewhere) had asked the Soviet Embassy for financial assistance. If such an explosive "assistance" intercept ever existed, official traces of it have now disappeared.[166]

Win Scott's claim of pre-assassination reporting on Oswald in the Cuban Embassy, never officially admitted or revealed, is corroborated also by Ray Rocca's deposition in 1978 to the House Select Committee.[167] Cumulatively these reports are further evidence that cables about Oswald in the Cuban Embassy reached headquarters by a back channel. This strengthens the hypothesis, explored in *Deep Politics II* (pp. 90–109), that there may have been a pre-assassination CIA operation involving Oswald (or at least someone in Mexico City pretending to be Oswald) and Cuba. Such an operation, at least in its Mexico City aspects, would almost certainly have been directed by David Phillips.

As noted elsewhere, there are other signs that pre-assassination knowledge involving Oswald and the Cuban Embassy has been suppressed. For some reason the FBI already associated Oswald with the Cuban Embassy in a memorandum of November 22, based on a phone call from the Legal Attaché in Mexico City.[168]

But Scott's claim in his manuscript is hard to reconcile with his reaction to the second "Phase-One" intercept (about Oswald's going to the Cuban Embassy for his address). If Scott did already know about intercepts linking Oswald to a visa application, there is no excuse for his having linked the address intercept to a Cuban assassination plot. If he did *not* know about the visa intercepts, it would appear that these "Phase-Two" intercepts were post-assassination fabrications, created *ex post facto* as part of a CIA cover-up.

The Importance of the Managed Oswald Stories

Most critics have given only passing attention to the role of the

Oswald Mexico stories in the aftermath of the Kennedy assassination. The "Phase-Two" accounts of his visit to the Embassies (to obtain a visa), because of their abundant corroboration, are almost universally accepted, even by severe critics of the Warren Commission narrative.[169] It is not my intention at this point to challenge the "Phase-Two" version, except to urge caution in accepting it. As noted in *Deep Politics II* (pp. 117–30), the CIA and FBI have also managed the visa story told by Silvia Durán on November 23, editing and re-editing this story on at least four different occasions.

I do wish to argue that these managed stories, fleeting and insubstantial though they are, were of central importance in determining the outcome of the Kennedy assassination investigation. In succeeding years, furthermore, the discredited "Phase-One" stories have been revived to manipulate public opinion, even after the CIA and FBI had agreed on a "Phase-Two" interpretation of Oswald's movements in Mexico City. In 2013, for example, the discredited Garro story of the twist party was revived in a mainstream book by Philip Shenon.[170]

Two of the key figures to keep the "Phase-One" stories alive in the early stages were CIA Counterintelligence Chief James Angleton, and his subordinate Raymond Rocca, C/CI/RAG (Research and Analysis Group). In late January 1964 Rocca sent a memo to the Warren Commission with a section on Kostikov, with a last sentence containing a new reason to suspect a suspicious Kostikov-Oswald connection:

> Kostikov is believed to work for Department Thirteen of the First Chief Directorate of the KGB. It is the department responsible for executive action, including sabotage and assassination. These functions of the KGB are known within the Service itself as "Wet Affairs" (*mokryye dela*). The Thirteenth Department headquarters, according to very reliable information, *conducts interviews or, as appropriate, file reviews on every foreign military defector to the USSR to study and to determine the possibility of using the defector in his country of origin.*[171]

This last sentence so concerned another Counterintelligence [CI] officer in Soviet Russia Division that he dictated a memo to file concerning it.

> I called Tom Hall [CI/RAG] to inquire about the source of the statement included in the last sentence of para 17 of Rocca's memo. Rocca called me sometime later and said that the source was AELADLE [Anatoliy Golitsyn, Angleton's preferred Soviet defector]. It seems that he made the statement to C/CI [Angleton], who, himself, drafted and inserted the sentence in question.[172]

This is one of the rare occasions when Angleton himself is visible in the JFK record. Note that he calls his preferred KGB defector "very reliable;" this was at a time when another KGB defector with a "Phase-Two" message, Yuri Nosenko, had been isolated by Angleton from the Warren Commission and confined in a specially-constructed room.[173]

The opposing views of an Oswald-KGB relationship had by now produced, among other things, a battle between two KGB defectors, each with their supporters inside the CIA. This conflict ultimately contributed to a showdown in 1974, when CIA Director Colby fired Angleton and reconstructed the Counterintelligence staff. In the wake of Angleton's departure the CIA conducted an internal review of its JFK assassination records, releasing some of them to the Church Committee and later the House Select Committee on Assassinations [HSCA]. At the same time watered-down Angletonian innuendos about Oswald and Kostikov were leaked to the public, notably in the 1978 book *Legend*, by Edward J. Epstein.[174]

To this day both "Phase-One" and "Phase-Two" versions are trotted out from time to time. These control public perceptions of the Kennedy assassination and seize the debate from genuine critics who have less access to the media. In November 1976, for example, David Phillips of the CIA Station gave a new conspiratorial "Phase-One" spin to the intercepts. At a time when student activists were pressuring Congress to reopen an inquiry into the

Kennedy assassination, former Warren Commission member David Belin countered with a proposal for an inquiry to see if there was "there is any credible evidence of a foreign conspiracy."[175] Backing this demand was a lengthy secret memorandum written in 1975 by Angleton's deputy, Ray Rocca, the CIA liaison to the Rockefeller Commission.

Phillips lent strength to this "Phase-One" alternative by telling the *Washington Post*, falsely, that he had authored the Mexico City cable on the first intercept; and that Oswald had told the Soviets, "I have information you would be interested in, and I know you can pay my way to Russia."[176] But there was nothing about this alleged offer in Phillips' memoir published two years later: a "Phase-Two" account that admitted someone else had written the cable.[177]

Privileged authors, those who (unlike the rest of us) are able to interview CIA officers and quote from unreleased classified documents, continue to dominate the U.S. media with their dance between "Phase-One" and "Phase-Two" accounts of Oswald. Gus Russo, for example, writes of the "tantalizing leads about a possible Cuban conspiracy with Lee Harvey Oswald."[178] He claims, very misleadingly, that "The CIA was unsuccessful . . . in preventing the arrest" of Silvia Durán, which (although opposed by the CIA in Washington) had in fact been ordered by CIA Station Chief Scott. Referring to the questions prepared by Scott about possible Cuban or Soviet involvement, he calls them the "most critical questions surrounding the assassination." Russo states, against the available evidence, that "Duran's Mexican interrogators chose not to ask" them.[179] To assert this, he has to overlook the contrary testimony of Durán herself, partially corroborated by a CIA informant (LIRING-3, since identified as Carlos Delmar Jurado),[180] whom Russo cites elsewhere as "a CIA contact viewed as very reliable by the agency."[181]

The opposite "Phase-Two" stance in this propaganda duet is assumed by Gerald Posner. Posner dismissed the claims of Alvarado ("now so discredited that few repeat his story"), five years before Russo would re-open questions of why the claims of this "young Nicaraguan" were so "quickly disregarded."[182] Posner found Garro's story "highly unlikely," and unsupported.[183] Russo faulted the CIA in Mexico (i.e. Win Scott) for reaching "the wrong conclusion," when it reported that "[The fact] that Sylvia Duran had sexual intercourse with Lee Harvey Oswald . . . adds little to the case."[184] With both of these books receiving rave reviews from the *New York Times*, it is hard for the American public to look behind this ballet of bestsellers, and discern the actual dynamics of case management.

The Intercepts, the Cover-Up, and the Assassination Plot

With the wholesale releases of the cable traffic in the 1990s, there is more and more recognition that the CIA and FBI, in the days after the assassination, engaged in a cover-up. Richard Mahoney reports that Bobby Kennedy, on November 29, asked Hoover if Oswald had been "connected with the Cuban operation [Mongoose] with money;" and received only a guarded reply, "That's what we're trying to nail down now."[185] According to Mahoney,

> It was obvious . . . to anyone in the know that the CIA, in particular Allen Dulles, a Warren Commission member, had covered up the CIA's violent relationship with anti-Castro Cubans and the fact that Oswald, as Senator Schweiker later said, "had the fingerprints of Intelligence all over him."[186]

Even Gus Russo, whose book is throughout a defense of CIA integrity, concedes that the CIA withheld information that "could have given the public the misperception that the Agency had a relationship with Oswald."[187] But according to Russo, Dulles' cover-up activities on the Warren Commission were intended chiefly to protect Bobby Kennedy, rather than the CIA.[188] "A full disclosure of Mexico City matters," Russo argues, "would have bared the Kennedys' plans to murder Fidel Castro. . . . Such a disclosure would certainly have diminished JFK's mystique as an innocent martyr."[189] (In other words, what I shall call in Chapter 6 a "Phase-Three" story.)

Both of these two variant explanations focus on a cover-up designed to cover up anti-Castro assassination plotting in 1963:

plotting in which both CIA personnel (certainly) and Bobby Kennedy (possibly) were involved. But neither Mahoney nor Russo point out the degree to which the 1963 post-Mongoose plotting involved the sources and managers of the Oswald Mexico City stories.

The Sources of the Stories and the ZR/RIFLE Assassination Project

In the pages to follow, I shall show how Staff D, the small CIA unit responsible for SIGINT (signals intelligence), and thus for electronic intercept operations, was also the unit which housed the CIA's ZR/RIFLE assassination project. The Mexican DFS, which supplied the raw intercept data to the CIA in Mexico City, also overlapped in many ways with the Cubans and organized crime personnel picked for the CIA-mafia anti-Castro assassination plots.[190]

It is possible that the special circumstances in Mexico City explain why the CIA's generic assassination project, ZR/RIFLE, was housed within the Staff D's intercept operations. ("ZR" normally prefixed the cryptonym for a intercept program.) In his hunt for killers, ZR/RIFLE chief William Harvey searched for individuals with criminal connections.[191] The Mexico City intercept operation against the Soviet Embassy was by far the largest and most important CIA intercept program anywhere in the world.[192] And the DFS, the local intelligence service on which the CIA relied to man its listening posts, was probably the intelligence service with the profoundest links to the international drug traffic and to American organized crime.

For example, the brother-in-law of Luis Echeverría Alvarez, in 1963 the main liaison between Win Scott and the DFS, was Rubén Zuno Arce, who during Echeverría's term as President of Mexico emerged as a top drug trafficker, eventually jailed for the murder of a DEA agent (*Los Angeles Times*, 3/25/93). Such direct family links between Mexican politicians and the drug traffic were unfortunately not uncommon.

Here is the gist of the DFS-drug-organized crime relationship, as set out in *Deep Politics II*:

The DFS was involved in the LIENVOY intercept project and probably manned the listening posts. The DFS may have been assisted in this LIENVOY project by Richard Cain, an expert telephone tapper and adjunct to the CIA-Giancana [ZR/RIFLE] assassination connection, when he was in Mexico City in 1962 as a consultant to a Mexican Government agency. Richard Cain at the time was also part of that Dave Yaras-Lennie Patrick-Sam Giancana element of the Chicago mob with demonstrable links to Jack Ruby in 1963, and the HSCA speculated that Cain may have been part of the 1960–61 CIA-Mafia plots against Castro. [Cain's CIA file, according to a later CIA memo, "reflects that . . . in 1963 . . . he became deeply involved in the President Kennedy assassination case.][193]

Since 1995 new releases from Cain's FBI file have revealed that the file identified Cain not with the CIA or its Bay of Pigs Cuban Front the FRD, but as "a former United States Army Military Intelligence Officer.[194]

Unmistakably Staff D, the small secretive part of CIA in which the CIA-Mafia plots were housed, controlled the LIENVOY intercept intake inside the Mexico City CIA station (Anne Goodpasture, the responsible officer, was a member of Staff D). If Richard Cain trained and possibly helped recruit the Mexican LIENVOY monitors, then the CIA-DFS LIENVOY collaboration would present a matrix for connecting the CIA's internal mishandling of Oswald information to the behavior of Ruby and other criminal elements in Dallas. It would also put the CIA-Mafia connection, through Staff D, in a position to feed to the CIA the false intercept linking a false Oswald to a suspected Soviet assassination expert (Kostikov), the intercept that became a major pretext for creating a Warren Commission to reach the less dangerous conclusion of a lone assassin.

There are contextual corroborations of this matrix. Both Ruby and the DFS had links to the Mexico-Chicago drug traffic, dating back to the 1940s. The DFS and the Mexican drug traffic became increasingly intertwined after 1963; the last two DFS Chiefs were indicted, for smuggling and for murder; and the DFS itself was nominally closed down in the midst of Mexico's 1985 drug scandals.[195]

To this we should add that Nicaraguan security forces, to whom Alvarado reported, were also deeply implicated under Somoza in the international drug traffic. Indeed military intelligence officers from Mexico to Panama in this period frequently exhibited the same pattern: involvement with each other, with the drug traffic, and with the CIA.[196]

Involvement with drug-trafficking was associated with other criminal activities, notably the smuggling of stolen U.S. cars. Miguel Nazar Haro, a key DFS official who was also a CIA asset, handled requests for information with respect to Lee Harvey Oswald from the CIA, and eventually from the HSCA.[197] Eventually Nazar Haro was indicted in California as part of a $30 million car theft ring.[198]

We have seen that Alvarado himself was part of this milieu. As CIA cables reveal, his reports on Communists for Nicaraguan intelligence reached the CIA through his superiors. And the man to whom he reported, Gustavo Montiel of Nicaraguan Military Intelligence, was accused years later of being behind a "massive car theft ring" in the 1970s, which was run by another undercover informant against subversives, Norwin Meneses Canterero.[199]

Norwin Meneses became the key figure in a Contra-drug connection exposed by Gary Webb; CIA cables released in connection with Webb's charges confirm that already in the Somoza era Meneses "was called the kingpin of narcotics traffickers in Nicaragua."[200] Yet Meneses was able to move in and out of the United States with impunity in the Contra period. This immunity aroused suspicions in law enforcement circles that Meneses enjoyed CIA protection, just as undoubtedly the CIA intervened to remove Nazar Haro from the list of DFS agents indicted in California for car smuggling.[201]

It is highly unlikely that Scott and the other CIA Station officers were unaware of the corruption with which they were dealing, but of which their cables mention nothing. Indeed Scott was a personal beneficiary, having accepted from his friend Miguel Nazar Haro a Cadillac for his personal use.[202]

New Revelations about Staff D, the DFS, and ZR/RIFLE

There are new revelations which strengthen the importance, in the ZR/RIFLE assassination nexus, of the Mexico City connection between Staff D and the DFS. The first is the importance of Mexico City to Staff D operations globally. As already noted, Mexico City was the site of the largest CIA intercept operations around the globe, as it afforded the CIA the opportunity to target one of the largest KGB outposts outside of the Soviet bloc.[203] Anne Goodpasture, who supervised the intercept operations in the Mexico City station, was a member of Staff D. She was also a co-author of the suspect cable naming Oswald and Kostikov, MEXI 6453, which I have characterized as evidence of a conspiracy.

As Chief of Covert Action in the Mexico City CIA Station, and later as Chief of Cuban Operations, David Phillips oversaw these intercept operations. Simultaneously he held a second operational responsibility in the Special Affairs Staff, which in 1963 was coordinating all covert operations (including assassinations) against Castro. Some of these anti-Castro Cuban assets were based in Mexico City, and two of these in particular have been linked to the Kennedy assassination.

The first is Isidro (or Eusebio) Borja, the Mexican–born Cuban military chief of the exile group DRE, the Directorio Revolucionario Estudiantil. At the 1995 meeting in Nassau between Cuban and American students of the assassination, the Cubans reported that according to their files Borja was back in Mexico in 1962–63, as an asset of Phillips. This is quite credible, given Borja's Mexican background, plus the DRE's role in propaganda activities for the Bay of Pigs, for which Phillips was responsible. Borja in 1963 was one of the DRE Cubans being financed by Clare Boothe Luce (see Chapter 6).

The Cubans, who had seen a photograph of Borja, also suggested that Borja might have been the alleged Mexican observed in the photographs of Oswald leafleting in New Orleans.[204] More relevant in my view is Borja's responsibility for the DRE's military arms procurement program in 1963, which brought the DRE to Dallas and possible contact (according to a book by Ray and Mary La Fontaine) with both Oswald and Jack Ruby.[205] Of particular interest is the fact that arms were being supplied by a Captain of the U.S. Army at Fort Hood (Capt. George Nonte), the army base in Texas which for some reason maintained an intelligence file both on Oswald and his alias "A.J. Hidell."[206]

The second of Phillips' anti-Castro Cuban assets was Bernardo de Torres, the assassination suspect referred to by Gaeton Fonzi as "Carlos."[207] De Torres also developed close relationships with the DFS and has been accused of smuggling drugs out of Mexico with the knowledge of Nazar Haro.[208]

Bernardo de Torres has further been established as a contact of David Sanchez Morales.[209] Morales was a CIA officer and killer who "was well known as the Agency's top assassin in Latin America." He also openly described Kennedy's conduct during the Bay of Pigs operation "as *traición* (betrayal)."[210] According to a friend, Morales once ended an anti-Kennedy tirade with the words, "Well, we took care of that son of a bitch, didn't we?"[211]

Since the 1950s Morales' career had closely paralleled that of his friend David Phillips: in Caracas, on the Guatemala operation, on the Bay of Pigs, and by 1963 at the JM/WAVE station. Two witnesses have stated that when Morales was stationed at JM/WAVE in Miami, and Phillips in Mexico City, "Morales would frequently travel from . . . Miami to Mexico City."[212] Two of Morales' friends said that Morales spoke of having taken part in the killing of Che Guevara (1967), and also of "a leader of the government in Chile" (either General Schneider in 1970 or President Allende in 1973).[213] The former assassination at least would have been while under the direction of David Phillips, who was in charge of the CIA's program to prevent Allende from assuming office.[214]

But in 1963 Morales was also meeting with the former principals of the ZR/RIFLE plots, William Harvey and John Rosselli, for purposes which are unexplained, and were possibly unauthorized.[215] Rosselli, an associate of Richard Cain from Chicago, had been the principal mob participant in the ZR/RIFLE project to assassinate Castro.[216] But by 1963 Harvey, after infuriating both Robert Kennedy and CIA Director McCone, had been taken off anti-Castro operations and reassigned as CIA Station Chief in Rome. The FBI had Rosselli under close observation in 1963; and allegedly overheard him and Harvey indulge themselves "by saying nasty things about Bobby Kennedy."[217]

Another significant revelation is the presence in William Harvey's ZR/RIFLE files of Harold Meltzer, who in the 1940s helped build up the Mafia's Mexico City drug connection.[218] According to Richard Mahoney,

> In 1975, the Church Committee catalogued Harvey's ZR/RIFLE files and found the dossier of one Harold Meltzer, whom Harvey had described as "a resident of Los Angeles with a long criminal record." What the ZR/RIFLE memo did not say was that Meltzer was a longtime collaborator and sometime shooter for Rosselli. Who, if not Rosselli, would have introduced him and vouched for him to Harvey? It was yet another indication that the alliance between Harvey and Rosselli went far deeper than the one-shot joint venture to kill Castro. What sealed their relationship was a venomous hatred of the Kennedys, and their collaboration in the sensitive art of murder.[219]

And what Mahoney does not mention is that both FBN and FBI files linked the Mexican drug connection to Jack Ruby. Ruby's contacts with Mexican drugs are first reported in 1948, but seem to have been reactivated in 1963. At least one old collaborator of Meltzer in the Mexican drug traffic, Paul Roland Jones, contacted Ruby in Dallas just before the assassination.[220]

It is clear that throughout 1963, members like David Morales of the CIA's Special Affairs Staff, designated to co-ordinate operations against Castro (including new assassination projects), maintained contact with Cuban and other enemies of the Kennedys. What has become clear only recently is that David Phillips, when he acquired his second role in the fall of 1963 as Chief of Cuban Operations in Mexico City, now answered in this capacity to the

Special Affairs Staff.[221] Phillips was in effect rejoining the officers he had worked with on the Bay of Pigs in 1961, at which time he had been responsible for propaganda operations against the newly-created Fair Play for Cuba Committee.[222]

From about October 1 to October 9 Phillips made a quick trip, authorized by the Special Affairs Staff, to Washington and then Miami.[223] On October 1 the Mexico City CIA station also sent a cable directing that a diplomatic pouch, sent on October 1 to Washington, should be held in the registry until picked up by "Michael C. Choaden" (i.e. Phillips) presently TDY (temporary duty) HQS."[224-225]The date October 1 catches our eye, inasmuch as it is the date of the alleged Oswald-Kostikov intercept. One is also struck by Phillips' presence in the Miami JMWAVE station from October 7–9. There are reports that Rosselli, who had good standing in the JMWAVE station, met on two occasions in Miami in early October with Jack Ruby.[226]

Phillips' trip coincides curiously with a significant change in the contents and handling of Oswald's 201 file. Up to late September 1963, incoming documents about Oswald had been referred to the CI/OPS and SR/CI (Soviet Russia/Counter-intelligence) desks.[227] But there was a new addressee for the next Oswald document, an FBI Report of September 24 from New Orleans about Oswald's arrest in August 9 after distributing Fair Play for Cuba leaflets. This was "Austin Horn" of SAS/CI (replacing the usual SR/CI), whose name appears next to the date stamp "8 Oct 1963."

This exclusion of SR/CI, coupled with the initial exclusion of the report (entitled "Lee Harvey Oswald") from Oswald's 201 file, helps explain how an unwitting member of the SR/CI staff (Stephan Roll) could clear an outgoing cable that stated, falsely, that

Latest HDQS info [on Oswald] was ODACID [State Department] report dated May 1962 [!] saying ODACID had determined Oswald is still US citizen and both he and his Soviet wife have exit permits and Dept State had given approval for their travel with their infant child to USA.[228]

Of the six officers responsible for drafting and signing this important cable, only one, Jane Roman of CI/LS (Counterintelligence/
Liaison), had seen the incoming FBI report of September 24 that
disproved their text.

David Phillips is the one man who seems to cover all aspects
of the CIA-Oswald operation and cover-up in 1963. David Phillips
even had one friend, Gordon McLendon, in common with Jack
Ruby. McLendon, a sometime intelligence officer and Dallas owner
of radio stations, had known Phillips since both men were in their
teens. (The two men would in the 1970s join in forming the Association of Former Intelligence Officers.)[229] McLendon was close to
two other wealthy men in Dallas who have attracted the attention
of JFK researchers, Clint Murchison and Bedford Wynne.[230]

What was not yet known is why McLendon, whom Ruby
described as one of his six closest friends, embarked on a sudden
and surprising trip with his family to Mexico in the fall of 1963.[231]

Conclusion: The CIA, Drugs, and History

By looking closely at the Mexico Oswald stories, and particularly
at their genesis in the corrupt drug-linked Mexican DFS, we have
learnt more about the CIA role in covering up important clues
about the Kennedy assassination. We have seen also that the CIA
drew on the resources of intelligence agencies whose power was
grounded in the local drug traffic, not just in Mexico, but also in
Nicaragua.

Later in this book, we shall see the illicit drug traffic as a
shadow nexus behind other figures who figure in the story of the
John F. Kennedy assassination, such as Jack Ruby, Sam Giancana,
John Roselli, John Martino, and Richard Cain. It will I think prove
relevant that key CIA figures, notably William Harvey and James
Angleton, had direct or indirect links to just these elements in
organized crime.[232]

This situation, an interaction between what is documented and
what is not, also forces us to enlarge our thinking about history.
As we have seen, history is defined in dictionary terms as a narrative or record of what is known. A successful assassination plot,

by contrast, represents an interruption of this record by the unre-corded, the unknown. Thus the defense of succeeding political legitimacy becomes indistinguishable from a defense of the integrity and dominance of the public historical record. This defense propels people to trivialize the assassination as an accident, the work of a "lone nut."

Those of us who genuinely wish to see overt, rational forces prevail in the world must reject such a superficial and spurious defense of our institutions. The ideal embraced by our society, that it be based on truth and openness, is not a cynical cliché, but a real condition for our institutional health. The pursuit of leads hinted at in this essay may seem frustratingly difficult, esoteric, and above all slow. But to abandon this pursuit is to break faith with the American dream, indeed the dream of enlightenment itself.

3

Oswald, the CIA, and the Hunt for Popov's Mole

One of the most brazenly deceptive sentences in the Warren Report was the claim that the Warren Commission had "thoroughly investigated Oswald's relationships prior to the assassination with all agencies of the U.S. government."[233] In fact the Commission, already disturbed by reports that Oswald had been an FBI informant, had publicly declined even to look at Oswald's Headquarters FBI file.[234]

As noted in Chapter 2, the CIA file on Oswald forwarded to the Commission had been altered to disguise one of the false allegations in it; and this alteration had been further disguised with a falsely dated transmittal slip.[235] The Warren Commission staff did not pursue this discernible anomaly, while Chief Justice Warren again took pains to note in the public record that he had declined to review the CIA file at all.[236] As far as can be determined, the Warren Commission and its staff never reviewed relevant Oswald files in Army Intelligence, Marine Intelligence, and Air Force Intelligence (OSI).

Did Warren decline to review the most basic Oswald files because he rightly suspected they would undermine the desired picture of Oswald as a "loner" without governmental connections? In fact Oswald's pre-assassination files in the U.S. Government were voluminous: there were at least thirteen files in the State

Department alone, plus at least two further CIA files on Oswald never offered to the Warren Commission.[237] They were also replete with demonstrable anomalies and falsehoods: so many falsehoods that we can refer to the book-length body of pre-assassination Oswald documents as "the Oswald legend."

From the CIA files now released we know there has been, since 1960, a great deal of CIA deception from many different officers with respect to Oswald. Most of this is probably attributable to a legitimate counterintelligence operation, rather than an assassination conspiracy. Some of it, especially after the assassination, is probably cover-up. As for the residue, the surplus deception, I shall leave the reader to decide whether or not some of the lies of the late David Atlee Phillips ("Michael C. Choaden") fall into this category.

As I have said before, the existence of a large CIA deception operation with Oswald does not in any way prove that the CIA was behind the assassination of the President. It does however make it probable that we should include among the assassination conspirators one or more individuals witting of the CIA operation. For much of Oswald's strange behavior in the last six months of his life, including his conflicting performances in New Orleans as first an anti-Castro and then a pro-Castro activist, appears to have been in fulfillment of some as yet unrevealed intelligence agenda.

What can be said with more confidence is both simple and important. From 1959 through October 1963, the Oswald files were the subject of attention, manipulation, and deceptive reporting, from a number of senior Counterintelligence Operations officers. The easiest and most likely explanation for this manipulative and deceptive behavior is that these files were part of a significant, sophisticated, multi-agency counterintelligence operation. I shall suggest that at least one phase of this operation was a search for a mole inside the CIA.

If so there was probably at least one operational file on Oswald in addition to the three CIA files on Oswald referred to above. This would not be so unusual. From other newly-released CIA documents we learn that the CIA (or at a minimum the CIA Office of Security) was accustomed to maintain dual files on individuals, one overt and one covert. At least four Counterintelligence (CI) Operations officers handled the CIA's Oswald documents before the assassination.[238]

A further conclusion is even simpler. It is highly unlikely that, in the last four weeks of his life, Oswald could have shaken free from this hidden legacy, and become what we have always been officially told he was: a lone nut without significant connections to any governmental agency.[239] On the contrary, Oswald's last weeks saw recurring encounters between Oswald and various Cubans and Americans with intelligence connections.[240]

The Pre-Assassination Oswald Documents as a Counterintelligence "Marked Card" Operation

In 1994 I suggested that Lee Harvey Oswald, or more specifically the government documentation on Oswald, was used by the Counterintelligence Staff of the CIA in its obsessive search for a mole inside the U.S. government. CI/SIG, the Counterintelligence Special Investigation Group, the group charged by CIA Counterintelligence Chief James Angleton with the search for the mole, opened a 201 file on Oswald in 1960. The file, I suggested, became the control point for a "marked card" operation, in which falsified bits of information, like bent cards, were passed through the system to see where, and by what route, they ended up.[241] This article will look more closely at how that "marked card" operation worked. It will conclude that, however important and sensitive the search for the mole may have been, one or more other important covert operations were piggy-backed upon the mole search.

From his alleged defection to Russia in 1959, to his alleged visit to Mexico in 1963, Oswald's files in at least seven federal government agencies (CIA, State, FBI, ONI, OSI, Marine G-2, INS) became repositories for more and more conspicuously or subtly variegated data. At least some of these "marked cards" were invented inside the counterintelligence system, and some of them inside CI/SIG itself. For example "Lee Henry Oswald," the CIA's name for its Lee Harvey Oswald file, was a name invented in December 1960 by Ann Egerter of the CI/SIG Staff.[242] The 201 file opened in this name remained tightly restricted by CI/SIG, so that they could keep track for almost two years of whoever had had access to it.

A classic example of card-marking was the generation in October 1963 of two CIA messages about Oswald, by two teams, each of which included Ann Egerter of CI/SIG, Stephan Roll of the Soviet Russia Counterintelligence Staff, and Jane Roman of the Counterintelligence Liaison Staff. Both messages were released, to different addressees, on the same day, October 10, 1963. Both cables were in response to the incoming information that someone who identified himself as Lee Oswald had spoken to the Soviet Embassy in Mexico City. They were sent to different audiences, including CIA officers whom we know Angleton suspected of being a mole.

In one of the two cables, drafted on the same day by the same people, Oswald was described as "approximately 35 years old . . . about six feet tall."[243] In the other, he was a 23-year-old measuring five feet ten.[244] There were other invented differences. Ignorance or inattention cannot explain this obvious deception; indeed Jane Roman, confronted by John Newman with the second cable, admitted to him, "I'm signing off on something [the cable] that I know isn't true."[245]

Both John Newman and I have argued that by 1963 Oswald was being used in other covert operations, specifically against the Fair Play for Cuba Committee.[246] But the CI Staff's bifurcation of its Oswald information, into two different forms for different audiences, is the classic "marked card" operation that characterizes a molehunt. If your sources tell you later that an outside party has heard Oswald is aged 35, you have clearly narrowed your search for the source of the leak. (An outside report of him as 23 would not tell you anything, because in real life Lee Harvey Oswald was indeed 23).

Another in-house name for this marked information is a "barium meal."[247] The same procedure was followed, again by the Soviet Russia Counterintelligence Staff, in the nine-year search for the mole Aldrich Ames:

Then the barons of the Soviet division began devising
ways to test their communications links, the wiring that
connected the CIA's headquarters with Moscow. They
would pump the system full of bogus information and see
if the system leaked. It was a procedure similar to doc-
tors injecting radioactive barium into a patient's blood-
stream so that X rays could detect flaws in the veins and
arteries. If the trick worked, the Soviets would pick up on
the false information and act on it. That might reveal the
location of a weak link in the CIA's chain of command and
communications.[248]

This particular barium meal revealed nothing, perhaps because
Ames, the actual source of the leaks, was himself serving as Chief
of the Soviet Russia Counterintelligence Staff.

The key to this method lies in the altering of information,
analogous to the use of the radioactive barium isotope. Borrowing
yet another analogy from science, I shall call this method *allotropy*,
the creation of one or more variants of an information datum; and
each consciously differentiated variant I shall call an *allotrope*.
Analysis of Oswald's 201 file will reveal numerous and sustained
instances of allotropy, beginning with his alleged defection to Russia in 1959.

There are three different ways in which one can visualize the
relationship of Oswald to this molehunt. One possibility is that
Oswald himself was under suspicion.[249] The best rebuttal to this
hypothesis is that Oswald himself was (as we shall see) used to
help generate the allotropic barium meal; thus he is unlikely to
have been the suspect. A second possibility is that Oswald followed U.S. orders as a molehunter's catspaw, serving as bait to
catch others at a higher level. (It is extremely unlikely that he was
more than a low-level pawn in a larger tightly-held operation that
was mostly beyond his comprehension.) A third possibility is the
mixed hypothesis, that Oswald, in fulfilling the agenda of one U.S.
covert operation, aroused suspicions among other U.S. operators
who were not in on the secret.[250]

Angleton's Molehunt, Pyotr Popov, and the U-2

The evidence considered in the present essay will strengthen the second possible thesis, that Oswald himself was a low-level part of a CI search for a leak or mole. It will suggest that this search was a major one involving five or more U.S. government agencies, and we shall dwell in particular on the active Oswald investigation pursued by the Air Force Office of Special Investigations (OSI).

There are six major reasons why we should consider the hypothesis that the Oswald files were designed to function as part of a marked card or barium meal operation. The first is that those in charge of the Oswald 201 file, Birch D. O'Neal and Ann Egerter (alias Betty Eggeter), were both in the very small and secret Counterintelligence Special Investigation Group (CI/SIG), whose unique assignment was to supervise the hunt for moles, using standard devices such as a "marked card" operation.[251] (For reasons never adequately explored, O'Neal as Chief of CI/SIG continued to be the recipient of post-assassination cables about Oswald, as late as 1965).[252]

The second reason is that Counterintelligence *Operations* Officers, housed in the CI/OPS group, the SR/CI (Soviet Russia Counterintelligence) Branch, and WH (Western Hemisphere Division) were the largest group handling most of the incoming and outgoing Oswald documents. There were at least four such operations officers involved, including Jean Evans, the Chief of Counterintelligence Operations (C/CI/OPS). We shall see that two of them (William Potocki and D. Lynch) apparently coordinated the operation whereby a falsified or "marked" State Department despatch ("A-273" of 4/13/61) was introduced into CIA files.

The third reason is that (as we shall see) the Angletonian molehunt was triggered by a report from a KGB double agent (Pyotr Popov) that the KGB had detailed information about the then-secret U-2 program. Oswald was knowledgeable about the U-2 from his stint at Atsugi in Japan; and I shall argue that his otherwise inexplicable talk in Moscow of sharing his information with the KGB (said to American officers, not to Soviet ones!) is explainable as part of a test for leaks on just this subject.

The fourth reason is that William Hood, reportedly the newly-created Chief of Operations for the Western Hemisphere Division (WH/COPS), signed as Authenticating Officer for the clearly deceptive cable of October 10, 1963, in which it was falsely reported that "latest HDQS info [on Oswald] was [State] report dated May 1962," about Oswald's plans to return from the Soviet Union.[253] Hood was a long-time counterintelligence ally of Angleton, with a career-long interest in the Popov case and resulting molehunt, about which he subsequently wrote a book.[254]

The fifth reason is that some of those minor officials suspected of being a mole after Popov's revelations were on the distribution lists of "marked" Oswald documents. A symptomatic example is Russell Langelle, Popov's case officer at the time of his arrest. Both Hood and Langelle appear to have shifted from Soviet to Western Hemisphere affairs at about the time that Oswald became actively interested in Cuba and allegedly visited Mexico City. (Thus an Oswald document routed to Langelle was signed by William Hood, both men having long been deeply implicated in the Popov case.)

The sixth reason is that, for whatever reason, information in the Oswald files is recurringly altered, falsified, or given distinctive variant versions: serving, in effect, as "marked cards." Even routine documents appear to have been crafted with great deliberation. A brief request to the Navy for Oswald's photograph, for example, required coordination by six officers whose names appear on the file copy (at least three of these were from the Counterintelligence Staff).[255]

In this investigation, we shall observe some anomalies which corroborate the thesis of a molehunt; but we shall also see others (such as consistent efforts to conceal his background) which this thesis does not explain. Thus I shall argue not just the thesis that Oswald's falsified file was part of a molehunt, but also the more speculative thesis that behind the highly classified molehunt lurked one or more other covert operations, even more secret.

In Chapter 4 I will consider whether Oswald, or at least the Oswald file, may not have been at the center of a profound U.S. internal conflict, one transcending even the CIA, over the role of the U.S. in the cold war. It is relevant to observe at this point that Angleton's search for a mole was part of a profound division within the CIA on perhaps the most profound of foreign policy issues: how should the U.S. respond to signs of liberalization within the Soviet Union.

The First Reports of Oswald in the Soviet Union

Among Aldrich Ames' responsibilities for the CIA when he served overseas was to coordinate "double agent operations that the U.S. Army and Navy were running against the Soviets—that is, American dangles pretending to cooperate with the KGB."[256] Other studies of U.S. intelligence confirm that the running of "dangles"—personnel offering to share information with or work for the Soviet enemy—was the special responsibility of military intelligence, but coordinated with the CIA.[257]

Oswald's alleged defection to the Soviet Union in 1959 has the earmarks of a classical "dangle." The first State Department cable on his visit to the Moscow Embassy reported that Oswald "says has offered Soviets any information he has acquired as enlisted radar operator."[258] The follow-up despatch from Embassy official Richard Snyder, who interviewed Oswald, added that Oswald "intimated that he might know something of special interest."[259]

This of course was an understatement. Oswald's work in the Marines as a radar operator at Atsugi had exposed him to knowledge of the super-secret U-2 program, a fact so sensitive and important it was omitted in 1964 from the Warren Report's biography of Oswald, and in 1979 from the HSCA Report.[260] The same two Reports suppressed one of Oswald's most intriguing acts: his declaration in the US Moscow Embassy of his intention "to make known [to the Soviets] such information concerning the Marine Corps and his specialty as he possessed".[261]

All the alarms in Washington should have gone off if Oswald's threat were possibly a real one. The failure of the dogs to bark, of the various agencies to follow up, is in fact the most obvious clue that Oswald's threat was part of his performance as a dangle. Although the initial response of ONI to the news had indicated "continuing interest" in this "intelligence matter," the matter of Oswald's threat seems never to have been pursued by any agency.[262]

Even Snyder, the man to whom Oswald oddly reported this self-incriminating threat, concluded that it was a performance. "Snyder's hypothesis was that Oswald assumed the KGB had bugged the American Embassy, and 'was speaking for Russian ears in my office.'"[263] If so, this was a highly inefficient way for Oswald to communicate his threat to the Soviets. One explanation, offered many years ago by Snyder, is that Oswald might have "thought he was establishing credibility with Russian ears-in-the-wall [electronic surveillance]."[264] Interestingly, the KGB (according to Norman Mailer) also assumed that Oswald's talk of offering information was addressed to their microphones in the wall.[265]

Oswald's talk, in the presence of U.S. officials, of giving information to the Soviets, was if taken at face value an extraordinarily reckless performance. Legally, it amounted to no less than a threat to commit espionage. As a Marine still in the Corps (even if released to "inactive duty"), he should normally have been arrested on the spot by the Marines responsible for the U.S. Embassy's security.

Thus one has to agree with Mailer's KGB sources (against Snyder) that Oswald's performance for the microphones would normally diminish his credibility with the KGB. The straightforward way for him to establish this credibility would have been to share his highly desirable intelligence with them directly.

The example of Oswald will show how the different operations of a dangle and a barium meal would work more efficiently together. Common to both is the need to make the subject *interesting* to the KGB. Intelligence about the U-2, "the most important single source in the U.S. perception of the Soviet threat," certainly would have caught the KGB's attention.[266] Yet we now have two books about Oswald purporting to be based in part on KGB files and witnesses. They both, in different ways, claim that Oswald's threat to give the KGB information was never fulfilled. Nechiporenko states unambiguously that Oswald's threat to offer information was made inside the U.S. Embassy, but never directly to the KGB.[267] Mailer's composite KGB source, "General Marov," is quoted as saying that the KGB "did not seek to debrief him overtly . . . 'Certainly no official debriefing. This is not only my opinion but my information.'"[268]

We shall return in a later essay to the possibility that, despite the combined testimony of U.S. and KGB officials, Oswald did offer, successfully, information about the U-2: if not to the KGB, then possibly to the rival GRU. (From as early as 1964, some U.S. personnel have assumed that information from Oswald helped the USSR to down Gary Powers' U-2 in May 1960, resulting in the cancellation of a proposed summit meeting between Eisenhower and Khrushchev.)[269] In the absence of that hypothesis, the "dangle" operation seems subordinate to the barium meal: that is, the testing of the Embassy's security to see if the threat leaked to the Soviets.

The case for a barium meal is strengthened when we look at the allotropy in Richard Snyder's two written responses to the "threat," Moscow Cable 1304 of October 31, and Despatch 234 of November 2. Snyder's cable reported, "Mother's address and his last address US 4936 Collinwood St., Fort Worth Texas;" but this was not true, and had not been since May 1957. In fact his mother's address in 1959 was 3124 West Fifth Street, Fort Worth; and this was the address that Oswald had used on his passport application of September 4.[270] (We cannot tell if that home address was ever inscribed in Oswald's passport; the home address is effaced and apparently had been before Snyder examined it.)[271]

Snyder is by all accounts an intelligent, literate, Harvard-educated career State official, who in the past had worked for the CIA.[272] His getting things wrong about Oswald is thus more plausibly explained as part of a counterintelligence operation, than as incompetence. In his ensuing despatch of November 2, Snyder blamed Oswald himself for the (incorrect) Collinwood address, but Snyder then compounded this allotropy with others, at least one of which was of his own making:

> Oswald gave his last address in the United States as that of his mother at 4936 Collinwood Street, Fort Worth, Texas. A telegram subsequently received at the Embassy for him indicates that a brother, Robert L. Oswald, resides at 7313

Davenport, Fort Worth, Texas. He stated that he was discharged from the U.S. Marine Corps on September 11,
1959. Highest grade achieved was corporal. Oswald evi-
dently applied for his passport to the Agency in San Francisco while still in service.[273]

This paragraph is dense with allotropes, not all attributable to
Oswald. Oswald was not "discharged;" he was released from
active duty, but was still in the Marine Corps Reserve. His highest
grade was not "corporal," but private first class.[274] Finally and most
importantly, the passport, which was not only examined by Snyder
but retained by him, indicates clearly that it was issued, not in San
Francisco, but in Los Angeles.[275]

Both the stale address allegedly offered by Oswald, and Snyder's own allotrope, the lie that Oswald's passport was applied for
in San Francisco, are part of a repeated pattern in Oswald's 201 file.
One effect of this misinformation, as of similar allotropes generated by the FBI and CIA, is to render the real Oswald untraceable
(except through his brother, another ex-Marine), and also to seg-
regate the information being collected about him from other files
(such as Oswald's passport file in Los Angeles).

Keep in mind that Oswald had allegedly said he would offer
Soviet officials information about his "specialty" as a Marine
Corps radar operator. This threat to commit espionage was heavily
marked in pencil by someone in Washington, and small wonder.
A straightforward response would have been to begin investigating the self-declared spy at once. To prepare for this, Snyder
should have reported immediately anything relevant to such an
investigation.

His cabled response was the opposite: to report as fact an
alleged address that was in fact no longer true ("Mother's address
and his last address US 4936 Collinwood St., Fort Worth, Texas"),
and to omit, indeed suppress, the valid, documented address of
Oswald's brother that was written in the passport itself ("7313
Davanport [i.e. Davenport] St., Fort Worth").[276] That some kind of
complex game is being played here seems likely, even more so in
the light of Snyder's evasive response in 1994 to a question about

this omission. After I had discussed this problem with John Newman in August 1994, Newman

> asked Snyder [on August 21, 1994] why he did not mention this address in 1959. Snyder's reply was that Oswald had probably written the Davenport address in ["above the excised address"] after Snyder gave Oswald his passport back in 1961.[277]

This is fudging the issue. The "Davanport" address is entered *twice* on the first page (not, as Newman writes, on the photograph page) of the passport (18 WH 161). One of these entries is in place of the deleted ("excised") home address, and indeed this entry was probably written in later. But the other address (of his brother, the person to notify "in case of death or accident") was presumably written in when Oswald received his passport in 1959. Thus Snyder's "explanation" does nothing to explain why this important information was not forwarded.

(A Digression) Looking Ahead: The State Department Variants of 1961

The State Department and Snyder would continue to behave oddly on the matter of Oswald and his passport. In Headquarters Instruction A-173 of April 13, 1961, Snyder was instructed by the State Department Passport Office in Washington that Oswald's passport could be returned to him "if he presents evidence that he has arranged to depart from the Soviet Union."[278] This unambiguous instruction is marked and commented on in the Moscow copy. In a despatch numbered 809, of May 26, 1961, Snyder wrote a complex reply to this instruction. Yet when Oswald turned up at the Embassy, in July, Snyder returned the passport the same day, even though Oswald had no evidence that he had "arranged to depart," and would not have such evidence for almost another year.[279]

These State Department documents appear to have been part of an allotropic barium meal being dispersed widely through the

Washington bureaucracy. Eighteen copies of Despatch 809 were distributed to at least five divisions of the State Department, with another fifteen allocated to the CIA. Meanwhile the copies were differentiated allotropically. At least one copy was filed in the Moscow Embassy with its original despatch number, 809, still visible under a typed alteration.[280] But other copies (both in State and over in CIA) were filed with this number clearly retyped (on page one, but not pages two and three) to read "806."[281]

A similar fate awaited the original Instruction A-173 of April 13, 1961. In October a copy was thermofaxed and sent over to CIA, where it was presumably filed by Ann Egerter of CI/SIG, who was in charge of Oswald's 201.[282] That thermofax has however never been released by the CIA. What we have in Oswald's 201 file, as released, is a new copy of A-173, completely retyped, and headed "A-273." This copy was originally stored in a different CIA Oswald file, #351–164 of the Office of Security.[283]

One can see from this how the allotropic barium meal would help pinpoint the leak. KGB references to "809," or "A-173," would implicate those with access to one set of files. "806," or "A-273," would implicate a different group. If this allotropic hypothesis is correct, we can conclude two things about the search for the mole. It was widespread, involving those who worked in the Soviet field both in State and the CIA.[284] And it was relatively high-level, involving inside CIA the restricted groups with access to either Oswald's 201 file (in CI), or his Office of Security file #351–164.

With the releases in the 1990s from the Assassination Records Review Board (ARRB), we learned that one CIA officer was responsible for bringing State despatches "806" and "A-273" to the CIA. This was D. Lynch, an operations officer in the Soviet Russia Counterintelligence Branch. To some extent at least Lynch must have been witting of the game being played. What Lynch actually requested in late 1961 were State Despatches A-173 (the correct number) and "806" (the revised number). A note on his order card indicates that A-173 was "still on order, 5 Oct 61"—exactly the date that a thermofax copy of it was sent over from Robert D. Johnson of the State Department Passport Office (presumably in response to a follow-up request of that day).[285] As noted above, a retyped and falsified "A-273" was eventually placed in the Oswald Security file.

It would appear however that Lynch was being guided in his handling of the Oswald materials, by someone else, an unidentified "WP." Most likely this was William Potocki of the Counterintelligence Operations Branch, where the molehunt operation was housed.[286]

The complex game was being played in the State Department as well, and once again we find Richard Snyder at the center of it. For Snyder was the author of Moscow Despatch #809, which went into the Moscow Embassy file ("XIII") as #809, and reached a Headquarters State file ("X") as #806.[287] Yet when Snyder wrote again about Oswald on July 11, 1961, he too now referred to his earlier despatch as "Embassy's D-806."[288] Somehow he was in sync with the Headquarters officer who, on the same day July 11, also sent a letter referring to "Despatch No. 806."[289]

Snyder was also responsible for the despatch at this time of Oswald's passport renewal application, and also for a "copy" of it (which in fact was not a copy) in the Moscow files. Here again we have an extreme example of allotropy and bifurcation. The Washington version clearly read "I have been naturalized as a citizen of a foreign state." With a different typewritten deletion, the Moscow version read, "I have *not* been naturalized as a citizen of a foreign state."[290]

The Warren Commission was concerned about the content of the Washington version; but did not ask the more relevant question: Why had Embassy typists prepared and Snyder signed two different and opposing versions of what were supposed to be (but were not) identical duplicates?[291] Allen Dulles dominated the Warren Commission discussion of this anomaly, which he dismissed as "a mistake."[292]

In this case, we may be faced with a different phenomenon, not pre-assassination allotropy, but a desperate post-assassination attempt to obfuscate a glaring anomaly in the pre-assassination record. Warren CE 947, allegedly the Moscow copies of Oswald's declaration, reinforced (with the statement, "I have not been naturalized as a citizen of a foreign state") the State Department position that Oswald had not taken actions to renounce his citizenship. It was only received by State in Washington on June 3, 1964, or weeks after the Warren Commission had raised a question about the earlier version ("I have been naturalized as a citizen of a foreign state"), which seemed at odds with that position.[293] On June 10, 1964, one week after the new version was received in State, Dulles used it to rebut Congressman Ford's understandable concern (reflecting, as Ford always did, that of the FBI) that Oswald *had* renounced his citizenship (5 WH 359).

Robert Johnson, who answered Lynch's request for "D-806," may have been witting as well. Although in 1961 he was Chief Counsel for the Passport Office, he had formerly served in the State Department Office of Security, which both housed many CIA officers under cover and collaborated with the CIA in its molehunt. Mr. Johnson would later tell Mr. Sourwine of the Senate Internal Security Subcommittee that he "regularly" performed "confidential," "very important" services for other "agencies of the Government."[294]

Hiding Oswald's Origins: Allotropic Variants from the FBI

Snyder's two communications about Oswald in 1959 were not the only ones to introduce confusing but trackable allotropes, some of which effectively made Oswald himself untraceable. In 1960 a similar game was played by the FBI and the CIA, indeed by the molehunting Ann Egerter herself.

Some of the FBI's allotropy appears to have been created with the cooperation of Oswald's mother Marguerite. As John Newman has noted, Marguerite Oswald took a number of steps in 1960 which led to the multiplication of government files and documents on her son. She herself told the Secret Service that in February 1960 she contacted FBI Agent "Fannan" (presumably Dallas FBI Agent John W. Fain), who recommended that she get in touch with "some senators and congressmen and people" about her son's defection.

> Mr. Fannan (phoenetic [sic]) recommended that I write
> to Sam Rayburn, Secretary Herder [sic] and Congressman

Wright of Fort Worth. I wrote a letter to the three men and
made copies. My reason for that was before my marriage,
I worked for attorneys, and I know that where anything is
important, you should have something to back it up. The
letter [sic] stated the circumstances and I made this clear
and underlined it. As I say, I have a copy of the letter, *the
same letter sent to the three representatives.*[295]

However the three letters, far from being the same, constitute
another important instance of allotropy. On March 6, 1960, she
wrote to Congressman Jim Wright a letter about Lee, in which she
informed him, "According to the UPI Moscow press, he appeared
at the U.S. Embassy renouncing his U.S. citizenship."[296] The next
day she wrote to Secretary of State Christian Herter to say the
exact opposite: that Lee had *not* renounced his citizenship.

All I know is what I read in the newspapers. He went to
the U.S. Ambassy [sic] there and wanted to turn in his U.S.
Citizenship and had applied for Soviet Citizenship. However the Russians refused his request but said he could
remain in their country as a Resident Alien. *As far as I
know he[?] is still a U.S. citizen.*[297]

As Agent Fain must have known, the cognitive dissonance between
these two conflicting statements was destined to fill numerous files
and keep bureaucrats busy for months. Marguerite's statement,
that Oswald *had* renounced his citizenship, was soon officially
recorded by Fain himself in his FBI Report on Oswald of May 12,
1960, and transmitted to the Office of Naval Intelligence (ONI) on
May 26. As we will see in Chapter 4, it would generate a fat Marine
file leading in August to Oswald's undesirable discharge.

John Fain would compile a total of four substantive reports on
Lee Harvey Oswald over the next thirty months. The first three are
interesting chiefly for their allotropic variants, which are numerous and sustained enough to be grouped into two categories. The
first are variants or even errors which are glaring. The cumulative
effect of these is the same as Snyder's communications from the

Moscow Embassy, to ensure that any efforts to contact Oswald's family would be channeled through his brother Robert at the Davenport address, instead of through his mother. Marguerite's married name, which was actually Mrs. Robert Edward Lee Oswald, was rendered as "Mrs. Edward Lee Oswald" in the 1960 report.[298] Her maiden name, which was actually Marguerite Claverie, was rendered in the July 1962 report as "Margaret Clavier."[299]

Like Snyder, Fain also supplies useless, stale-dated addresses for Marguerite. In the four reports he supplies a total of four addresses (including one in Waco), none of them current, none of them useful.[300] For example, the July 12, 1962 report claims that "Margaret Clavier Oswald, nee Clavier ... currently resides at Vernon, Texas."[301] This was not true. For some months she had been residing in Crowell, Texas; and had so notified the State Department in March.[302] By the time of Fain's report it was probable (though there is considerable obfuscation about this) that she had already moved to 1501 West Seventh Street in Fort Worth, where Lee and Marina joined her after Oswald's return from the Soviet Union. (1501 West Seventh is the address on Oswald's employment application of July 13 to Leslie Welding Company).[303]

As we shall see, Fain knew there was something tricky if not conspiratorial about Marguerite's addresses; namely, that she could be reached via the quite different address and telephone number in the Fort Worth phone book, even though she did not actually reside there. But he reserved what he knew for the Administrative pages of his 1960 Report, which (unlike the rest) did not circulate outside the FBI.

This conscious withholding of Marguerite's most serviceable address is a sign that Fain's flood of trivial disinformation was a deliberate stratagem, and probably part of a barium meal. Indeed we can trace the passage of Fain's barium (or allotropes, or "marked cards") through the FBI into other agencies. The May 1960 Fain Report for example reached the CIA almost immediately, and in John Newman's words

took a lengthy and interesting ride through the Agency's Directorate of Operations. This journey through the "spook," or so-called "dark side" of the CIA included stops at several points in James Angleton's counterintelligence staff and at nearly half the branches and offices in [the] Soviet Russia division.[304]

As Newman notes elsewhere, Angleton at this time believed that there was "a mole buried deep within Soviet Division."[305] The barium was being directed to the area of suspicion.

Hiding Oswald's Origins: More Allotropic Variants from FBI, CIA, and from Oswald Himself

A few weeks later, the May 1960 Fain Report was distilled by Ann Egerter of CI/SIG into the following short allotropic gem:

> Born 18 October 1939 in New Orleans, Louisiana, Lee *Henry* Oswald joined the United States Marines at the age of seventeen. . . . After receiving an honorable *discharge* from the Marines on *3 September 1959* [it was actually 4 September 1959] Oswald visited his mother in *Waco*, Texas [instead of Fort Worth]. . . . Shortly thereafter he appeared at the United States Embassy in Moscow and *renounced* his U.S. citizenship.[306]

This short biography was included in a list of American defectors sent over to Hugh Cumming at the State Department, which at the time was being investigated by the House Un-American Activities Committee (HUAC) for harboring Soviet agents. Unlike some others in the list (such as Robert Edward Webster's) Oswald's biography was classified "SECRET," which of course made it easier to channel under controlled circumstances.

Egerter's biography of "Lee Henry Oswald" was part of a "List of American Defectors" prepared at the State Department's request.[307] A sign that the Oswald bio was barium to find a leak is that one of the contributors to the list was Otto Otepka of the State Department Security Office.[308] Otepka was the State Department's Angletonian, a man (close to Robert Johnson) recruited by

Republicans in the McCarthy era to weed out "undesirables," after the furor over Alger Hiss.[309] For years Otepka focused attention on a file of defectors (including Oswald) which Kennedy liberals in the State Department found in Otepka's safe, when they fired him (allegedly for illicit leaks to Congress) in November 1963.[310]

The FBI itself may have been under suspicion. As John Newman has noted, the Fain report of May 1960 was not routed into the FBI Headquarters file on Oswald, as one might expect, but was housed in a different file.[311] At different points in his narrative, Newman documents how CIA, FBI, and State files all share this phenomenon of bifurcated Oswald information that is divided into different files.[312] This phenomenon of "bifurcation" is hard to explain by the single hypothesis of what Newman calls "a counter-intelligence 'dangle' of Oswald in the Soviet Union."[313] But it makes perfect sense as part of a "marked card" operation in which differently marked cards are being parked in different files.

Thus strengthened in the hypothesis that the allotropes are significant, and not random, we should look more closely at two other marked cards supplied by Fain. One is Marguerite's allegation, later denied by Oswald, that Oswald "took his birth certificate with him" when he left for the Soviet Union.[314] This unsupported allegation was escalated by an FBI cable into the statement that "since Oswald had his birth certificate in his possession, another individual may have assumed his identity."[315]

Drawing attention to the Fain Report and Marguerite's statement that Oswald "had taken his birth certificate with him," Hoover then used this bizarre notion in a letter to the State Department Security Office: "Since there is the possibility that an imposter is using Oswald's birth certificate, any current information the Department of State has concerning subject [i.e. Oswald] will be appreciated."[316] This request effectively empowered the FBI's eyes and ears in the State Department Security Office (Emery Adams and Otto Otepka) to investigate what the State Department was doing on the Oswald case.

I shall suggest later that, although the allusion to the birth certificate was an irrelevant pretext, Hoover's speculation (possibly prompted from other sources) was a shrewd one.

An Allotropic Variant and Oswald's Arrest in Dallas

I would like to digress for a moment about a second marked card, which, trivial as it may sound, came to play an important role in Dallas on November 22, 1963. This was Marguerite's voluntary description to Fain of Oswald's height as "5'10'" and his weight as "165 pounds."[317] This allotropic variant of Oswald's height and weight (together with the false father's name "Edward Lee Oswald") was then recorded by the INS on an information form widely disseminated through the U.S. Government: to the CIA, and back to the FBI itself.[318]

It was not accurate. As the FBI knew, Oswald when entering the Marines had been measured at 5'8", weighing 135 pounds (and again at 131 pounds).[319] The heaviest Oswald was ever actually weighed at was 150 pounds, when he joined the Marine Reserves in 1959.[320] Oswald was measured again in 1963, after his first arrest in New Orleans, at 5'9", 136 pounds.[321] After his second arrest, in Dallas, he was measured at 5'9", 131 pounds.[322]

Never at any time did any measurement or acquaintance corroborate Marguerite's allotropic description of her son as 5'10", 165 pounds. Yet this was the description of Kennedy's suspected assassin broadcast by the Dallas Police 15 minutes after the shots were fired in Dealey Plaza.[323] Soon afterwards the Dallas Police turned over to the FBI their alleged source, the only other person besides Marguerite who was ever alleged to have given this description of Oswald.

This witness was Howard Brennan, who told the FBI that in one of the Texas School Book Depository windows he had seen a gunman "about 5'10" tall and around 165 pounds in weight."[324] How Brennan could have actually seen this is unclear; in a later interview he admitted that he had been "able to observe Oswald's head and shoulders in the window and possibly as far down as Oswald's belt."[325] Yet the Warren Report treats Brennan as its star eyewitness, even though (as it later concedes), Brennan did not make a positive identification of Oswald in a November 22 lineup.[326]

Let me specify what conclusions can and cannot be drawn from all this. Clearly the allotropic Oswald variants of 1959 and

1960 could not have contemplated a presidential assassination plot in 1963, of a president who was not yet even elected. On the other hand, the plotters of 1963, in designating Oswald as the alleged assassin, appear to have built their stratagem on knowledge about the information, much of it false, that had been accumulated about Oswald in government files. If so, they must have known also that the subject of Oswald was one so sensitive to government secret operations, that it was certain to trigger an official cover-up.

The Multi-Agency Charade of Oswald's Discharge and of Marguerite's Addresses

We have seen that there are numerous allotropic variants generated in successive documents from Snyder in State, Fain in the FBI, and Egerter in the CIA. These variants share certain features, above all in rendering Oswald difficult to trace, except through his brother (also an ex-Marine). In other words, if this was a marked card operation, it was a high-level, far-reaching one, one not simply confined to CI/SIG operating inside the CIA. A secret shared by many agencies was precisely the kind of secret which could eventually compel the collusion of many agencies, perhaps even reluctantly, in an official cover-up of the assassination.

A symptom of this inter-agency collaboration can be found in the falsified home address supplied on October 31, 1959 by Snyder in State, as "4936 Collinwood St., Fort Worth." Two days later a J.M. Barron, of the Op-921D1 section in the Office of Naval Intelligence (ONI), wrote a memo on Oswald "for the file" with the altered spelling "4936 Collinswood;" and immediately arranged for a copy of this file memo to be delivered by hand to a Mr. Wells in the FBI.[327] Two years later, FBI Agent Fain generated a third spelling of the irrelevant address, "4936 Collingwood," in yet another dose of barium for the much-tested CIA Soviet Russia Division.[328]

As we shall discuss further shortly, many different agencies were collaborating to create an allotropic legend in Oswald's government files. The clearest evidence of this is a Marine Headquarters

Cable of 8 March 1960 to the Commander of Oswald's Marine Air
Reserve Training Command:

> Arrangements being made with a federal invest[igative]
> agency to furnish you with rpt [report] which relates to
> PFC Lee Harvey Oswald. Upon receipt CMM you are
> directed to process PFC Oswald for disch[arge] IAW
> [in accordance with] Para 10277.2.f MARCORMAN X
> [Marine Corps Manual].[329]

This agency appears to have been the FBI, and the report, Fain's
report on Oswald of May 1960. This report contained the false
recollection by Marguerite, that Oswald had renounced his citizenship; and this recollection, converted by the FBI into a false
pseudo-fact, became the final basis for Oswald's undesirable discharge.[330] It would appear that the Marines had already decided in
March to discharge Oswald, even though the first official report
that Oswald had renounced his citizenship (Fain's report, based
on Marguerite's reading of a error-transmitting press account) was
not prepared until May 12.

Let us consider the prodigious bureaucratic result of Marguerite's dissonant communications. As we shall see in Chapter
4, he processing of Oswald's discharge became a bureaucratic
procedure swelling the files of ONI, Marine Intelligence, and
the Office of Special Investigations (OSI) of the U.S. Air Force.
Meanwhile the conflicting letters to Secretary Herter, stating
that Oswald *had* renounced his citizenship, and to Congressman Wright, stating that Oswald *had not* renounced his citizenship, bounced around the State Department, generating yet more
bureaucratic paper.[331]

We can summarize the hundreds of pages of documents by
saying that the Marines accepted that Oswald had renounced his
citizenship, and therefore discharged him.[332] Meanwhile the State
Department (which alone had the power to make this determination) concluded that he had not.[333] This difference within the
government about Oswald led to political maneuverings, as when
the State Department Security Office, dissenting from the State

Department viewpoint, in June 1962 apparently leaked its supporting evidence from the 1961 Fain report to the House Un-American Activities Committee.[334] The issue was still unresolved in 1963.[335]

The chief source of all this bureaucratic agitation, producing more than two dozen files in at least seven U.S. agencies, was nominally Marguerite Oswald. But we have already seen that in fact Marguerite did not initiate her actions on her own; she acted in response to the promptings of men like John Fain inside the U.S. Government. And Fain was not her only advisor. As she told the Secret Service and the Warren Commission, she was also told what to do on the discharge matter by a Marine Corps Captain in Fort Worth ("I wrote a letter, and was told how to write the letter").[336]

The discharge review was a charade. The military authorities knew very well that Oswald was in the Soviet Union, yet they sent him a registered letter (with the instructions, "Deliver *only* to addressee"), to an address, 3613 Harley, in Fort Worth.[337] Worse, Oswald had never lived at this address; still less was it the address which the Marine Corps Manual called for (his "last address on file").[338] As far as can be told, Marguerite did not live at this address either; but, luckily for the flow of the barium meal, she was able to sign for and respond to the letter.[339]

We know for a certainty that Marguerite did not live at the address supplied on her reply, 1410 Hurley, which was also on the address of the Marines' reply to her. Our source for this is John Fain, who shared with Headquarters an insight into the Marguerite address mystery he declined to put into his report. As he explained in his report's "administrative cover page" (which did not circulate),

On April 27, 1960, efforts were made to contact Mrs. Oswald at this address [1605 Eighth Avenue, Marguerite's address with her telephone number in the Fort Worth telephone directory] with negative results. The telephone operator advised that all calls made to WAlnut 3-0659 [her listed number] were temporarily being handled by WAlnut 3-0572, which is listed to Velma Marlin of 1410 Hurley

Street, Fort Worth, Texas. Velma Marlin is employed as cashier at the "Fort Worth Star Telegram," a daily newspaper in Fort Worth. Upon contact with Miss Marlin, she advised that Mrs. Marguerite Oswald is currently employed "out of town" and that her son Robert L. Oswald is believed to know her address. Upon contact with Robert L. Oswald, on April 27, 1960, he advised that . . . she could be reached at 1111 Herring Avenue, Waco, Texas.'[340]

Using the language of spycraft, we can say that Velma Marlin was a cut-out or message drop, receiving mail which was then somehow relayed to Marguerite. Marguerite also used Velma Marlin's address, 1410 Hurley, in her correspondence with Albert Schweitzer College, and the State Department. Replies reached Marguerite without being forwarded, even though she was supposedly living in Waco.[341]

It is interesting that Velma Marlin was an employee of a newspaper, the *Fort Worth Star-Telegram*, that had helped generate the news stories about Oswald which Marguerite cited in her productive letters to U.S. government figures. It was a *Star-Telegram* reporter who first told Robert Oswald in October 1959 of his brother's defection, and then prompted the two cables which he sent to Lee and to Secretary of State Herter.[342] As we shall see, these cables also contributed significantly to the flow of bureaucratic barium.

Oswald, the U-2, and OSI

Fain had stumbled on to evidence that a complex game, involving a cut-out outside the government, was being played with Marguerite's phone number and address. His response to this discovery was complex, and illuminating. On the one hand he acted as if not in on the secret, and reported Velma Marlin's role as if learning it for the first time. On the other hand he made sure (by referring the information to his Administrative pages) that the secret was kept within the Bureau. In a straightforward investigation he might have quizzed Velma Marlin about her unusual relationship to Marguerite's telephone. (We may add that a responsible investigation of the Kennedy assassination in 1963 would have gone back to Velma Marlin, and the reasons for this use of her as mail-drop.)

I conclude that Fain knew that his own activities were part of a larger game transcending his knowledge, and suspected that Velma Marlin and the *Fort Worth Star-Telegram* were part of this game also. In retrospect, this seems likely. By suggesting that Robert write cables to Herter and Lee, the anonymous *Star-Telegram*-reporter in 1959 seems to have played for Robert the role which "Fannan" (Fain) soon played for his mother, and with equally productive bureaucratic results.

The alert reader may recall that the first of these cables was referred to in Snyder's initial despatch from Moscow. It also formed part of a UPI story published in Japan (but apparently not elsewhere). This led to further inquiries from Oswald's half-brother John Pic, stationed there in the U.S. Air Force.[343] The result was an Air Force Office of Special Investigations (OSI) file, opened in the name of Pic, but in fact preoccupied with Oswald. It (along with Oswald's ONI file) slowly filled with interminable exchanges between OSI and ONI on the subject of Oswald's discharge.

No one, to my knowledge, has ever pointed out that the first military intelligence agency to have shown an active interest in investigating Oswald was the Air Force OSI. On February 19, 1960, at about the time Fain suggested that Marguerite write her letters, an OSI inquiry to the FBI about Oswald resulted in Oswald's fingerprint record being supplied to OSI.[344] On March 8, 1960, an L.E. Cole of OSI reviewed Oswald's Passport file at the State Department. This is the only recorded instance of such a military review.[345] Almost certainly the OSI's inquiry was related to the Marines' decision the same day to initiate the processing of Oswald for discharge (pending receipt of an investigative report).[346]

It makes perfect sense that OSI would be conducting such an investigation, if the files on Oswald were related to a molehunt. As Newman records, Angleton's intense search for a mole in 1959 was triggered by a report from CIA's own mole in the KGB, Pyotr Popov. Popov transmitted a drunken boast that the KGB had many technical details on the high-altitude U-2, one of the U.S. government's most tightly-held secrets.[347] The Air Force was the primary support branch for the U-2 program, and inevitably OSI would be tapped to participate in a search for leaks. (We shall see in a moment that there are striking matches between the CIA's response to the Popov story and reported events in the life of Lee Harvey Oswald.)

The *Fort Worth Star Telegram* was published, until his death in 1955, by Amon G. Carter, Sr., one of the most powerful civilian backers of the U.S. Air Force in the nation. After his death his place as publisher, and as director of American Airlines, was taken by his son Amon G. Carter, Jr. Marguerite herself had once been employed in the house of Amon Carter, either the father or the son.[348]

The Carters, and especially the father, can be characterized as pillars of the air force industrial complex. Director and National Governor of the Air Power League from 1947 to 1955, the senior Amon Carter was personally responsible for the location near Fort Worth of Carswell Air Force Base, headquarters for the 8th Air Force (one of the addressees in the Pic-Oswald OSI file).[349] Carter was also responsible for the location near Fort Worth of the World War II plant producing the B-24 bomber; this same plant after World War II became the Convair plant of General Dynamics.

As I have noted elsewhere, Oswald and Marina on their arrival in Fort Worth in 1962 appear to have enjoyed a special connection with the Convair plant's Director of Security, Max Clark, and his Russian wife.[350] We have learned from recent CIA releases that both CIA and OSI kept files on Max Clark from the 1950s, that Max Clark had a security clearance of Top Secret, and that Max Clark was temporarily cleared by CIA in 1959 for a covert operation.[351]

Finally Carter is said to have been "also personally responsible for the location of the helicopter branch of Bell Aircraft . . . in Tarrant County" near Fort Worth.[352] This was the plant where Michael Paine was employed in classified work for which he required a security clearance.[353]

There were others besides Max Clark and Michael Paine who maintained connections between Oswald and the air force industrial complex. Even George de Mohrenschildt, so often described as the Oswalds' babysitter, made his first trip to visit the Oswalds in the company of a Col. Lawrence Orlov; and Orlov like Clark was a veteran of the U.S. Air Force, as well as a good friend of the local CIA representative, J. Walton Moore.[354] There may even have been an OSI agent at the Dallas School Book Depository on November 22, who drove back from there to the Dallas Police Station with Dallas Detective Jack Revill.[355]

After the assassination moreover, the OSI produced a witness, Palmer McBride, who (until the FBI toned down his story) described Oswald as someone "preaching the Communist doctrine," who "stated he would like to kill President Eisenhower."[356] It is a theme of this book that such "Phase-One" stories (especially from witnesses who later recanted or modified them) should be considered an integral part of a pre-assassination plan to induce an official cover-up.[357]

The CIA's Popov Flap and Oswald

Though it is reasonable to assume that OSI would be called into an investigation of leaks in the U-2 program, coordination of such an inquiry would remain the responsibility of the CIA. And we have seen that Angleton had decided he was hunting, not just for a leak, but for a mole.

Angleton's molehunt began in 1958, when the CIA learned from KGB officer Popov that the KGB knew details about the U-2. It escalated considerably on October 16, 1959, when Popov was arrested on a Moscow bus. Also seized and soon expelled was Popov's American case officer at the U.S. Embassy, Russell Langelle. Popov and Langelle had been caught red-handed in the act of passing notes.[358]

Although there were many other possible explanations for Popov's arrest, Angleton became more and more convinced that a mole in the CIA had betrayed him. Reinforced in this conviction by the KGB defector (or pseudo-defector) Anatoliy Golitsyn, Angleton's list of suspect CIA officers (mostly in Soviet Russia Division) grew to include forty names, of which we know twenty-three. Among those eventually suspected by Angleton of being this mole were a number who were assigned to read the documents (radioactive barium) being circulated on Lee Harvey Oswald. Two of these were David Murphy (who in September 1963 became head of the Soviet Russia Division) and Popov's case officer Russell Langelle.[359]

The Oswald barium seems to have channeled closely in response to changes in Langelle's career. After being expelled from the USSR in 1959, Langelle was given a cover assignment on January 10, 1960 in the State Department's Office of Security. (We have seen that in 1960 inquiries about Oswald were directed to this Office of Security by J. Edgar Hoover.)

By 1963 Langelle was assigned to the Western Hemisphere section of the Operations Branch of the Soviet Russia Division (SR/O/WH). Oswald's parallel shift of interest from Russia to Latin America meant that his documentation followed Langelle in his move. Even after the assassination, on November 25, 1963, a message about the recorded telephone intercepts of Oswald in Mexico had only two individual names on its internal distribution list. One of these was "SR/O/WH/Langelle."[360]

We also see an overlay between the Popov-generated mole-hunt and the Oswald documentation flow if we focus, not on those targeted like Langelle, but the targeters. As Newman points out, Birch D. O'Neal, who became Chief of the CI/SIG in charge of the molehunt, appears to have received the original Snyder despatch on Oswald in November 1959.[361] Four years later O'Neal became the initial CIA spokesperson on Oswald after the assassination; it was he who told the FBI (falsely) that there was no CIA-generated material "in CIA file regarding Oswald".[362] A key figure was Ann Egerter of CI/SIG, who opened the 201 file on Oswald, kept it in her office, and kept records also of who had been allowed to see it.

There are other examples. William Hood, who signed off on the post-assassination letter addressed to Langelle, was a long-time counterintelligence ally of Angleton's, even though he was assigned in 1963 to the post of Western Hemisphere Division Chief of Operations. He took a special interest in the Popov case, and wrote a book about it, *Mole*, for he had been Vienna Chief of Station when Popov was originally recruited there. If as I believe

Hood was also the pseudonymous "L.N. Gallary" who signed for
Oswald cables going outside the CIA, then on October 10 he personally authenticated two conflicting and irreconcilable cables
about Oswald.[363]

Finally it should be mentioned that many of those in William Sullivan's Division Five of the FBI who handled the Oswald
file were men who were simultaneously involved in aspects of
Angleton's counterintelligence war against the KGB. A prominent
example is Don Moore, the FBI's Soviet counterintelligence chief,
who handled the FBI's interviews of the Soviet defector Golitsyn.[364] As supervisor of the FBI's Counterintelligence Division,
Moore represented the FBI on the joint CIA/FBI panel created to
oversee the molehunt. The other permanent FBI members were
Assistant Director William Sullivan and Sam Papich, the FBI liaison to Angleton's Counterintelligence Staff. Moore, Sullivan, and
Papich all handled the Oswald file.[365] In addition, Elbert Turner,
whose name appears in the last outgoing FBI Headquarters pre-
assassination message on Oswald, was also the FBI agent in charge
of feeding doctored secrets to the KGB through the Soviet double
agent Shadrin.[366]

In the game of molehunting, of course, the distinction between
targeter and targeted is not a secure one. The situation is somewhat like the parlor game of Murder, in which the culprit is (or
at least was in the eyes of Angleton) likely to be one of the investigators. Thus both Murphy and Bagley were at first prominent in
the CIA molehunt, and eventually were added to Angleton's list of
forty suspects. In the same period they were fed bits of the allotropic barium meal.

There is a third overlay between the Popov story and the Oswald
story, which may possibly be coincidental. It is that October 16,
1959, the day Popov was pulled off a Moscow bus, is also the day
on which, we are told, Lee Harvey Oswald arrived in the same city.
Oswald's unexplained talk of espionage in the U.S. Embassy, just
fifteen days later, makes perfect sense as a test for leaks in response
to Popov's arrest.

The problem with this hypothesis, and the best argument that
the coincidence in dates is just that and nothing more, is that

Oswald is supposed to have arrived in Moscow, not after Popov was arrested, but just a few hours before. Thus if Oswald's performance was a response to fears that a mole blew Popov's cover, one is forced to imagine other possibilities. The most probable is that the CIA had wind of Popov's impending downfall, before it occurred. (A likely time might have been in early September, when Oswald's abrupt "hardship discharge" from the Marines was precipitously arranged for).[367]

Oswald's departure for the Soviet Union could quite easily have been in response to the signs the CIA picked up in the summer of 1959 that the KGB was now aware of Popov's role as a double agent. According to David Martin, the quality of the intelligence supplied by Popov fell off in the summer of 1959, and this was taken as "an almost certain sign that he had come under KGB control."[368]

The Surplus of Deception: A Molehunt? Or Also Something More?

I find that the most coherent explanation for the many anomalies recorded in this essay, and above all the allotropic variants of Oswald data generated by Snyder, Fain, Marguerite Oswald, Egerter, and Roman, is that the anomalous Oswald documentary record was authorized as part of a barium meal in search for a mole.

In saying this, I do not rule out the possibility that some other operation was piggy-backed upon the molehunt. If we review the whole picture, there seems to be a surplus of deception, more complicated wrinkles to the Oswald story than the molehunt by itself would have required. I refer to such odd details as the half-executed renunciation, the leaving of the passport in the U.S. embassy, etc.

Perhaps the most striking of these excess deceptions is the consistent effort, from many agencies, to make Oswald untraceable, or at least unattributable. This might suggest, as I wrote many years ago, that Oswald was being "sheep-dipped," and provided a legend, for some covert assignment.[369] (As someone who had lived in both

America and the Soviet Union, whose citizenship was now being questioned, and who had voiced major criticisms of both countries, he had acquired a "legend" that would make any questionable action virtually unattributable to any single nation.)

So let me in closing offer, as a pure speculation that cannot be proven, an example of how an authorized counterintelligence molehunt could serve as a platform for a still more sensitive program. Recall that 1959, the year of Oswald's deception, was the year in which Vice-President Nixon, through his assistant, Marine General Robert E. Cushman, allegedly began to pressure the CIA on the elimination of Fidel Castro.[370] Simultaneously the CIA had since the early 1950s been developing long-range plans for a standing assassination capability, using assets with legends to make them untraceable.[371]

I do not myself believe that Oswald was a good marksman and likely assassin. But his legend as a defector with an ambiguous U.S.-Soviet background, whose citizenship and whose ideological alignment were now both in question, was a perfect legend for the job. Furthermore the documentary record on Oswald, beginning with the UPI story on the weekend of his defection, was salted with references to his interest in going to Cuba.[372]

Consider now that, by leaving his passport with Snyder in the U.S. Embassy for almost two years, the CIA could conceivably have in that time frame have given the passport, and with it the legend, to someone else. The passport was not returned to Oswald until July 1961, after the failure of the Bay of Pigs, and apparent termination (at least for a while) of assassination planning. Of course there are many problems with such a scenario. My point is merely to demonstrate how one operation could become the basis for a different one.

It is far less fanciful to consider that in 1963 the products of the Oswald barium meal operation were used to double for a propaganda operation whose purpose was to neutralize the Fair Play for Cuba Committee. We know that the Oswald-Bringuier "debate" in New Orleans with a representative of the Cuban Student Directorate (DRE) was relayed by the Miami JMWAVE CIA station to Headquarters, for possible broadcast over the JMWAVE station's

radio facility JMHOPE. The same document suggests that Ed But-
ler, the central propagandist in the debate, was a CIA asset with
the cryptonym "AMCOUP-1." The tape itself had reached the CIA
with the label, "From DRE to Howard."[373]

("Howard" has since been identified, by researcher Jefferson
Morley from a CIA document, as George Joannides, an expe-
rienced career CIA officer known at the time only as a liaison
between the CIA and the House Select Committee on Assassinations. Because I mistrust all CIA "revelations," I continue to
believe it is possible that "Howard" here was in fact not Joannides
but Howard Hunt. The veteran CIA propagandist Howard Hunt
had long been particularly close to the DRE, and his specific duty
in 1963 was "to coordinate DODS [Division of Domestic Opera-
tions] foreign & domestic propaganda operations.")[374] One can see
how a report on Oswald's alleged visit to the Soviet Embassy in
Mexico, the pretext for the bifurcated cables of October 10 1963,
could also be considered grist for a propaganda operation, if not
actually a product of it.

In the course of time, I believe, those who plotted the death of
President Kennedy turned the available secrets and public legend
of Oswald to their own purposes. With their plot centered on a
suspect who had been the subject of a sensitive government operation, an eventual cover-up was virtually guaranteed. Let me suggest further that we can see where a covert maneuver, ostensibly
designed as part of the CI search for a molehunt, was also inexcus-
ably manipulated to facilitate the assassination of John F. Kennedy.
I am referring to the previously mentioned CIA messages 74673
and 74830 of October 10, 1963, the first sent to the FBI and the
second to Mexico City. As pointed out earlier, the messages served
as a "barium meal" by supplying falsified and mutually incompatible weight, height, and age data for the same person, "Lee Henry
Oswald."

The message to FBI (and State and Navy, DIR 64673), in par-
ticular, was relatively brief. Incredibly, it failed to transmit to the
FBI anything about "Oswald"'s alleged contact with Kostikov.
This should have been an urgent matter: in the previous May,
CIA and FBI had had exchanged correspondence as to whether

Kostikov was or was not a KGB "wet affairs" expert in charge of assassinations.[375]

There is no excuse for this failure, but there is a reason. If the FBI had been warned that Oswald had said he had been with Kostikov, whom the FBI thought was an assassination expert, Oswald would have been at a minimum put under surveillance in Dallas. It appears that Oswald had already become the designated culprit in the plot to kill, and people under Angleton in CI/CIA were taken a necessary step to protect him.

They were not alone. On October 9, 1963, the day of the Kostikov cable, an FBI agent, Marvin Gheesling, removed Oswald from the FBI watch list for surveillance.[376] This was in the wake of FBI reports from New Orleans about Oswald's pro-Castro political activity there.

It cannot escape notice that Marvin Gheesling was in the Intelligence Division headed by William Sullivan, a political ally of Angleton.

APPENDIX: CIA PERSONNEL AND ANOMALIES IN THE OSWALD FILE (January 1996)

The names that follow are of CIA officers, agents, and assets who before the assassination became involved with the handling of information with respect to Lee Harvey Oswald. Some of these individuals (marked with a double asterisk) were also involved directly or contextually in anomalies with respect to this information: i.e. paradoxes (unexplained behavior), errors, falsifications (deliberate errors), and/or deceptions (extended falsifications).

I have argued elsewhere that we can distinguish between three kinds of official deception with respect to Oswald. There are those who commit deception as part of an authorized intelligence or counterintelligence operation (see Jane Roman below). There are those who commit deception to protect (or cover up) an authorized operation (see Richard Helms below). Finally there are those who are guilty of what we may call surplus deception: deception that is not justifiable in terms of the CIA's mission and which appears to further or protect an *unauthorized* operation: the murder of the President.

The purpose of the rather dry analysis which follows is to show that there has been a great deal of CIA deception from many different officers with respect to Oswald. Most of this is probably attributable to a legitimate counterintelligence operation, rather than an assassination conspiracy. Some of it, especially after the assassination, is probably cover-up. As for the residue, the surplus deception, I shall leave the reader to decide whether or not some of the lies of the late David Atlee Phillips ("Michael C. Choaden") fall into this category.

OFFICERS HANDLING THE OSWALD RECORDS
HEADQUARTERS: PRE-ASSASSINATION
PLANS DIRECTORATE (CLANDESTINE SERVICES)

Thomas Karamessines, Assistant Director of Plans [to DDP Richard Helms] (ADDP). Signed as Releasing Officer for deceptive cable DIR 74830 of 10/10/63 on "Lee Henry Oswald," stating "latest HDQS info was [State] report dated May 1962] about Oswald in Soviet Union planning to travel home." (Scott, *Deep Politics II*, 28; cf. Newman, *Oswald and the CIA*, 405, 502). Unclear whether Karamessines witting. Cf. Egerter, Roman, "Scelso," Bustos.

According to James Hosty, Karamessines after the assassination "went down to Mexico to 'call off the investigation'" (Newman, *Oswald and the CIA*, 382). Hosty writes that the order to desist came from President Johnson in the White House (Hosty, *Assignment: Oswald*, 221).

COUNTERINTELLIGENCE STAFF

James Jesus Angleton, Chief, Counterintelligence Staff (C/CI). In charge of the CIA's molehunt. His name does not appear on any pre-assassination Oswald records. However the recurring presence of two of his top molehunting allies (O'Neal and Evans, each chief of a different CI group) indicates a coordinated operation in which C/CI would have had to give direction. The further presence of SR/CI/OPS officials, whose activities were also coordinated by Angleton, gives additional corroboration of Angleton's oversight.

According to Tom Mangold, "the molehunt required the highest executive clearance—the tacit support, at least, of the DCI, the Deputy DCI, and the Deputy Director of Operations [Plans in 1963]" (Mangold, *Cold Warrior*, 245). If so, a molehunt Counterintelligence operation with Oswald as subject would have involved Dulles and McCone (DCIs), Gen. Earle Cabell (DDCI), and Richard Helms (DDP).

After the assassination, Angleton served as a back channel to Allen Dulles on the Warren Commission (11 AH 479); Angleton designated CI/SIG "the central point of assassination-related information made available to the FBI" (11 AH 476; cf. 11 AH 57).

Counterintelligence Special Intelligence Group (CI/SIG)

Birch D. O'Neal, Chief, Special Intelligence Group (C/CI/SIG, x5367, 6227). In charge of Angleton's molehunt. Signature on CIA copy of first Oswald despatch, Amembassy Moscow 234 of 11/2/59. Presumably responsible for failure to pursue as espionage case.

Birch D. O'Neal (from HSCA Deposition #014735 of 6/20/78) "had jurisdiction over the HT-LINGUAL Project files" (AR 205; cf. 11 AH 476n at fn 10). These included what the CIA itself called "a separate Oswald HT/LINGUAL file" (Newman, *Oswald and the CIA*, 285), HT/LINGUAL being the CIA's highly secret mail opening program.

**After assassination, the FBI reported that O'Neal (falsely) told FBI there was no CIA-generated material "in CIA file regarding Oswald" (Warren Commission CD 49.22). In fact Ann Egerter of O'Neal's CI/SIG had helped generate three cables on Oswald, one of which (DIR 74673 of 10/10/63) was addressed to FBI.

After November 26, 1963, coordinated GPFLOOR [Oswald] investigation, especially of Alvarado, with "John Scelso" [Whitten], C/WH3 (e.g. NARA #104-10015-10236).

****Ann Egerter** (CI/SIG; Room 1408J, x2621). Author of SECRET falsified biographical note on "Lee Henry Oswald," making him effectively untraceable.

**On 12/9/60, opened 201 on "Lee Henry Oswald," in which she thereafter deposited FBI and other documents on Lee Harvey Oswald (NARA #104-10015-10002). Action officer on file, over which she maintained control (meaning that she kept track of whoever requested to see the file).

**On 10/10(?)/63, recipient after Jane Roman of DBA 52355 (FBI Letterhead Memorandum of 9/24/63 on Oswald). This reports Oswald arrested in New Orleans on 8/9/63; yet Egerter and Roman together help draft DIR 74830 of same date, 10/10/63, stating "latest HDQS info was [State] report dated May 1962] about Oswald in Soviet Union planning to travel home." (Scott, *Deep Politics II*, 28; cf. Newman, *Oswald and the CIA*, 405, 502). Cf. Roman.

**On 10/10/63, one of three CIA officers (cf. Roman, Roll) co-ordinating two mutually contradictory cables (DIR 74673, 74830 of 10/10/63) with differing descriptions of Oswald (NARA #104-10015-10052).

Counterintelligence Operations Group (CI/OPS)

Jean E. Evans, Chief, Counterintelligence Operations Group (C/CI/OPS). Responsible for counterintelligence operations to discover mole. First named recipient of FBI Fain Report on Oswald dated 5/12/60. Also recipient of FBI Fain Report of 7/3/61 (NARA #104-10015-10041). Cf. Newman, *Oswald and the CIA*, 159-60, 493-94.

COPS (Evans?) recipient of file copies of CI-drafted letters of 3 Nov 60 and 21 Nov 60 to State re defectors (including Oswald). (Sckolnick 21, 24.)

**Copies of all CIA Oswald cables (MEXI 6453 of 10/8/63; DIR 76743 of 10/10/63; 74830 of 10/10/63; MEXI 6534 of 10/15/63, and DIR 77978 of 10/24/63) referred "info" to CI/OPS, along with SR/7 (?SR/CI?).

William Potocki (CI/OPS). Referred FBI Hosty memo of 9/10/63 by Jane Roman (NARA #104-10015-10045). Cf. Newman, *Oswald and the CIA*, 348, 501.

**Probably the "WP" who asked Lynch of SR/CI/P in 1961 "to pull together all refs to [Oswald], before learning that Ann Egerter of CI/SIG "either holds the 201-289248 or has it restricted to her" (NARA #104-10015-10040). This leads to the planting of falsified State Department records in CIA files (cf. Lynch).

On January 22, 1964, Potocki initialed routing sheet for DBA 20883 (FBI Fain Report of 8/30/62 on Oswald, initiating process whereby this report is marked "for inclusion OSWALD's 201 file." Cf. Newman, *Oswald and the CIA*, 499.

(FNU) Hughes (CI/OPS/WH). Coordinated drafting of DIR 77978 of 10/24/63, along with Reichhardt (AC/WH3), and Roll, (SR/CI/A/WH). This brief cable asked the Navy for two copies of their most recent photo they have of "Lee Henry Oswald." With a total of six officers in on the drafting, including one from CI/OPS/WH, it would appear that the cable was part of a counter-intelligence operation. (NARA #104-10015-10049)

Hughes (CI/OPS/WH). Recipient of CSCI-3/778,826 of 11/25/63, covering Oswald LIENVOY transcripts, suggesting that these were part of a Western Hemisphere CI/OPS operation. (NARA #104-10015-10257)

Counterintelligence/ International Communism (?) Branch (CI/IC)

H. Recipient of DBF 82181 (FBI Fain Report of 7/3/61 on Oswald). (NARA #104-10015-10041). Cf. Newman, *Oswald and the CIA*, 159-60, 493-94.

CT. On routing sheet for DBA 51407 (FBI Hosty Report of 9/10/63 on Oswald). (NARA #104-10015-10045, Cf. Newman, *Oswald and the CIA*, 501.).

CT. On routing sheet for DBA 52355 (FBI Letterhead Memo-randum of 9/24/63 on Oswald).

CI/IC. "Info" recipient of MEXI 6453 of 10/8/63, reporting Lee Oswald phone call to Soviet Embassy 10/1/63 (NARA #104-10015-10047; Cf. Newman, *Oswald and the CIA*, 509).

Counterintelligence/ Liaison (CI/LS)

**Jane Roman (CI/LS). On 10/4/63, recipient of DBA 52355 (FBI Letterhead Memorandum of 9/24/63 on Oswald). This reports Oswald arrested in New Orleans on 8/9/63; yet Egerter and Roman together help draft DIR 74830 of same date, 10/10/63, stating "latest HDQS info was [State] report dated May 1962] about Oswald in Soviet Union planning to travel home." (Scott, *Deep Politics II*, 28; cf. Newman, *Oswald and the CIA*, 405, 502). Cf. Egerter

   **Jane Roman (CI/LS). Forwards DBA 52355 (FBI Letterhead Memorandum of 10/24/63 on Oswald), not to Egerter and Oswald's 201 file, but to Horn of SAS/CI (q.v.).

   **Jane Roman (CI/LS). Releasing officer on two outgoing CIA Oswald cables (DIR 74673 of 10/10/63 and DIR 77978 of 10/24/63; 104-10015-10052 and 104-10400-10308), Coordinating officer on draft of DIR 74870 of 10/10/63, with different description of "Lee Henry Oswald." (104-10015-10049). Conceded to John Newman that, on DIR 74870, "I'm signing off on something that I know isn't true" (Newman, *Oswald and the CIA*, 405, cf. 511-13).

SOVIET RUSSIA DIVISION

Soviet Russia/Counterintelligence Branch: SR/CI (Before 1962, Counterespionage Branch: SR/CE)

Tennent ("Pete") Bagley, C/SR/CI after Fall 1963. (Active on Oswald case post-assassination, suggesting on 11/23/63 a conspiratorial Oswald-Kostikov assassination link. Case officer for Yuri Nosenko.)

William C. Bright (SR/CE; later SR/RISB/P). Recipient of Fain Reports of 5/12/60 and 6/7/61 on Oswald. (Newman, *Oswald and the CIA*, p. 160, calls him C/SR/CE.)

"JMA," C/SR/CI/P [Project?]. Recipient of D. Lynch's routing sheet for XAAZ 9644 (AmEmb Moscow Despatch "806" [809] of 5/26/61; NARA #104-10015-10040). Cf. Potocki (CI/OPS), Newman, *Oswald and the CIA*, 495.

D. Lynch (SR/CI/P, Room 1044AJ; later SR/CI/P/OP). Orders three State Dept. Oswald despatches in 1961 (AmEmb Moscow 234 of 11/2/59, A-173 of 4/13/61, and AmEmb Moscow D-"806" [809] of 5/26/61; NARA #104-10015-10002)

Lynch ("dl") completed routing sheet for XAAZ 9644 (AmEmb Moscow Despatch "806" [809] of 5/26/61; NARA #104-10015-10040). Cf. Potocki (CI/OPS), Newman, *Oswald and the CIA*, 495.

Lynch author of note of 28 Sept 61 to CI/SI[G] concerning Marina Oswald, nee Prusakov, "in response to request for information on Lee Harvey OSWALD" (NARA #1993.07.02.13:25:25:180530; Sckolnick, 52; Response to HSCA request of 9 Mar 1978).

Miss Geneva Shiflet (Room GH0909, x5308). Receives "A-273" [A-173] of 4/13/61 from Robert D. Johnson of State Dept. Passport Office (18 WH 369; cf. 11 WH 197), in response to request by Lynch (NARA #104-10015-10002).

**Stephan Roll (SR/CI/A). On 10/10/63, one of three CIA officers (cf. Egerter, Roman) co-ordinating two mutually contradictory cables (DIR 74673, 74830 of 10/10/63) with differing descriptions of Oswald (NARA #104-10015-10052; Sckolnick, 116-20).

Stephan Roll (SR/CI/A). Coordinated drafting of DIR 77978 of 10/24/63, along with Reichhardt (AC/WH/3), and Hughes (CI/OPS/WH). This brief cable asked the Navy for two copies of their most recent photo they have of "Lee Henry Oswald." With a total of six officers in on the drafting, including one from CI/OPS/WH, it would appear that the cable was part of a counterintelligence operation. (NARA #104-10015-10049).

TR (?Tom Ryan?) (SR/CI/K [?KGB?]). Recipient of DBA 51407

(FBI Hosty Report of 9/10/63 on Oswald). (NARA #104-10015-10045). Cf. Newman, *Oswald and the CIA,* 501.

Russell Langelle (SR/O/WH). Like Hughes, recipient of CSCI-3/778,826 of 11/25/63, covering Oswald LIENVOY transcripts, suggesting that Langelle may have been working earlier with Hughes (CI/OPS/WH) on a Western Hemisphere CI/OPS operation. (NARA #104-10015-10257). For SR/O/WH, cf. Agee, *Inside the Company,* 499.

Russell Langelle (SR/O/WH). According to Tom Mangold, Langelle was one of forty senior CIA officials investigated in connection with Angleton's and CI/SIG's molehunt (Mangold, *Cold Warrior,* 246, 414).

WESTERN HEMISPHERE DIVISION (WHD)
Operations Branch

William J. Hood, Chief of Operations (WH/COPS). Signed as Authenticating Officer for deceptive cable DIR 74830 of 10/10/63 on "Lee Henry Oswald," stating "latest HDQS info was [State] report dated May 1962] about Oswald in Soviet Union planning to travel home." (Scott, *Deep Politics II,* 28; cf. Newman, *Oswald and the CIA,* 405, 502). If indeed Hood was WH/COPS than he probably was responsible for the deception. Cf. Egerter, Roman, "Scelso" [Whitten], Bustos. See next two items.

Hood had an operational interest in Pyotr Popov, the KGB double agent whose report on the U-2 and subsequent arrest in Moscow triggered the CI/SIG molehunt. Hood was in Vienna when Popov was recruited there. Hood was C/CI/OPS in 1973 when Colby forced his retirement along with Angleton (C/CI) and Ray Rocca (C/CI/R&A). Hood after retirement wrote a book (*Mole*) about the Popov case. Cf. Mangold, *Cold Warrior,* 320.

According to Philip Agee, in 1963 Hood "had the newly created job of Chief of Operations" for WHD (*Inside the Company,* 320, cf. 610). If so, then Hood shifted his attention from SR to WH in the same year that the Oswald documents were similarly rerouted. Cf. also Langelle.

William Hood is possibly identical with "L.N.Gallary" (see next entries).

"L.N.Gallary, C/WH/R" (?William J. Hood, WH/COPS?). Signed as Authenticating Officer for deceptive cable DIR 74673 of 10/10/63 to FBI, etc., re "Lee Henry Oswald" (NARA #104-10015-10052; PS #61-26). This cable in response to MEXI 6453.

"L.N.Gallary, C/WH/R" (?William J. Hood, WH/COPS?). Signed as Authenticating Officer for DIR 77978 of 10/24/63, co-ordinated by Reichhardt (AC/WH3), Roll, (SR/CI/A), and Hughes (CI/OPS/WH). This brief cable, in response to MEXI 6534, asked the Navy for two copies of their most recent photo they have of "Lee Henry Oswald." With a total of six officers in on the drafting, including one from CI/OPS/WH, it would appear that the cable was part of a counterintelligence operation. (NARA #104-10015-10049).

Note that the name "L.N. Gallary" (or "Gallery") is found only on cables addressed outside the CIA.

"Mexico Branch" (North American Branch, WH/3)

"John Scelso," [John Whitten] Chief, WH/3 [North American Branch] (C/WH/3). Recipient of DBA 51407 (FBI Hosty Report of 9/10/63 on Oswald). (NARA #104-10015-10045; cf. Newman, *Oswald and the CIA*, 501.) On 10/10/63, presumably after signing off on Hosty Report of 9/10/63, co-ordinated draft DIR 74830 of same date, 10/10/63, stating "latest HDQS info was [State] report dated May 1962] about Oswald in Soviet Union planning to travel home." (Scott, *Deep Politics II*, 28; cf. Newman, *Oswald and the CIA*, 405, 502). Cf. Egerter, Roman.

Bernard E. Reichhardt, Acting(?) Chief, WH/3 (A/C/WH/3). Coordinated drafting of DIR 77978 of 10/24/63, along with Roll, (SR/CI/A), and Hughes (CI/OPS/WH). This brief cable asked the Navy for two copies of their most recent photo they have of "Lee Henry Oswald." With a total of six officers in on the drafting, including one from CI/OPS/WH, it would appear that the brief cable was part of a counterintelligence operation. (NARA #104-10015-10049).

Charlotte Bustos (WH/3/Mexico, x5940). Recipient by routing stamp of MEXI 6453 of 10/8/63, reporting Lee Oswald phone call to Soviet Embassy 10/1/63 (NARA #104-10015-10047; cf. Newman, *Oswald and the CIA,* 509).

    **Charlotte Bustos Originating Officer for deceptive cable DIR 74673 of 10/10/63 to FBI, etc., re "Lee Henry Oswald" (NARA #104-10015-10052). This cable in response to MEXI 6453, referred to Bustos for action.

    **Charlotte Bustos Originating Officer for deceptive cable DIR 74830 of same date, 10/10/63 (NARA #104-10400-10308), stating "latest HDQS info was [State] report dated May 1962] about Oswald in Soviet Union planning to travel home." The two cables 74673 and 74870 disseminate mutually incompatible descriptions of Oswald (Scott, *Deep Politics II,* 28; cf. Newman, *Oswald and the CIA,* 405, 502). Cf. Egerter, Roman, "Scelso."

    Charlotte Bustos-Videla. On 12/3/76 she told Scott Breckinridge of the CIA Office of Legal Counsel "that she got involved [in Oswald matter] from the Cuban angle, not from the Soviet point of view" (Breckinridge Memo for the Record of 12/3/76; NARA #104-10095-10001). This is anomalous, since none of the incoming FBI reports on Oswald were routed to Bustos or her division (cf. Horn below), and none of the incoming or outgoing CIA cables which Bustos saw or drafted ever mentioned Cuba. This confirms the argument in Newman that additional Mexico City cables (whose existence has hitherto been suppressed) discussed Oswald's visits to the Cuban Embassy (Newman, *Oswald and the CIA,* 414-19, citing Kalaris memo of 9/18/75, NARA #104-10051-10173).

T[erry?] Ward (WH/3/Mexico, x5940). Originating Officer for DIR 77978 of 10/24/63, co-ordinated by Reichhardt (AC/WH3), Roll, (SR/CI/A), and Hughes (CI/OPS/WH). This brief cable asked the Navy for two copies of their most recent photo they have of "Lee Henry Oswald." With a total of six officers in on the drafting, including one from CI/OPS/WH, it would appear that the cable was part of a counterintelligence operation. (NARA #104-10015-10049).

SPECIAL AFFAIRS STAFF (SAS) [Anti-Castro Operations]

Austin Horn, SAS/CI. The officer to whom Jane Roman routes the last three FBI reports on Oswald (DBA 52355 of 9/24/63, LHM on Oswald's arrest; DBA 55777 of 10/25/63, DeBrueys Report; DBA 55715 of 10/31/63, Kaack Report; all from New Orleans). Jane Roman's role in thus separating incoming from outgoing Oswald communications is apparently deceptive. Cf. Roman.

The deflection of the last three incoming FBI reports on Oswald to SAS/CI is of interest because of the movements between Mexico City and HQ in this fall 1963 period of David Atlee Phillips and Balmes ("Barney") Hidalgo. See below.

LD (Leonard Dooley?). Initials for Horn on routing sheet of DBA 52355 (FBI Letterhead Memorandum of 9/24/63 on Oswald).

B. PRE-ASSASSINATION: PHILLIPS
SPECIAL AFFAIRS STAFF (SAS)

Samuel Halpern, Executive Officer (SAS/EXEC). Releasing Officer for cable DIR 73214 of 4 Oct, advising WAVE Station in Miami of impending visit 10/7 and 10/8 1963 of David Phillips, newly appointed "Chief PBRUMEN [Cuban] Ops in Mexi" (NARA #104-10086-10003).

Military Operations Branch (MOB)

Arthur A. Maloney, Chief (C/SAS/MOB). Authenticating Officer for cable DIR 73214 of 4 Oct, advising WAVE Station in Miami of impending visit 10/7 and 10/8 1963 of David Phillips, newly appointed "Chief PBRUMEN [Cuban] Ops in Mexi" (NARA #104-10086-10003).

John Tilton (SAS-MOB, x6963). Originating Officer for cable DIR

73214 of 4 Oct, advising WAVE Station in Miami of impending visit 10/7 and 10/8 1963 of David Phillips, newly appointed "Chief PBRUMEN [Cuban] Ops in Mexi" (NARA #104-10086-10003).

SAS/PMPS (?Paramilitary and Psychological Operations?)

J. Albert Hoeser (SAS/PMPS). Coordinating Officer for cable DIR 73214 of 4 Oct, advising WAVE Station in Miami of impending visit 10/7 and 10/8 1963 of David Phillips, newly appointed "Chief PBRUMEN [Cuban] Ops in Mexi" (NARA #104-10086-10003).

C. R. Hallowell (WH-3/CA). Coordinating Officer for cable DIR 73214 of 4 Oct, advising WAVE Station in Miami of impending visit 10/7 and 10/8 1963 of David Phillips, newly appointed "Chief PBRUMEN [Cuban] Ops in Mexi" (NARA #104-10086-10003; PS #62-184).

POST-ASSASSINATION
MEXICO CITY STATION

Winston Scott ("Willard C. Curtis"), Chief of Station (COS): LITEMPO case officer. Asked Echevarria to have Silvia Duran arrested (MEXI 7029).

Originator of MEXI 7127: As of morning of 29 Nov 63, "LITEMPO-4 'doubts' story and will begin work to 'break' Alvarado" (MEXI 7127 of 29 Nov).

Also originator of MEXI 7156 of 29 Nov: LITEMPO-4 ("who is a very intelligent officer") on morning Nov 29 saw Alvarado for one hour, "believed Alvarado story a fantastic lie;" saw Alvarado for three hours in afternoon "'inclined' believe Alvarado telling truth in general outline; but believes he mixed up on dates" (MEXI 7156 of 29 Nov, 290046Z [i.e. evening of Nov. 28], Incoming 30 Nov 70530 [i.e. this OPIMMEDIATE cable, which might have delayed announcement of Warren Commission on 29 November, was itself held up for over 24 hours]). Scott the originator of MEXI 7127 and 7156.

****Ann Goodpasture** ("R.B. Riggs"). Assistant to COS. Added description of mystery man to MEXI 6453 of 10/8/63. Author of bowdlerized Chronology (Wx-7241 of 1967). Originator of MEXI 7023: "Station unable compare voice as first tape erased").

****George Munro** ("Jeremy K. Benadum") Liaison with LITEMPO-4 ((Fernando Gutiérrez Barrios, Assistant Director of the DFS). Received second version of alleged Duran statement of 11/23/63 from LITEMPO-4 (#104-10068-10084).

****Alan White** ("R.L. Easby"), Deputy Chief of Station (DCOS): Originator of many cables dealing with photos of Cuban Embassy from LIERODE Base: MEXI 7021, 7035, etc. Also at meeting of Scott with Ambassador Mann (MEXI 7053). Originator of cables on Duran interview: MEXI 7046 (Oswald "said he Communist," etc.), 7054 ("Regret complete recheck shows tapes for this period already erased").

Soviet Bloc Section

Herbert Manell ("G.F. Gestetner"), Chief.[377] Sends most cables dealing with physical and electronic surveillance of Soviet Embassy: MEXI 6534 of 10/15/63 asking HQ to pouch photo of Oswald, MEXI 7014 of 11/22/63 (first known post-assassination Oswald cable), MEXI 7024, 7027, 7032, 7034, 7038, 7044 (LIEN-VOY), 7047 (LIFEAT), 7050 (LIENVOY), 7051, etc.

Barbara Murphy Manell ("L.A. Dillinger").[378] Soviet Case Officer Originator of MEXI 6453 of Oct. 8, 1963, containing second para (by Ann Goodpasture, Lopez Report. 136-37), with description of mystery man,. Wife of "Gestetner" (Lopez Report, 51, cf. 171).

4

Oswald, Marine G-2, And
The Assault On The State Department

Introductory Abstract

As we saw in Chapter 3, the special handling of Lee Harvey Oswald
by the State Department swiftly aroused (by as early as 1960) the
suspicions of individuals in the FBI, the Office of Naval Intelligence
(ONI) and Marine intelligence, as well as of Hoover's allies (notably Otto Otepka) in the State Department's own Office of Security.
We know this chiefly from Oswald's ONI records, where we also
learn that there were confidential ONI messages on Oswald (alias
"Harvey Lee Oswald"), stored in Marine G-2 (intelligence) files
that were never seen by the Warren Commission.

The charade of Oswald's discharge from the Marine Reserve
in 1960 was an operation coordinated by Marine G-2 and ONI
Counterintelligence. The procedure leading to Oswald's discharge
involved a challenge to State's determination that Oswald had not
revoked his U.S. citizenship, leading Otto Otepka, in a series of
vain efforts, to attempt to pry loose confidential information about
Oswald from files in other parts of the State Department.

Otepka eventually shared his understandable suspicions about
State's handling of Oswald with the Senate Internal Security Subcommittee (SISS). For this Otepka was first reprimanded, and
then fired from his position in November 1963. After this the SISS

in 1964 publicly explored Otepka's concern that Oswald's passport application had been mishandled by the State Department.

The uproar over the Otepka case in 1963 became one more battle in an on-going war between elite (above all State) and anti-elite (FBI, military intelligence) factions in the U.S. Government, the latter backed by the SISS and virulently anti-Kennedy right-wing organizations, notably in Dallas. The drilling and ransacking of Otepka's safe in November 1963 by Kennedy-appointed officials (later forced under Johnson to resign) reveals how deeply this conflict divided elements inside the bureaucracy.

Oswald's Suppressed ONI and Marine G-2 Records

Lee Harvey Oswald's defection to the Soviet Union in 1959 was immediately described as an "intelligence matter" by the Navy's Office of Naval Intelligence.[379] In ensuing years the military intelligence agencies continued to collect information about him. Since the publication of the Warren Report we have seen the belated release of documents on Oswald from ONI (the Office of Naval Intelligence), from Army G-2 (Army Intelligence) and even OSI (Air Force Intelligence), the first of the military intelligence agencies to consult Oswald's security file in the State Department.

Oswald however did not serve in the Navy, Army or Air Force; like his brother Robert he was a Marine. In October 1959, at the time of his defection, he was no longer on active duty, but had transferred six weeks earlier to the Class III Ready Marine Corps Reserve (19 WH 665). We shall see that over three years Marine G-2 (Intelligence) both received and disseminated records concerning Oswald, regionally and at Marine HQ. Nevertheless, despite Marine G-2's sustained interest in Oswald, we still have only three or so documents clearly generated by Marine G-2, all unclassified, and presumably a tiny fraction of the whole. (These large gaps in what is available suggest the existence of a second system for classified records, one never shared with the Warren Commission.)

The Warren Commission appears to have ignored the question of Oswald's Marine G-2 file (or files). In taking testimony from Lt.

Col. Allison Folsom, head of the Marine Headquarters Personnel Records Branch, John Hart Ely of the Warren Commission staff claimed to "have here Oswald's Marine records," while introducing a copy of Oswald's personnel file into the record (8 WH 304). Col. Folsom, in turn, also referred to the personnel file as "the official record held by the Marine Corps of Lee Harvey Oswald" (ibid.).[380]

This personnel file appears to be a compilation (whether from before or after the assassination is not clear).[381] It collects copies of correspondence on Oswald from the files of at least three and probably more Marine Commands under which he served.[382] As published as Folsom Exhibit No. 1 (19 WH 656-768), this personnel file contains only unclassified documents and information. There are no overt references to Marine G-2, and only one passing reference to the existence of confidential intelligence records on Oswald in the Department of the Navy.

This reference is in a letter of 29 July 1960, recommending Oswald's discharge from the Marines. The letter mentions two confidential reports from the Ninth (Chicago) Naval District [ND] Intelligence Office [DIO], which it cites as follows:

DIO, 9th ND confidential report serial 02049-E of 8 Jun 60.

DIO, 9th ND confidential report serial 02296-E of 27 Jun 60.[383]

Years later, replying affirmatively to a request for these DIO reports from researcher Paul Hoch, the Naval Investigative Service (NIS) supplied two records. These established a fact not available from the rest of the personnel file: that Marine G-2 (in regional offices as well as at Marine HQ) received documentary information from this ONI District Intelligence Office concerning Oswald.[384]

In addition at least one of these G-2 records listed Oswald by a slightly different name. This alternative name, which eventually was used by at least three different military intelligence sources, was "Harvey Lee Oswald."[385] This "Harvey Lee Oswald" reference was no accidental anomaly, but part of a larger inter-agency pattern, so widely dispersed that it suggests an official intelligence deception (and possible earlier set of files on "Harvey Lee Oswald"). The name

"Harvey Lee Oswald occurs for example in Mexico City Legat (FBI) files, and in the "JKB version" of the Mexican Government report on Silvia Durán's interrogation after her arrest.[386]

The Mary Ferrell Foundation database contains 314 documents referring to "Harvey Lee Oswald," from the CIA, FBI, Secret Service, Dallas Police Department, military intelligence, and Warren Commission testimony.[387] (One such record is the CIA file copy of a *Washington Post* photo caption describing Marina, on February 3, 1964.)[388] A consistent pattern of behavior in different agencies since the assassination has been the tendency to suppress these references to "Harvey Lee Oswald," and replace them by the more standard "Lee Harvey Oswald."[389] But to my knowledge the earliest "Harvey Lee Oswald" document we now possess is 9th Naval DIO Serial 02296-E of 27 Jun 60.

Both these missing DIO documents were addressed to the Commander, Marine Air Training Command, Glenview, "(ATTN: G-2)." (The Naval Air Station at Glenview, Illinois, supported the Marine Air Reserve.) More importantly, both were classified "confidential" (19 WH 672, cf. 703). This would explain their absence (apart from a single reference) from the unclassified Oswald personnel file: classified intelligence information concerning Oswald (or "Harvey Lee Oswald") was apparently stored in a different set of G-2 files, perhaps at Marine Headquarters and certainly at the Marine Air Reserve Headquarters in Glenview.

Marine G-2 has been remarkably loath over the years to yield up these two DIO records, even though their content, apart from the anomalous "Harvey Lee Oswald" name, would appear to be innocuous. On November 23, 1963, the day after the assassination, the General Counsel of the Department of Defense, John McNaughton, noticed the existence of the two missing DIO records and "expressed a strong desire to review" them; he apparently never was given this opportunity.[390] Two months later, the Warren Commission, having learned of the ONI interest in Oswald, asked for documentation of this. In response to this request, McNaughton's assistant, Frank Bartimo, again asked the Director of Naval Intelligence in writing to see the two missing DIO records.[391] Apparently he never received them.[392]

It is clear, as we shall see, that Marine G-2 at Marine Head-quarters was also actively interested in Oswald. Indeed the ONI cable referring to Oswald's defection as an "intelligence matter" also spoke of the "continuing interest of [Navy] HQ, Marine Corps and U.S. intelligence agencies."[393]

We know furthermore that the Marine G-2 HQ did receive classified intelligence on Oswald. The CIA on October 10, 1963, sent a Secret cable to the Navy, reporting that someone identifying himself as Lee Oswald had been in contact with the Soviet Embassy in Mexico City. Like the first Navy cable about Oswald's defection, the action copy of this cable was referred to "92" (the Office of Naval Intelligence). Handwritten on this copy are the words, "Passed to G-2—USMC 10/11/63."[394]

ONI and the Deception of the So-Called ONI "File on Oswald"

In response to a Warren Commission request of February 18, 1964, John McNaughton's office supplied what it referred to as "the complete file of the Office of Naval Intelligence on Lee Harvey Oswald."[395] In fact this file was not complete. More importantly, it was only created on November 22, 1963, from Oswald records that apparently were stored earlier in two or three files, some of which possibly had a different subject or subjects.

In the Archives version of this ONI file, we find clues to its own creation on November 22, 1963. A memo to file of that date by the duty officer in the ONI Support Center refers to both an "ONI investigative file" (possibly from Op921D, investigations) and a "supplemental file," (possibly from Op921E, counterintelligence). Later the duty officer learned "of a request being prepared from General [Joseph] Carroll of DIA [the Defense Intelligence Agency, a recent McNamara creation] to see the file on Oswald." Advised of this request, ONI Chief Admiral Rufus Taylor gave instructions "to *prepare a file* for him to be passed to General Carroll."[396]

It was this newly prepared file (now referred to as "the file on OSWALD" or "original OSWALD file") that (according to General Carroll) was seen by DOD General Counsel John McNaughton (ONI-254), during an emergency meeting of senior civilians in the office of Assistant Secretary of State Fred Dutton.[397] According to notes the same day from this duty officer's superior, Admiral Taylor initially "was cautious about passing file to DIA," but then told the IDO [Intelligence Duty Officer, Lt. Cdr. Hammer or Hamner] "to *prepare a file* for review by him and for agent to take file for DIA to read and for agent to return."[398] A mysterious note the next day reads "briefed Taylor on 3 files."[399] The haste in the preparation of this "file on Oswald" may explain the absence in the originally released ONI file of cited relevant documents, and the presence of supposedly irrelevant documents, such as documents from Oswald's court martial in June 1958, not present in Oswald's Marine personnel file, and not (in the Warren Commission version of events), an intelligence matter.[400]

The details of this file-preparation suggest conscious deception by ONI on November 22, both of General Carroll (the Kennedy-McNamara appointee as head of DIA), and subsequently of DOD General Counsel John McNaughton. It was from reviewing the ONI "file on Oswald" that McNaughton requested three documents, referred to in the file, which he never got to see.[401] The grounds for not transmitting the three serials was in each case the same: they were just transmittal letters. When McNaughton requested verification of this, the reassuring message was passed up to him that there were no other contents.[402] Thus he apparently never learned what each of the serials would have confirmed: that ONI, and its District Intelligence Office in Chicago, were sharing confidential information on Oswald (or Harvey Lee Oswald) with Marine G-2, specifically towards the goal of effecting Oswald's predetermined "discharge."

As we look more closely at this ONI-Marine G-2 collaboration, we shall see that it has the marks of a counterintelligence operation, indeed of an official "deception" (to use an intelligence term of art) with respect to Oswald. There is of course nothing in this fact per se to link either ONI or Marine G-2 to the assassination.

What is more alarming is the refusal by ONI, on November 22, to share their actual records with even Joseph Carroll, the Air Force General and former FBI Agent who in 1961 was appointed by Kennedy to be the first head of the Defense Intelligence Agency. The DIA represented an attempt by Kennedy and McNamara to establish some kind of civilian control over the military intelligence agencies, an attempt that the armed services resisted.[403]

Particularly alarming is the deceitful withholding at that time of three records which (unlike most of the others) constituted strong clues to the existence of the counterintelligence collaboration. In suggesting to their superiors that the three withheld records added no information, senior naval officers were deceptive. Admiral Taylor's decision to have a file prepared, rather than share raw data, is further evidence that the original files with Oswald records contained truths quite different than those eventually given to the public.

The Collaboration Between ONI and Marine G-2 to Arrange for Oswald's "Discharge"

The true secret about the DIO documents which McNaughton never saw may have been the existence of the Marine G-2 files which contained them. In fact the personnel file can be considered to be no more than the outermost tegument or covering of inter-agency intrigues, hidden in classified Marine and Navy files.

One of these intrigues was the orchestration of events to arrange for Oswald's discharge from the Marines. We saw in Chapter 3 that this discharge was based on virtually worthless "evidence" that Oswald had "revoked" his citizenship, evidence not available from his personnel file. There is a page of remarks from the July 1963 review of Oswald's discharge, missing in the personnel file, that contains the following information:

> Oswald was discharged on the approved recommendation of a Board of Officers, based on CNO ltr OP-921D/ck serial 015422P92 of 4 Aug 60. The CNO ltr is not on file in Oswald's file jacket.[404]

The August 4 serial likewise was not seen by the Warren Commission (cf. 19 WH 690-92, where this page is missing).

[Further evidence of the serial's sensitivity came in 1975, when it was requested by the Schweiker-Hart Senate Subcommittee assessing the "Performance of the Intelligence Agencies" in "The Investigation of the Assassination of President John F. Kennedy." A Committee staff member, Alton Quanbeck, in a letter to the Special Assistant to Defense Secretary Donald Rumsfeld, noted that "The files we received on Oswald" did not contain the August 4 serial and several other records, and asked the Department of Defense to supply them. The request was forwarded to a Mr. John O. Marsh, Jr., who was overseeing current investigations of the JFK assassination in the White House on behalf of Ford's Chief of Staff (and Rumsfeld's protégé) Richard Cheney.[405] (Cheney had just succeeded Rumsfeld as President Ford's Chief of Staff, after the so-called Halloween Massacre on October 31, 1975.)[406] There is no sign in the Schweiker-Hart Report that the request was honored.]

The appearance of a review process to achieve the result of Oswald's discharge was misleading. In fact the discharge was already predetermined by two branches of Marine Headquarters, the Discipline Branch (Code DMB) and Marine G-2 (Codes DK and DKE), with Marine G-2 playing the key coordinating role.[407] In this matter, as throughout the file, events in Oswald's life were directed by branches of Marine HQ, whose files have never been released.[408]

In this matter, an inter-agency co-ordinating role was played by the Security Division of ONI (OP921), including the Programs Section of Naval Counterintelligence (OP921E2 of ONI). We learn from Oswald's ONI file that Marine G-2 (using the Codes DK and DKE) had a series of phone conversations with and resulting correspondence from ONI, concerning Oswald and his impending discharge.[409] Above all, G-2 received (from ONI who in turn transmitted key documents from FBI and OSI) the "evidence" which arranged for Oswald's discharge from the Marines. Specifically, G-2 sent the original Speedletter of 8 March 1960, directing that Oswald be processed for discharge.[410] It also received the ONI file and letter on Oswald (the missing Op 921D/ck serial 015422P92 of 4 Aug 60), which became the "basis" for Oswald's discharge on August 17.[411]

Like the Warren Commission after them, the elaborate files compiled from ONI and G-2 records ignore the two most important intelligence aspects of Oswald's career: 1) as a radar operator, Oswald knew a lot about the once highly-classified U-2 program; and 2) when the U-2 was still a tightly held secret, Oswald had reportedly said in Moscow he had "offered Soviets any information he has acquired as enlisted radar operator."[412]

Deception can be detected as early as the Naval Counter-intelligence reply of 4 November 1959 to this news. It said that "possibility exists [Oswald] may have had access to Confidential info" (18 WH 116). In fact Oswald's superior, John Donovan, testified under oath that Oswald "must have had secret clearance to work in the radar center, because that was a minimum requirement for all of us" (8 WH 298).

This deception was maintained after the assassination by Marine G-2. In a carefully drafted statement for the Warren Commission, Marine G-2 addressed the matter of Oswald's clearance in language which, while technically accurate, was wholly misleading:

> Oswald was granted a final clearance on 3 May 1957 to handle confidential matter. *There is no evidence contained in the personnel file* that . . . he was granted access to any information of higher than confidential characterization.[413]

Of course not; as we have seen, the personnel file was an unclassified one, almost devoid of reference to classified Oswald records. (Suppressing the qualification about "no evidence," the HSCA Report drew the unjustified inference that "Oswald had a security clearance of confidential, but never received a higher classification.")[414]

It is possible, however, that the Marine Intelligence interest in Oswald dates back to before his alleged "defection" to the Soviet Union. It has not been explained why Oswald's officer signed an affidavit in support of Oswald's passport application on September 4, 1959, or why his passport application (to visit Russia!) should refer to a Defense Card which in theory was only issued one week later.[415] Oswald's Marine Corps Air Station (MCAS) at El Toro, California, approved Oswald's release from active duty in

September, on the ground that his mother in Fort Worth needed his support (WR 688-89; 19 WH 665). Yet the records suggest that Marine authorities knew very well that Oswald would soon leave the U.S., even while the same people pretended to think that he was going to work in Fort Worth.[416]

Perhaps the greatest paradox about the Marine G-2 and ONI records on Oswald is that they show sustained interest in learning more from the State Department about Oswald's alleged renunciation of citizenship; but never, apparently, about his self-confessed offer of espionage.

The Use of Oswald's "Discharge" to Focus Investigation, Not on Oswald, but the State Department

From Oswald's ONI file, we also have one Marine G-2 memo asking Naval Intelligence to obtain from the State Department "a signed copy of Oswald's statement of 31 October 1959" in which he reportedly renounced his United States citizenship.[417] (It would appear from the ONI copies that correspondence to Oswald, signed by the Assistant Director of Personnel, was in fact drafted as a Code DKE letter, i.e. by G-2).[418] This was just one shot in an important inter-agency drama concerning Oswald, of which there is no trace in Oswald's personnel file.

The thrust of this inquiry from Jerome Vacek of G-2 was a continuing one in the Oswald ONI file: to extract information from a conspicuously reluctant State Department:

> Will you [Pross Palmer of ONI Counterintelligence] get in touch with your State Department contacts [the State Department Office of Security] with view toward obtaining for HQMC retention a signed copy of OSWALD's statement of 31 October 1959 in which he "revokes" his United States citizenship with view toward coming a citizen of the U.S.S.R. *Congressional interest is likewise anticipated.*[419]

ONI's State Department contacts, the McCarthyite Office of Security, gave this assignment to one of their most notorious and controversial Red-hunters, Otto Otepka (26 WH 45).

The efforts of Vacek, Palmer, and Otepka were unsuccessful. The State Department replied (as it had before) that "it is considered . . . that Mr. Oswald . . . has not expatriated himself."[420] There is no sign that Oswald's two requests for revocation (18 WH 108-09) ever reached the eager eyes of ONI and Marine G-2. Indeed from the outset the State Department appears to have resisted resolutely, even deceptively, the efforts of G-2 and ONI to poke into the Oswald affair. Early efforts by ONI to obtain an Embassy airgram about Oswald's renunciation were apparently rebuffed with the answer that the airgram had not been retained: the State Department "destroys files every month."[421] This answer was untrue, indeed barely credible; the airgram (G-184 of 7 Nov 59) was still in existence, and can be read today in the National Archives.[422] In each of three subsequent assaults on the State Department fortress, the results were similarly unsuccessful.[423]

The FBI joined Marine G-2 and ONI in requesting the State Department for more information about what they had about Oswald. A now famous FBI letter, asking about "Oswald's "renunciation of his American citizenship," justified its request for "any current information" by the intriguing "possibility that an imposter is using Oswald's birth certificate."[424]

Less than a week later, Marguerite also zeroed in on the controversial issue of renunciation, in a letter of June 8, 1960, to Mr. Haselton of State's Office of Special Consular Services. Referring to her earlier letter of March 7 on the same subject, Marguerite wrote that she "would like to know if Lee had signed the necessary papers renouncing his citizenship or is he still a citizen of the United States."[425] Both Hoover's letter and Marguerite's generated the same answer from the relevant officials, that the State Department had "no information."[426]

What began as a barrage of ONI and Marine G-2 questions to State became increasingly a challenge to State's authority. Unquestionably, only the State Department could rule on the issue of

Oswald's renunciation, which according to its complex policy was a procedure that had not been completed.[427] Repeatedly, ONI and G-2 were informed that, in State's view, Oswald was still a citizen. Just as insistently, U.S. Naval and Marine records continued to state the opposite, that Oswald had indeed revoked or renounced his citizenship.[428]

As we shall see, this issue was still unresolved at the time of the Kennedy assassination. Clearly, as long as Kennedy was President, State had little to fear from the challenges to its ruling on Oswald in ONI and Marine G-2 records. However, after the assassination, the latter were reinforced by hostile challenges to State's ruling, in the Senate Internal Security Subcommittee, and also in the House of Representatives.[429] It is striking that the evidence for Oswald's alleged revocation of his citizenship, as supplied by the FBI, should turn out to be nothing more that Marguerite's memory of a newspaper report.[430]

The FBI-Supplied "Basis" for the ONI/G-2-Arranged "Discharge"

The first available evidence of on-going contact between ONI and Marine G-2 with respect to Oswald is an Confidential ONI file reference, dated February 4, 1960, to a conversation two days earlier between Lt. j.g. [George M.] Fredrickson of ONI and Captain Steele of Marine G-2. The topic is Oswald's recent defection to the USSR, or more specifically State Department reporting of this event.[431] There are other such references to such telephone conversations, whose content remains hidden even in the confidential ONI letters withheld from the unclassified Oswald personnel file.[432] It is not clear whether records were ever kept of these phone conversations or of the bureaucratic initiatives which gave rise to them. We do however have the names of at least six personnel involved; but as far as I know, the Assassination Records Review Board (ARRB) never asked them whether such records ever existed.[433]

Even without such records, it is clear from their context that the ONI-G-2 telephone conversations concerned plans to arrange for Oswald's discharge from the Marines, on grounds that he had revoked his U.S. citizenship.[434] These conversations, moreover, were part of a larger inter-agency operation, or deception, in which the real target may not have been Lee Harvey Oswald at all. It is striking that ONI and G-2 continued to have phone conversations and other communications concerning Oswald after his return to the United States, without any apparent suggestion that Oswald himself should be contacted or debriefed.

A chronology of events in 1960 reinforces this sense of inter-agency collaboration in deception. The chronology shows that the ONI/G-2 conversations on February 2 and August 2, 1960 were key events in the sequence, along with synchronous developments at OSI and the FBI, and above all steps attributed to Oswald's mother Marguerite. According to the Oswald personnel file, Oswald's discharge "was based on reliable information which indicated that he had renounced his U.S. citizenship" (19 WH 690). This "reliable information," persistently repeated in FBI and military intelligence records, was just as persistently discredited by the competent authorities in the State Department.

The deciding evidence of his renunciation, which for the Marines overrode repeated State Department rulings, was Marguerite's recollection of a newspaper story, as narrated by her (after consulting with Marine personnel in Fort Worth) to FBI Agent John Fain. John Fain then compiled a report of 5/12/60, concerned with Oswald but placed in a different file ("Funds Transmitted to Residents of Russia"). This confidential report transmitted Marguerite's recollection that Oswald was "reported to have renounced his U.S. citizenship and . . . sought Soviet citizenship" (17 WH 700). This FBI report was placed in Oswald's ONI file and then shown to Marine G-2, under cover of the missing 4 Aug 1960 letter which in turn became the "basis" for Oswald's discharge.[435]

I have written about the charade of Oswald's discharge extensively elsewhere, Here I shall merely point out that the crucial 8 March speedletter (from Marine HQ G-2) directed the processing of Oswald for discharge, on the basis of evidence from "a federal investigative agency" which had not yet been furnished. This travesty of "review" was further compounded by sending Oswald's notice to appear to a fictitious address, "3613 Hurley, Fort Worth," where neither Oswald nor his mother had ever lived, at a time when the Marines knew very well he was in the Soviet Union.[436] Yet the recommendation for Oswald's discharge contains the remark that Oswald "refused to answer correspondence" (19 WH 699).

In the published documentary record of this travesty, falsifications abound. For example the envelope for the June 24 "3613 Hurley" letter carried the Certified Mail Stamp No. 2154584 (19 WH 716). Yet when copies of the Marine Corps correspondence were first introduced into the Warren Commission record, the "3613 Hurley" letter of June 24 was suppressed; at the same time the Mail Arrival Notice for Certified Mail No. 2154584 was entered into evidence, with the different address "1410 Hurley." (16 WH 587).[437]

The upshot of all this activity was that, in August 1960, Oswald was given an undesirable discharge, on the reported information in a news story (as recalled by his mother to the FBI) that Oswald had renounced his citizenship while in the Soviet Union.[438]

Oswald, the FBI, Otto Otepka, and the Congressional Hunt for Subversives

Oswald's subsequent appeal of this decision continued the inter-agency bombardment of the State Department with questions about Oswald's alleged renunciation of U.S. citizenship. In this campaign I suspect that a coordinating role was played by J. Edgar Hoover.

FBI collaboration with ONI and Army Intelligence went back at least to the 1930s, and became more collusive in these three agencies' intensive, but ultimately unsuccessful, campaign to block the creation of a post-war Central Intelligence Agency. (In this campaign, overt opposition was led by Army General G.V. Strong, former head of Army G-2; but Hoover, behind the scenes, supplied much of the ammunition Strong and his allies used.)[439] Senator Joe McCarthy's charge in 1950 of Communists in the State Department, it later became clear, was drawn from confidential FBI reports, "reworded, then laundered, usually with military intelligence acting as the go-between."[440]

The end result of McCarthy's charge was the hiring of one of his Congressional allies, ex-FBI agent R.W. "Scotty" McLeod, to be a Hoover spy overseeing the State Department's Office of Security: "Through McLeod and his cadre, Hoover was tapped into every part of the State Department."[441] When John Foster Dulles finally got rid of McLeod, his mantle fell chiefly to Otto Otepka, a Security Officer soon suspected of leaking not only to Hoover but also to Congress.

The battle-lines established in these old conflicts, with State on one side, FBI and military intelligence on the other, reappear in the extended inter-agency conflict over Oswald's alleged renunciation. The available records raise the possibility that ONI and Marine G-2 files on Oswald were manipulated to learn more about one of Hoover's oldest targets (so-called "liberals" in the State Department). To this end confidential information on Oswald's defection, after Vacek's Marine G-2 inquiry, clearly reached Hoover's Congressional allies, the House Committee on Un-American Activities (HUAC), and the Senate Internal Security Subcommittee (SISS). Two unanswered questions are: when, and by whom?

Did HUAC in 1962 receive a confidential FBI report on Oswald (with synopsis "Subject later renounced U.S. citizenship and sought to become a citizen of Russia")? Such might appear to be the case from a notation ("HCUA—6-12-62") on a State Department transmittal slip for Fain's report on Oswald of July 1961.[442] Did this in turn have to do with Vacek's unexplained statement, three months earlier, that "Congressional interest is likewise anticipated"?[443] Researchers could inquire whether any records concerning Oswald can be located in the surviving files of HUAC and the SISS, which might answer this question.

In 1962 ONI and Marine G-2 were intimately aware of HUAC and SISS interest in possible State Department subversion. Increasingly this demonstrated itself in the form of SISS concern for the welfare of Otto Otepka, which bears on the Oswald matter because Otepka had been since 1959 the Oswald-watcher in the State Security Office.[444]

Congressional concern about State "subversives" (to use Otepka's term)[445] had revived in 1959, when business interests and

Republicans began to allege that two State Department employees, Roy Rubottom and William Wieland, were responsible for "losing" Cuba to Castro. Subpoenaed by SISS, Otepka testified that he had dissented from the decision to clear Wieland for duty. This was followed by President Kennedy's public defense of Wieland at a press conference, and also by a series of increasing restrictions on Otepka's activities inside State.

This radically escalated the tension between the Kennedy Administration and the Senate Internal Security Subcommittee, whose Chairman, Senator Eastland of Mississippi, opposed the President on civil rights matters as well. Increasingly the cause of Otto Otepka was taken up by right-wing journals and journalists, the American Security Council, the Hearst press, and the John Birch Society. By 1963 the case of Otto Otepka was a talking point of right-wingers like Robert Morris of Dallas, a former general counsel of SISS who opposed Kennedy's policies on issues such as race, the Test Ban Treaty, and Vietnam. A former district naval intelligence officer from 1941 to 1946, Morris in 1962 took leave from his post as president of the Catholic University of Dallas, to deal full time with what he called "a time of great crisis in the United States."[446]

Otepka, the Oswald Records, and Counterintelligence Operations

The increasing controversy about Otepka did not help his situation inside the State Department. In 1963 Otepka's phone was tapped; his safe (containing documentation on Oswald) was drilled open on orders from his superiors. Finally, on November 5, 1963, 17 days before the assassination, Otepka was removed from his post, after being accused of having passed confidential State Department documents to his friends in Congress.[447] (Otepka denied this charge.)

What obsessed Otepka in his final years of diminished power was the question of defectors to the Soviet Union. He later told Bernard Fensterwald that his safe was drilled a day or so after Oswald obtained his second passport in June 1963. Nothing was in there, he said, except his research on defectors: "which are ours and which are theirs?" Otepka later confirmed to Eastland's Sub-committee that in his safe he kept information on defectors, specifically including Oswald.[448]

I interviewed Otto Otepka at length in 1978; he impressed me as a sincere anti-Communist who from his vantage point had rightly concluded that there was far more to the Oswald case than met the eye. He observed, for example, that State Department procedures had been violated when Oswald, a former defector, received a new passport on June 25, 1963, one day after applying for it. (Just two days later, on June 27, Otepka was permanently separated from his office and his defector file.)[449] Otepka also found suspicious Oswald's receipt of a Soviet visa in just two days, when the normal waiting period was one to two weeks.[450]

Otepka's concerns about State's handling of Oswald were publicly articulated, after the assassination, in the Senate Internal Security Subcommittee. In the summer of 1964, Subcommittee Counsel Julien Sourwine, obviously well-briefed, grilled Otepka's Kennedy-appointed boss, Abba Schwartz, about the handling of Oswald's first and second passports.[451]

In my view Otepka was quite justified in finding Oswald's treatment by State to be anomalous. (The Warren Commission shared this concern.) I believe however that the explanation is not to be sought in KGB subversion, but in Washington, possibly in a CIA/State-coordinated counterintelligence operation, of which Otepka (like his allies) might have been unaware.

I have suggested elsewhere that Oswald's discharge was itself part of this counterintelligence operation, and that the true purpose of the discharge was to generate paper about it. Much of the documentation over Oswald's discharge has the marks of what in counterintelligence is called a "barium meal:" the flooding of a communications network with deliberately altered information, to see if and where this altered information ends up in enemy (in this case, KGB) hands. As I showed in Chapter 3, altered details recur in the Oswald documents of the CIA, FBI and State Department.

This argument, if correct, would imply that some individuals inside the FBI and Navy counterintelligence establishments would have been at least partially witting to the fact that the Oswald records concealed an intelligence operation. Those partially witting (because they were directed to perform certain anomalous tasks) must have lived in a milieu of colleagues who, not witting, would naturally have become increasingly suspicious of what was going on.

The overall behavior of Hoover, Otepka, and others, suggests that these men were not only unwitting but highly suspicious, and anxious to get to the bottom of the matter. Even to know that the CIA and State were behind the Oswald operation would not appease those who had argued for years that the CIA and State harbored red subversives.[452]

It might appear that the Oswald files ended up being a battleground between two opposing counterintelligence operations. One, eschewing publicity, sophisticated, was centered in CIA and State, and looked for an individual or individuals who might be moles. Suspicion of this operation led to a second, retaliatory counterintelligence operation. This one was more populist, questioning elite procedures, and invoking press support outside the Administration altogether.

The methods of the two counterintelligence operations were antithetical. The first one, truly a hunt, wished secretly to identify a mole or moles not yet identified. The second wished (at times in public) to gather derogatory information about government opponents whose identity was familiar.

With so few confidential ONI and Marine records on Oswald available, we know too little at present to speculate about the extent to which ONI and Marine G-2 operatives were participants in, as well as targets of, the original molehunt operation. These files are confusing: they contain traces both of a witting collaboration in a broader interagency molehunt operation, and of countermeasures to learn what that operation was.

It is for example possible that some ONI-Marine G-2 records are themselves part of the "barium meal." There are examples of altered details in Oswald's Marine and ONI documents, but not enough to demonstrate by themselves an established pattern.[453] More suggestive of interagency collaboration is an artificial delay in the records of ONI, CIA, and FBI together, so that key files on Oswald in all three agencies were only opened belatedly in the four months after the election of Kennedy.[454] An unexplained comment in the last new file to be so opened ("Now you can make contact") suggests that this synchronized delay was deliberate and coordinated, in accordance with a still unexplained inter-agency agenda.[455] It is also striking that after November 22, 1963, all relevant agencies (ONI, Marine G-2, Army Intelligence, CIA, FBI, and even State) responded similarly: they all withheld pertinent Oswald records from their superiors and/or the Warren Commission.[456]

Against these similarities in the Oswald records of all agencies, one has to note an antithetical strain in those of ONI, Marine G-2, and FBI: to acquire and even disclose secrets about Oswald held inside suspect areas of the State Department. These areas were so esoteric, so unknown to most people, that the "Congressional interest" referred to by Jerome Vacek would most likely be that of the obsessive HUAC and SISS.

Military Intelligence and the Assault on State from the Radical Right

What we know of the sociology of ONI and Marine G-2 corroborates their sympathy to the hunt for subversives in government. Glenview Naval Air Station, the site of the Marine G-2 regional detachment to which we found documents addressed, had been for years a center for right-wing political activity. In the 1930s the Ninth Naval District had organized reserve intelligence teams to ferret out intelligence on radicals and pacifists.[457] In 1960, while Marine G-2 and ONI shuffled their Oswald records, Glenview Naval Air Station played host to a five-day school of the Christian Anti-Communist Crusade (CACC), led by Dr. Fred Schwarz. The faculty, which included several Navy officers, pursued the Crusade's theme that Communist fifth columnists and their "stooges" could be found both on American college campuses and in the policy-making levels of the Federal Government. The Glenview Crusade was later criticized in the *New York Times*, on the ground that "it held up to ridicule and criticism certain established foreign policy positions of the Federal Government that the Navy was required to support."[458]

It should be understood that the CACC was not a local ad hoc group, but an international organization that for decades worked in many countries, notably the Philippines, in conjunction with the World Anti-Communist League and later the National Endowment for Democracy.[459] It should be noted furthermore that the Glenview CACC Crusade of 1960 was not campaigning against the "established foreign policy positions" of Kennedy, but of Eisenhower.

One key figure in the Glenview CACC Crusade was Jack Mabley, the president of Glenview Village from 1957 to 1961.[460] Mabley happened to be a close friend of the important Chicago mob figure, FBI informant, and sometime CIA asset Richard Cain, who as we saw in Chapter 2 was identified in his FBI file as "a former United States Army Military Intelligence Officer.[461] Mabley was also a columnist for the *Chicago Daily News*, and Cain at one point was hoping to travel to Cuba as a journalist for both the *Chicago Daily News* and *Life* Magazine.[462]

Indeed the Glenview Naval Air Station, by supporting Schwarz and his Crusade, was lending respectability to the Crusade's sustained onslaught against another part of the government: the accommodators in the U.S. State Department. In a 1961 rally at the Hollywood Bowl, addressed also by C.D. Jackson of *Life* Magazine and by future President Ronald Reagan, the only speeches reported by *Nation* reporter Fred Cook both assaulted State. Admiral Chester Ward (USN, Retd.) demanded that Kennedy "get rid of the architects of accommodation, the foreign policy advisers who give President Kennedy bad advice." Ex-FBI Agent Cleon Skousen, until 1960 an employee of the American Security Council (ASC), called for an investigation "to root out the 'small left-wing group in the State Department' that has been the source of all our troubles."[463]

Both events, in short, were rather typical examples of the military politicking (and budget-buttressing), which in 1961 was challenged by President Kennedy and Defense Secretary McNamara, supported by a lengthy memorandum from Senator Fulbright.[464]

(The Fulbright memo summarized the five-day 1960 Conference at Glenview.)[465] Among the military bases known to have supported the Crusade was the Eighth Naval District station in Algiers, Louisiana, which as it happens was the other Naval District Office handling Oswald's Marine reserve records.

C.D. Jackson's presence at the Crusade event reflected the backing for Schwarz from those, primarily defense contractors and other U.S. corporations, who saw in the President's foreign policy of negotiation a threat to their stake in the Cold War.

> When *Life* ran a skeptical story about Fred Schwarz, the outcry from Schwarz's backers, some of whom were national advertisers, induced *Life*'s publisher, C.D. Jackson, to fly to a [1961] Schwarz rally in the Hollywood Bowl and offer a public apology. "I believe we were wrong," Jackson said, "and I am profoundly sorry. It's a great privilege to be here tonight and align *Life* magazine with Senator Dodd [the SISS Vice-Chairman], Representative Judd, Dr. Schwarz and the rest of these implacable fighters against communism."[466]

The Crusade was backed principally by the ideological Eversharp Corporation, one of whose directors was Otepka's backer, former SISS counsel Robert Morris in Dallas. When eventually General Edwin Walker was fired for inculcating his troops in Germany with Birchite propaganda, he too joined forces with Robert Morris in Dallas.[467] Other major funding for the CACC came from international oil companies, above all from the Pew Memorial Trust and the Richfield Foundation. It reported a gross income of $1.2 million in its peak year of 1961.

Eversharp and other defense-related corporations also backed the American Security Council, which not only generated propaganda against proposed treaties with the Soviet Union but lobbied vigorously against them in Washington.[468] The American Security Council's files on over a million Americans established an industrial security database for American corporations, much like that established by naval intelligence at Glenview in the 1930s.

The ASC also claimed that "during 1960, eight government agencies and two Congressional committees obtained information from the Council's Research and Information Center on a regular basis."[469] One can reasonably conclude that among these consultants of the ASC Center were the SISS and ONI. William J. Gill, national editor of the *ASC Washington Report*, wrote a best-selling book, *The Ordeal of Otto Otepka*, endorsing Otepka's attack on the subversives of the State Department.[470] Editor-in-Chief of the same journal was Rear Admiral Chester C. Ward, whose meetings in 1961 with the radical right (while still an active Navy officer) were criticized (along with General Walker's activities) in Senator Fulbright's memorandum.[471]

After the assassination, a major attack on the legitimacy of the Warren Commission was published by the John Birch Society, through its chief spokesman Revilo Oliver.[472] Oliver, according to one of his books, was during World War II "Director of Research in a highly secret agency of the War Department [the Army Security Agency]." In the same book he revealed that he had resigned from the John Birch Society in 1966, convinced by then that its leader, the "little shyster" Robert Welch, had operated the John Birch Society "under the supervision of a committee of Jews."[473]

Oliver's self-acknowledged "racialism" is consistent with his role as featured speaker at an April 1963 meeting of the racist Congress of Freedom, about which more in Chapter 5. An informant, Willie Somersett, later told the Miami Police that at this meeting, "in a generalized feeling, there was indicated the overthrow of the present government of the United States." This included "the setting up of a criminal activity to assassinate particular persons." The same informant reported that "membership within the Congress of Freedom, Inc., contain [sic] high ranking members of the Armed Forces that secretly belong to the organization."[474]

In his *American Opinion* articles for the John Birch Society, Oliver challenged the constitutional authority for heading off an impending SISS investigation of the murder by the creation of a Warren Commission.[475] Oliver was questioned extensively about his opinions, and more importantly their sources, by the Warren Commission. Counsel Jenner elicited the significant fact that

Oliver relied heavily on his "research consultant" Frank Capell, who in turn had "the cooperation of many former intelligence officers of the Army and former members of the FBI."[476]

This presumably was a reference to the anti-Kennedy Foreign Intelligence Digest, a group uniting Frank Capell with army intelligence veterans like General Willoughby, and funded by the family of Dallas billionaire H.L. Hunt.[477] The Commission may well have been concerned by the ability of Oliver and Capell accurately to cite rumors already lodged in confidential intelligence files.[478]

Oliver and his friends continued to target the State Department in particular.[479] Echoing the concern of Otepka, Frank Capell wrote in his journal that "In spite of all that was known about [Oswald], a new passport was issued within twenty-four hours."[480] Earlier, right-wing Representative John Ashbrook, in a statement cited by Oliver, told the Congress that "any investigation of the assassination of John F. Kennedy must center upon the State Department's role in bringing defector Lee Harvey Oswald back to the United States."[481]

Alleging management and suppression of news by newspapers like the *Washington Post*, Ashbrook tellingly introduced a single news story: one which does indeed sound like an establishment defense of State, another shot in the great bureaucratic feud over Oswald's renunciation of citizenship:

> The American consul who handled the case of Lee Oswald when the accused Presidential assassin tried to renounce his U.S. citizenship in Moscow in 1959 says he has been ordered by the State Department not to discuss the case. Richard Snyder . . . said that Oswald's case was now under judicial investigation and, therefore, it would not be appropriate to say anything. Snyder did indicate, however, that Oswald never formally renounced his U.S. citizenship.[482]

Question: Was Oswald's Mission to Moscow a Test by Marine G-2 of State?

Ashbrook's interest reinforces a question that has haunted me for decades, but for which I cannot supply a certain answer: was

Oswald's trip to Moscow in 1959, and his apparently staged threat to tell the Soviets what he knew, not just a USG probe of the KGB, and not just a CIA search for Popov's mole, but a Marine G-2 probe of "liberals" (presumably including Richard Snyder) in the State Department? The chief evidence for this is the actual failure of the military agencies at the time to respond to a threat of espionage that should have alarmed them greatly. The lack of a vigorous response would make sense if ONI and Marine G-2 were witting of Oswald's game.

The chief argument against this explanation is the evidence, examined in Chapter 3, that Snyder himself was cognizant of Oswald's game, and playing a concurrent game himself. Furthermore, Jim Angleton's Counter-Intelligence (CI) shop in CIA in May 1960 compounded the game by inventing a legend, and a file which they controlled and manipulated, about a "Lee Henry Oswald." These and other facts confirm me in my belief that the Oswald trip was indeed part of a search for what I have called "Popov's mole" in the KGB.

But intelligence agencies are known to "piggy-back" operations inside other, duly authorized operations. So one can still ask the unanswerable question: Did anti-Eisenhower officers in Glenview, when asked to release Oswald for a CIA CI operation, give him a second mission: to test whether State would protect an American who talked treason while threatening to renounce his citizenship? The record is clear that Marine G-2 personnel at Glenview were not satisfied with how State handled the Oswald case, and in fact took steps to counter it.

This train of thought leads to yet another question. If officers at Glenview could successfully use Oswald's record in order to piggy-back their own CI investigation inside an authorized CIA one, could further steps have been taken in 1963 by someone witting to use the Oswald legend in a plot against the president?

There is missing evidence, perhaps still available, that might cast light on the first of these questions. I refer to the Confidential G-2 and ONI files that contained the two l messages discussed earlier: "9th ND confidential report serial 02049-E of 8 Jun 60," and "CNO Ser 015422P92 of 4 Aug 60."

We have seen that the first was denied to both McNamara and later the Warren Commission, the second was denied to the Church Committee (after interventions by White House Chief of Staff Dick Cheney and the office of Defense Secretary Donald Rumsfeld).

It would appear that something is still being covered up.

Conclusion: The Growing Opposition to Presidential Leadership

The growing support for the Birchite and American Security Council (ASC) right-wing was illustrated in 1961, when the collective clout of corporate advisers persuaded C.D. Jackson to fly out to a Christian Anti-Communist Crusade rally in Los Angeles, and apologize for criticisms *Life* magazine had made about the CACC.

Opposition was clearly growing to the Eisenhower consensus that had dominated U.S. policy thinking for eight years. And as is well known, Eisenhower fought back in his Farewell Address of the same year: "we must guard against the acquisition of unwarranted influence, whether sought or unsought, by the military–industrial complex" (of which the ASC was the principal Washington lobby).

Less known is that the text of Eisenhower's speech was prepared outside his own bureaucracy. Ike turned instead to his brother Milton, who directed the drafting of the speech in conjunction with a Johns Hopkins professor of political science, Malcolm Moos.[483] Eisenhower knew very well he was challenging forces at work in his own government. (An earlier draft had warned about the military-industrial-congressional complex.)

Mutual mistrust between the presidency and the military bureaucracy became much greater in the Kennedy administration. This was specially true after JFK's negotiated settlement of the Cuban Missile Crisis in 1962, which U.S. Air Force General Curtis LeMay publicly denounced as "the greatest defeat in our history."[484]

As is well known, Kennedy's response to the threat he had faced in that crisis of mutual nuclear annihilation was directly and dialectically opposite. On June 10, 1963, in his American University commencement speech, Kennedy called for a shift from "a strategy of annihilation" to "a strategy of peace," in which both America and Russia would guard the world against war. As a first step he announced an instant unilateral suspension of nuclear bomb testing.

Like Eisenhower before him, Kennedy went outside the national security bureaucracy for his speechwriters.

> In preparing the address, Kennedy had limited the discussion to a handful of White House advisers, including [Ted] Sorenson, who did the principal drafting, as well as [McGeorge] Bundy, [Arthur] Schlesinger, and Tom Sorenson, Ted's brother, an official at the United States Information Agency. McNamara, Rusk, and [Joint Chiefs Chairman Maxwell] Taylor were only told about the speech two days before Kennedy delivered it. He did not want predictable quibbling from the principal national security bureaucracy officials. . . . His caution was borne out by instant objections from Taylor that the Joint Chiefs could not endorse a unilateral suspension of atmospheric tests.[485]

In the months leading up to the speech, Kennedy had also resorted to secret personal communications with Khrushchev in Moscow, via the secret private diplomacy conducted with his approval by Pope John XXIII and a peripatetic American journalist, Norman Cousins.[486] It is possible that U.S. intelligence services became aware of this private diplomacy; if so, some must have thought it no less than treasonable.

And in the same year 1963, as we shall see in Chapter 7, Kennedy encouraged the making of a movie, *Seven Days in May*, to alert America to the increasing risks of a possible coup d'état from a small but determined military conspiracy.

The American deep state, relatively strong and united through the 1950s, was beginning to become deeply polarized, or dyadic. And with the Kennedy brothers' search for an end to the Cold War, by the unusual step of going outside channels, it was beginning to seem to more than just Birchers that that there was indeed a treasonable conspiracy in the White House.

5

The Dyadic Deep State and Intrigues Against JFK

Introductory Summary

In this chapter we will examine how numerous anti-Communists in what I have called the Birchite anticommunist complex were mobilized against Kennedy while alive, and presented false theories about his assassination after (and possibly even before) his death.

One chief reason for the Birch Society dislike of Kennedy was his failure to invade Cuba: first after the collapse of the Bay of Pigs operation, and again one year later in the Cuban Missile Crisis. Those in the military who wished also to attack the Soviet Union were still further appalled by Kennedy's rapprochement with Khrushchev after the Missile Crisis. This became evident with the President's American University speech of June 10, 1963, when he called for a "reexamination" of American attitudes towards Russia, and warned that a course towards nuclear confrontation would be "evidence only of the bankruptcy of our policy—or of a collective death-wish for the world."

Many also disliked the Kennedy brothers for their response to a 1962 riot at Ole Miss with more than twelve thousand U.S. Army soldiers, climaxing a fixed battle that left two people dead.[487] When Robert Kennedy then remanded General Edwin Walker, one of

the mobilizers of the mob at Ole Miss, for psychiatric examination, "The John Birch Society and other far-right groups heralded
this as an example of the 'Kennedy police state.'"[488]

In my recent book, *The American Deep State*, I focused on the
dominant internationalism in this country of Wall Street and big
oil. I had only a couple of paragraphs in which I acknowledged that
there was also an entrenched resentment in this country towards
Wall Street, which dated back to even before the Civil War. This
chapter will look at that widespread, entrenched resentment
among prominent people, especially but not just in the American
South and Southwest.

This will force us to recognize that the American deep state is
one whose very power generates, dialectically, a powerful opposition. In *The American Deep State* I devoted only a few lines to
the oppositional faction of right-wing Texas oilmen and the John
Birch Society, opposed to the relative internationalism of Wall
Street. But under Kennedy (as for the next two decades) America
was so deeply divided, from top to bottom, that it was, for a while,
in effect a dyadic deep state.

In this situation the presidency was, not just under Kennedy
but also under his next four successors, no longer the prevailing
power.

Milteer, Del Valle, Giannettini, and Northwoods

Before discussing the Birch Society in more detail, this chapter will
begin with what a right-wing extremist, Joseph Milteer, predicted
about the Kennedy assassination. From this we will look at related
efforts inside the government, to falsely implicate in the assassination a Cuban, Paulino Sierra Martinez, who had been assigned to
work on defusing the risk of a U.S.-Soviet confrontation, by Robert Kennedy's friend Enrique Ruiz-Williams.

But we shall also look at Milteer's association with senior military veterans, such as former Marine General Pedro del Valle, and
other prominent figures who in the 1960s were discussing among
themselves possible assassinations and even a possible military
coup d'état.[489]

Joseph Milteer, an organizer of the reactionary National States Rights Party, has drawn the attention of Kennedy researchers because of his statement, on November 9, 1963, that the best way to get the president would be "From an office building with a high-powered rifle." When asked whether "they are really going to kill him," he replied, "Oh yeah, it is in the working."[490]

Whether or not this constituted a prediction has been debated. But many believe Milteer's statements should have been taken more seriously at the time by J. Edgar Hoover at FBI Headquarters, who instead went out of his way to discredit them.[491]

Unquestionably Milteer made a second prediction that proved to be accurate. This was that there would be "a propaganda campaign put on how to prove to the Christian people of the world that the Jews, the Zionist Jews, had murdered Kennedy."[492] There was indeed such a campaign put on by the John Birch Society, the earliest stage of which fulfilled a trail of pre-assassination reports set in place, partly by outsiders close to the Minutemen, and partly by Richard Cain. The trail led, I believe falsely, to Paulino Sierra.

The connection between Milteer's prediction and Cain's activities, even if proven, might be written off as a lower-level conspiracy involving marginal people out of control. I try in this paper to sketch a deeper pattern in which these particular events grew out of disaffection with the Kennedys at a higher level, even inside the White House.

Milteer implicated in this propaganda campaign an "International Underground," and was himself involved with the Constitution Party of retired Marine General Pedro del Valle, an avowed believer in the need for an American coup d'état. It is widely alleged in Europe that in late 1961 del Valle invited an Italian expert on false-flag terrorism, Guido Giannettini, to lecture to active American military personnel in Annapolis on techniques of a coup d'état (a subject on which he was well versed).

A few weeks later such ideas, many of them to do with false-flag terrorism, were formulated by American military themselves in the documents we know as Operation Northwoods. These ideas were solicited by General Edwin Lansdale, whom the Kennedys had put in charge of Operation Mongoose, at a time when

Lansdale already knew that pretexts for war were wholly incon-sistent with the low-level campaign which the Kennedys wished at that time.

The historical record is quite clear that President Kennedy was opposed to the idea of initiating a U.S. invasion of Cuba, which Northwoods proposals were designed to bring about. But there are signs that the proposals began to be implemented in his presi-dency even before his assassination. And the assassination itself can be seen as a case of false-flag terrorism, thanks to false "Phase-One" stories which some in the CIA and military disseminated at first, implicating Cuba and the USSR.

The facts known about the Northwoods proposals do not establish a direct link between Northwoods and the Dallas assas-sination; but they do demonstrate on-going survival of an unau-thorized, contumacious state of mind. I believe them to be relevant above all because they illustrate part of a larger disturbing picture. This is that for fifty years after World War Two, there was a group inside and outside government, not restricted to the military, that wished to use the full resources of U.S. strength to destroy the Soviet Union and its clients.[493]

Every post-war president before Reagan, including Eisen-hower, aroused seditious hostility because of their refusal to endorse this dangerous policy direction. But no president aroused as much seditious hostility as John F. Kennedy.

The Predictions of Joseph Milteer

Shortly before the Kennedy assassination, a Southern racist and activist, Joseph Milteer, predicted to a Miami police informant, William Somersett, how the murder would be done: "from an office building with a high-powered rifle."[494] Beyond question, Milteer was an organizer for two racist parties, the National States Rights Party of former Admiral John G. Crommelin, and the Con-stitution party of former Marine General Pedro Del Valle. In Octo-ber 1963 Milteer was at a meeting of the Constitution Party, along with General Del Valle, Curtis Dall of the Liberty Lobby (a former son-in-law of Franklin Roosevelt) and Colonel Arch Roberts who had been the architect of General Edwin Walker's "Pro Blue" program in the military.[495]

In addition Milteer had attended an April 1963 meeting in New Orleans of the Congress of Freedom, Inc., which had been monitored by an informant for the Miami police. Miami Detective Lochert Gracey's report of the Congress included the statement that "there was indicated the overthrow of the present government of the United States," including "the setting up of a criminal activity to assassinate particular persons." The report added that "membership within the Congress of Freedom, Inc., contain high ranking members of the armed forces that secretly belong to the organization."[496]

The Congress of Freedom meeting, and Gracey's report of it, have received too little attention. There is however an account of it in a book about the Martin Luther King assassination by Stuart Wexler and Larry Hancock, *The Awful Grace of God*. In their words, this was

> a meeting of elite figures, devoted to the cause of white supremacy, who secretly discussed deploying strike teams to kill a host of (mostly Jewish) public figures. This meeting . . . included "high-ranking industrialists, bankers, and insurance executives" with "access to great amounts of money."[497]

In other words the Congress of Freedom was an example of the dyadic or dialectical nature of the American deep state, with at least some groups in it dedicated at that time to the removal of others.

Milteer did not just predict to Somersett the mode of assassination. As many critics have noted, he had also predicted the cover-up: "They will pick up somebody within hours . . . just to throw the public off."[498] After the assassination, Milteer added further details about the cover-up, three of which deserve far more attention than they have generally received.

The first is Milteer's remark to Somersett that Oswald's "group was infiltrated by the Patriot underground," and that arrangements had been made "from there to have the execution carried out."[499] Like other critics, Dick Russell assumes that this group was Oswald's chapter of the Fair Play for Cuba Committee (FPCC).[500]

Milteer's remarks about the infiltration of Oswald's group were corroborated by a much more established figure, former U.S. Ambassador Clare Boothe Luce. On October 25, 1975, she phoned CIA Director William Colby to tell him that in 1962 and 1963 she had been sponsoring anti-Castro activities by the Cuban exile Directorio Revolucionario Estudiantil (DRE); and that right after the assassination one of her protégés had phoned to say that "Oswald had tried to penetrate their little cell [and] that they ruined around and did a counterpenetration job on Oswald."[501]

As we shall see in Chapter 6, Luce's report fitted closely with Oswald's interactions with DRE contacts while he was in New Orleans. The problem here with both reports is that, according to the Warren Commission, Oswald's FPCC chapter consisted of himself alone; he did not have a group.

However, as I have written before, Dallas Sheriff "Buddy" Walthers had reported that there was a Cuban exile group on Harlendale Street in Dallas, "possibly connected to the 'Freedom for Cuba Party' of which Oswald was a member."[502] The FBI identified the group as a chapter of Alpha 66 and "an organization 'United to Liberate Cuba,'" presumably the coalition Alpha 66-SNFE-30th November.[503]

There is abundant evidence that this group *was* infiltrated by U.S. right-wingers, like Richard Lauchli (a Minuteman), Steve Wilson, and Dennis Harber, whom Milteer would have considered patriots.[504] And a CIA asset ("AMTAUP-2") on November 24 also advised the CIA JMWAVE station in Miami that the leader of the group in Dallas, Manuel Rodriguez Orcarberro, "was known to be violently anti-Kennedy."[505] (Station chief Theodore Shackley forwarded this information to Washington.)

The Milteer and Luce reports become more meaningful and sinister if we understand Oswald's group to have been the left-wing Alpha 66-SNFE Chapter-30th November chapter, which in 1963 was receiving funds from Paulino Sierra as part of an effort to persuade the group to move outside the United States. As we shall see, Sierra engaged on this project after encouragement from Enrique Ruiz Williams and ultimately Robert Kennedy.[506] Right-wingers in the Cuban exile movement would have had a motive to frustrate these efforts to reduce tensions between the United States and the Soviet Union.

Milteer's second prediction was that "there would be a propaganda campaign put on how to prove to the Christian people of the world that the Jews, the Zionist Jews, had murdered Kennedy."[507] Eventually this prophecy was fulfilled publicly by Revilo P. Oliver's articles for *American Opinion*, the journal of the John Birch Society. Earlier retired Admiral John Crommelin shared with the editors of *The Thunderbolt* (organ of the racist National States Rights Party) "the reasons Kennedy was assassinated by the Communist-Jewish conspiracy."[508] (The editors of *The Thunderbolt* were Edward R. Fields and James K. Warner. Milteer twice mentioned Edward Fields in his post-assassination ramblings with Somersett.)

But the campaign Milteer accurately predicted began much earlier, on November 26. On this day an ATF informant, Tom Mosley, reported to the Secret Service that one day *before* the assassination he had heard a Cuban member of the 30th November Movement, Homer S. Echevarria, say: "We now have plenty of money—our new backers are Jews—as soon as we (or they) take care of Kennedy. . . ."[509]

I am convinced that the trail planted by Mosley was false. Moreover it falsely linked the 30th November Movement (whose "new backers are Jews") both to the assassination and (in Secret Service reports) to Paulino Sierra Martinez. In fact two different operations were being conflated: illegal arms purchases by Isidro Borja and the Cuban exile DRE, and Paulino Sierra›s legal efforts to form a junta to arm and remove other aggressive Cuban activist groups, including the merged groups Alpha 66, SNFE, and the 30th November Movement.

Part of the purpose of Sierra's program was to persuade these groups embarrassing U.S.-Soviet relations to relocate outside the United States. Less militant groups like Artime and the MRR, or JURE, had already relocated voluntarily. Sierra was attempting to lure the recalcitrant remainder to leave as well.

I repeat: in this activity, Sierra was following the guidance of Enrique Ruiz Williams, who in turn was working, outside CIA channels, with Robert Kennedy. The erroneous Secret Service reports about Paulino Sierra and the assassination came too late to explain by themselves Robert Kennedy's reported comment to Haynes Johnson and/or Ruiz Williams, on the afternoon of November 22, that "one of your guys did it."[510] But the summary of FBI and CIA reports released in Appendix X of the House Assassination Committee Report makes it clear that Mosley's report meshed with a misleading trail, implicating Sierra with Mosley's Minuteman contact Richard Lauchli, which was reportedly already in place before the assassination.[511]

The propaganda campaign Milteer discussed focused on a pamphlet he himself intended to write and distribute "throughout the world laying the murder of Kennedy at the foot of the Jews."[512] However Milteer linked his "propaganda campaign", and himself, to an "International Underground, which is dedicated to destroy the Jews," of which his own "Constitutional Party of America would be used as part."[513]

Milteer and Pedro del Valle

Milteer was not fantasizing when he spoke of an "International Underground, which is dedicated to destroy the Jews," of which his own "Constitutional Party of America would be used as part."[514] His remarks, even if not as well informed as he professed, suggest that he was to some degree privy to the intentions and connections of the Constitution Party's leading theoretical spokesman, former Marine General Pedro del Valle.

Del Valle had so many international connections that it is idle to speculate what Milteer was referring to by the party's International Underground. One possibility would be the Shickshinny Knights of Malta, which I have discussed elsewhere for their many links to the handling of the Kennedy assassination story.[515] But del Valle, like his friend Willoughby, traveled regularly to Europe and specifically Spain and Italy. He maintained contact with his old friend Prince Valerio Borghese, whose picture appears in del

Valle's autobiography.[516] In December 1970 Borghese, "the Black Prince" would attempt a brief attempt at a military coup d'état in Italy, a coup inspired by the ideas of his associate Giannettini.[517]

Del Valle's main network, operating within the Constitution Party, was the Defenders of the American Constitution (DAC). This was an organization of retired high ranking American military officers (including Admiral Crommelin), many of them like himself veterans of the General MacArthur's army apparatus in the Far East.[518] Del Valle had created the DAC in 1953, after helping to found the Constitution Party in 1952, in order to run the unwilling MacArthur as a third-party candidate for president.[519]

The Constitution Party presidential candidate in 1960 was Brig. General Merritt B. Curtis USMC (Ret.), the Secretary and General Counsel for the DAC. But as Kevin Coogan has written,

> The DAC's role in the Constitution Party seems to have served another purpose as well since there is evidence that the DAC attempted to organize "militia type" networks under the guise of electoral politics. Del Valle's papers show that the former general played a role in the creation of a shadowy paramilitary network that divided up sections of the United States into four "zones." In a 7/23/1963 letter to Brig. General W.L. Lee, USAF (Ret.), del Valle said that it was agreed to organize everything "under cover of voter organization [for the Constitution Party], which is not inconsistent with our being an effective state militia as well."[520]

Coogan also depicts del Valle's recurring, if ineffective, attempts to construct a neo-fascist international:

> After the war del Valle maintained good ties with Italy's "Black Prince" Junio Valerio Borghese, whom he had first met during the Ethiopia campaign.[521] . . . Del Valle was also close to Franco's Spain. Through his good friend, the Madrid-based [Spanish Ambassador] Marques de Prat y Nantouillet, who headed a rightwing religious movement

called Active United Christians, del Valle met Franco in 1952. . . . He returned to Spain on other occasions, most notably in 1964 when he tried to help the Marques put together an anti-communist "worldwide Christian movement" with proposed financing from Arab nations and far right Texas millionaires.[522]

Convinced as he was that America was "in the power of the Zionist-Marxist minority," del Valle called for the "organization of a powerful armed resistance force to defeat the aims of the Usurpers and bring about a return to constitutional government."[523] Later he suggested in a private 1966 letter to a right-wing friend, Mary Davidson, that the solution to America's problems was clear: "the only way to cut the Gordian knot is by a military coup d'état."[524]

Del Valle took practical steps towards this goal: Together with Charles Willoughby, Lt. Gen Charles B. Stone,[525] and other military officers, he allegedly backed

a tactical guide, or manual of arms for the future, called the *John Franklin Letters* which suggested that "Patriotic underground armies should be established, named the 'Rangers,' who should train to assassinate, sabotage, and overthrow the 'People's Democracy.'"[526]

In the short term the *John Franklin Letters* served as a tactical guide for the "Rangers" established in California by William Gale, the California Chairman of del Valle's Constitution Party.[527] In time they would allegedly inspire *The Turner Diaries*, which in turn would be said to have guided Tim McVeigh in carrying out the 1995 Oklahoma City bombing.[528]

Del Valle may by the 1960s have been far closer to racists like Milteer than to Washington. The same was true of his colleague from the days of the Japan occupation, Gen. Charles Willoughby (born Weidenbach). Willoughby in retirement maintained associations with the racist ex-Nazi Walter Becher, and defended the racist *American Mercury* against the "stupid intolerance" which made William Buckley urge him to resign from it.[529] But Willoughby also kept up correspondence with CIA Director Allen Dulles, at least until the latter's firing by Kennedy after the Bay of Pigs.[530] And in 1955 Army Chief of Staff General Maxwell D. Taylor "personally wrote Willoughby, 'a distinguished alumnus of the Army', to enlist his help 'in interpreting the Army to the American people.'"[531]

Del Valle, Borghese, and Parallel Structures

Whether del Valle knew it or not, his hopes for a military coup d'état was the thinking also of his friend Prince Valerio Borghese. Borghese in the 1960s was in the course of creating in Italy a two-tier organization, similar to del Valle's, in preparation for a coup. This was disclosed at the trial of Borghese and Italian secret service chief Vito Miceli for their role in Borghese's abortive attempt at a coup d'état in December 1970. At the trial of Borghese and Miceli in 1997, the latter testified:

> "There has always been a certain top secret organisation, known to the top authorities of the state and operating in the domain of the secret services, that is involved in activities that have nothing to do with intelligence gathering." Likewise, a colonel called Amos Spiazzi, who was investigated for his links with the Borghese coup and the Bologna bombing, talked of an "organisation operating within the armed forces, that did not have any subversive intention, but was set up to protect the state from the possibility of a Marxist advance." A few days ago, Mr Spiazzi, who was acquitted in the trials, said proudly he had been a member of "Operation Gladio" since 1960.[532]

Earlier, in 1968, Borghese, using ideas from Giannettini, had organized a Fronte Nazionale, implementing the concept of an overt organization, "known as Group A and a secret, military wing known as Group B, . . . recruiting people for use in 'unscrupulous' activities."[533] He contemplated the use of bombs, falsely attributed to the left, to persuade the public to accept right-wing authority.

It would be very wrong to think that Prince Borghese and his ideas were as marginal in Italy as were del Valle's in the United States. Since the end of World War Two, fear of a democratic Communist takeover had obsessed the Italian establishment, NATO, and the United States. According to Roberto Faenza, William Harvey, when CIA Station Chief in Rome, suggested that the head of the Italian intelligence service SIFAR "use his 'action squads' to 'carry out bombings against Christian Democrat Party offices and certain newspapers in the north, which were to be attributed to the left.'"[534]

Borghese's Front is said to have been encouraged by his long-time associate James Angleton, who had saved Borghese from a partisan firing squad in 1945.[535] At the time of the coup Borghese's financial position may have been secured by Michele Sindona, the alleged banker for the Sicilian mob who knew Nixon and is said to have offered $1 million to Nixon's election campaign in 1972.[536]

But the details of Borghese's intricate coup plans can be traced to the so-called Pollio Institute conference in Rome, 1965, when theorists put forward what would later become known as "the strategy of tension."[537] At this conference Guido Giannettini, the intellectual father of the strategy of tension, argued for the use of "parallel and 'camouflaged' organizations" (such as we have seen implemented by both del Valle and Borghese).[538] Also advocated was the idea of false-flag terrorism: having the right infiltrate the left in order to attack the state (Cf. what Milteer claimed had happened in the Kennedy assassination).[539]

Del Valle, Giannettini, and the Strategy of Tension

In a paper submitted to the conference, Giannettini described a program leading from propaganda to infiltration to action. This last could be either violent or legal.[540] In the paper Giannettini wrote that in Italy the appropriate choice was for legal rather than violent action. He was dissembling. Giannettini was later to become notorious, after it was disclosed that he had planned the celebrated bombing of Milan's Piazza Fontana in 1969, in which sixteen people were killed. Although anarchists took part in these bombings, and were initially blamed for them, it developed that the anarchists had been infiltrated, and that the bombings were in fact part of a "strategy of tension" orchestrated by Italian military intelligence.[541]

Similarity of ideas does not of course prove a connection between them. But there would be such a connection if, as has been frequently claimed, in November 1961 General Pedro del Valle invited Gino Giannettini to give a three-day lecture course in Annapolis, possibly at the US Naval Academy, on "Techniques and Possibilities of a Coup d'État in Europe."[542]

We have to view this claim, which was first presented in garbled form, as unproven.[543] It has served the purposes of both Italian right-wing terrorists, like Giannettini, and also their left-wing opponents, to blame the United States for approving or even overseeing all of the violent bombings and coup attempts of the 1970s.[544]

At the same time, the claim is both plausible and, if true, extremely significant. For if true, it would suggest that del Valle's privately expressed desire for a coup d'état was shared, as early as 1961–62, with

1) Giannettini and perhaps others in the realm of international neo-fascism, and

2) more importantly, still others in the active U.S. military.

Other sources attest to the growing rebelliousness in the U.S. military at this time. Perhaps the most famous example is General Edwin Walker, and his Pro-Blue education program for the 24th Army Division stationed in West Germany. By 1962 Walker, now retired, was leading the small-scale insurrection at "Ole Miss" when U.S. federal marshals enforced the enrolment there of the first African-American student, James Meredith. In November 1963 Walker's aide Robert Surrey produced and distributed in Dallas the "Wanted for Treason" leaflet in which Kennedy was accused of "betraying" Cuba.[545]

Still later, attacking the UN and the Council on Foreign Relations, Walker challenged what he called the "no win" policies of the "fifth column conspiracy and influence in the United States" in US Government, and what Arch Roberts called "the mindless march toward a socialist America."[546]

Even before Truman's dismissal of General MacArthur in 1952—the event which roused del Valle to found the Constitution Party—a number of senior military officers had been increasingly alienated by the recurring failure of United States presidents to use America's overwhelming military strength for decisive victory. Key crises that revealed this alienation were the Kuomintang collapse in mainland China, or what Sen. Knowland called the "betrayal" of Chiang Kai-shek (1949), the siege of Dien Bien Phu in Indochina (1954), the Bay of Pigs (April 1961), and the Berlin crisis (summer 1961).

An inspirational book for those in seditious opposition was Col. John Beaty's *The Iron Curtain Over America* (1951, but still in print in 2005), arguing how Jews (who Beaty termed "Khazars") had captured the Democratic Party in their search for world dominion.[547] Among the prominent retired generals who endorsed the book when it appeared were Lt. General George Stratemeyer and Lt. General Pedro A. del Valle.

Those hating Kennedy from this perspective did not hesitate to try to draw the disgruntled anti-Castro Cubans to their cause. A flyer dated April 18, 1963, distributed to Cubans in Miami, stated,

> Only through one development will you Cuban patriots ever live again in your homeland as freemen, responsible as must be the most capable for the guidance and welfare of the Cuban people. . . . If an inspired Act of God should place in the White House within weeks a Texan known to be a friend of all Latin Americans . . . though he must under present conditions bow to the Zionists who since 1905 came into control of the United States, and for whom Jack Kennedy and Nelson Rockefeller and other members of the Council of Foreign Relations and allied agencies are only stooges and pawns.[548]

Kennedy counted active as well as retired military officers among his enemies. James Galbraith has revealed how, in the midst of the 1961 Berlin crisis, Kennedy angered the U.S. generals, and possibly Allen Dulles, by rejecting "the military's drive for a vast U.S.

nuclear build-up," and possible first strike as well.[549] A few days later Kennedy was told of a study by White House aide Carl Kaysen "that showed that a 'disarming first strike' against Soviet strategic forces could be carried out with a high degree of confidence that it would catch them all on the ground."[550]

Galbraith also notes the report of Nikita Khrushchev that, at the peak of the Cuban Missile Crisis in 1962, Robert Kennedy told the Russian ambassador, Anatoly Dobrynin:

Even though the President himself is very much against starting a war over Cuba, an irreversible chain of events could occur against his will . . . If the situation continues for much longer, the President is not sure that the military will not overthrow him and seize power. The American military could get out of control.[551]

In his book *Body of Secrets*, James Bamford recalls the concern at that time: how the Fulbright Committee's investigation of Gen. Walker's Pro-Blue program, citing the recent example of the OAS revolt in France, had warned of the "considerable danger" in programs such as Walker's. He quotes from a mainstream book of 1963, *The Far Right*, which also cited the OAS example:

Concern had grown that a belligerent and free-wheeling military could conceivably become as dangerous to the stability of the United States as the mixture of rebelliousness and politics had in nations forced to succumb to juntas or fascism.[552]

It is high time for this country to conduct a dispassionate examination of the degree of military alienation in the Kennedy years, and the possibility that this was a factor in the 11/22 assassination. But significantly, the nation cannot yet agree whether the U.S. disaster in Vietnam should be attributed to military coercion of the White House, or White House coercion of the military.[553]

From the vantage point of the 21st Century, we can now look back and see that, for sixty years after World War Two, there has been a faction inside as well as outside the U.S. Government—a faction concentrated in the military but not by any means restricted to it—who have been committed to the use or threat of

U.S. strength as a means of eliminating first the Soviet Union and then perhaps Russia as a threat to the United States.

Gareth Porter's excellent book, *Perils of Dominance*, shows how the chief opposition to such belligerence before 1980 came not from civilian bureaucrats but from the White House. This explains why Robert Welch of the once-powerful John Birch Society targeted even Eisenhower as "a dedicated conscious agent of the communist conspiracy."[554] By 1962–63 Kennedy was far more controversial.

I believe it is important to explore the issue of seditious rebelliousness within as well as outside the U.S. armed forces. An important first step would be to learn

1) whether del Valle did in fact bring Giannettini to Annapolis for a discussion of a "European" coup d'état.

2) if so, who was responsible for the invitation, and who were the audience. I consider it unlikely that it would have been restricted to the military.

Giannettini, the OAS, Philippe Thyraud de Vosjoli, and Dallas

I believe the claim of the Giannettini visit is plausible, for three reasons. First, it is plausible because both men believed in the necessity of coup d'état, although their views were not widely shared. Second, it is plausible because two reputable sources making the claim have studied the documentation supplied by Giannettini when he negotiated his surrender in 1977 to Judge Loreto d'Ambrosio, the magistrate investigating the Piazza Fontana bombing.[555]

Third, it is plausible because of the date suggested of late 1961. The coup d'état in Europe discussed must have embraced the successful coup of the Algerian colonels in 1958, ending the French Fourth Republic and installing de Gaulle, and also the unsuccessful follow-up coup of April 1961, of what became the Organisation de l'Armée Sécrète (OAS), led by former General Challe and Jacques Soustelle.

Not generally known was the fact that Giannettini was a principal representative in Italy of the OAS, and may even have participated in preparations for the April '61 plot.[556] Giannettini's theory and practice of indiscriminate terror against civilians followed the ideas of revolutionary war as practiced by the French colonels in Algeria.[557]

At the time of the April 1961 coup French journals like *Le Monde* and *L'Express* had charged that some CIA officers had met with Soustelle and encouraged it. In response, the *New York Times* conceded that CIA officials had dined at a luncheon with Soustelle in Washington. As James Reston wrote in the *New York Times*, the CIA

> was involved in an embarrassing liaison with the anti-Gaullist officers who staged last week's insurrection in Algiers.... [The Bay of Pigs and Algerian events have] increased the feeling in the White House that the CIA has gone beyond the bounds of an objective intelligence-gathering agency and has become the advocate of men and policies that have embarrassed the Administration.[558]

Three days later the *Times* ran the CIA's exculpatory explanation: that the lunch had been arranged in the French Embassy by a French Embassy official who was present throughout, "and thus there could have been no dark conspiracy."[559] This is an admission of extreme relevance to those researchers who have been interested in the presence of OAS Army Captain Jean Souetre in Dealey Plaza on 11/22/63.[560] For the French Embassy official who arranged the luncheon must almost certainly have been Philippe Thyraud de Vosjoli, the French intelligence (SDECE) representative in Washington. For de Vosjoli was a double agent working for the CIA, and close also to OAS leader Soustelle.

Thyraud de Vosjoli's double-agent status is described in a second book by Frédéric Laurent and an Italian, Fabrizio Calvi, a book based on ten years' study of the immense documentation on the Piazza Fontana bombing:

> In the early 1960s Thyraud de Vosjoli, a fugitive from the French secret services who had taken refuge in the United

States, served as an intermediary between certain leaders of the CIA (including Richard Helms) and one of the principal organizers of the OAS, Jacques Soustelle.[561]

The next sentences describe how in the same period certain ex-OAS cadres were picked up for service in the United States: "One of these was Captain Souetre. At the time Jean Souetre worked with the anti-Castro Cuban refugees attached to the CIA."[562] Souetre went on to join the OAS veterans who regrouped in Portugal as Aginter-Presse, a service in support of the Portuguese intelligence network PIDE (and also, according to European sources, a service operating as an asset of the CIA).[563]

Thyraud de Vosjoli's service as a CIA double agent is discussed in Tom Mangold's biography of de Vosjoli's good friend James Angleton. Angleton's aide Clare Petty told Mangold how Angleton's famous black-bag entry into the French Embassy in Washington was achieved very simply: "De Vosjoli remained inside the embassy after business hours and let Jim and the team in." Like Souetre, de Vosjoli worked with anti-Castro Cubans, and transmitted reports to the CIA—quite possibly from DRE—about Soviet missiles in Cuba.[564] (De Vosjoli had been filing intelligence reports since 1951 directly to Allen Dulles in the CIA.)[565]

In September 1963 de Vosjoli was suddenly recalled to Paris, but he declined to return, fearing, as he told Mangold, that he might be killed there. Instead Mangold relates how de Vosjoli, on learning that Kennedy had been assassinated, immediately "fled south to Mexico," where he "stayed for several months with Frank Brandstetter, a Hungarian-American friend who ran the Las Brisas holiday resort" in Acapulco.[566]

For over a year Brandstetter, an U.S. Army Reserve Colonel, had been receiving sensitive information in Acapulco from de Vosjoli about allegations of Communist penetration of the French intelligence service SDECE, information which Brandstetter in turn would take to U.S. Army Intelligence (ACSI) in Washington, resulting in at least one "one-on-one meeting with Vice President Lyndon Johnson and his senior advisers in the White House."[567]

Two relevant details suggest that the two men may have had some degree of special knowledge about Dallas.

1) According to his autobiography, de Vosjoli's flight south to Brandstetter was in response to the news that John F. Kennedy had been assassinated. For unexplained reasons, he responded to the event by immediate departure from Washington to Las Brisas.[568] Sources in Dallas have claimed that de Vosjoli actually met Brandstetter at the latter's residence in Dallas, right after the assassination.

2) Frank Brandstetter, before being hired by Hilton International to run the Las Brisas Hotel in Acapulco, had been a member of Army Intelligence Reserve in Dallas, where he still maintained a residence. One of his biographies reveals that he was close to a number of people who figure in the events of November 22. His Army Intelligence Reserve unit included Dallas Police Department Deputy Chief George Lumpkin, the commander of his Intelligence Reserve Unit there,[569] and was headed by Colonel John A. Crichton.[570]

In Chapter 7 I will describe how these two men in Dallas, Lumpkin and Crichton, participated in what can only be called the conspiratorial manipulation of Marina Oswald's testimony in the first hours after the assassination, in order to create the "Phase-One" impression that the Soviet Union may have been involved.[571]

Brandstetter and Crichton shared a professional interest in Soviet oil. The 488th Strategic Intelligence Reserve unit was engaged on a study, in which both men collaborated, "of the capability of Soviet oil fields." After the break-up of the Soviet Union in the 1990s, as we shall see in Chapter 8, Crichton was one of the U.S. oilmen who went on to explore the newly available oil and gas reserves of Central Asia.[572]

In addition Brandstetter, like de Vosjoli, had been a close associate of David Atlee Phillips since their days together in pre-Castro Cuba.[573] Brandstetter was also close to Phillips's (and Jack Ruby's) friend Gordon McLendon; and when traveling used McLendon, who was also in Army Intelligence, as a contact point through whom the Army could reach him.[574]

In 1975, in response to the post-Watergate pressures in Congress and elsewhere to investigate the CIA, Phillips and McLendon formed the Association of Former Intelligence Officers (AFIO). Brandstetter

> urged Phillips to expand his group to include not only former CIA officials, but also officers from other intelligence services, such as the army, navy, and air force. Accordingly, Phillips, with the approval of other CIA members, organized the Association of Former Intelligence Officers (AFIO). It was Brandy's responsibility to recruit the nucleus of former heads in the intelligence community, now retired, to represent the army, navy and air force.[575]

Giannettini, False-Flag Terrorism, and Operation Northwoods

If the story of the Giannettini visit to Annapolis is true, it might indicate that del Valle's interest in a coup d'état was not confined to a lunatic fringe, but shared within the active U.S. forces. It would also lead to a second question: is it a pure coincidence that the visit of Giannettini, the principal author of what came to be known as "the strategy of tension," was followed very shortly by the first known U.S. official documents proposing a false-flag strategy of tension?

I am referring of course to all the Operation Northwoods documents produced by the military for General Lansdale in March 1962, and submitted as part of Lansdale's White House Cuba Project, which we remember as Operation Mongoose. These documents were released by the Assassination Records Review Board, but only reached a wide American audience in James Bamford's *Body of Secrets*.

Here is Bamford's summary of the Northwoods documents, which by now are well known:

> The plan, which had the written approval of the Chairman [Gen. Lyman Lemnitzer] and every member of the Joint Chiefs of Staff, called for innocent people to be shot on American streets, for boats carrying Cuban refugees

fleeing Cuba to be sunk on the high seas, for a wave of violent terrorism to be launched in Washington, D.C., Miami, and elsewhere. People would be framed for bombings they did not commit. . . . Using phony evidence, all of it would be blamed on Castro.[576]

Once again, these ideas are pure Giannettini, whom as we saw was the intellectual author of the Piazza Fontana massacre eight years later. One does not need to go to Italians for such perverse ideas: Bamford notes that Eisenhower himself, in January 1961 told Lemnitzer that if Castro failed to supply a reason for invading Cuba, perhaps

the United States "could think of manufacturing something that would be generally acceptable." What he was suggesting was a pretext—a bombing, an attack, an act of sabotage—carried out secretly against the United States by the United States.[577]

This may be the origin for the plan, which failed at the last minute, for a simulated attack on Guantanamo to accompany the Bay of Pigs invasion. (For complex reasons, the anti-Castro Cubans designated to come ashore, led by Nino Diaz, never landed.)[578] More importantly, on February 2, 1962, Gen. William H. Craig, on behalf of the Joint Chiefs of Staff, submitted a memo to Lansdale suggesting a number of false-flag scenarios. Once again these included riots and sabotage to simulate an attack on Guantanamo.[579]

Bamford focuses very narrowly on Lemnitzer's fury and frustration with the "new and youthful Kennedy White House." He fails to mention that if (as I agree) the Northwoods proposals were a rebellious response to the restrictions imposed on Operation Mongoose by the Kennedy brothers, the man initially responsible for the rebellious response was not Lemnitzer but General Edwin Lansdale, the man entrusted by the Kennedys to be Chief of Operations for Operation Mongoose.

The JCS Northwoods documents make it very clear that Lemnitzer produced them in response to a request from Lansdale on March 5, 1962, for a "brief but precise description of pretexts which would provide justification for US military intervention in Cuba."[580] Although Lansdale's memo is not reproduced, we find identical language in a related Lansdale memo the next day to Richard Goodwin in State:

> At the 5 March meeting chaired by Secretary Rusk, on our favorite subject, the Secretary spoke of "other tracks" which might be opened for the U.S. to achieve its objective. He mentioned proof of "their" plots in Latin America, as an example. Also, there was joking reference to a "Bay of Pigs" in, perhaps, Guatemala, as a notional clandestine action for which "they" could be blamed.
>
> General Taylor has asked me to report on these alternate "tracks," among other things, to the Special Group he chairs. I intend to complete this report on Friday, 9 March. Thus, request that you provide me the section on alternate "tracks" Secretary Rusk sees as possibly open to the U.S., by Thursday, 8 March. I plan to include this, as the State response, in my report. Alexis Johnson was present when Secretary Rusk mentioned this, and perhaps could be of assistance.
>
> Along these same lines, and in response to direction, I am asking the Defense representative (Gen. Craig) to give me *a brief but precise description of pretexts* which the JCS believes desirable if a decision is ultimately made to use direct *military intervention*. I would appreciate it if you could provide a companion statement, a brief but precise description of pretexts which the State Department believes desirable in connection with any such direct military intervention.[581]

But as endlessly reiterated in the *Foreign Relations of the United State* (FRUS) records, the objective of the Cuba Project, from its inception on November 30, 1961, was "to help the Cubans overthrow the Communist regime from within Cuba."[582] This language is repeated in all the major documents in the FRUS, including the one preceding Lansdale's memo of March 6.

By early 1962 this limited objective, defended by State, had led to disagreements similar to those over Laos and Vietnam. The JCS, joined by CIA Director McCone and Special Group Chairman Gen. Maxwell Taylor, felt that the program should not be undertaken without establishing conditions which would permit the United States to "help" with external military force.[583]

At a Special Group meeting on January 25, CIA Director McCone warned that "popular uprising within Cuba could be brutally suppressed . . . unless the U.S. is prepared to give overt assistance."

> In commenting on Mr. McCone's last point, General Taylor [Chairman of the Special Group] noted that the CIA paper of the 24th appears to question the feasibility of the basic objective of overthrowing the Castro regime without overt U.S. military intervention, and that it suggests the need to accept in advance of implementing the Project the definite possibility of having to use U.S. forces. He said that in his view more than contingency plans *are required* and that, so far as possible, authority should be obtained in advance to undertake major moves which might be required as circumstances develop. He conceded that it may be impossible to get such a firm determination very far in advance. The Group agreed, however, that every effort should be made to line up various situations that might arise, and to formulate recommended policy to capitalize on these situations at the proper time.[584]

The result was a "working level draft regarding the use of U.S. military forces in support of the Cuba project." But the draft was a compromise leaving both State dissatisfied (it contemplated military intervention too readily) and also the military dissatisfied (the conditions for military involvement were too restrictive).[585] After discussion of the draft at a Special Group meeting with McNamara on February 26, Lansdale "was asked to submit a plan for an initial intelligence collection program only."[586]

Given this imposed restriction, Lansdale's request to Lemnitzer, for pretexts for military intervention, seems inexcusable and hostile, almost insurrectionary. In his request to the Joint Chiefs of March 5, Lansdale has escalated from the earlier search to establish "conditions" for military support, to a search for "pretexts" for military intervention.

It is probable however that Lansdale in his March 5 request for pretexts, and Lemnitzer in his response, had the support (as Lansdale noted in his request) of General Taylor. On March 5, the day of Lansdale's memo to the JCS, Taylor also drafted a memo (with contributions from McGeorge Bundy and John McCone) that endorsed the hard Lansdale line. Its first substantive sentence reiterated the Lansdale position, already rejected by Robert Kennedy, that

> In undertaking to cause the overthrow of the target government, the U.S. will make maximum use of indigenous resources, internal and external, but *recognizes that final success will require decisive U.S. military intervention.*[587]

It is clear that President Kennedy decisively rejected the italicized language when it was submitted to him on March 16:

> The President also expressed skepticism that in so far as can now be foreseen circumstances will arise that would justify and make desirable the use of American forces for overt military action. It was clearly understood no decision was expressed or implied approving the use of such forces although contingency planning would proceed.[588]

Whatever the fate of the specific Northwoods documents, it seems quite clear that false-flag ops were subsumed about this time into the U.S. repertory, even after Gen. Lemnitzer was replaced as JCS Chairman by the Kennedys' favorite General, Maxwell Taylor. In May 1963, Taylor and McCone had resumed talk of a military attack on Cuba; and the DOD Caribbean Survey Group revived some of the Craig proposals of February 2 for false-flag violence, including once again a simulated attack on Guantanamo. It assumed "that US military intervention in Cuba is necessary," and concluded:

> The United States should intervene militarily in Cuba and could (a) engineer provocative incidents ostensibly perpetrated by the Castro regime or (b) foment a revolt in Cuba".[589]

In the context of Kennedy's efforts to defuse the threat of nuclear war with the Soviet Union, this document is almost insurrectionary. This was six months after Kennedy, to resolve the Missile Crisis in October 1962, had given explicit assurances to Khrushchev, albeit highly qualified, that the United States would *not* invade Cuba.[590] And we have to keep in mind that some of the Joint Chiefs were furious that the 1962 Missile Crisis had not led to an invasion of Cuba.

This dissident military-CIA intrigue was being implemented as late as the month of the assassination. One of the Northwoods proposals had been for "'Cuban' shipments of arms which would be found, or intercepted, on the beach."[591] On November 3, 1963, just such a "Cuban" arms cache was discovered on the beach in Venezuela, on the eve of a presidential election there.[592] A year later an alleged shipload of North Vietnamese arms was discovered in a South Vietnamese cove. This arms cache, and the one in Venezuela, were widely denounced at the time, I believe correctly, as U.S. propaganda operations.[593]

The CIA certainly exploited them. On November 19, 1963, Helms showed Robert Kennedy a Cuban rifle from the cache, as well as blueprints for a coup by Castro against the Venezuelan president.[594] Eleven days later, on November 30, McCone showed President Johnson "the evidence that proved absolutely that arms had been imported into Venezuela from Cuba;" and called for an immediate "series of steps" through the Organization of American States (OAS), leading to "even to possible invasion" of Cuba.[595]

By this time, of course, some hawks in the U.S. government had a new argument for attacking Cuba: the assassination of President

Kennedy. Michael Beschloss has written that, at 9:20 AM on the morning of November 23, CIA Director John McCone briefed the new President. In Beschloss's words: "The CIA had information on foreign connections to the alleged assassin, Lee Harvey Oswald, which suggested to LBJ that Kennedy may have been murdered by an international conspiracy."[596] In other words, a "Phase-One" analysis of the assassination was proposed by the CIA Chief to the President.

One has to ask whether, if U.S. officials were implementing false-flag scenarios of violence abroad, they could have also done so with respect to the Kennedy assassination. Even if we cannot establish a direct link between Northwoods and 11/22/63, we can document the on-going survival of an unauthorized, contumacious state of mind.

The Kennedy Assassination as a False-Flag Operation, and Paulino Sierra Martinez

Ever since they were exposed in Bamford's *Body of Secrets*, the Web has pullulated with texts linking the Kennedy assassination to the Northwoods scenarios. Most of these have focused on what I have called the "Phase-One" efforts, some of them involving cables from CIA and U.S. Army Intelligence, to link Oswald to either the Soviet Union or Cuba.

I myself believe that a false Oswald may have impersonated the Dallas one in an overheard Mexico City phone call, and thereby created "evidence" in CIA files that he had been in touch with the Soviet diplomat and KGB officer Valeriy Kostikov, whom some in Washington believed argued was a KGB "wet affairs" expert in charge of assassinations.[597] On November 23, Pete Bagley in the CIA Soviet division wrote to Richard Helms:

> According to an intercepted phone call in Mexico City, LEE OSWALD was at the Soviet embassy there on 28 September 1963 and spoke with . . . Kostikov . . . a case officer in an operation which is evidently sponsored by the KGB's Thirteenth Department (responsible for sabotage and assassination).[598]

(A cruder example of false-flag propaganda was the Army cable from Texas suggesting that "information obtained from Oswald revealed that he had defected to Cuba in 1959 and is card-carrying member of Communist Party."[599])

The false evidence from Mexico was contained in a telephone intercept supplied by the crime-linked Mexican DFS. As I wrote in Chapter 2, the DFS may have been assisted in their intercept project by Richard Cain, an expert telephone tapper from Chicago, when he was in Mexico City in 1962 as a consultant to a Mexican Government agency.[600]

Cain's expertise was in electronic surveillance, most notoriously the tapping of telephones. In the period 1950–52 he had tapped the telephones of Cuban revolutionary leaders in Miami on behalf of Batista; in 1960 he was approached by his former employer to install phone taps on behalf of former Cuban President Prío.[601] According to an obituary notice in the *Chicago Tribune*, the CIA had engaged Cain in 1960 because of his Havana mob contacts, and also to wiretap the Czech embassy in Havana.[602]

Richard Cain at the time was also part of that Dave Yaras-Lennie Patrick-Sam Giancana element of the Chicago mob with demonstrable links to Jack Ruby in 1963, and the House Select Committee on Assassinations speculated that Cain may have been part of the 1960–61 CIA-Mafia plots against Castro.[603] (Cain had indeed worked with the CIA's FRD front in the Bay of Pigs operation.)

But what is relevant here is Cain's role in the pre-assassination falsification of files with respect to Paulino Sierra Martinez, linking Sierra falsely to the mob, to illegal arms sales, and ultimately to the alleged Jewish sponsors of the Kennedy assassination. Here it is certain that Richard Cain played a role, and at the invitation of a member of the CIA's SAS staff—the successor group to William Harvey's Task Force W that had worked with Lansdale on Mongoose.

Available CIA and FBI files on Sierra suggest that through 1963 both agencies were curious and even suspicious about Sierra's intentions. Using at least two and perhaps three of Hunt's future Watergate burglars, notably Bernard Barker, CIA in Miami

observed Sierra closely. Then on August 19, 1963, "Horace Goe-
let" [Stanley Figolak], a member of the CIA HQ SAS staff, flew to
Chicago for a meeting he had requested with Richard Cain and the
head of the local CIA Domestic Contact Service.[604]

An internal report ten years later says that at this meeting

> Cain was told of Agency requirements in general, and
> agreed to assist the Agency by providing information on
> undercover activities of the Cubans, especially Paulino
> Sierra and his contacts.[605]

Cain soon submitted information concerning a prospective arms
purchase in the Chicago area by the Directorio Revolucionario
Estudiantil (DRE)—specifically by a "Torres" (who was later identified as the DRE's military chief Juan Francisco Blanco Fernandez), and by an unidentified "Miro Cardoza."[606]

The CIA files so far released do not show any Cain reports
naming Sierra. However there is an August 9 report from Cain,
entitled "Cuban Exiles' Interest in Purchasing Arms/Financial
Contribution/ From Chicago Underworld."[607] This sounds very
much like other allegations from this period in the CIA's Sierra file,
and may have been the cause of "Goelet"'s sudden trip to Chicago
on August 19.[608]

Immediately after the assassination, Cain told both the CIA
and the press that in February 1963 the Fair Play for Committee in Chicago had discussed assassinating the President, and
that Oswald might have visited Chicago in April.[609] Another CIA
report says that "in 1963 [Cain] . . . became deeply involved in the
President Kennedy assassination case."[610]

The CIA was not alone in falsely linking Sierra to illegal arms
purchases. According to the Secret Service file on the assassination
which erroneously linked Sierra to the DRE arms purchases, the
name of Sierra as backer was supplied by a Chicago FBI agent.[611]
At the time Richard Cain was a top organized crime informant for
the Chicago FBI, and he reported to the same William Roemer
who in 1993 assured Gerald Posner that Ruby had no organized
crime connections.[612]

But perhaps the most damning portrayal of Paulino Sierra came sixteen years later, in a staff report prepared for the House Select Committee on Assassinations. We are indebted to the HSCA for having addressed the question of Paulino Sierra, which I believe brings us closer to the heart of the assassination conspiracy. But there are anomalies about the HSCA description of Sierra which are not only unfounded but egregious.

The HSCA Report says, with respect to the arms deal on which Cain had reported,

> The Secret Service . . . learned . . . that the arms deal was being financed through one Paulino Sierra Martinez by hoodlum elements in Chicago and elsewhere. . . . The committee did find that the initial judgment of the Secret Service was correct . . . It found, for example, that the 30th of November Group [said to be involved in the arms deal] was backed financially by the Junta del Gobierno de Cuba en el Exilio (JGCE), a Chicago-based organization run by Paulino Sierra Martinez. . . . Its purpose was to back the activities of the more militant groups, including Alpha 66 and the Student Directorate, or DRE, both of which had reportedly been in contact with Lee Harvey Oswald. Much of JGCE's financial support, moreover, allegedly came from individuals connected to organized crime.[613] . . . During its short life. JGCE apparently acquired enormous financial backing secured at least in part from organized gambling interests in Las Vegas and Cleveland. JGCE actively used its funds to purchase large quantities of weapons and to support its groups in conducting military raids on Cuba.[614]

But if we go to the supporting staff report, we find that the Secret Service never *learned* that the arms deal and Sierra's junta were being financed by hoodlums, it heard *rumors* to this effect:

> It was widely rumored that [Sierra's] money was actually from gambling interests of organized crime. . . . The committee hoped to determine exactly what means were

available to [his] group and from what source. . . . Pre-
liminary research also indicated that the Secret Service in
Chicago was investigating a "threat to the President" case
at the time of President Kennedy's assassination, in which
Paulino Sierra was of interest. The committee wished to
explore the nature of the allegation and the extent of Sierra's involvement in the case.[615]

The rumors were indeed there, and merited investigation. At least
some of them seem to have been contrived before the assassination, and appeared to implicate Sierra with men who soon became
suspects, notably Richard Lauchli, Steve Wilson, Manolo Aguilar,
and Loran Eugene Hall.[616] But the committee was more interested
in validating the rumors started by Richard Cain, than in investigating their sources.

One might think that before printing as fact libelous rumors
about Sierra and organized crime, a lawyer like Prof. Blakey would
have put these questions initially to Sierra himself. One would
expect also that the HSCA would have put its questions about
money to Sierra's employer, Union Tank Car General Counsel
William Browder. For the staff report notes that Browder "told
FBI agents that . . . he (Browder) kept the group's funds under
his control."[617] This was in fact the case, so that the Committee's
claims, if true, would implicate Browder as much as Sierra.

The HSCA did investigate the story, by requesting from the CIA
their files and index references on the informant (Thomas Mosley), the alleged originator of the story (Homer Samuel Valdivia-
Echevarria), Paulino Sierra and his Junta associate Reinaldo Pico
(who in the Nixon era was briefly arrested with Watergate burglar
Frank Sturgis for his physical assault on Daniel Ellsberg),[618] and
Interpen members like Manolo Aguilar.[619] But the HSCA never
asked either Sierra or Browder concerning the allegations against
them in CIA files.

I myself, almost as soon as this staff report was published in
1979, spent hours with both Sierra and Browder. Although much
about the Sierra operation remains a mystery to me, my condi-
tional conclusions at the time were that

1) Sierra and Browder were *not* handling money from organized crime, and indeed had immediately reported what appeared to be approaches by the mob to the FBI.

2) Sierra and Browder were *not* spending their money, as the staff report alleges, "on arms and equipment" from Richard Lauchli, "Gerry Patrick Hemming associate, Steve Wilson," and Dennis Harber.[620]

3) The activities of Sierra and Browder had been prompted by a telephone call which they took to be from Robert Kennedy's associate Enrique Ruiz Williams. At a time when Robert Kennedy was trying to end exile raids from the mainland United States, Sierra would try, using the promise of money as incentive, to persuade the most resistant Cuban groups to join a united junta and leave for new bases in Latin America.

I might add that Browder was a senior vice-president of Union Tank Car and who went on to be president of the Chicago Crime Commission—not the kind of person likely to disburse organized crime funds for raids that the Attorney General was trying energetically to stop.

From Sierra and Browder I consistently gained an almost opposite picture—namely, that at the request of Robert Kennedy's friend Enrique Ruiz-Williams, Sierra was trying to provide financial and other arrangements for the most violently anti-Kennedy Cuban groups for two purposes: a) to remove themselves from the United States to a foreign country, and b) to join a junta in unity with the rest of the Cuban exile anti-Castro movement. In short, he was not financing military raids from the U.S., as the HSCA Report asserts; he was trying to reward the groups for *ending* such raids and moving elsewhere.

This campaign was part of the overall strategy of the Kennedys in 1963. As the HSCA reported, "Suddenly there was a crackdown on the very training camps and guerrilla bases which had been originally established and funded by the United States."[621] The leading Cuban groups, Artime's MRR and Manolo Ray's JURE, left voluntarily for Nicaragua and the Dominican Republic. Sierra struggled to have Alpha 66 and the SNFE join them. (By September the U.S. Government had issued "strong warnings" to six

Americans who had been backing Alpha 66 raids against Soviet ships.[622])

As AP reported on May 10, 1963, Ruiz-Williams was seeking to unify Cuban refugees into a single "junta in exile," a short version of the actual title of Sierra's Junta del Gobierno de Cuba en el Exilio (JGCE).[623] In his book *Ultimate Sacrifice*, Lamar Waldron reported that he heard from Ruiz-Williams that the third of the "five fingers" of Ruiz-Williams' junta (after Artime's MRR and Ray's JURE) was Eloy Gutierrez Menoyo of the SNFE, with his new SNFE base in the Dominican Republic.[624] Specifically he wrote that Menoyo was "receiving support from the Kennedys, both directly and through Harry [Ruiz-Williams]."[625] The HSCA reports Menoyo and SNFE as part of Sierra's campaign, inadvertently corroborating that Sierra's activities were authorized.[626]

The Committee, despite its claims, did not go to the most obvious sources for Sierra's and Browder's funds—the two men themselves. Worse, the Report and staff report cherry-picked the files available to them to present innuendos about organized crime, while discounting Sierra's claims to establishment respectability.

There is not a word in the staff report about what I was able to establish from the public record: Sierra's meeting on August 17, 1963 with John H. Crimmins, the State Department's Coordinator for Cuban Affairs.[627] (In his memo of the meeting, which I was able to obtain from the JFK Library, Crimmins noted that "the Attorney General had been talking to Enrique Ruiz Williams and that, as a result, Dr. Sierra would be calling [Crimmins] for an appointment.")[628]

And the distorted HSCA summary of Sierra's CIA files omits his credible report that he met in Washington in April 1963 with Allen Dulles, Gen. Lucius Clay (then the senior partner of Lehman Brothers, a group with Cuban interests), and Morris Leibman, a representative of the American Security Council. It would appear that Sierra's objectives and plans were co-ordinated with those of the influential Citizens Committee for a Free Cuba (CCFC), a report on which was included in Sierra's CIA file.

Why did the HSCA distort and suppress with respect to Sierra? For years I have suspected that, at a minimum, the Committee did not want to reveal how some CIA officials, and in particular "Goe-let" from the Special Affairs Staff, may have transmitted a false trail from Richard Cain, leading to Sierra and thus possibly to Robert Kennedy. Instead of investigating and exposing Cain's false picture of Sierra, the Committee appears to have refined and perfected it.[629]

I don't wish to close on too negative a note about the House Select Committee on Assassinations. Their depositions of CIA officers, declassified by the JFK Records Act of 1994, have done much to clarify the complex tale of Oswald's relationship to U.S. intelligence.

But the record is clear that distortions of the truth, to establish Oswald as a lone assassin, did not end with the Warren Commission. This suggests that, although Milteer and his racist circles may have had some insight into the Kennedy assassination, there were others inside the government who had then, and have still, a secret to hide.

In 1963 the Kennedy Administration was deeply divided over the issue of whether to commit U.S. forces in warfare against communism, whether in Cuba, Laos, or Vietnam. Sierra was relevant to this controversy, insofar as his desultory efforts, to remove the more violent Cuban groups to new locations outside the United States, were working to remove a *casus belli* between the United States and the Soviet Union.

Because of the elaborate higher-level preparations for the assassination, I am inclined to doubt that the actual shooting of the President in Dallas was left to anti-Castro Cubans. I do believe however that the struggle over the Cubans' future brought more solidly into line a conspiracy uniting forces—including the mob, some CIA officers, and both active and retired military—which were both inside and outside the U.S. government.

The fate of Cuba was of course not the only issue in which Kennedy faced fierce controversy. Perhaps the best summation of what made him so controversial can be found in his two speeches of June 10 and June 11, 1963. The first, at American University, called for a fresh approach to the Cold War, and spoke of peace "as the necessary rational end of rational men." The second, on television, called for civil rights legislation, and addressed the question "whether all Americans are to be afforded equal rights and equal opportunities." Given America's divisions in 1963, such strong affirmations of American ideals reached outside the usual constricted limits of political discourse, and courted disaster.

6

William Pawley, the Kennedy Assassination, and Watergate

"All of the Cubans and most of the Americans in this part of the country believe that to remove Castro you must first remove Kennedy, and that is not going to be easy."[630]

"You put me in an awful position. . . . We are all in a kind of box at this point, and we really in conscience cannot sit on all this stuff . . ."[631]

In his major work, *Politics as a Vocation*, the sociologist Max Weber defined the state as an entity which successfully claims a "monopoly on the legitimate use of violence."[632] That claim has never been successfully upheld in the United States, where in cities like Chicago and New Orleans it was for decades standard to accept that mob murders go unsolved.

Nor are mob members the only victims. In November 1977 William C. Sullivan, head of the FBI's Intelligence Division was shot in what passed for a hunting accident; but his friend, Journalist Robert Novak, later wrote, "Bill told me I would probably read about his death in some kind of accident but not to believe it. It would be murder."[633]

One can debate whether Sullivan was in fact murdered. But fourteen months earlier, on September 21, 1976, a sophisticated bomb killed former Chilean Foreign Minister Orlando Letelier and an American friend while they were driving to work down Washington's fashionable Embassy Row. It is clear that both the CIA and its Chilean counterpart DINA were involved in the initial cover-up. Yet only four low-level Cuban exiles were ultimately convicted of the crime.[634]

In 1943, the prominent Italian-American anti-fascist editor, Carlo Tresca, was murdered in the streets of New York. The case against New York Mafioso, Carmine Galante of the Bonanno family, might have seemed airtight; he was under surveillance at that time, for parole violation, and thus was placed in the murder vehicle at the time and place of the killing. But he was not arrested or brought to trial. Shortly afterwards a leading anti-Communist informant for the FBI claimed to have learnt that the Communist Party was responsible for the killing.[635]

In 1956, a distinguished émigré scholar from the Dominican Republic, Jesus de Galindez, was kidnapped on the streets of New York and flown to his home country, where he was almost certainly murdered by order of his political enemy, the dictator Trujillo. In this case, a former FBI agent, John Joseph Frank (who had worked for the CIA as well as a Trujillo lobbyist) pleaded *nolo contendere* for his role in chartering the kidnap plane; he was let off with a $500 fine. Ten years later *Life* reported that the plane had been chartered by Mafioso Bayonne Joe Zicarelli, another member and a 'fast' friend of Trujillo whom he had supplied with over $1 million worth of arms.[636]

As recounted by the governing media, these four deaths—at least three of them murders—might seem unrelated. But a much more coherent picture of a milieu uniting them emerges if we look at the life and achievements of a man I consider a preeminent representative of the American deep state—former Ambassador William D. Pawley. Pawley's rich and varied life will enable us also to see a continuity between the deep state milieu of his day and the later secret "Continuity of Government" planning (COG) or what in the Pentagon was referred to as the Doomsday Project—secret planning for the "suspension of the constitution."[637]

Although most Americans act as if they do not know it, COG measures—1) warrantless surveillance, 2) warrantless detention, (including unprecedented abridgments of the right to *habeas corpus*), and 3) unprecedented steps towards the militarization of domestic security and law enforcement—were at least partially implemented on September 11, 2011; and are still in effect.

William Pawley as an Exemplar of the Deep State Milieu

A new biography by Anthony Carrozza of William Pawley clarifies the millionaire's status as a friend and adviser to presidents, despite his reactionary views that often made the State Department and even the CIA reluctant to deal with him. His ability to modify and on occasion even overturn official U.S. policies easily qualifies him to be considered part of that partly invisible milieu I have clumsily called the American "deep state," a milieu both inside and outside government with the power to steer the history of the public state and sometimes redirect it. It would be wrong to think that Pawley had such power only because of his personal wealth and connections. I hope to show that from the beginning of his career to his sudden death by a gun wound, Pawley always acted in conjunction with other powerful people from both the overworld and the underworld—in short, with what I have called other dark forces of the deep state.

What particularly caught my eye in this new biography by Anthony Carrozza was a new detail, which others might not consider as important as I do, adding to Pawley's previously known links to the background of the Kennedy assassination. I shall argue that this seemingly trivial detail is evidence of the deep state's presence in that background.

The key to Pawley's controversial status was that he made (and sometimes lost) his fortunes under foreign dictators he was personally close to: Chiang Kai-shek in China, Presidents Prio and Batista in Cuba, and Rafael Trujillo in the Dominican Republic. Long after the U.S. Government ceased to support these men, Pawley maintained their confidence, which was one of the reasons elements of the U.S. Government chose on occasion to use him as an asset.

Another reason is that all these dictators had developed contacts with the U.S. underworld, often because of their involvement in the trafficking of opium and heroin into America. As we shall see, Pawley himself had at least one CIA-linked mob contact, John Martino.[638]

The book shows how Pawley's personal wealth and associations enabled him at times to mount his own foreign policy, one supported by friends inside government and also by other wealthy individuals and corporations who saw their wealth or policy objectives doomed by the fall of strongmen like Chiang Kai-shek and Batista. Among Pawley's closest influential friends were Henry Luce of Time-Life, Henry's wife Clare Boothe Luce, Allen Dulles, and Richard Nixon (who according to Anthony Summers had his own web of associations to men who had links to organized crime).[639] All of these people shared what has been called Pawley's "pathological hatred of [Fidel] Castro."[640]

On at least two occasions I believe Pawley's support for a minority right-wing clique led to significant and lasting changes to American foreign policy. The first was after Chiang Kai-shek's expulsion from mainland China to the island of Taiwan, when "Pawley became the point man for an end run around American policy toward Taiwan."[641] It was the official policy of the U.S. State Department under Dean Acheson to plan for a containment policy in East Asia in which Taiwan would not be defended. But Pawley persuaded Acheson to allow for Chiang in Taiwan to be assisted by "a small group of American civilian, economic, industrial and [retired] military advisors."[642]

This plan when implemented, apparently with assistance from at least one underworld figure along with Frank Wisner's Office of Policy Coordination (OPC), became a significant factor in the survival of an independent Taiwan, and also in the growth of the post-war Asian drug traffic.[643] (Though the Pawley biography by Anthony Carrozza does not mention this, Pawley was also "instrumental in setting up the infamous Civil Air Transport [CAT, later Air America], an airline that later became notorious for ferrying drugs from the Golden Triangle in Asia."[644]) The Taiwan plan also enabled the notorious "China Lobby" to continue to lobby and pass money to the American Congress, helping illicit Asian funds to secure among other things the election to the presidency of Richard Nixon in 1968, and again of Ronald Reagan in 1980.[645]

The Carrozza biography describes Pawley's lobbying for a private Taiwan defense mission as a one-man campaign. But the definitive history of the Korean War by Bruce Cumings shows how the end run around the State Department was fostered by other important individuals inside and outside government, including General Douglas MacArthur as the head of U.S. forces in Japan, MacArthur's intelligence chief Charles Willoughby, former OSS Chief William Donovan,[646] mob figure Sonny Satiris Fassoulis, and "Texas oilmen" presumably including H.L. Hunt.[647]

(This ad hoc coalition was not all-powerful, and fell apart the next year when H.L. Hunt tried and failed to promote Macarthur, after he was relieved of his command by Truman, as a candidate for the presidency. This fluidity is an example of why I argue that the so-called "deep state" should not be seen as a structure, but as a system.)

With the support of elements from the same milieu, Pawley affected U.S. policy again under Eisenhower, with perhaps even more long-lasting and widespread consequences. By 1952 Frank Wisner's free-wheeling OPC had gone so far afoul of U.S. laws and policy that it incurred the wrath of both President Truman and CIA Director Walter Bedell Smith.[648] As a result OPC was merged into the CIA and was known thereafter as the CIA's Department of Plans.

However Smith's and Truman's intentions of curbing OPC were soon thwarted, thanks to their appointment of Allen Dulles, an OSS veteran who was again a practicing Wall Street lawyer, to be the CIA's assistant director in charge of the former OPC.[649] Wisner's OPC "cowboys," now merged into the CIA's new Department of Plans, continued to operate as before, especially after Dulles was promoted by Eisenhower to become the new CIA Director.

But tensions and ill-will continued in the Department of Plans, between the veterans of OPC and those of the old CIA's Office of Special Operations (OSO). Matters came to a head in 1954, with the CIA's preparation to overthrow the Guatemalan government of Jacobo Arbenz in operation PBSUCCESS. Eisenhower asked his friend Pawley to participate in a planning group for the operation, along with the Latin American representative of U.S. Steel.

Eventually Arbenz was defeated, with the aid of three planes paid for by Pawley's personal advance of $150,000 to the Nicaraguan government of Anastasio Somoza.[650] Pawley was personally commissioned by his friend President Eisenhower to obtain the planes, after the two men heard first hand from Allen Dulles that the chances of winning without them were "Nil."[651]

More importantly for American history, Pawley noticed that plans for PBSUCCESS were being leaked to the U.S. press, and he learned that the source was a high official in the CIA's Department of Plans (presumably an old-guard opponent of the ex-OPC "cowboys"). Pawley brought the problem of the inside leaking to Eisenhower, "whose response surprised him, 'I want you to conduct a thorough investigation of the covert side of CIA operations for me.'"[652] Pawley declined to lead the new commission, giving as a reason "a possible breakdown in the special relationship Pawley had with [the] Dulles brothers." Instead Pawley's old friend Gen. Jimmy Doolittle became head of the Commission, with Pawley as a member.[653]

The Doolittle Commission's report in 1954 led to a complete victory for the OPC faction in the Department of Plans.[654] In addition to purging old officers deemed inefficient, the report also urged that the CIA become an "organization more effective, more unique, and, if necessary, more *ruthless* than that employed by the enemy."[655] The door was opened to far larger CIA operations, including the waging of a war with a drug-financed army in Laos.[656] "Dirty tricks" such as assassinations were now sanctioned as a covert adjunct to U.S. foreign policy. Today, with use of lethal drones at the core of the U.S. war on terror, it might be said that illegal "dirty tricks" have *become* U.S. foreign policy.

Seen from a different perspective, the Doolittle Commission represented a consolidation of control over the CIA by Allen Dulles, Wisner, and the OPC. Behind Pawley's recommendation more than one historian has seen the hand of Dulles himself.[657] (Pawley had the reputation of being a member of the CIA's "Old Boys network and . . . especially close to CIA Director Allen Dulles.")[658]

My chief criticism of Carrozza's excellent biography is that it repeatedly highlights Pawley's image as a maverick lone entrepreneur. In fact Pawley consistently acted in concert with other influential figures from the overworld, united in lobbying groups for the military-industrial complex like the American Security Council [ASC] and the Committee on the Present Danger [CPD]. Carrozza does note how in 1969 Pawley used the newsletter of the American Security Council (ASC) to publish his recommendation that Nixon's withdrawal plans for Vietnam be supplemented by unleashing "the armed forces of the Chinese Nationalists on Taiwan."[659]

But he treats as a personal initiative Pawley's publication in 1974 of a newspaper ad supporting "funding outlays of $20 billion for the B-1 bombers and Trident submarines."[660] In fact these two expensive and highly controversial weapons systems were being fiercely debated in post-Vietnam Washington, where the campaign on their behalf was being led by the American Security Council and later the Committee on the Present Danger (a member of which was Pawley's close friend Clare Boothe Luce, the wife of Henry Luce of Time/Life).[661]

Pawley's actions in short were not just idiosyncratic, but rooted in the agendas of the militarist sector of the overworld. Given Pawley's status in this overworld, and above all his ease of access to Dulles and his circle, including Henry Luce (another personal friend), one has to ask whether Pawley did not have high-level support in the following episodes, detailed in Carrozza's book, with respect to both Cuba and possibly even the Kennedy assassination.

Suppressed Information about Oswald's First Approach to Carlos Bringuier: He Was Taped

If Carrozza is to be believed, Pawley's well-known role as a supporter of anti-Castro activities outside the CIA made him aware of an important tape of Lee Harvey Oswald in New Orleans, a tape which for some reason did not reach the Warren Commission, and would seem to contradict the account of Oswald's activities in the Warren Report.

An early and energetic opponent of Fidel Castro, Pawley (according to historian David Kaiser) "may have been the man who first suggested to Ike that Castro should be assassinated."[662] From the time of Castro's takeover, Pawley became a well-known backer of anti-Castro operatives. Many of these he vetted and then referred to the CIA's JM/WAVE station in Miami, with such regularity that he was assigned his own special CIA cryptonym, QDDALE. But his own preferences for a post-Castro leadership were wealthy Batistianos like Dr. Antonio Rubio Padilla, who was too reactionary for the CIA, too reactionary even for conservative CIA officer Howard Hunt.[663]

Pawley in short was acting as a spokesman for those forces in Cuba, including both Cuban landowners and businessmen, and also American corporations like American and Foreign Power, who ran the risk of losing their Cuban investments, even under the kind of moderately conservative government with which the CIA hoped to replace Castro. The same was true of those mob owners of Havana casinos who had not, like Meyer Lansky, had the foresight to hedge their political bets, by developing new casinos in the Bahamas.

Thus it was no accident that Pawley, in his Cuban policies, according to Carrozza, also dealt with mob and casino-related figures who were also too shady for the CIA: "Pawley's involvement with anti-Castro groups brought him in contact with shadowy figures such as Mafia gangster John Martino, Watergate figures Frank Sturgis and Howard Hunt, and an unidentified anti-Castro youth who tape-recorded Lee Harvey Oswald during an interview when Oswald tried joining a New Orleans anti-Communist group as a hired gun."[664] (This last claim is not supported; and according to the book's Index, Pawley's contact with the unidentified youth is not referred to again.)

This reference to a tape-recording of Oswald resurrects the unresolved allegation of Pawley's close friend and political ally Clare Boothe Luce, about a story from her "young friend," the skipper of one of the anti-Castro DRE raider boats she and Pawley were sponsoring. Luce claimed that her friend (to whom she gave the pseudonym "Julio Fernandez"), told her the night of Kennedy's assassination that he "had these tape recordings of Oswald" in New Orleans, tapes which included Oswald's "bragging that

he could shoot anyone, even the Secretary of the Navy."[665] Luce
phoned CIA Director William Colby about the story on October
25, 1975, telling him chiefly about the tapes.[666]

This story, never explained, supplies an alternative to the FBI
and Warren Report account of Oswald's contact in early August
1963 with New Orleans DRE delegate Carlos Bringuier in his shop
Casa Roca, a remarkable visit even before this new information.
Oswald's behavior on this occasion was unique: instead of talking
about Marxist politics, Oswald (according to FBI interviews of the
two witnesses) said

> that he knew enough about explosives to be able to blow
> up the new bridge that crossed the Mississippi River from
> New Orleans to Algiers, Louisiana. Oswald also mentioned
> that he knew how to derail a train which could be easily
> accomplished by placing a chain around the railroad tracks
> and securing it with a lock.[667]

To my knowledge this is the only occasion on which Oswald is
said to have presented himself as a demolitions expert. There are
far more stories in which he is said to have presented himself as a
marksman, as Oswald did in Clare Boothe Luce's account (from
her skipper friend "Julio Fernandez") of what Oswald said, in
which Oswald told his anti-Castro group in New Orleans "he was
an ex-Marine and would be happy to shoot Castro. He . . . seemed
to be offering himself as a hired gun."[668]

The tape-recording, not known from any other sources, puts
the Oswald-Bringuier meeting in a completely new light. The reference to the taper as an "anti-Castro youth" would seem to refer
to either Philip Geraci III (then aged 15) or Vance Blalock, two
teenagers who were present when Oswald reportedly offered his
services as an explosives expert to Carlos Bringuier of the DRE.[669]
Until now all commentators, including David Kaiser and myself,
assumed that the presence of the teenagers was purely accidental,
and their testimony reliable.

If Oswald's presence was tape-recorded, we would be forced to
reexamine that assumption. It would also draw attention to two

curious details in the Warren version. The first is that a fifth person was also present, a fat man who "came in and showed Carlos this broken radio that he had, so Carlos left and he started fixing the radio and left us to talk to ourselves."[670] This "broken radio" that needed "fixing" could very possibly have been the tape recorder (in 1963 tape recorders were far bulkier and more difficult to disguise than they are today).

The second detail is that both Geraci and Blalock testified (in divergent and mutually exclusive versions) that, after Oswald left, they "started following him home."[671] In Luce's version as she told a journalist in 1975, "Fernandez'"s contacts also "followed him and found he was in a Fair Play for Cuba Communist cell."[672]

We seem to have two different accounts of the same event. The FBI and Warren Commission version, as we might expect, is a "Phase-Two" version, in which nothing conflicts with the picture they present of Oswald as a lone assassin. Geraci and Blalock were interviewed by the Warren Commission but said nothing about having taped him (10 WH 76, 82). The Luce-Hernandez version, in contrast, is a "Phase-One" story, in which Oswald appears as a hired gun who may have been working ultimately for Castro: "The young Cuban who called me," Mrs. Luce continued, "said that there was a Cuban Communist assassination team working some-where—in Dallas, New Orleans, or wherever . . . [and] Oswald was their hired gun."[673]

Luce's Cuban added, somewhat paradoxically, that Oswald, before deciding to work for Castro, "had tried to report the Communist plans to the FBI some time before the assassination."[674] This switch from anti-Castro to pro-Castro roles for Oswald, unlikely as it may sound, closely mirrors the Warren Report's account of Oswald between August 5 and August 9, 1963. Bringuier himself told the *Washington Post* after the assassination that on August 5 "I thought he might be an agent for the FBI or the CIA," before Bringuier caught him on August 9 distributing leaflets from the pro-Castro Fair Play for Cuba Committee.[675] As we shall see, I gave reasons in *Deep Politics and the Death of JFK* to believe Bringuier's suspicion was well-founded.[676]

Bringuier, Sturgis, Interpen, and the Lake Pontchartrain Training Camp

If in fact Oswald was taped in Bringuier's store, the "anti-Castro youth" who did it is most likely Philip Geraci, who had previously contacted Bringuier. Two years later, in 1965, the FBI prepared a Letterhead Memorandum on Geraci, under the rubric "Bombing Matters –Threats," which was also distributed locally to Army and Navy Intelligence and the Secret Service.[677] Geraci, now 17, had just run away from home; he was reported to be "mentally disturbed," with "an interest in guerrilla warfare, explosives, and the organizing of groups." He was also active in a group calling itself "Sons of the Confederacy," engaging in guerrilla war games.

Geraci had undergone psychiatric treatment; according to his psychiatrist, he was "highly concerned about a possible communist takeover in this country . . . and wanted to do something about it himself [as] evidenced by his desire to join 'Alpha 66.'" Three years later, a subsequent FBI memo of October 1968 reported that Geraci had indeed "affiliated" with some anti-Castro Cubans, possibly Alpha 66. Picked up in the same month of May 1965, he had been committed to an insane asylum, but after release he served in Vietnam.[678]

Perhaps the most relevant information in the 1965 memo concerned young Philip's father, Philip Geraci, Jr. The senior Geraci reported that he worked for the Mason-Rust Company, which maintained the buildings of the Michoud plant of NASA in New Orleans. In this capacity he held a "secret clearance."[679] In addition his son's gang had considered planting a fake bomb contrivance at Michoud "for the avowed purpose of showing the public that the security regulations were not strict enough."[680]

This background may explain why the FBI opened an inter-agency file on this missing 17-year old under the heading of "Bombing Matters." Let me repeat my argument in *Deep Politics and the Death of JFK* that Oswald's visit to Bringuier was as an informant in the FBI investigation of a potential bombing matter, the FBI's recent raid of a nearby explosives cache at an anti-Castro training camp:

Oswald's initial meeting of August 5, 1963, with the DRE's
Carlos Bringuier [was] only five days after the FBI had
raided the dynamite cache next to the DRE's secret training camp. Bringuier, with good reason, took Oswald's offer
to him "to train Cubans in guerrilla warfare" as proof that
he was not a "loner," but someone with knowledge of the
DRE's secret links to both the arms cache and the training
camp.

Bringuier's argument was indeed an almost unanswerable
one. As he pointed out to the Warren Commission, the presence of the training camp "was not generally known. . . . I
believe that was the only time here in New Orleans that there
was something like that" (10 WH 43-44). Bringuier went on
to suggest that Castro might have given Oswald this privileged information. Back in August, however, Bringuier had
had the opposite reaction: "I thought he might be an agent
from the FBI or the CIA, trying to find out what we might be
up to." Bringuier's logic here is of major importance. Oswald
had to be working for one side or the other; he could not
have been acting alone.[681]

I also drew attention to two other matters. The first was that
Oswald (according to Geraci) asked Bringuier "was he connected
with the Cosa Nostra" (10 WH 77), at a time when (according to
the Church Committee) "underworld figures" were indeed, as the
FBI knew, involved with the cache and training camp. ("La Cosa
Nostra" had been for over a month the FBI's in-house term for the
Mafia, but the public did not learn this until it was used in the *New
York Times* on August 5, 1963, the very day of Oswald's interview.)

The second, which I previously thought to be unrelated, is
that Oswald's previous employment at the Reily Coffee Company might have been connected to surveillance of candidates for
employment at the Michoud NASA plant. In July 1963 Oswald
told an acquaintance, Adrian Alba, "that he was leaving [Reily] for
Michoud" (10 WH 226; cf. 23 WH 709); and some of his Reily co-
workers also talked of making the move.[682] (Those actually moving
to Michoud included his supervisors, John Branyon and Alfred

Claude.)[683] I cited this Michoud syndrome, not as conclusive proof that Oswald was an informant, but as part of an ongoing pattern suggesting that Oswald had been regularly employed as an informant in industrial security matters.

I conclude from all this:

1. It is likely that Oswald was indeed taped when he first spoke to Bringuier, and the young man who brought the tape to Pawley may also have been Luce's "young friend."

2. The tape should have reached the Warren Commission but apparently did not—even though, according to Luce, she told her friend in November 1963 to take the tapes to the FBI. Luce later claimed that her Cuban told her the FBI took the tape, then "roughed them up and told them to scram and keep their mouths shut."[684]

3. There was more to the Oswald-Bringuier meeting than met the eye. Specifically, if he was taped, it is unlikely that the encounter was as spontaneous as presented in the Warren Report.[685]

Oswald may indeed have talked to Bringuier of assassinating Castro. If Oswald's questioning of Bringuier was indeed, as I suggested in *Deep Politics*, part of an investigation, then the most innocent explanation of the taping would be that that too, was sanctioned as part of that investigation. However another supplementary explanation is also possible: that Oswald was maneuvered into contacting Bringuier as part of a preparatory legend anticipating that he would become the designated culprit in the November assassination.

Pawley may not have been at arms' length from this preparation. It is highly probable that he was not at arms length from the Lake Pontchartrain training camp. Let us recall that the Schweiker-Hart Committee reported that "anti-Castro exiles and underworld figures . . . were operating the guerrilla training camp in July 1963."[686] It is not clear who these "underworld figures" were, but a CIA memo about Lake Pontchartrain activities in 1962 points to the Intercontinental Penetration Force (Interpen) of

Gerald Patrick Hemming and Frank Sturgis (aka Frank Fiorini).[687] This confirms the report of Warren Hinckle and William Turner that the camp "had been set up [in 1962] by Gerry Hemming and Frank Sturgis at the request of the New Orleans branch of the Cuban Revolutionary Council," whose Secretary for Propaganda was Carlos Bringuier.[688]

What makes this fact especially interesting is that, in the first half of 1963, Hemming and Sturgis had also been involved in Pawley's most significant contribution to the background of the JFK assassination, the so-called Bayo-Pawley raid into Cuba. (In addition Hemming reportedly received some funds for Interpen from a meeting in Dallas attended by Clint Murchison, Nelson Bunker Hunt, and Col. Brandstetter's friend Gordon McLendon.)[689]

Pawley, Sturgis, Hemming, Martino, and the Bayo-Pawley Plot

We now know that Pawley, Hemming, and Sturgis (along with John Martino) were actively involved with the Miami CIA Station in a conspiratorial penetration of Cuba in April 1963, the so-called Bayo-Pawley plot (known to the CIA as Operation TILT).

The Bayo-Pawley story has been told many times. David Kaiser, relying on the congressional testimony of Loran Hall, has seen in it the hand of Martino's associate John Roselli, and concludes that, in the Bayo-Pawley plot, "Roselli and Trafficante were using Martino and Pawley as cut-outs to enlist the help of the CIA."[690] The Carrozza account differs from Kaiser's in attributing a more forceful role to Pawley, claiming that it was Pawley himself who "began assembling a team [which] included mob figures, Cuban exile leaders, CIA operatives, and mercenary soldiers, some of whom would become well known names during the Watergate investigation a decade later."[691]

David Kaiser, in contrast, claims that Pawley "became a pawn in an elaborate scheme hatched by John Martino."[692] But Pawley's and Martino's outlooks on Cuba were so similar, that there is no need to think that one of them duped the other. (It is symptomatic of their convergence that both men used the anti-communist writer Nathaniel Weyl to ghost-write their memoirs.)[693] Pawley,

Martino, and Weyl all had links to the John Birch Society, which Gus Russo and others have also linked to the Lake Pontchartrain training camp.[694]

What is certain is that *Life* Magazine helped finance the raid, and sent Richard Billings to join the expedition as a reporter. And *Life* was not alone in financing Bayo-Pawley; in addition, a CIA internal memo reported that "James [i.e. Julien] Sourwine, counsel to the Senate Internal Security Subcommittee [SISS], was involved in financing the operation which has come to be known as the Bayo-Pawley raid."[695]

Life had financed a number of other anti-Castro Cuban raids in 1963, notably those of Alpha-66.[696] The raids of Alpha 66, and its spin-off, Comandos L, had been targeting Soviet ships in Cuban waters, hoping to wreck the U.S.-Soviet agreement over Cuba that had been reached after the Cuban Missile Crisis. (The terms of that agreement had not been fully disclosed, but were generally understood to include a U.S. promise not to invade Cuba if the Soviet Union proceeded to withdraw its missiles and most of its troops.)[697] On March 18 Alpha 66 attacked the Russian freighter Lvov at Isabela de Sagua in Cuba; nine days later Comandos L blew up the Soviet freighter Baku in Caibarién, ruining 10,000 bags of sugar.[698] These anti-Soviet raids had the blessing and financial backing of Henry Luce and his Time-Life empire, which allegedly "spent close to a quarter of a million dollars during 1963–1964 on the renegade Cuban exile commandos."[699]

The raids also drew the attention of the Kennedy White House. On March 30, 1963, the U.S. State and Justice Departments (the latter of course headed by Robert Kennedy) jointly announced that they would take "every step necessary" to ensure that raids by Cuban exiles against Cuba were "not launched, manned, or equipped from U.S. territory." Surveillance of the exiles and their bases was immediately intensified.[700]

This was one day after CIA Director McCone had recommended that the U.S. not prevent the raiders from using the U.S. as a base.[701] It was also about this time that Harry Ruiz-Williams initiated contact with Paulino Sierra, to have groups like Alpha-66 relocate their base of activities to a base outside the United States.

"Eddie Bayo" (Eduardo Perez), one of the best-known Alpha 66 raid leaders, was chosen to lead the Bayo-Pawley mission. In addition, Pawley told Ted Shackley of the CIA's Miami JM/WAVE Station "that Martino was to play a role in the operation."[702] This seems an odd requirement if the purpose of the mission was (as Pawley told Shackley) to extricate Soviet technicians who would testify to the on-going presence of Soviet missiles in Cuba. But it makes perfect sense if (as Carrozza suggests) Pawley knew that this was planned to be (or at least look like) an assassination mission, which members of the mob (Roselli and Sam Giancana, according to participant Loran Hall) were also paying for.[703]

Jack Anderson's "Phase-Three" Report of a "Political H-bomb," and Watergate

Pawley's biographer, Anthony Carrozza, corroborates the story given in 1976 by one of the participants, Loran Eugene Hall, and endorsed by David Kaiser: that a deeper purpose of this raid was to assassinate Castro.[704] And Carrozza speculates that the team of Cubans exfiltrated into Cuba for this purpose may have been the team that (according to a John Roselli story published by Jack Anderson) came "back to the United States as the team that killed President Kennedy and set up Oswald as the fall guy."[705] Anderson referred to this possibility as "a political H-bomb."[706]

In other words, Carrozza gives support to a story first spread by Martino and Roselli in 1963 (and reported by myself three decades later) both of whom "told the FBI that the assassination of John F. Kennedy had been Castro's retaliation for Kennedy's CIA-Mafia plots against himself, even to the point of Castro's having 'turned' an assassination team and sent it back to Dallas."[707]

This "retaliation" story was first published nationally by Jack Anderson, after meeting with Roselli's lawyer Edward P. Morgan, on March 3, 1967. I suspect however that it was circulated much earlier, and may even have been the substance of the long discussion between John McCone and Robert Kennedy on the afternoon of November 22, 1963.[708] We know that on that same afternoon RFK voiced a version of what I have called the "Phase-Three" "retaliation" theory when he spoke to his Cuban friend Harry Ruiz-Williams. According to journalist Haynes Johnson, who was present, Kennedy turned to Williams that fateful afternoon and said, "One of your guys did it."[709] What makes the quote so meaningful is the fact that in 1963 RFK, at odds with CIA plans for the replacement of Castro, was using Williams as his go-between with Cuban exiles for alternative covert operations not sponsored by the CIA.[710]

From early in his presidency, Lyndon Johnson also reportedly believed, perhaps from what he was told by CIA director McCone, that JFK was killed in retaliation for U.S. assassination plots against Castro.[711] Joseph Califano, a former Army member of the Cuban Coordinating Committee under both JFK and LBJ, later formulated this belief more precisely as a "plot that backfired" theory:

> I have come to share LBJ's view [that Castro "got him first"]. . . . Over the years I have come to believe that the paroxysms of grief that tormented Robert Kennedy for years after his brother's death arose, at least in part, from a sense that his efforts to eliminate Castro led to his brother's assassination.[712]

I like to think of the "plot that backfired" theory as a "Phase-Three" story, because of my arguments elsewhere that it, and more specifically the Bayo-Pawley mission, was planned precisely to coerce the CIA, *Life,* and perhaps even the Kennedy family, "into an assassination cover-up."[713] For many years I have suspected that the true target of the Bayo-Pawley mission was neither the mythical Soviet defectors, nor even to assassinate Castro, but President Kennedy, on a level even deeper than its avowed intention to sabotage Kennedy's policy of détente with Cuba and the Soviet Union.

As Robert K. Brown and Miguel Acoca wrote in their 1976 account, "The Bayo-Pawley Affair," "It was a plot to destroy President Kennedy politically, and the CIA played a major role. Without the CIA, in fact, the weird adventure could not have taken place."[714] It is indeed true that proof of missiles in Cuba would have completely discredited Kennedy's claim to have successfully resolved the Cuban Missile Crisis, and put an end to his efforts to develop a policy of détente towards the Soviet Union.

No Soviet defectors were actually obtained, so the plot might at first glance seem to have been ineffective. That however did not at all impede the use of the "Phase-Three" retaliation story as post-assassination political blackmail. By enlisting two regular CIA personnel from Shackley's JM/WAVE station ("Irving C. Cadick" and "Oliver E. Fortson"),[715] and also Richard Billings from *Life* magazine, the plot may have helped ensure that the CIA, *Life*, and others would later engage in a post-assassination cover-up.[716]

The plot may also have blackmailed Robert Kennedy: Brown and Acoca report (as Kaiser and Carrozza do not) that the organizers of the raid had at the outset brought in a wealthy Kennedy supporter, Theodore Racoosin; Racoosin reported later that he had contacted "someone in the White House, who had authorized him to organize meetings of Cuban exile leaders, in order to obtain information on the CIA's Cuban operations."[717]

Such an authorization, if granted, would be enough to explain why Robert Kennedy "immediately moved to shut down" Roselli's "Phase-Three" story when Jack Anderson published it in March 1967. According to David Talbot, Kennedy first requested "a copy of the FBI memo on the . . . meeting when he was first informed by the CIA about the Mafia plots." and the arranged to have lunch, on March 4, 1967, with CIA Director Richard Helms. Three days later, on March 7, 1967, the *Washington Post* finally published a bowdlerized version of the March 3 Jack Anderson column. It no longer contained Anderson's reference to "a political H-bomb—an unconfirmed report that Senator Robert Kennedy (Dem-N.Y.) may have approved an assassination plot which then possibly backfired against his late brother."[718]

One does not have to believe in the truth of the "Phase-Three" "plot that backfired" story to believe in the importance of it. Robert Kennedy was not the only major figure to feel threatened by Anderson's "political H-bomb;" so, four years later, did President Nixon. In January 1971 a Jack Anderson column reported again about CIA plots, this time naming mob figure John Roselli, ex-CIA officer William Harvey, and CIA contract agent Robert

Maheu, their go-between in the CIA-mafia plots of 1960 (plots involving Nixon but not Kennedy). In 1971 Anderson asked again, "Could the plot against Castro have backfired against President Kennedy?"[719]

As I noted in 1976, the column "caused a flurry of investigative memos inside the Nixon White House," including a warning from one of the White House "dirty tricks" operatives, Jack Caulfield, that "Maheu's covert activities . . . with CIA . . . might well shake loose Republican skeletons from the closet."[720] According to Anthony Summers, Attorney General John Mitchell promptly phoned Maheu, who was currently "under pressure to appear before a grand jury in connection with a Las Vegas gambling prosecution," and arranged a deal whereby, in exchange for Maheu's silence on "the entire Castro story," Maheu would not have to testify.[721]

This was noted and investigated by two members of the staff of the Senate Watergate Committee, Terry Lenzner and Mark Lackritz, who concluded that White House concern about Anderson's "Phase-Three" story "could have been a possible motivation for the [Watergate] break-in to the office of the DNC."[722] The two staffers questioned Caulfield about his "skeletons" memo. Anthony Summers writes that "Caulfield first asked to go off the record. After discussion in private, he conceded that his reference to 'covert activities' related to [Anderson's] Castro plot revelations."[723]

At the end of a lengthy chapter, Summers concluded,

Nixon had good reason to fear exposure of his part in the Cuban intrigues. The information marshaled here shows starkly why it was that in 1971, in the wake of the Anderson articles and the Maheu scare, he renewed his demands for the CIA's files on the Bay of Pigs. He hoped, to be sure, that they contained embarrassments for the Kennedys. At the same time, he knew the agency's records probably contained material compromising to himself. Nixon needed to see them, as he explained to [his aide John] Ehrlichman, in order to know what to "duck," to "protect" himself.[724]

In January 1974 Senator Sam Ervin, Chairman of the Senate Watergate Committee, rejected the request of the staffers Lenzner and Lackritz to issue subpoenas to their witnesses.[725] But six months later, on the "smoking gun" tape which led promptly to his resignation, Nixon was heard by the committee to say to his chief of staff Bob Haldeman, "Look, the problem is that this [Watergate break-in] will open the whole Bay of Pigs thing."[726] Summers notes that Haldeman later wrote in his memoir that "It seems that in all those Nixon references to the Bay of Pigs, he was actually referring to the Kennedy assassination."[727]

And it was in response to Nixon's order to Haldeman that Haldeman contacted CIA Deputy Director Vernon Walters; and that Acting FBI Director Gray, after a visit from Walters, ordered that the FBI in Mexico temporarily not interview Mexico CIA Station officer George Munro, a friend of Howard Hunt's, about Watergate.[728] As noted in Chapter 2, Munro (with the CIA pseudonym JKBenadum) was the CIA liaison with the DFS phone surveillance program that allegedly hear a "Lee Oswald" speak about his meeting with Kostikov.

Let me close this section with a letter from Pawley to Richard Nixon, dated April 15, 1963, three days before Pawley contacted Shackley about Operation TILT:

> Focusing again on Cuba, Pawley recounted the disastrous decisions that both the Eisenhower and the Kennedy administrations had made. There was only one way out of the mess, according to Pawley: "All of the Cubans and most of the Americans in this part of the country believe that to remove Castro you must first remove Kennedy, and that is not going to be easy."[729]

These were suggestive words to communicate to the man who, along with Allen Dulles, had back in 1960–61 supported Pawley's efforts for a more decisive anti-Castro policy than that adopted by Eisenhower and Kennedy.[730]

Why Did Clare Boothe Luce Not Release Her Oswald Story Until 1975?

Pawley and Luce were enthusiastic supporters of Nixon in his 1968 campaign to be elected president, and Pawley joined the "Ambassadors for Nixon Committee."[731] But their support predictably waned with Nixon's moves in 1971–72 to redefine America's relationship to China and the Soviet Union. Pawley wrote in his unpublished memoir, "Russia is Winning," that "The whole pattern is now colored with a thin, pasty coating called 'detente,' a Communist tactic to prepare the trusting democracies for the kill . . . It can end only in surrender."[732]

After Nixon's resignation in 1974, Pawley was even more uncomfortable with the foreign policy of his successor Gerald Ford. In 1975 the John Birch Society publication *American Opinion* quoted Pawley as stating that Kissinger, whom Ford had retained as Secretary of State, "scares me to death."[733] Pawley was particularly incensed to learn that Ford and Kissinger might lend support to a move in the Organization of American States (OAS) to lift economic and diplomatic sanctions against Cuba.[734]

It was inevitable that Pawley's political preference in 1976 would be for his friend, and Ford's opponent in the primaries, Ronald Reagan, whom Pawley had urged Nixon to consider as his vice-presidential choice in 1968.[735] Clare Boothe Luce was also a supporter of Reagan in both 1976 and 1980. Moreover she was a member of two important neocon groups that helped prepare for the 1980 "Reagan Revolution," by lobbying for an end to détente and an increase in defense spending. These were the Committee on the Present Danger (1976) and the Coalition for Peace through Strength (1978), of which Reagan also was a member.[736] In 1981 Reagan rewarded Luce for her efforts with a seat on the President's Foreign Intelligence Advisory Board (PFIAB).

More importantly, in 1964 both Pawley and Mrs. Luce had been important figures in the campaign to elect their friend Barry Goldwater as president. Clare Boothe Luce seconded the nomination of Goldwater at the Republican Convention, and thereafter co-chaired a Citizens group (with General James Doolittle) to elect him. Pawley meanwhile had served as chairman of Florida Citizens for Goldwater-Miller.[737] After Goldwater's ignominious defeat in 1964, Mrs. Luce continued to be close to him, dining with him at least twice (in 1965 and again in 1967) along with their mutual friend William Buckley.

With the unprecedented resignation of Nixon in 1974, American politics were left in disarray, with both left and right struggling (and expecting) to prevail in the post-Nixon era. Major topics, usually too sensitive for public discussion, were briefly debated in both Congress and the media, including the size of the post-Vietnam defense budget, the future of the CIA, and even the CIA's possible past involvement in assassinations. At the time there was an unprecedented outpouring of books attacking the CIA from both the left and the right.[738]

In this post-Watergate turmoil Democrats and Republicans in the Senate agreed to the formation of the Church Committee to investigate the CIA and FBI. On this Committee the Republicans were represented by Senator John Tower as Co-Chair, and also Senator Goldwater.

Inside the Church Committee the contest between the advocates or a more open America versus the advocates of a more authoritarian one became crystallized about the question of who had been responsible for past assassinations: the Kennedys or others in the government. In his massive defense of the "Phase-Three" story, Gus Russo sums up the positions of Republican Senators Schweiker and Goldwater:

> Senator Richard Schweiker headed the Church Committee's investigation into the Kennedy assassination's possible connection to intelligence activities. He has said, "My impression is that the presidents not only knew but ordered these policies by and large . . . Past presidents have used the CIA as their secret police at home and their secret army abroad."
>
> Perhaps the most forthright Committee member was Senator Barry Goldwater of Arizona. At the time of the

hearings, Goldwater remarked that there was friction on the Committee between "those who want to protect the Kennedys and those who want to tell the truth." Years later, he stated it more succinctly, saying, "We spent nine of the ten months trying to get Kennedy's name out of it." When asked by the press who was behind the attempts on Castro's life, Goldwater motioned towards the White House and said, "Everything points right down there."[739]

Goldwater's description of the Democrats' behavior in the 94th Congress is corroborated by the Democrats' subsequent behavior in the 95th. A new House Select Committee on Assassinations (HSCA), first set up in 1976, was severely reorganized by Democrats in 1977 and put in the hands of Robert Blakey, who had been a former close ally of Robert Kennedy in the Justice Department. Although the HSCA achieved much of value, it also studiously avoided the Bayo-Pawley story. The HSCA Report did not mention it, nor did it point out that the HSCA Report's author, HSCA editorial director Richard Billings, had himself been a participant in the Bayo-Pawley mission.

But the CIA appears to have been as industrious in protecting its secrets as the Kennedy loyalists. The CIA gave an undercover assignment to one of its officers, psychological warfare expert George Joannides, and assigned him to work as its liaison officer with the HSCA. The Committee never learned that Joannides had also been the case officer for the Cuban exile group DRE, whose publicity director Carlos Bringuier had been repeatedly in contact with Lee Harvey Oswald.[740]

In the course of their debates, the Church Committee established a subcommittee "to review the role of federal agencies in investigating the Kennedy assassination."[741] Goldwater's viewpoint was represented on the subcommittee by Senator Richard Schweiker, a Republican from Pennsylvania. According to Church Committee investigator Gaeton Fonzi, the subcommittee was established on September 8, 1975.

Clare Boothe Luce's Discussion of the Tapes with William Colby

The appointment of the Schweiker Subcommittee had one interesting consequence: Clare Boothe Luce's decision to go public with
her "Phase-Three" story that Oswald had been "turned" by Castro.
In Fonzi's words.

> Right after Schweiker announced the formation of his Ken-
> nedy assassination Subcommittee, he was visited by Vera
> Glaser, a syndicated Washington columnist. Glaser told him
> she had just interviewed Clare Boothe Luce and that Luce had
> given her some information relating to the assassination. Sch-
> weiker immediately called Luce and she, quite cooperatively
> and in detail, confirmed the story she had told Glaser.[742]

It is not clear whether she told Schweiker about the tapes. We do
know that on October 25 she told CIA Director William Colby
about the tapes in a phone call, saying, "I have a big problem, a
case in conscience." (Of course, since obstruction of justice is a
crime, she might also have worried she had a legal problem.)

Luce told Colby she had discussed the matter with a mysterious Justin McCarthy, a fellow-Catholic who, with Pawley, had persuaded her to finance raids on Cuba by the DRE. McCarthy when
first approached by Luce refused categorically to share anything
with Schweiker, even in a closed session.

> Mrs. Luce: . . . He said, "All these fellows on the Hill give a
> damn about is a big headline and political attention, and if
> this should involve my testifying and some of my fellows
> got bumped off, or their apparat shut down, I could not live
> with myself, so I will not testify."

McCarthy went on to describe to Luce how he and the DRE (in
Luce's words to Colby)

> "did one operation with CIA, as a result of which all the
> Cubans involved were caught and killed, and I do not want

any part with the CIA." I said, "You have me really over a barrel." I said, "Justin, I have to tell to tell someone, is there anyone you trust?" He said . . . Bill Colby . . . "He is a daily communicant" —

Mr. Colby: No, no.

Mrs. Luce: I did not disillusion him. In any event, if only to put my own mind at rest since . . . yes, they did turn over the tapes to the FBI but they kept copies. . . . I do not know what to say if he [Senator Schweiker] calls again . . . I leave it with you."[743]

Six days later, Colby spoke to Luce in a second phone call:

Mr. Colby: I called Justin McCarthy. We had a long chat. he does not want me to do anything about, but I said you put me in an awful position. . . . I think both of us are (hung?) with a rather tantalizing story. . . . The only real thing is the thing about the tapes and the photos and the allegations about the FBI. I tried to (argue?) him into figuring out some way in getting rid of those but keeping himself out of the act.

Mrs. Luce: He called me back and said he talked with you and that you left him in a box, and I think he feels now that there is some kind of a question of conscience involved. He said, "I am going to let you and Bill Colby decide what is best to do." . . . Why don't we suggest that he bring you or me . . . the tapes and photos if he has copies of them.

Mr. Colby: And then you pass them over to Schweiker.

Mrs. Luce: And let them decide. . . .

Mr. Colby: I think that is a good idea. You say that you and I have talked, and we are all in a kind of box at this point, and we really in conscience cannot sit on all this stuff—all these charges that there is remaining evidenced that (can't read next word) was held back and disappeared . . ."[744]

The end of Colby's last sentence is unknown; only the first page of the second phone call transcript has survived. We have no evidence, however, that the tapes ever reached Senator Schweiker.

We do know that by the end of the day of the second phone call, October 31, 1975, Colby had been dismissed as CIA Director by Ford's White House Chief of Staff Donald Rumsfeld and his assistant Dick Cheney. This was part of the notorious "Halloween Massacre" that also ended Henry Kissinger's career as National Security Adviser.[745]

The Impact of the Church and Schweiker Investigations

It makes strong political sense that Luce would be less reluctant to see the explosive tapes story aired in 1975. Nixon was no longer there to be protected; the president who might be injured by it now was Gerald Ford; and Ford, besides having been a member and spokesman for the Warren Report,[746] was the leader of the anti-Reagan forces in the Republican Party, and perhaps above all the protector of Henry Kissinger with his hated policy of detente.

But if Luce's decision to release her story at this time was partly political, she may have badly underestimated its political explosiveness. This was clearly shown in the case of the Jack Anderson version of the "Phase-Three" story. Eventually the Church Committee would document how both the Secret Service and the FBI found Jack Anderson's story too hot to handle (5 AH 80-82). The reaction of the CIA was different: after LBJ asked DCI Richard Helms about it (having been alerted by Earl Warren, who had heard about it from Drew Pearson before the March 1967 story), the CIA produced an Inspector-General's Report of over 100 pages, which even then (at least in the version released) dealt only obliquely and evasively with Anderson's story.[747]

Buried near the end of the CIA I-G Report was a section headed with the ominous question, "Should we try to silence those who are talking or who might later talk?"[748] The Report's response to the question was low-keyed and quite benign, ending two pages later with the sentence, "There might be some value to be gained from endorsing [Robert Maheu's] suggestion that he approach [Edward P.] Morgan and perhaps Roselli and urge discretion."

But in 1975, after Nixon's two CIA directors (James Schlesinger and William Colby) had demanded an accounting of the CIA's past illegalities, the CIA was in a far more desperate plight than it had been back in 1967. We have to ask whether it is only coincidental that the years 1975–78 saw so many violent deaths among those involved in the CIA-mafia plots, and more specifically with the Bayo-Pawley plot.

On June 19, 1975, "a week before his scheduled appearance before the Church Committee to be questioned about the CIA-Mafia plots . . . Sam Giancana [was] shot in the back of the head with a .22-caliber pistol."[749] John Martino also died in May 1975, allegedly after telling his wife, a business partner, and a journalist friend that he had been peripherally involved in the plot to kill Kennedy.[750] After John Roselli had testified to the Church Committee, his mutilated body, on August 7, 1976, was discovered in Biscayne Bay, floating in an oil drum. Committee investigator Gaeton Fonzi records the deaths of three other witnesses he had planned to question: Oswald's friend George de Mohrenschildt by alleged suicide, former Cuban president Carlos Prio by suicide, and Cuban exile leader Manuel Artime, weeks after his diagnosis with cancer.[751]

Extensive as it is, Fonzi's list of witness deaths is not complete. William Harvey, a CIA officer who was also a friend of Roselli and one of the three sources Anderson named for his "backfire" story, testified to the Church Committee in 1975; on June 8, 1976, he died suddenly, at age 60, from a heart attack.[752] William C. Sullivan, head of the FBI's Intelligence Division that so strangely handled (or mishandled) Oswald's FBI files in the weeks before the assassination, was shot in November 1977 with a high-powered rifle, by a hunter who claimed to have mistaken him for a deer. As noted earlier, journalist Robert Novak, a friend of Sullivan, later wrote, "Bill told me I would probably read about his death in some kind of accident but not to believe it. It would be murder."[753]

Then on May 8, 1978, David Morales, the CIA Operations officer who is said to have selected his close friend Mickey Kappes for Operation TILT, died, after having reportedly told friends, "I was in Dallas when I, when we got that mother fucker, and I was in Los Angeles when we got the little bastard."[754]

But there is one death in particular that could suggest that Clare Boothe Luce may have underestimated the political explosiveness of "Phase-Three" stories. It can be seen also as an ironic comment on the fluidity of the dark forces underlying American politics, and the danger of dabbling with them. I shall close with a quote from Gaeton Fonzi's description of how in early 1977 he began to continue his investigations on behalf of the recently created House Select Committee on Assassinations:

> On my official first day, I sent to Washington a list of witnesses I planned to interview . . . William Pawley was near the top of that list. Exactly one week later [on January 7, 1977], William Pawley, in bed in his mansion on Miami Beach with a nervous ailment [shingles], put a gun to his chest and committed suicide.[755]

Although I have never heard of any other person committing suicide because of shingles, Pawley's death by itself proves nothing at all. However I believe that this story of a "Phase-Three" story that was indeed a political H-bomb, makes at least two things clear. The first is that President Kennedy was not assassinated by a marginal neglected loner who was quickly killed, but by some deep enduring force in our society, with the power to affect bureaucratic behavior.

And despite their lip service to the findings of the Warren Report, a lot of public figures knew this, and felt very threatened. Pawley in particular attracts our attention, because of his ability to draw on the resources of other governments he had done business with, not just the United States.

7

The JFK Assassination and Later Deep Events: Watergate, Iran-Contra, and 9/11

Since writing these chapters, I have come more and more to analyze recent American history in the light of what I call structural deep events: events, like the JFK assassination, the Watergate break-in, Iran-Contra, or 9/11, which repeatedly involve law-breaking or violence, are mysterious to begin with, are embedded in ongoing covert processes, have political consequences that enlarge covert government, and are subsequently covered up by systematic falsifications in the mainstream media and internal government records.[756]

The more I study these deep events, the more I see suggestive similarities between them, increasing the possibility that they are not unrelated external intrusions on American history, but parts of an endemic process, sharing to some degree or other elements from a common source.[757]

For example, one factor linking Dallas, Watergate, Iran-Contra, and 9/11, has been the involvement in all four deep events of personnel involved in America's highest-level emergency planning, known since the 1950s as Continuity of Government (COG) planning, or more colloquially inside the Pentagon as "the Doomsday Project."[758] A few of these actors may have been located at the top, as overseers of the secret COG system. Others—including some I shall discuss in this chapter—were located further down in its secret communications network.

I see this planning group as one among many in what I have chosen to call the American deep state, along with agencies like the CIA and NSA, the private groups like Booz Allen Hamilton to which more than half of the US intelligence budget is outsourced,[759] and finally the powerful banks and corporations whose views are well represented in the CIA and NSA. But if only one group among many, those in the COG planning group are also special, because of their control of and access to a communications channel, not under government control, that can reach deeply into the US social structure, manipulate it, and permanently affect it. I discuss all these matters at some length in *The American Deep State*.

COG planning was originally authorized by Truman and Eisenhower as planning for a response to a crippling atomic attack that had decapitated government. In consequence its planning group contemplated extreme measures, including what *Miami Herald* reporter Alfonso Chardy in 1987 called "suspension of the Constitution."[760] And yet in Iran-Contra its asset of a secret communications network, developed for the catastrophe of decapitation, was used instead to evade an official embargo on arms sales to Iran that dated back to 1979.[761] I wish to propose here that the network may have been similarly misused in November 1963, to piggy-back another operation on it.

The Iran-Contra misuse has been well-documented. Oliver North supervised the sale of arms to Iran by using his resources as the National Security Council action officer for COG planning, under cover of a "National Program Office" that was overseen by then Vice-President George H. W. Bush.[762] North and his superiors could thus use the COG emergency network, known then as Flashboard, for the arms sales to Iran that had to be concealed from other parts of the Washington bureaucracy as well as the public. So when North had to send emergency instructions for arms delivery to the US Embassy in Lisbon, instructions that directly contravened the embargo prohibiting such sales, he used the Flashboard network to avoid alerting the Ambassador and other unwitting personnel.[763]

The documented example of Iran-Contra allows me to explain what I am saying about the users of the COG network, and also what I am not saying. Let begin by emphasizing what I wrote in Chapter 1: I am *not* saying that a single "Secret Team" has for decades been using the COG network to manipulate the US Government from outside it. There is no evidence to suggest that North's actions in Iran-Contra were known to any of his superiors other than CIA chief William Casey and probably George Bush.

The point is that a very small group had access to a high-level secret network outside government review, in order to implement a program in opposition to government policy. They succumbed to the temptation to use this secure network that had been designed for other purposes. I have argued elsewhere that this secure network was used again on 9/11, to implement key orders for which the 9/11 Commission could find no records.[764] Whether it was also used on that day for illicit purposes is not known.

It is certain that the COG emergency network program survived North's demise, and continued to be secretly developed for decades, at a cost of billions, and overseen by a team including Dick Cheney and Donald Rumsfeld. It is relevant that the two men's presence on the committee spanned three administrations— those of Reagan, Bush I, and Clinton—even though at one point under Clinton neither man (while planning for suspension of the constitution) held a position inside the U.S. government. And on 9/11 COG plans were officially implemented for the first time, by Vice-President Cheney and Defense Secretary Rumsfeld, the two men who had planned them for so many years.[765]

Whether or not they knew about Iran-Contra, Cheney and Rumsfeld were on the COG planning committee with North at the time North used the COG network to implement arms sales to Iran. There is no such obvious link between COG planning and Watergate, but the involvement of COG personnel in Watergate is nonetheless striking. For example, John Dean, perhaps the central Watergate figure, had overseen secret COG activities when serving as the associate deputy attorney general.[766]

James McCord, one of the Watergate burglars, was a member of a small Air Force Reserve unit in Washington attached to the Office of Emergency Preparedness (OEP), that was assigned "to draw up lists of radicals and to develop contingency plans for censorship of the news media and U.S. mail in time of war."[767] His unit was part of the Wartime Information Security Program (WISP), which had responsibility for activating "contingency plans for imposing censorship on the press, the mails and all tele-communications (including government communications) [and] preventive detention of civilian 'security risks,' who would be placed in military 'camps.'"[768] Warrantless detention was one of the three key features of COG planning, along with warrantless sur-veillance and militarization of homeland security. All three were implemented on 9/11.

McCord had not just a covert appointment but a pronounced right-wing politics, wherein he was not a loner. In a post-Watergate fire at his home, where much evidence was burned, he was assisted by his close associate Lee R. Pennington, Jr. Pennington in turn

> was director of the Washington office of the ultraconserva-tive American Security Council (ASC). He was also, and had been for more than fifteen years, a contract agent of the CIA's Security Research Staff.[769]

In the case of the JFK assassination, I wish to focus on two men in Dallas who functioned as part of the communications network of the Office of Emergency Planning (OEP), the agency renamed in 1968 as the Office of Emergency Preparedness (to which McCord was attached), and renamed again in 1982 as the National Program Office (NPO, for which Oliver North was the action officer).[770]

These two men in Dallas were Winston Lawson, the Secret Service advance man who from the lead car of the motorcade was in charge of the Secret Service radio channels operating in the motorcade; and John (Jack) Crichton, the army intelligence reserve colonel who with Deputy Dallas Police Chief George Lumpkin contributed to a "Phase-One" story, when they selected the Russian interpreter for Marina Oswald's first DPD interview.[771]

Lawson has drawn the critical attention of JFK research-ers, both for dubious actions he took before and during the assassination, and also for false statements he made after it. For example, Lawson reported in writing after the assassination that motorcycles were deployed on "the right and left flanks of the President's car" (17 WH 605). On the morning of November 22, however, the orders had been changed (3 WH 244), so that the motorcycles rode instead, as Lawson himself testified to the Warren Commission, "just *back* of the President's car" (4 WH 338; cf. 21 WH 768-70). Captain Lawrence of the Dallas Police testified that that the proposed side escorts were redeployed to the rear on Lawson's own instructions (7 WH 580-81; cf. 18 WH 809, 21 WH 571). This would appear to have left the President more vulnerable to a possible crossfire.[772]

Early on November 22, at Love Field, Lawson installed, in what would become the lead car, the base radio whose frequencies were used by all Secret Service agents on the motorcade. This radio channel, operated by the White House Communications Agency (WHCA), was used for some key decisions in Dealey Plaza before and after the assassination, yet its records, unlike those of the Dallas Police Department (DPD) Channels One and Two, were never made available to the Warren Commission, or any subsequent investigation. The tape was not withheld because it was irrelevant; on the contrary, it contained very significant information.

The WHCA actually reports to this day on its website that the agency was "a key player in documenting the assassination of President Kennedy."[773] However it is not clear for whom this documentation was conducted, or why it was not made available to the Warren Commission, the House Select Committee on Assassinations, or the Assassination Records Review Board (ARRB).[774] It should have been.

For one thing, the WHCA tape, as some have alleged, may contain the "key" to the unresolved mystery of who, after the shooting, redirected the motorcade to Parkland Hospital. The significance of this apparently straightforward command, about which there was much conflicting testimony, is heightened when we read repeated orders on the Dallas Police radio transcript to "cut all traffic for the ambulance going to Parkland code 3" (17 WH 395). For the ambulance in question having nothing to do with the president (whose shooting had not yet been announced on the DPD radio). In fact the ambulance had been dispatched about ten minutes before the assassination to pick someone from in front of the Texas School Book Depository (TSBD), who was wrongly suspected of having suffered an epileptic seizure.[775]

Lawson later reported to the Secret Service that he heard on his radio "that we should proceed to the nearest hospital." He wrote also that he "requested Chief Curry "to have the hospital contacted," and then that "Our Lead Car assisted the motorcycles in escorting the President's vehicle to Parkland Hospital" (17 WH 632), cf. 21 WH 580).[776] In other words, after hearing something on the WHCA radio, Lawson helped ensure that the President's limousine would follow the route already set up by the motorcycles for the epileptic. (In his very detailed Warren Commission testimony, Lawson said nothing about the route having already been cleared. On the contrary he testified that "we had to do some stopping of cars and holding our hands out the windows and blowing the sirens and horns to get through" (4 WH 354).

The WHCA radio channel used by Lawson and others communicated almost directly to the WHCA base at Mount Weather in Virginia, the base facility of the COG network. From there, Secret Service communications were relayed to the White House, via the

> batteries of communications equipment connecting Mount Weather with the White House and "Raven Rock"—the underground Pentagon sixty miles north of Washington— as well as with almost every US military unit stationed around the globe.[777]

Jack Crichton, head of the 488th Army Intelligence Reserve unit of Dallas, was also part of this Mount Weather COG network. This was in his capacity as chief of intelligence for Dallas Civil Defense, which worked out of an underground Emergency Operating Center. As Russ Baker reports, "Because it was intended for 'continuity of government' operations during an attack, [the Center] was fully equipped with communications equipment."[778]

In retrospect the Civil Defense Program is remembered derisively, for having advised schoolchildren, in the event of an atomic attack, to hide their heads under their desks.[779] But in

1963 civil defense was one of the urgent responsibilities assigned to the Office of Emergency Planning, which is why Crichton, as much as Secret Service agent Lawson, could be in direct touch with the OEP's emergency communications network at Mount Weather.

Jack Crichton is of interest because he and DPD Deputy Chief George Lumpkin of the 488th Army Intelligence Reserve unit (two friends, as we saw earlier, of Col. Brandstetter as well as of each other), were responsible for choosing a Russian interpreter for Marina Oswald from the right-wing Russian community.[780] This man was Ilya Mamantov, who translated for Marina Oswald at her first DPD interview on November 22. What she allegedly said in Russian at this interview (as mistranslated by Mamantov) was later used to bolster what I have called the "Phase-One" story, still promoted from some CIA sources, that Russia and/or Cuba were behind the assassination.

As summarized by the FBI, Mamantov's account of Marina's Russian testimony linked it to a gun owned by Oswald in the Soviet Union:

> MARINA OSWALD advised that LEE HARVEY OSWALD owned a rifle *which he used in Russia about two years ago.* She observed what she presumed to be the same rifle in a blanket in the garage at [Ruth Paine's residence] . . . MARINA OSWALD stated that on November 22, she had been shown a rifle in the Dallas Police Department. . . . She stated that it was a dark color like the one that she had seen, but she did not recall the sight.[781]

Mamantov's "Phase-One" assassination clue was later discarded, even though it had supporting evidence at the time, also discarded. At the time the story was supported; in particular there was another discarded "Phase-One" story, an army cable from an officer in the Dallas Police Department intelligence section, who like Crichton and Lumpkin was also in Army Intelligence:[782]

Following is further information on *Oswald, Harvey Lee* [sic] . . . Assistant Chief Don Stringfellow, Intelligence Section, Dallas Police Department, notified 112th INTC [Army Intelligence] Group, this Headquarters, that information obtained from Oswald revealed he had defected to Cuba in 1959 and is a card-carrying member of Communist Party."[783]

This cable was sent on November 22 from the Fourth Army Command in Texas to the U.S. Strike Command at Fort MacDill in Florida, the base poised for a possible retaliatory attack against Cuba.[784]

Today the cable utterly lacks credibility, but at the time there was supporting evidence for each of Stringfellow's two points. Stringfellow may have heard Oswald was a Communist from his boss in the Intelligence Section, Jack Revill, who reported on November 22 in a memo to his boss, Special Services Bureau chief W.P. Gannaway, that Oswald "was a member of the Communist Party."[785] We now know that a probably false "Oswald" did present a "Communist Party card" (presumably also false) at the Cuban Consulate in Mexico City.[786] (Stringfellow, Revill, and Gannaway were all reportedly in Army Intelligence, i.e. Reserve.)[787]

And the false story that Oswald had visited Cuba would seem to be vaguely corroborated by what Hoover told Robert Kennedy on the afternoon of November 22:

I related that Oswald went to Russia and stayed three years, came back to the United States in June 1962, and went to Cuba on several occasions but would not tell us what he went to Cuba for.[788]

Hoover's statement is one more indication that (as we saw in Chapter 4) there may have been an earlier file in circulation, perhaps on a "Harvey Lee Oswald," to which he and possibly Stringfellow may have had access.

The discarded "Phase-One" story from Stringfellow in Dallas is of interest, and should persuade us to look at the discarded corroborations for the discarded Mamantov "Phase-One" story. His specific details—that Marina said she had seen a rifle that was dark and scopeless—were confirmed in an affidavit (signed by Marina and Mamantov, 24 WH 219) that was taken by DPD officer B.L. Senkel (24 WH 249). They were confirmed again by Ruth Paine, who witnessed the Mamantov interview, (3 WH 82). They were confirmed again the next night in an interview of Marina by Secret Service Agent Mike Howard, translated by Mamantov's close friend Peter Gregory.

(Both Gregory and Mamantov worked in the oil industry; Mamantov in particular worked for Sun Oil [9 WH 103, 105], and was personally close to John G. ["Jack"] Pew Jr., who oversaw the Sun Oil and Pew family interests in the Spindletop oil field of Texas. Jack Pew in turn was a spiritual heir of his relative, Sun Oil president J. Howard Pew, "a leading supporter of Rightist causes in the United States, [who] at one time served on the Editorial Advisory Committee of the [John Birch Society's] American Opinion magazine.")[789]

A Secret Service transcript of the Mike Howard interview reveals that the source of these details about a dark and scopeless rifle was not Marina, but her supposed translator, Gregory:

(Q) This gun, was it a rifle or a pistol or just what kind of a gun? Can she answer that?

(A) It was a gun

Mr. Gregory asked: Can you describe it?

NOTE: Subject said: I cannot describe it because a rifle to me like all rifles.

Gregory translation: She said she cannot describe it. It was sort of a *dark* rifle just like any other common rifle . . .

Subject in Russian: It was a hump (or elevation) but I never saw through the scope. . . .

Gregory translation: She says there was an elevation on the
rifle *but there was no scope*—no telescope.[790]

We have to conclude not just that Gregory had falsified Marina's
testimony ("a rifle to me like all rifles"); but had done so concert-
edly with his friend Mamantov, who later testified no less than
seven times to the Warren Commission that Marina had used the
word "dark" to describe the gun.

There were others in Dallas who claimed that Oswald's gun
indeed had been scopeless, until Oswald had a scope installed on
it by Dallas gunsmith Dial Ryder. The Warren Report elaborately
refuted this corroborated claim, and concluded that "the authen-
ticity of the [gun] repair tag" used to support it was "subject to
grave doubts" (WR 317).

We can see here, what the Warren Commission did not wish
to see, signs of a conspiracy to misrepresent Marina's testimony,
linking Oswald's gun to a dark and scopeless rifle he had in the
Soviet Union.

Our concerns that Mamantov misrepresented her lead us to
concerns about why two Army Intelligence Reserve officers from
the 488th unit (Jack Crichton and Deputy DPD Chief George
Lumpkin) selected Mamantov as her interpreter. Our concerns
are increased when we see that B.L. Senkel, the DPD officer who
took Marina's suspect affidavit, was the partner of F.P. Turner, who
collected the dubious rifle repair tag (24 WH 328), and that both
men spent most of November 22 with DPD Deputy Chief Lumpkin. For example, they were with Lumpkin in the pilot car of the
motorcade when Lumpkin was communicating (via the WHCA
network) with Winston Lawson in the lead car behind them.

I conclude that when we look at the conduct of the three men
we know to have been parts of the COG emergency communications network in Dallas, we see patterns of sinister behavior
that also involved others, i.e. conspiratorial behavior. These con-
catenated efforts to implicate Oswald in a "Phase-One" conspiracy narrative lead me to propose another hypothesis for which
I have neither evidence nor an alternative explanation: namely,
that someone on the WHCA network may have been the source

for the important unexplained description on the Dallas Police tapes of a suspect who had exactly the false height and weight (5 feet 10 inches, 165 pounds) recorded for Oswald in his FBI and CIA files.

Note that there are no other known sources ascribing this specific height and weight to Oswald. For example, when he was arrested and charged in Dallas that same day, Oswald was recorded as having a height of 5'9 ½ inches, and a height of 131 pounds.[791] The first reference to Oswald as 5'10", 165 pounds, was that offered by Oswald's mother Marguerite to FBI Agent Fain in May 1960, when Oswald himself was absent in Russia.[792]

The DPD officer contributing the description on the Police Channel was Inspector Herbert Sawyer, who allegedly had heard it from someone outside the Texas School Book Depository (TSBD) whom he could not identify or describe.[793] The Warren Report said categorically that his source was Howard Brennan (WR 5), and that on the evening of November 22, Brennan "identified Oswald as the person in the lineup who bore the closest resemblance to the man in the window but he said that he was unable to make a positive identification" (WR 145). But there are many reasons to doubt Brennan was the source, starting with conflicts in Brennan's own testimony.[794]

There is another strong reason to doubt that the source was Brennan. Brennan testified later to the Warren Commission that he saw his suspect in a window of the Texas School Book Depository, "standing up and leaning against the left window sill." Pressed to describe how much of the suspect he saw, Brennan answered, "I could see probably his whole body, from his hips up. But at the time that he was firing the gun, a possibility from his belt up" (3 WH 144).

The awkwardness of Brennan's language draws attention to the fundamental problem about the description. It is hard to imagine anyone giving a full height and weight estimate from seeing someone who was only partially visible in a window. So there are intrinsic grounds for believing the description must have come from another source. And when we see that the same description is found in Oswald's FBI and CIA files —and nowhere else that we know of—there are reasons to suspect the source was from government secret files.

We have seen that there was interaction in Dallas between the WHCA and DPD radio channels, thanks to the WHCA portable radio that Lawson had installed in the lead car of the presidential motorcade.[795] This radio in turn was in contact by police radio with the pilot car ahead of it, carrying Dallas Police Department (DPD) Deputy Chief Lumpkin of the 488th Army Intelligence Reserve unit.[796] At the same time, as noted above, it was in contact with the COG nerve center at Mount Weather, Virginia. And Mount Weather had the requisite secret communications to receive information from classified intelligence files, without other parts of the government being alerted.

Permit me at this moment an instructive digression. It is by now well established that Kennedy in 1963 was concerned enough by "the threat of far-right treason" that he urgently persuaded Hollywood director John Frankenheimer "to turn [the novel] *Seven Days in May* into a movie."[797] In this book, to quote Wikipedia, a

charismatic superior officer, Air Force General James Mattoon Scott, intend[s] to stage a coup d'état. . . . According to the plan, an undisclosed Army combat unit known as ECOMCON (Emergency COMmunications CONtrol) will seize control of the country's telephone, radio, and television networks, while the conspiracy directs the military and its allies in Congress and the media from "Mount Thunder" (a continuity of government base based on Mount Weather).[798]

We have seen that in 1963 Kennedy had aroused major right-wing dissatisfaction, largely because of signs of his increasing rapprochement with the Soviet Union. The plot of *Seven Days in May* reflects the concern of liberals at the time about generals like General Edwin Walker, who had resigned in 1961 after Kennedy criticized his political activities in the Army. (As we have seen, Walker had given his troops John Birch Society literature, along with the names of right-wing candidates to vote for.)[799] We can assume however that Kennedy had no firm evidence of a Mount Weather conspiracy: if he had, it is unlikely his response would have just been to encourage a fictionalized movie.

It is important at this stage to point out that, although COG elements like Mount Weather were considered part of the Pentagon, the COG "government in waiting" was at no time under simple military control. On the contrary, President Eisenhower had ensured that it was broadly based at the top outside government, so its planners included some of the nation's top corporate leaders, like Frank Stanton of CBS.[800] By all accounts of COG leadership in the decades after Reagan took office in 1981, this so-called "shadow government" still included CEOs of private corporations, like Donald Rumsfeld and Dick Cheney, as well as three former CIA directors, Richard Helms, James Schlesinger, and George Bush.[801]

Alfonso Chardy wrote in 1987 that the "virtual parallel government" empowering North to run Iran-Contra had also developed "a secret contingency plan that called for suspension of the Constitution, turning control of the United States over to FEMA."[802] Subsequently North was questioned in the Iran-Contra Hearings about this charge, but was prevented by the Committee Chairman, Democratic Senator Inouye, from answering in a public session.[803]

Later, investigating the powerful COG planning group, CNN called it "a hidden government [in the USA] about which you know nothing."[804] James Mann emphasized its hawkish continuity, unaffected by changes of presidency in the White House:

> Cheney and Rumsfeld were, in a sense, a part of the permanent, though hidden, national security apparatus of the United States, inhabitants of a world in which Presidents come and go, but America always keeps on fighting."[805]

Going one step further, Andrew Cockburn quoted a Pentagon source to support a claim that a COG planning group under Clinton was now for the first time staffed "almost exclusively with Republican hawks." In the words of his source, "You could say this was a secret government-in-waiting. The Clinton administration was extraordinarily inattentive, [they had] no idea what was going on."[806]

The Pentagon official's description of COG planners under Clinton as a "secret government-in-waiting" (which still included both Cheney and Rumsfeld) is very close to the standard definition of a cabal, as a group of persons secretly united to bring about a change or overthrow of government. A very similar situation existed under Jimmy Carter, when some of those who would later figure in Iran-Contra (notably George H.W. Bush and Theodore Shackley) worked with chiefs of foreign intelligence services (the so-called Safari Club) "to start working with [former DCI Richard] Helms [then U.S. Ambassador to Iran] and his most trusted operatives outside of Congressional and even Agency purview."[807] This group began by backing guerrilla forces in Africa (notably UNITA of Jonas Savimbi in Angola), which they knew would not be backed by the CIA under William Colby or Stansfield Turner.[808]

But some in the Safari Club, notably Alexandre de Marenches of the French spy agency SDECE, became involved with Casey, Bush, Shackley, and others in a 1980 plot—the so-called Republican "October Surprise"—to prevent the reelection of Jimmy Carter. The essence of this plot was to frustrate Carter's efforts to repatriate the hostages seized in the U.S. Tehran Embassy, by negotiating a Republican deal with the Iranians to delay the hostages' return. (The hostages in fact were returned hours after Reagan took office in 1981.)[809]

This Republican hostage plot in 1980 deserves to be counted as a fifth structural deep event in recent US history, along with Dallas, Watergate, Iran-Contra, and 9/11. Unquestionably the illicit contacts with Iran established by the October Surprise Group in 1980 became, as Alfonso Chardy wrote, the "genesis" of the Iran-Contra arms deals in 1984–86.[810]

In an important interview with journalist Robert Parry, the veteran CIA officer Miles Copeland claimed that a "CIA within the CIA" inspired the 1980 plot, having concluded by 1980 that Jimmy Carter (in Copeland's words) "had to be removed from the presidency for the good of the country."[811] Copeland made it clear to Parry that he shared the view that Carter "represented a grave threat to the nation;" and former Mossad agent Ari Ben-Menashe told Parry that Copeland himself was in fact "the conceptual father" of the 1980 arms-for-hostages deal, and had "brokered [the] Republican cooperation with Israel."[812] And Copeland, together with his client Adnan Khashoggi whom he advised, went on with Shackley to help launch the 1984–85 Iranian arms deals as well.

However, just as Fletcher Knebel in *Seven Days* may have over-estimated the military component in the COG Mount Weather leadership, so Copeland may have dwelt too exclusively on the CIA component behind the October Surprise Group. In *The Road to 9/11*, I suggested that this CIA network overlapped with a so-called "Project Alpha," working at the time for David Rockefeller and the Chase Manhattan Bank on Iran issues, which was chaired by the veteran establishment figure John J. McCloy.[813]

I will conclude by again quoting James Mann's dictum that the Mount Weather COG leadership constitutes a "permanent, though hidden, national security apparatus of the United States, . . . a world in which Presidents come and go, but America always keeps on fighting."[814] And I would like readers to contemplate that elements of this enduring leadership, with its ever-changing mix of CIA veterans and civilian leaders, may have constituted "a secret government-in-waiting," not just under Clinton in the 1990s, not just under Carter in 1980, but also under Kennedy in November 1963.

8

The Fate of Presidential Challenges to the Deep State (1963–1980)

In the days after Kennedy's death, the U.S. media rushed to assure the American public that the president had been killed by a lone assassin, Lee Harvey Oswald. Two days later millions watched Oswald get shot on network television.

But governments overseas saw the assassination as the work, not of a lone nut, but of a right-wing conspiracy. Reports to this effect soon began reaching Moscow.

> A source in Mexico City reported that the leader of the Mexican senate had quoted President Lopez Mateos as saying that Kennedy had died at the hands of "extremely right-wing elements that did not like his policies, especially his policy toward Cuba."
>
> These Mexican hunches were bolstered by KGB information from its network in the French government. "The Quai d'Orsay," it was reported to the Kremlin, "has come to the conclusion that Kennedy's assassination was organized by extremely right-wing racist circles, who are dissatisfied with both the domestic and foreign policies of the slain president, especially his intention of improving relations with the Soviet Union." The French permanent representative to the UN, according to Soviet intelligence, believed

that the assassination was a "carefully organized act" by a determined group on the far right of American politics.[815]

Soon Khrushchev would receive a cautious corroboration of conspiracy from an unusual informal source, JFK's close friend William Walton. Walton flew to Moscow on November 29, with a private message from Robert and Jacqueline Kennedy. Bobby and Jackie

> wanted [Walton] to meet with Georgi Bolshakov, the man who for twenty months around the time of the Cuba missile crisis had served as the Russian end of a secret link between the White House and the Kremlin. The Kennedys wanted the Russian who they felt best understood John Kennedy to know their personal opinions of the changes in the US government since the assassination. . . .
>
> "Dallas was the ideal location for such a crime," Walton told the Soviet intelligence officer. "Perhaps there was only one assassin, but he did not act alone." Bolshakov . . . listened intently as Walton explained that the Kennedys believed there was a large political conspiracy behind Oswald's rifle. Despite Oswald's connections to the communist world, the Kennedys believed that the president was felled by domestic opponents.[816]

Bobby used Walton to assure Moscow that, although LBJ might not continue the Kennedy program of increasing détente with the USSR, Bobby himself intended to run for the presidency; and if elected would work to bring John F. Kennedy's ideas to fruition.[817]

In this book I have presented corroborating evidence that many of the events leading up to the assassination, such as the Bayo-Pawley plot, grew out of right-wing opposition to Kennedy's policy of increasing détente with Moscow. Two different visions of U.S. foreign policy clearly divided Kennedy from others, such as William Pawley, who were also powerful in America's dyadic deep state. Kennedy's vision of détente and coexistence, clearly articulated in his American University speech of June 10, 1963, was less popular inside the American bureaucracy than the competing vision of U.S. global dominance, or hegemony. This was shared by those, including Air Force General LeMay, who believed that the Cuban Missile Crisis should have been resolved by a successful U.S. invasion of Cuba.

The two visions had been at odds in Washington since the late 1940s, when the coexistence model of conducting foreign relations through the United Nations was supplemented by the rollback policies implemented, covertly at first, by the misnamed Office of Policy Coordination (OPC); and later advocated overtly by Republicans in the 1952 election. The tension between the two visions underlay the debates in the JFK White House over Cuba and Vietnam. And the tensions between them grew even greater when America eventually withdrew from Vietnam, leaving open the question whether America should cut back on its wartime defense budget, or increase it in the interests of establishing and maintaining a permanent U.S. hegemony.

For almost two decades after the JFK assassination, elements of both policies, détente and dominance, characterized U.S. foreign policy. After the Reagan Revolution of 1980 it became increasingly clear that U.S. Soviet policy had rejected détente for hegemony.

Underlying this significant shift foreign policy was a deeper if less visible shift in the relationship between public power and what I have called the deep state. In the pivotal decades of the 1960s and 1970s five presidents sought to restrain the deep state powers of the CIA and Pentagon, or what Eisenhower, in his farewell speech of 1961, called the military-industrial complex. And as we shall see, the political careers of all five presidents—Kennedy, Johnson, Nixon, Ford and Carter—were cut off in ways that were unusual. The first, Kennedy, was assassinated. Another, Nixon, was forced to resign. None of the three others was able to enjoy a second term.

When Eisenhower warned against the military-industrial complex in 1961, the values, institutions and resources that comprised it were still competing with alternative more peaceful prospects for American society. Today these values not only dominate both parties, but are also threatening both these parties from even further to the right. A good measure of this change is that liberal

Republicans are as scarce in the Republican Party today as Gold-water Republicans were scarce in that party back in 1960.

That change has been achieved partly by money, but partly also with the assistance of deep events as defined in the last chapter: events, beginning with the Kennedy assassination, but continuing with Watergate, the 1980 October Surprise, Iran-Contra, and 9/11.

In saying that these deep events have contributed collectively to a major change in American society, I am, once again, *not* attributing them all to a single agent or "secret team." Rather I see them as flowing in part from the dialectical processes of violent power itself, power associated with and deployed in the service of the global expansion of American military might, which (as history has shown many times) has the effect to transform both societies with surplus power and the individuals exercising that power.[818] Insofar as these power processes govern America without deriving from its constitution, we can say that they derive from the milieu of the American deep state.

Military and CIA Resentment of Presidential Strategies

We can trace what has happened over fifty years through the dra-matic change in presidential attitudes toward the Soviet Union. Kennedy and above all Nixon believed in détente with the Soviet Union. Starting under Ford and Carter, and climaxing with Rea-gan, elements in the United States set out to help destroy what Reagan called "the evil empire." Saudi Arabian wealth and influ-ence approved of this change and may have been a factor in achieving it.[819]

The last major achievement of the dove faction was Kennedy's peaceful resolution of the Cuban Missile crisis in 1962. But the Joint Chiefs had been eager to engage with the Soviet Union, and were furious that Kennedy denied them this chance. Air Force Chief General Curtis LeMay "called the settlement 'the great-est defeat in our history,' and urged a prompt invasion."[820] Earlier LeMay had called Kennedy's blockade tactic "almost as bad as the appeasement at Munich;" and had threatened to take his dissent public.[821]

There are abundant corroborations for this alarming standoff between the president and his Joint Chiefs. Daniel Ellsberg, who worked in the Pentagon in 1964, told David Talbot that after the Cuban Missile settlement "there was virtually a coup atmosphere in Pentagon circles . . . a mood of hatred and rage. The atmosphere was poisonous, poisonous."[822] Disagreements over how vigorously to pursue the Vietnam War later divided President Johnson from many of his generals, split his party, and finally persuaded LBJ not to run for re-election.

Many of my generation thought of LBJ in those days as a warmonger. We were not then aware of the degree of rebelliousness inside the armed services, against the limits LBJ set on that war, in order to avoid conflict with the Soviet Union. By 1967, U.S. airmen had begun making unauthorized attacks on Soviet ships in Haiphong harbor, much as in 1963 crews of Alpha-66 (a Cuban exile group connected to U.S. Army Intelligence) had attacked Soviet ships in Havana.

In June 1967 U.S. airmen, in the midst of delicate Washington-Moscow negotiations over the Six-Day War, shot up the Soviet ship *Turkestan* in Haiphong harbor and killed one of its seamen. For that episode three U.S. airmen were ultimately court-martialed. One was convicted, for "destroying U.S. government property" (the flight film in the planes' gun cameras) and "processing the film in an unauthorized manner." Even this penalty, a $600 fine, was ultimately set aside. This bizarre episode was only one of many such attacks, as I detailed in *The War Conspiracy*.[823]

These right-wing resentments survived into the era of Nixon, who also struggled to fight in Vietnam without provoking a response from the Soviet Union. The two years of the Watergate crisis saw a president forced into resignation by a number of forces, both pro- and anti-war. But the key figures in the initial Watergate break-in itself—Howard Hunt, James McCord, G. Gordon Liddy, and their Cuban allies—were all far more anti-Soviet than Nixon and Kissinger. And the end result of their machinations was not finalized until the so-called Halloween Massacre in 1975, when Kissinger was ousted as National Security Adviser and Vice President Nelson Rockefeller was notified he would be dropped from the 1976 Republican ticket. This major shake-up was engineered by two other right-wingers: Donald Rumsfeld and Dick Cheney in the Gerald Ford White House.[824]

In this period Admiral Elmo R. Zumwalt, Jr., came close to accusing Nixon and Kissinger of treason and Kissinger of being a Soviet sympathizer.[825] A book co-authored by retired admiral Chester Ward and published in 1975 charged that Kissinger was not just a Soviet sympathizer but a conscious Soviet agent.[826]

We have to consider that it was no accident that two deep events, the Kennedy assassination and Watergate, cut off the presidencies of both Kennedy and Nixon, both bitterly resented by their generals, and also the only presidents not to serve full terms in the postwar era. Less conspicuously, their successors, Ford and Carter, were also afflicted by deep divisions within their respective administrations. Following the wishes of Congress,

> Gerald Ford and Jimmy Carter carried out the largest number of revisions to presidential directives since Eisenhower, carefully rewriting each of the [COG] emergency documents, aware of changes in the Cold War (and the country) since Ike's Time, and the recent massive unlawfulness on the part of the secret services.[827]

Not coincidentally, each of them faced divisions among their supporters; and they became the first and second incumbent presidents to be defeated for reelection since Herbert Hoover in 1932.[828]

The military figures who protested against presidential restraints on their proposals were not alone in Washington: there was also CIA resistance to presidential efforts to control the agency. The most striking example is perhaps the 1980 election campaign that launched the Reagan Revolution. Robert Parry has demonstrated that this election was preceded by a number of illegal actions—climaxing in the Republican October Surprise—in which both veterans and active employees of the bureaucratic deep state—no longer the servant of the public state but its master—played a significant role. The events of the Republican October Surprise have been characterized—by myself among others—as an

escalated reprise of dirty tricks between Republicans and Democrats.[829] It is closer to the truth to see them as Robert Parry has
done, as in part a CIA revolt (in alliance with Israel) against Jimmy
Carter and his CIA Director Stansfield Turner.[830]

The antagonism between CIA operatives and the White House
did not begin with Carter. It was so acute right after the Bay of Pigs
and the firing of CIA Director Dulles that Kennedy told one of the
highest officials of his Administration that he wanted "to splinter
the C.I.A. in a thousand pieces and scatter it to the winds."[831] In
1972 Nixon fired Helms after the Watergate break-in because he
believed Helms "was out to get him;" and he gave orders to Helms's
replacement, James Schlesinger, "to turn the place inside out."[832]

Neither Kennedy nor Nixon finished their terms, let alone
their intention to bring the CIA under control. But their successive firings of Dulles and Helms left a toxic resentment inside
CIA, especially after Nixon's CIA Director James Schlesinger then
purged more that five hundred analysts and more than one thousand people in all from the clandestine service.[833] CIA veteran Ara-
bist Archibald Roosevelt, who was a significant player along with
former CIA Director Bush in the October Surprise, believed that
Nixon's appointees as CIA Director—James Schlesinger and William Colby—"had both . . . betrayed their office by pandering to
politicians."[834]

CIA resentment and concern was not just directed against
presidents. The CIA's Operations Division was also determined to
fight a number of limitations imposed on it in the mid-1970s by
the responses of a Democratic Congress to the recommendations
of the Senate Select Committee chaired by Senator Frank Church.
As a result, even before Carter's election, a number of the CIA's
allied intelligence services, in France, Egypt, Saudi Arabia, Iran,
and Morocco, had allied in the so-called Safari Club to serve as an
alternative source of funding and financing of covert operations.[835]

In this they used the resources and networks of the drug-
laundering Bank of Credit and Commerce International (BCCI).
CIA assets like Adnan Khashoggi and Bruce Rappaport, assisted
by officially retired CIA personnel like Miles Copeland and Jerry
Townsend, were part of this global BCCI network. Former Saudi

intelligence chief Prince Turki bin Faisal, a key figure in the Safari Club, once admitted candidly to a Washington audience that the Safari Club, operating at the level of the deep state, was expressly created to overcome the efforts of Carter and Congress to rein in the CIA:

> In 1976, after the Watergate matters took place here, your intelligence community was literally tied up by Congress. It could not do anything. It could not send spies, it could not write reports, and it could not pay money. In order to compensate for that, a group of countries got together in the hope of fighting Communism and established what was called the Safari Club.[836]

The plight of Jimmy Carter in 1979–80 epitomizes how weak a president can become when he loses the mandate of heaven from the American deep state. First he expressed his determination not to admit the deposed Shah of Iran into the United States, knowing very well that this might result in the seizure of the U.S. Embassy in Tehran.[837] But soon thereafter Carter was coerced by the Rockefellers and their man in the White House, Zbigniew Brzezinski, to do just that.[838] (Carter, in caving in to Rockefeller's demands, reportedly asked, "What are you guys going to recommend that we do when they take our embassy and hold our people hostage?")[839]

In the remaining months of his presidency, his popularity was battered by long waits at gas stations and convenience stores, in a gas shortage generated chiefly (as we shall see) by the major oil companies.[840] We can see Carter as a victim of the top-down power of the deep state, which would mean that Carter himself, like Kennedy and Nixon before him, was not on top.

Carter's defeat by Reagan in 1980 ended two tumultuous decades in which one president (along with his brother) was assassinated, the next chose not to run for re-election, the next was forced to resign, and the two last, despite their incumbencies, failed to be re-elected. In every case, one way or another, tensions between the presidents and the deep state helped terminate the careers of those in the White House.

The 1980 Defeat of Jimmy Carter

The Safari Club was an alliance between national intelligence agencies that wished to compensate for the CIA's retrenchment in the wake of President Carter's election and Senator Church's post-Watergate reforms.

After Carter was elected, the Safari Club allied itself with Richard Helms and Theodore Shackley against the more restrained intelligence policies of Jimmy Carter, according to Joseph Trento. In Trento's account, the dismissal by William Colby in 1974 of CIA counterintelligence chief James Angleton,

> combined with Watergate, is what prompted the Safari Club to start working with [former DCI Richard] Helms [then U.S. Ambassador to Iran] and his most trusted operatives outside of Congressional and even Agency purview. James Angleton said before his death that "Shackley and Helms . . . began working with outsiders like [Kamal] Adham and Saudi Arabia. The traditional CIA answering to the president was an empty vessel having little more than technical capability."[841]

Trento adds that "The Safari Club needed a network of banks to finance its intelligence operations. With the official blessing of George Bush as the head of the CIA, Adham transformed . . . the Bank of Credit and Commerce International (BCCI), into a worldwide money-laundering machine."[842] Trento claims also that the Safari Club then was able to work with some of the controversial CIA operators who had been forced out of the CIA by Turner, and that this was coordinated by Theodore Shackley.

> Shackley, who still had ambitions to become DCI, believed that without his many sources and operatives like [Edwin] Wilson, the Safari Club—operating with [former DCI Richard] Helms in charge in Tehran—would be ineffective. . . . Unless Shackley took direct action to complete the privatization of intelligence operations soon, the Safari Club would not have a conduit to [CIA] resources. The

solution: create a totally private intelligence network using CIA assets until President Carter could be replaced.[843]

During the 1980 election campaign each party accused the other of plotting an October Surprise to elect their candidate. Subsequently other journalists, notably Robert Parry, accused CIA veterans on the Reagan campaign, along with Shackley, of an arguably treasonable but successful plot with Iranians to delay return of the U.S. hostages until Reagan took office in January 1981.[844]

According to Parry, Alexandre de Marenches of the Safari Club arranged for William Casey (a fellow Knight of Malta) to meet with Iranian and Israeli representatives in Paris in July and October 1980, where Casey promised delivery to Iran of needed U.S. armaments in exchange for a delay in the return of the U.S. hostages in Iran.[845] Parry also suspects a role of BCCI in the subsequent flow of Israeli armaments to Iran.

De Marenches was also a member of the Pinay Circle, "an international right-wing propaganda group which brings together serving or retired intelligence officers and politicians with links to right-wing intelligence factions from most of the countries in Europe." At a June 1980 meeting of the Pinay Circle "attention was turned towards the American Presidential election that was to bring Reagan to power."[846] (David Rockefeller reports in his *Memoirs* that at one point in his life he was usually the only American present at meetings of the Circle.)[847]

A more usual explanation for Carter's defeat in 1980 was the second oil shock of 1979–1980, in which an acute gas shortage led to both a sudden increase in prices and long gas lines at service stations. It is customary for establishment scholars to blame the shortage on political upheavals in Iran, which led to "a cutoff of Iranian oil."[848]

However Robert Sherrill's close analysis of the American oil industry demonstrates that American oil companies, not Iranian turmoil, were primarily responsible for the gas shortage:

U.S. companies were up to their own strategy. . . . Although in fact America was importing more oil in January and

February [1979], during the Iranian shutdown, than it had imported during the same period in 1978, major oil importers pretended that the Iranian "shortage" . . . was real. It was the excuse they gave for slashing the amount of gasoline they supplied to their retail dealers. . . . A CIA study showed that in the first five months of the year, at a time when the Administration was deploring our oil shortage, U.S. companies exported more oil than they had in those glut years 1977 and 1978.[849]

The oil majors' manipulation of domestic oil prices, combined with Carter's failure to bring the hostages home, combined to cause the first defeat for an elected president running for reelection, since that of Herbert Hoover in 1932.

Not mentioned by either mainstream journalists or Sherrill was the role quietly played by Saudi Arabia in augmenting the 1979 gas crisis: "The Saudis had cut production by nearly 1 million barrels a day to 9.5 million at the start of the year [1979], and in April 1979 they made a second cut to 8.5 million. The Saudis had the capacity to produce 12 million barrels a day at that point."[850]

The Saudi manipulation of gas prices reflected their acute displeasure with the Camp David Accords of 1978, which did nothing to change Israeli control of Jerusalem.[851] But what concerns us here is that the concerted policy of big oil in 1979 was closely aligned with their deep state allies in the Saudi government and the Safari Club, to the severe detriment of Americans and their nominal government, the beleaguered Carter administration.

The oil shock and gas shortage contrived by big oil in 1979, together with the October Surprise, were the chief factors in enabling the subsequent Reagan Revolution. This in turn opened the door for a new phase in "continuity of government" or COG plans, that were secretly prepared over two decades by planners like Donald Rumsfeld and Dick Cheney, and then implemented on 9/11.

Conclusion

The door was opened to the Reagan Revolution, and the emergence of two-party agreement on a so-called "Washington consensus" in economics, by which we can mean here the increasing deregulation of the private sector and privatization of the public sector.

A crucial step in this was Reagan's decisive end to four decades of power-sharing between labor and capital, by decisively crushing the 1981 strike of the Professional Air Traffic Controllers Organization or PATCO. This completed the transformation of the Republican Party of the 1950s (when the Goldwater conservatives were a fringe minority) into that of the 1980s (when Goldwater was now to the left of the new conservative majority). The era of the Council on Foreign Relations and the Committee for Economic Development had been supplanted by the era of the Heritage Foundation and the American Enterprise Institute.

The era of Nixonian and Trilateral détente was also officially ended by NSDD-32 of May 20, 1982, which declared as America's "formal goal the reversal of Soviet power in the region" of Eastern Europe.[852] The actual language of NSDD-32 was a little less stark: "To contain and reverse the expansion of Soviet control and military presence throughout the world."[853] But the enshrining of the word "reverse" signified a revolution. In the words of Reagan's first National Security Adviser, William P. Clark, ""In NSDD-32, . . . we attempted to forge a multi-pronged strategy to weaken Soviet influence and strengthen indigenous forces for freedom in the region."[854] In promoting NSDD-32, Clark's true goal may have been to go even farther, having persuaded Reagan that the Soviet Union could be pushed to the edge of collapse.[855]

U.S. oil interests, having become excited by the oil and gas reserves of the Caspian Basin, had a motive for this collapse (and helped induce it by participating in an orchestrated reduction of oil prices).[856] By 1991 there were already "ongoing negotiations between Kazakhstan and the US company Chevron;" and other corporations soon joined in the search.[857] As we saw in Chapter 5, one of the many U.S. oilmen who joined the search was Army

Intelligence Reserve Col. Jack Crichton of the 488th Intelligence Unit.[858]

Many, including myself, can welcome the exit of the Soviet Union from its subject nations like Poland and Czechoslovakia, and even the now admitted fact that the CIA helped subsidize the authentic Solidarity resistance movement in Poland.[859] But success in the dangerous maneuvering of international politics encourages bureaucrats with limited vision and responsibility to overreach, and set in motion a dialectics they do not contemplate.

Such I believe was the consequence of demolishing the Soviet Union, and unseating Gorbachev. At the end Gorbachev and the leaders of the West, including Ronald Reagan, were working together to truly end the Cold War. Events since then are threatening to restore it.

Elsewhere I have observed how the latest stage of the Pax Americana resembles, ominously, the latest stage of the 19th Century Pax Britannica.[860] In both cases excessive dominance was followed by developing resistance abroad, leading to absurd local blowups, such as the grotesque U.S.-Russian confrontation over Georgia in 2008.[861] In Britain's case, the similar incidents at Fashoda (1898) and Agadir (1911) were symptoms of an impending dialectical build-up towards a disastrous World War.[862] The unnecessary tensions between Moscow and Washington over Ukraine have been feared by many observers as signifying a possible reprise of the folly of 1914.

It is clear that, since the time of Kennedy and before, there have been forces in America that would welcome a final confrontation between America and Russia. And for better or for worse, the forces wishing for détente have declined radically since the Kennedy presidency, and the prospects for U.S. hegemony have temporarily increased.

It is clear to me also we owe America's present unstable global situation in part to a sequence of covert dirty tricks—beginning, but not ending, with assassination.

ACKNOWLEDGMENTS

I have been helped by so many people on this project, and for so long, that it is hard to know whom I should thank first. But I will begin by thanking those who worked hard with me to edit this book: Rex Bradford, whose chief efforts were a decade ago, Bill Simpich, and Oliver Curme. I am also indebted to them in other ways: in particular to Rex and Oliver for creating the superb Mary Ferrell Foundation website, and Bill for his formidable use of it in *State Secret* and other publications. The work of these three has deepened the insights that all of us can now have on the John F. Kennedy assassination.

This is true of the work of others as well, some of whom are now dead. I think particularly of my longtime editor Mark Selden, who has helped me with so many books and essays, including a chapter in this book. I would also be remiss not to thank in particular John Newman, David Talbot, Paul Hoch, Josiah Thompson, Larry Haapanen, Mark Allen, William Turner, Gary Aguilar, Jefferson Morley, James Lesar, and Daniel Ellsberg, most of whom are cited in the footnotes to this book. Of all these authors, my longest relationship, lasting almost half a century, is with Paul Hoch, who secured the release of many of the ONI records I discuss in Chapter 4.

I wish also to thank my publishers Mark Crispin Miller and Philip Rappaport, whose idea it was that I should finally complete this book, so long unfinished. And thanks once again to my wonderful indexer, P.J. Heim.

Finally let me thank, once again as so many times before, my wife Ronna Kabatznick, a fine author whose prose may outlast my own.

ENDNOTES

1   Warren Commission Executive Session of Jan 22, 1964. http://www.mary-ferrell.org/mffweb/archive/viewer/showDoc.do?absPageId=172707.

2   Peter Dale Scott, *Deep Politics and the Death of JFK* (Berkeley: University of California Press, 1993).

3   Ibid., p.202. See 5WH205-206.

4   Peter Dale Scott, *Oswald, Mexico, and Deep Politics* (New York: Skyhorse Press, 2013). *Deep Politics II: Essays on Oswald, Mexico, and Cuba* was originally published by JFK Lancer in spiral-bound, and then republished by the Mary Ferrell Foundation. Page references in the two editions are identical.

5   Telephone conversation between the President and Senator Russell, Nov 29 1963, 8:55PM. http://www.maryferrell.org/mffweb/archive/viewer/showDoc.do?docId=912&relPageId=2.

6   See "The Fourteen Minute Gap," by Rex Bradford, as well as an update. Links to those essays as well as a short documentary film on the subject are available at http://www.maryferrell.org/wiki/index.php/The_Fourteen_Minute_Gap.

7   Bill Kelly, "The Railroading of LCDR Terri Pike," http://jfkcountercoup.blogspot.com/2011/10/railroading-of-lcdr-terri-pike-over.html.

8   5WH198. Predictably, Warren failed to engage Ruby on this. Ruby then said "Would you rather I just delete what I said and just pretend that nothing is going on?"

9   ZRRIFLE handwritten notes, p. 5. NARA # 180-10142-10336, http://www.maryferrell.org/mffweb/archive/viewer/showDoc.do?mode=searchResult&absPageId=1194584.

10 Hoover memo of conversation with Attorney General of 4:01pm, November

22, 1963. FBI HQ File 62-109060-59, http://www.maryferrell.org/mffweb/
archive/viewer/showDoc.do?absPageId=753904. Hoover told RFK that
Oswald "went to Cuba on several occasions but would not tell us what he
went to Cuba for." Hoover's memo records that he knew Oswald had spent
3 years in Russia, and so was not simply confusing the two countries.

11 http://jfkfacts.org/wp-content/uploads/2013/11/galbraith-on-jfk.pdf

12 This has come to light due to a new version of the Air Force One recording, found among the possessions of General Clifton, which is less edited
than the one formerly available. See http://jfkcountercoup2.blogspot.
com/2013/07/raab-on-clifton-tape.html

13 Sheldon Stern, *Averting the Final Failure: John F. Kennedy and the Secret
Cuban Missile Crisis Meetings* (Stanford: Stanford University Press, 2003),
121. LeMay's statement was a special dig at Kennedy, whose father as
Ambassador to England had opposed America's entry into World War II.

14 See   http://www.maryferrell.org/wiki/index.php/1963_Vietnam_With-
drawal_Plans for more information, and read the plans themselves at http://
www.maryferrell.org/mffweb/archive/viewer/showDoc.do?docId=122.

15 Hannah Arendt, *Between Past and Future: Eight Exercises in Political
Thought* (New York: Penguin Books, 1993), 93.

16 Hannah Arendt, *Crises of the Republic: Lying in Politics, Civil Disobedi-
ence, On Violence, Thoughts on Politics and Revolution* (New York: Har-
court Brace, 1972), 155. Cf. Jonathan Schell, *The Unconquerable World:
Power, Nonviolence, and the Will of the People* (New York: Metropolitan
Books/Henry Holt, 2003), 218.

17 Jacques Ellul, trans. Cecelia Gaul Kings, *Violence; Reflections From A
Christian Perspective* (New York: Seabury Press, 1969), 125.

18 Andrew Bacevich, "The Western Way of War Has Run its Course," CBS
News, August 4, 2010.

19 Uwe Klussmann, Matthias Schepp, and Klaus Wiegrefe, "NATO's East-
ward Expansion: Did the West Break Its Promise to Moscow?" *Spiegel
Online International*, November 26, 2009, http://www.spiegel.de/inter-
national/world/nato-s-eastward-expansion-did-the-west-break-its-
promise-to-moscow-a-663315.html: "After speaking with many of those
involved and examining previously classified British and German documents in detail, SPIEGEL has concluded that there was no doubt that
the West did everything it could to give the Soviets the impression that
NATO membership was out of the question for countries like Poland,
Hungary or Czechoslovakia."

20 Jack Matlock, "Who is the bully? The U.S. has treated Russia like a loser
since the end of the Cold War," *Washington Post*, March 14, 2014, http://

www.washingtonpost.com/opinions/who-is-the-bully-the-united-states-has-treated-russia-like-a-loser-since-the-cold-war/2014/03/14/b0868882-aa06-11e3-8599-ce7295b6851c_story.html.

21 Dana Priest and William Arkin, *Top Secret America: The Rise of the New American Security State* (New York: Little Brown, 2011), 52.

22 Peter Dale Scott, *The Road to 9/11: Wealth, Empire, and the Future of America* (Berkeley: University of California Press, 2007), 267.

23 Mike Lofgren, "A Shadow Government Controls America," Reader Supported News, February 22, 2014, http://readersupportednews.org/opinion2/277-75/22216-a-shadow-government-controls.

24 Peter Dale Scott, *The American Deep State: Wall Street, Big Oil, and the Attack on U.S. Democracy* (Lanham, MD: Rowman & Littlefield, 2014), 12–16.

25 Tim Shorrock, *Spies for Hire: The Secret World of Intelligence Outsourcing* (New York: Simon & Schuster, 2008), 6.

26 Scott, *The American Deep State*, 20–22.

27 Scott, *The American Deep State*, 109–24.

28 Peter Dale Scott, *The War Conspiracy: JFK, 9/11, And The Deep Politics Of War* (New York: Skyhorse, 2013), 171.

29 Peter Dale Scott, *Oswald, Mexico, and Deep Politics* (New York: Skyhorse, 2013).

30 There are previous examples where the actual events of American history are at odds with the public record. Allen Dulles represented the conventional view of John Wilkes Booth when he represented Booth to the Warren Commission as a loner, ignoring both the facts of the case and what is known now of Booth's secret links to the Confederate Secret Service (Scott, *Deep Politics*, 295; cf. William A. Tidwell, with James O. Hall and David Winfred Gaddy, *Come Retribution: the Confederate Secret Service and the Assassination of Lincoln.* [Jackson: University Press of Mississippi, 1988]).

31 *American Heritage Dictionary*, s.v. "history;" emphases added.

32 House Select Committee on Assassinations, *Report*, 249–50 (henceforward AR 249–50).

33 Rajeev Syal, "Drug Money Saved Banks in Global Crisis, Claims UN Advisor," *Observer*, December 13, 2009, http://www.guardian.co.uk/global/2009/dec/13/drug-money-banks-saved-un-cfief-claims; discussion in Peter Dale Scott, *American War Machine: Deep Politics, the CIA Global Drug Connection, and the Road to Afghanistan* (Lanham, MD: Rowman & Littlefield, 2010), 228–29.

34 For a candid account of how KMT China was torn between management

and suppression of the opium traffic, see Alan Baumler, "Opium Control versus Opium Suppression: The Origins of the 1935 Six-Year Plan to Eliminate Opium and Drugs," in *Opium Regimes: China, Britain, and Japan, 1839–1952*, ed. Timothy Brook and Bob Tadashi Wakabayashi (Berkeley and Los Angeles: University of California Press, 2000), 270–91. Baumler notes how "'The opium trade was a vital source of income and power for most of the colonial and national states of East and Southeast Asia" (270). I believe this state of affairs is less restricted, and has changed less, than his choice of terms implies.

35 These and other examples in Sally Denton and Roger Morris, *The Money and the Power: The Rise and Reign of Las Vegas and Its Hold on America, 1947–2000* (New York: Knopf, 2001), 185, 290, etc.

36 Peter Dale Scott, *Deep Politics and the Death of JFK* (Berkeley and Los Angeles: University of California Press), 1966), 207, 218–19.

37 For an instructive example involving Citicorp, America's largest bank, see Robert A. Hutchison, *Off the Books* (New York: William Morrow, 1986). This Citicorp scandal (one involving double bookkeeping and tax evasion rather than drugs) was richly documented by first the SEC staff and then a Congressional Hearing, yet it was successfully suppressed through political influence.

38 *New York Times*, 11/11/99: A Senate Committee "subpoenaed Citibank for transcripts of conversations among its private bankers on March 1, 1995, the day after Mr. Salinas had been arrested for murder. He has been convicted and is in prison in Mexico. In one conversation, the head of Citibank Private Bank, Hubertus Rukavina, asked whether Mr. Salinas's money could be moved from trust accounts in London to Switzerland, which has strict secrecy laws, according to the transcript."

39 Scott, *American War Machine*, 43–62.

40 Peter Dale Scott and Jonathan Marshall, *Cocaine Politics: Drugs, Armies, and the CIA in Central America* (Berkeley: University of California Press, 1998), 39.

41 Peter Dale Scott, *Deep Politics and the Death of JFK*, 104–05.

42 Elaine Shannon, *Desperados: Latin Drug Lords, U.S. Lawmen, And The War America Can't Win* (New York: Viking, 1988), 180.

43 Cf. James Mills, *Underground Empire: Where Crime and Governments Embrace* (New York: Dell, 1986), 840–43, 550.

44 CIA Cable MEXI 7041, 24 November 1963; NARA #104-10015-10070.

45 Mills, *Underground Empire*, 549–50; cf. Henrik Krüger, *The Great Heroin Coup: Drugs, Intelligence & International Fascism* (Boston,: South End Press, 1980), 178–79.

46 Cf. Scott, *Deep Politics and the Death of JFK*, 107–08.

47 Dorothy J. Samuels and James A. Goodman, "How Justice Shielded the CIA," *Inquiry* (October 18, 1978), 10–11. Discussion in Peter Dale Scott, *Drugs, Contras and the CIA: Government Policies and the Cocaine Economy. An Analysis of Media and Government Response to the Gary Webb Stories in the San Jose Mercury News (1996–2000)* (Los Angeles: From the Wilderness Publications, 2000), pp. 39–40. Samuels and Goodman summarize a little-noticed Report from the House Committee on Government Operations that I (even with the help of university librarians) have so far been unable to locate in Congressional Research Service indices. I have however located a second, follow-up report: U.S. Cong., House, Committee on Government Operations, *Justice Department Handling of Cases Involving Classified Data and Claims of National Security*. 96th Cong., 1st Sess.; H. Rept. No. 96–280. Washington: GPO, 1979.

48 I know of no adequate published account of this murder and cover-up. There is a veiled account of the "flap" in John Ranelagh, *The Agency: the Rise and Decline of the CIA* (New York: Simon and Schuster, 1986), 221.

49 Scott, *Drugs, Contras and the CIA*, 2, 12, 39–40.

50 Michael Beschloss, ed., *Taking Charge: The Johnson White House Tapes, 1963–1964* (New York: Simon & Schuster, 1997), 22.

51 Beschloss, *Taking Charge*, 23n, citing the National Archives. To my knowledge, no other researcher has yet discovered this memo. Cf. Chapter 3.

52 CIA Memo of November 23, 1963, from SR/CI Chief [Tennant Bagley] to ADDP [Thomas Karamessines], NARA #104-10436-10025, http://www.history-matters.com/archive/jfk/cia/russholmes/pdf/104-10436-10025.pdf.

53 Beschloss, *Taking Charge*, 23.

54 FBI Memo of November 22; NARA #124-10027-10395; 62-109060-lst nr 487.

55 James P. Hosty, Jr., *Assignment: Oswald* (New York: Arcade Publishing, 1996), 219.

56 Peter Dale Scott, *Deep Politics and the Death of JFK*, 275; *Oswald, Mexico, and Deep Politics*, 80–85.

57 Hoover memo of 11/22/63 (4:01 PM) to Tolson, Belmont, Mohr, etc., http://www.jfklancer.com/backes/newman/documents/hoover/Hoover_RFK.JPG.

58 Jack Anderson, *Peace, War, and Politics: An Eyewitness Account* (New York: Tom Doherty Associates, 1999), 115–16. Cf. Chapter 6.

59 CIA Cable MEXI 7072 262113Z; NARA #104-10015-10368.

60 House Select Committee on Assassinations, Staff Report, "Oswald, the CIA,

and Mexico City" ("Lopez Report"), https://www.maryferrell.org/mffweb/archive/viewer/showDoc.do?mode=searchResult&absPageId=68632, 174–75. On November 22 a State Department cable from Mexico City, announcing that Mexico had closed its U.S. border in response to the assassination, was distributed inside the Mexico City CIA Station to only three people. The two first were the Station's Chief, Winston Scott, and Deputy Chief, Alan White. The third was David Phillips, in charge of covert action against the Cubans (State Cable 269 of 22 November 1963, NARA #104-10015-10309).

61 FBI Memo from Branigan to W.C. Sullivan (Turner); (NARA #124-10027-10395; 62-109060-lst nr 487). Cf. Mexico FBI memo 105-3702-12, 11/23/63: "On 10/1/63, a person calling from the Cuban Embassy, Mexico City, to the Soviet Embassy, and speaking very bad Russian, identified himself as LEE OSWALD."

62 As re-released, the Lopez Report talks of reporting on Cuban Consulate employee Silvia Durán "from one of the Station's penetration agents, LI[redaction, "crypt"], at the Cuban embassy" (Lopez Report, 199; cf. 154). The context of the Lopez Report reveals that the penetration agent was Luis Alberu Souto, also known as LITAMIL-9 (NARA #104-10110-10192). When the HSCA tried to interview Alberu in Mexico, he was shielded by Mexican authorities until they left. For more on Alberu as LITAMIL-9, see Bill Simpich, *State Secret*, Chapter 3, http://www.maryferrell.org/wiki/index.php/State_Secret_Chapter3.

63 "Scelso" memo of 11 December 1963 to Deputy Director (Plans), "Plans for the GPFLOOR Investigation;" NARA #104-10018-10103. Cf. John Newman, *Oswald and the CIA* (New York: Carroll & Graf Publishers, 1995), 406.

64 Anderson, *Peace, War, and Politics,* 116

65 [LBJ:] "We've got to take this out of the arena where they're testifying that Khrushchev and Castro did this and did that and kicking us into a war that can kill forty million Americans in an hour" (Beschloss, *Taking Charge*, 67).

66 William Manchester, *The Death of a President, November 20-November 25, 1963* (New York: Harper & Row, 1967), 717; *Washington Post*, 11/14/93.

67 CIA Cable MEXI 7203 (NARA #104-10016-10020).

68 CIA TX-1915 of 23 Nov 1963 (NARA #104-10015-10055: "Silvia Duran, the girl who put Oswald in touch with the Soviet Embassy"); MEXI 7029 232048Z (NARA #104-10015-10091); MEXI 7072 262113Z (NARA #104-10015-10368).

69 CIA Cable MEXI 7046 of 23 November; NARA #104-10015-10274.

70 JKB[enadum] letter of 26 Nov with report in Spanish of Durán interview; under covering letter of 27 November; NARA #104-10015-10189, -10190. "JK Benadum" was the pseudonym used by George Munro, who was employed in sensitive positions by both the FBI and the CIA in Mexico City, according to Jefferson Morley, author of *Our Man in Mexico*. Cf. CIA Cable MEXI 7105 of 27 Nov (10-page Durán statement coming to Washington by hand 28 Nov); NARA #104-10015-10416.

71 In her 1995 ARRB deposition, Anne Goodpasture confirmed (p. 39) that "I think there was what they called back channel, but I don't know the details of it."

72 CIA Document CSCI-3/778,826 (NARA #104-10004-10257), 102–514.

73 Ibid.

74 Edited transcript of November 26 phone call between Cuban President Oswaldo Dorticos and Cuban Ambassador Joaquin Hernandez Armas; NARA #104-10015-10007: "They asked her . . . did she have personal relations with him—including intimate relations—and she denied them all. . . . She has black and blue marks on her arms, which she said she got during the interrogation process. They were squeezing her arms" (p. 12). On December 10 a CIA HQ report "translated" Hernandez as follows: "he says that Mexican police bruised Silvia DURAN's arms a little shaking her to impress her with the importance of his questions" (CIA Document XAAZ-17958 10 Dec 63; Summary of Oswald case prepared for briefing purposes; NARA #104-10018-10040).

75 Personal interview with Larry Keenan.

76 Warren Commission, Hearings, Vol. 26, 411, henceforward 26 WH 411. Diaz Verson's CIA cryptonym was AMPALM-26 (MEXI 7776 of 14 Jan 1964, NARA #104-10404-10089, p. 2).

77 House Select Committee on Assassinations, Hearings, Vol. 3, 87, henceforward 3 AH 87.

78 CIA Dispatch HMMA-32243 of 13 June 1967, covering TX-1937 of 26 May.

79 Ibid.

80 3 AH 86.

81 3 AH 91; cf. 3 AH 86. Note that the DFS exempted the Soviets from their hypothetical conspiracy, as did Ambassador Mann (Anthony Summers, *Conspiracy* [New York: McGraw Hill, 1980], 441).

82 CIA Cable MEXI 7054 241837Z, NARA #104-10015-10082.

83 3 AH 292–93.

84 Lopez Report, p. 200. "The Committee cannot definitely resolve whether Silvia Duran was a Mexican or American intelligence agent or source" (p. 201).

85 CIA memo of 25 November from "A.C. Plambeck" memo re Alvarado; NARA #104-10015-10301. Also CIA Cable MEXI 7069 262037Z, NARA #104-10015-10366 (Canadian hippie).

86 Hoover –LBJ phone call, 11/29/63, as shown in the Church Committee, Final Report, Book 5, "The Investigation of the Assassination of President John F. Kennedy—Performance of the Intelligence Agencies, 34; Beschloss, *Taking Charge*, 53. I have been unable to find any cable which documents the change in Alvarado's testimony, which may have been conveyed to Washington by telephone or back channel.

87 CIA Cable MEXI 7168 of 30 Nov 1963, NARA #104-10025-10177.

88 AR 244; Scott, *Deep Politics*, 38.

89 CIA Cable MEXI 7289 070145Z, NARA #104-10017-10030. A confused Alvarado accepted the negative results of the polygraph, stating "that he had utmost confidence" in it.

90 *Washington Post*, November 23, 1993; cf. Beschloss, *Taking Charge*, 53. In a memorandum of the same day Hoover noted that it was Johnson, not Hoover, who initiated the call (3 AH 476). The call logs of the LBJ Library (available on its website) indicate that the call was from Hoover to Johnson. The September 28 date coincided exactly with the date the Mexico City CIA Station believed Oswald to have been in the Cuban Embassy. I shall argue later that in fact he was not in the Embassy on that Saturday (when the Embassy was closed), even though someone using his name was creating that impression.

91 DIR 85714 291631Z, NARA #104-10015-10224.

92 DIR 85744 291915Z, NARA #104-10015-10228.

93 Warren Commission Document (henceforth WCD), 347, p. 12.

94 CIA Cable MEXI 7067 of 26 November, NARA #104-10015-10297.

95 Lopez Report, 127–28.

96 NARA #104-10015-10347. The identity of "L. F. Barker" with Robert Shaw is revealed by comparing item 10, listed as "Lawrence F. Barker," in the "subject card file" (NARA #104-10079-10049, 5) with item 10, listed as "Robert Tyler Shaw," in the "black notebook" (NARA #104-10079-10014, 4) provided by the CIA to the HSCA.
    Note this Mexico City flowchart that depicts Shaw as the man who "oversaw Cuban operatives". NARA #180-10113-10119, p. 11.

97 CIA Cable MEXI 7104 of 27 November, NARA #104-10015-10191.

98 3 AH 595 (FBI memo of December 12, 1963); Mexico City serial MC 105-3702-22 (Legat Cable to HQ of November 26, 1963).

99 Richard Millett, *Guardians of the Dynasty* (Maryknoll, NY: Orbis Books, 1977), 251.

100 Attachment to CIA Memo of 12 December 1963 from DDP to FBI, "Mexican Interrogation of Gilberto Alvarado;" NARA #104-10018-10043.

101 Gary Webb, *Dark Alliance: The CIA, The Contras, And The Crack Cocaine Explosion* (New York: Seven Stories Press, 1998), 55–56 (Montiel); Peter Dale Scott, *Drugs, Contras, and the CIA* (Sherman Oaks, CA: From the Wilderness Publications, 2000), 15 ("kingpin").

102 CIA Cable MEXI 7072 of 26 November, p. 4, #104-10015-10350.

103 For example a Mexican credit investigator, Pedro Gutierrez, wrote on December 2 to President Johnson that he had seen a Cuban in the Embassy count out dollars to an American, whom he later recognized as Lee Harvey Oswald (Coleman-Slawson Memorandum, 11 AH 161; cf. 24 WH 633, Summers, *Conspiracy*, 444, Gerald Posner, *Case Closed: Lee Harvey Oswald and the Assassination of JFK* [New York: Random House, 1993], 194.) Another example is the swiftly retracted claim that Luisa Calderon of the Cuban Embassy, whom Alvarado allegedly saw kiss Oswald, had prior knowledge of the Kennedy assassination. (AR 454, 4 AH 181, 11 AH 494).

104 FBI Memo of 27 November from DeLoach to Mohr, FBI File 62-109060-1571.

105 The "CIA man in Dallas" presumably refers to J. Walton Moore, an acquaintance if not associate of Oswald's friend and patron George de Mohrenschildt. Both de Mohrenschildt and his wife Jeanne have claimed that Moore had pre-assassination knowledge of Oswald (Summers, *Conspiracy*, 226–28).

106 CIA Cable DIR 85654 281520Z, NARA #104-100154-10438. "Clark" is presumably the FBI Legal Attache Clark Anderson, who joined with Scott and Mann in calling for the rearrest and "cracking" of Silvia Durán to corroborate the Alvarado story. In discrediting the rumor of the $5000 deposit, the CIA cable said that "ODENVY [FBI] here has just affirmed they never heard this story," a claim hard to reconcile with the FBI memo just quoted.

107 3 AH 300.

108 3 AH 300, Memo of conversation with Elena Garro de Paz; cf. 3 AH 297; Lopez Report, 217. The Garro story, like those of Durán and Alvarado, was a malleable and changing one. I have conflated the most prominent "Phase-One" details.

109 Scott, *Deep Politics*, 123; citing Warren Report (henceforth WR), 307.

110 The CIA originally reported that Silvia was arrested at home with husband and members of family who were having a party (CIA Cable MEXI 7054 of 24 Nov 1963, NARA #104-10015-10082). A CIA version of Silvia's November 23 interview (described in *Deep Politics II* as "DFS-2")

repeated that these others had all been picked up with Silvia because they were dining with her at Rubén Durán's home at the time of her arrest. The FBI version of the same interview (described in *Deep Politics II* as "DFS-4") indicated otherwise: that Silvia, Horacio, and Lidia were at Silvia's home, while Rubén and his wife were dining at their own home. See JKB Memo and attachment of 26 November, 1963, p. 7; NARA #104-10015-10190 (DFS-2); 25 WH 637 (DFS-4); *Deep Politics II*, 120–21. In her 1978 HSCA interview Silvia testified that Rubén had already been arrested before she went to his house from her own and was arrested in turn (3 AH 81).

111 Silvia's account of such interrogation (3 AH 86, 91) was earlier corroborated, as we have seen, by a State Department officer's claim to have heard from CIA Station Deputy Chief Alan White that the DFS interrogated Silvia on details of the Garro story (3 AH 292–93).

112 CIA Cable MEXI 7054 of 24 Nov 1963, NARA #104-10015-10082.

113 There is no proof that Garro shared her story in 1963. However in October 1964, when a version of the Garro story was first entered into the CIA Oswald file which we possess, Winston Scott noted that the "Garros [Elena and her daughter] have been talking about this for a long time" (Mexico City CIA TX-1928 n.d. (5 Oct 64), NARA #104-10016-10031).

114 See for example AR 249–50; Summers, *Conspiracy*, 373.

115 MEXI 6453 of 9 Oct 090043Z; NARA #104-10015-10047; 4 AH 212. The CIA Station later supplied an allegedly verbatim transcript of this conversation. In this transcript the person identifying himself as Oswald did not mention Kostikov as the cable suggested; he merely replied affirmatively when Obyedkov suggested that Kostikov was the Consul who had been spoken to on Saturday (Lopez Report 79). Was this transcript in fact a later "Phase-Two" rewrite to neutralize the "Phase-One" cable? This possibility seems less far-fetched when we see how the only other alleged Oswald allusion to Kostikov, the "Phase-One" "Kostin" letter of November 9, was similarly neutralized by the later presentation of a dubious alleged "draft," also "Phase-Two".

116 As noted in Chapter 1, some in the Mexico CIA Station personnel themselves doubted that the caller was Oswald. One of them wrote that "Both Mexican monitors . . . said *caller who called himself Oswald* had difficulty making himself understood both (as I recall) *in English* and Russian" (Handwritten note on Scott D. Breckinridge Memo for the Record of 12 December 1976, NARA #104-10095-10001, emphasis added). Corroborating evidence is provided by Dallas FBI chief Gordon Shanklin's report that in the days after the assassination his FBI agents listened to a copy of

a Mexico City tape purported to contain Oswald's voice. What they heard was a voice speaking in broken English who was not Oswald. (See http://digitalcollections.baylor.edu/cdm/compoundobject/collection/po-arm/id/786/rec/1, p. 39)

117 Phone call from Hoover to LBJ, 10:01 AM, 11/23/63 (Beschloss, *Taking Charge*, 23; Newman, *Oswald and the CIA*, 520).

118 Rex Bradford, "The Fourteen-Minute Gap," *Kennedy Assassination Chronicles*, Spring 2000, 28–32.

119 Letterhead Memo from Hoover to James J. Rowley, Secret Service, 11/23/63; AR 249–50; cf. FBI #62-109060-1133, NARA #104-10419-10022. (The drafter is SA Fletcher D. Thompson of Criminal Division, who on the next day flew to Dallas with SA Richard Rogge, to prepare memoranda on deaths of Kennedy and Oswald: 3 AH 465, 478, 479). Discussion below; Scott, *Deep Politics and the Death of JFK*, 41–45.

120 Address to November 1999 JFKLancer Conference, available on line at http://www.jfklancer.com/backes/newman.

121 CIA Cable MEXI 7023 231659Z (11:59 AM EST November 23), NARA#104-10015-10124.

122 "SUMMARY of Relevant Information on Lee Harvey OSWALD at 0700 on 24 November 1963," NARA #104-10015-10359. Reprinted in Hosty, *Assignment Oswald*, p. 289. Cf. CIA Memo of 11/23/63 to FBI, CSCI-3/778,826, NARA #104-10004-10257: "Voice comparisons indicated that the 'North American' who participated in several of these conversations is probably the person who identified himself as Lee OSWALD on 1 October 1963."

123 Anne Goodpasture comment on newspaper column by Robert S. Allen and Paul Scott (10/21/64) preserved in Mexico City Oswald file; NARA #104-10125-10001. See December 1995 ARRB Interview of Anne Goodpasture, p. 140: Q. "So did Mr. Feinglass then make that identification prior to the assassination?" A. Prior to the assassination and prior to Sylvia Duran's arrest. Q. Yes is the answer? A. Yeah."

124 FBI Cable of November 23 from Eldon Rudd to SAC, Dallas; FBI file MX 105-3702-12. Eldon Rudd was of course the FBI agent who reportedly had flown up the tapes the day before. In 1995 Anne Goodpasture told the ARRB that she thought Rudd "may have carried the tape dub [copy]." She suggested that the ARRB interview Rudd: "I think he refused to talk to the House Committee [on Assassinations] because he was a Congressman at that time" (ARRB Interview of Anne Goodpasture, 12/95, p. 146).

125 CIA Cable MEXI 7054 2401837Z (1:37 PM EST November 24), NARA

#104-10015-10082. The day before, at 2:11 PM EST, the station had reported it was "probable that Oswald conversation LIENVOY tapes erased" (CIA Cable MEXI 7024 23911Z, NARA #104-10015-10125).

126 E.g. CIA Memo to FBI of 23 November 1963, CSCI 3-778/826, NARA #104-10004-10257: "Voice comparisons [by Boris Tarasoff] indicated that the 'North American' who participated in several of these conversations is probably the person who identified himself as Lee OSWALD on 1 October 1963." Goodpasture wrote: "Douglas J. Feinglass [Boris Tarasoff] who did transcriptions says Oswald is identical to the person para one speaking broken Russian who called from Cuban embassy September 28 to Soviet embassy" (Memo from Mexico City station to CIA HQ, 11/23/63, NARA #104-10414-10330).

127 ARRB Counsel Jeremy Gunn in ARRB Deposition of Anne Lorene Goodpasture, December 1995, p. 147: "Q. I have spoken with two Warren Commission staff members who went to Mexico City and who both told me that they heard the tape[,] after the assassination obviously."

128 Church Committee Staff Memo of 3/5/76; NARA #157-10014-10168.

129 U.S. Cong., Senate, Select Committee to Study Governmental Operations, *Final Report, Book V, The Investigation of the Assassination of President John F. Kennedy: Performance of the Intelligence Agencies*; 94th Cong., 2nd Sess., Report No. 94-555.

130 Ibid., p. 102. The Report is dated April 23, 1976; it is possible that the 3/5/76 memo was prepared too late for inclusion.

131 AR 250.

132 One of the HSCA staff stressed to me that this evasive language had ben chosen "very, very carefully."

133 Warren Commission Exhibit 15, 16 WH 33.

134 WR 310; Warren Commission Exhibit 3126.

135 The importance of the alleged Kostikov-Kostin material was underlined in his autobiography by former FBI Director Clarence Kelley (*Kelley: The Story of an FBI Director* [Kansas City: Andrews McMeel, 1987], p. 293): "William C. Sullivan, assistant director in charge of security in Washington, was probably the highest FBI official, at that point, to review the Oswald file. What he discovered there must have astounded him. He read the data on the meeting between Oswald and Kostikov (Sullivan would have known exactly who Kostikov was), surmised the Cuban connection, viewed the CIA surveillance data on the Soviet embassy in Mexico City, studied FBI wiretaps involving Oswald and Kostikov, then read the November 9 follow-up letter from Oswald to the Soviet embassy in Washington. This information, it would surely have struck him, had such

dire international implications that the White House must be informed immediately."

136 WR 309–11; WCE 103, 16 WH 443; cf. 3 WH 14, 97; James Hosty, *Assignment Oswald*, 40–41, 85–86. Hosty claims that he received the draft on November 23, but this is uncorroborated. The draft does not form part of the inventory of items retrieved on that day from Ruth Paine's residence and typed three days later in the FBI office (24 WH 332–37). Hosty gives an elaborate explanation of why this draft was not filed by him in the regular way, but segregated in an envelope (Hosty, *Assignment Oswald*, 85–86; Curt Gentry, *J. Edgar Hoover: The Man and the Secrets* [New York: Norton, 1991], 546). An alternative explanation would be that knowledge of Oswald's Mexico trip, still classified because of its origin from a CIA intercept program, had not yet been shared with the Dallas police.

137 Ambassador Dobrynin in AP story, "Soviets Suspected Oswald Letter a Fake"; *Boston Globe*, 8/6/99, A8. This Soviet reaction was also headlined in Canadian newspapers, but omitted from George Lardner's account of the recently released "Yeltsin documents" in the *Washington Post*, 8/6/99. The full text is in Yeltsin Documents, p. 91; LS no. 0692061-26 Washington to Moscow cable of 27 November 1963: "*This letter was clearly a provocation*: it gives the impression we had close ties with Oswald and were using him for some purposes of our own. It was totally unlike any other letters the embassy had previously received from Oswald. Nor had he ever visited our embassy himself. The suspicion that the letter is a forgery is heightened by the fact that it was typed, whereas the other letters the embassy had received from Oswald before were typewritten." Cf. p. 91: "The embassy had suspicions about this letter the moment it arrived: either it was a forgery or was sent as a deliberate provocation. The embassy left Oswald's letter unanswered."

138 Warren Commission, CE 7–14 (16 WH 10–32); CE 986 (18 WH 501–35).

139 Yeltsin Documents, LS no. 0692061-8, Washington Embassy Cable 1967–1968 to Moscow, 23 November 1963. The cable notes that Marina's application had been rejected by a Foreign Ministry letter of October 7, 1963. The cable does not explicitly say that this information had been forwarded (as one would expect) to Marina, and there is no trace of such notification in the Warren Commission release of the Consulate-Oswald correspondence (WCE 986, 18 WH 501–35). But, whether the Oswalds had received news of the rejection or not, it is hard to believe that a genuine Oswald letter to the Consulate would pay such marginal attention to the issue.

140 The "Phase-Two" draft is thus exactly analogous to the "Phase-Two"

Kostikov intercept transcript indicating that Oswald had not in fact spoken of Kostikov (as the earlier "Phase-One" Kostikov intercept cable had suggested). Both "Phase-Two" documents purported to be earlier; but both in fact entered the record later. Even the draft had alleged corroboration, in the form of a handwritten draft which Ruth Paine allegedly made and gave to FBI Agent Bardwell D. Odum after the assassination. It too was withheld from the regular inventory of Oswald evidence (Hosty, *Assignment: Oswald*, 86). Ruth Paine testified about making this copy (3 WH 15, 52), but for unexplained reasons it (unlike the draft) was not introduced as a Warren Commission Exhibit (cf. 3 WH 52).

141 Jerry Rose, *The Fourth Decade*, November 1999, 5. I had not seen this article until after writing my own comments.

142 Ibid. Rose also pointed to real problems with the date of the postmark on the typed letter, and the unlikelihood that Oswald, having concealed the typed letter from Ruth Paine, would then leave his "draft" on her desk for her to pick up afterwards (cf. 3 WH 13–15).

143 Both the Walker note and the Mexican bus ticket were retrieved from the pages of books in Ruth Paine's house, both just when they were needed to fill gaps in the reconstructed "Phase-Two" account of Oswald's life. See Jim Marrs, *Crossfire* (New York: Basic Books, 2013], 261 (Walker note); Peter Dale Scott, "Some Familiar Faces Reappear in Monicagate." Pacific New Service, January 26, 1998 (ticket). (Other suspect evidence would include a silver Mexican coin, Spanish-English dictionary, silver bracelet for Marina, and postcards from Mexico City, all of which Ruth Paine confirmed seeing together in Marina's drawer; 3 WH 13).

144 We see evidence of this in the cover-up cable that the CIA sent to Mexico City shortly after noon on November 23. The cable reported the FBI as saying "that photos of man entering Soviet Embassy which MEXI sent to Dallas were not of Lee Oswald;" it said nothing about the voice on the tape which the FBI had also shown not to be Oswald's (DIR 84888 231729Z; NARA #104-10015-10115). The cable had an unusual releasing officer: William P. Hood, WH/COPS. Hood was the Chief of Operations for Western Hemisphere Division. More importantly, Hood was a senior Counterintelligence Officer who had been involved for some time on a highly sensitive case, a possible Soviet mole who had leaked information about the CIA's secret U-2 program. Before the assassination, William Hood had signed as Authenticating Officer for the misleading HQ cable in response to news of the Kostikov intercept (DIR 74830 of 10 October

1963; NARA #104-10015-10048. I will argue later that Oswald and his
files were manipulated as part of the search for this mole. See Chapter 3,
"Oswald and the Hunt for Popov's Mole."

145 Ruth Paine gave false or misleading testimony on a number of matters, but virtually always to corroborate a "Phase-Two" interpretation of
events.

146 CIA Cable MEXI 7023 231659Z; NARA #104-10015-10124.

147 26 WH 411.

148 Oleg M. Nechiporenko, trans. Todd B. Bludeau, *Passport to Assassination* (New York: Birch Lane/Carol, 1993), 75–81; see discussion in *Deep
Politics II*, 12–15.

149 "Interview with a KGB Colonel: Peter Dale Scott interviews Col. Oleg
Nechiporenko in Dallas" (videotape). For some years this videotape was
available from Prevailing Winds Research (#884) via a website (http://
prevailingwinds.org/videomain.html) that no longer exists.

150 According to a later CIA note, the monitors of the call said that the "caller
(who called himself Oswald) had difficulty making himself understood
both (as I recall) in English and in Russian" (Handwritten note on Scott
D. Breckinridge Memo for the Record of 12 December 1976; NARA
#104-10095-10001).

151 CIA TX-1915 of 23 Nov 1963; NARA #104-10015-10055. Cf. MEXI 7029
232048Z; NARA #104-10015-10091, in which Scott reports that he has
suggested to the Mexicans that they arrest Durán, citing an earlier cable
(MEXI 7025) with the full texts of the two "Phase-One" intercepts.

152 Scott's error in describing Rubén Durán as Silvia's brother, rather than
brother-in-law, is consistent with, and may have derived from, Garro's
recurring habit of describing the Duráns (as opposed to Rubén Durán's
wife) as her "cousins" (3 AH 295, 297, 305). Scott also supplied a wrong
address for Silvia, who told the DFS she lived at 143, Calles de Constituy-
entes. This may explain why the DFS went first to Herodoto #14, and only
arrested Silvia when she arrived there.

153 CIA TX-1907 of 27 Nov 1963; NARA #104-10015-10428.

154 CIA Memo of 24 or 25 November 1963, "Subject: Lee Harvey OSWALD,
also known as Lee Harry OSWALD; Alex HIDELL; Harvey Oswald
LEE," NARA #104-10195-10265, p. 3. Cf. Edward Jay Epstein, *Legend* (New York: McGraw Hill, 1978), 250; Gus Russo, *Live By the
Sword* (Baltimore: Bancroft Press, 1998), 344. The memo is undated
and unsigned, but is aware of Oswald's death on November 24. It mentions nothing about the claims made by Alvarado on November 25,
which were included in a list of questions compiled by Scott for the

Mexicans to ask after Durán's second arrest (MEXI 7124 282116Z; NARA #104-10016-10010).

155 CIA Cable MEXI 7072 262113Z; NARA #104-10015-10368.

156 Cover sheet to memo, in Scott's handwriting with initial: "Read to President on night of 25/XI/63—S." The *Washington Post* (November 14, 1993) concludes that the memo was read to President Johnson, but this is most unlikely. The Church Committee concluded (I believe correctly) that the person informed was "a senior Mexican government official" (Schweiker-Hart Report, 28).

157 CIA Cable MEXI 7033 of 23 November 232246Z; NARA #104-10015-10094.

158 Report in Spanish of November 26, 1963; retyped and transmitted by JKB (George Munro) to Mexico City CIA Station "Re: Lee Harvey Oswald and Silvia Tirado de Duran," NARA #104-10068-10084, p. 6. The report was prepared by "LI-4" (Fernando Gutiérrez Barrios, Assistant Director of the DFS) for "LI-2" (Gustavo Díaz Ordaz, Gobernación Chief and President-elect of Mexico). It was hand-carried to Washington on November 27 by a Headquarters CIA Officer, John Horton (CIA Cable MEXI 7105 of November 27, 1963, NARA #104-10015-10416). The report was retyped on the same machine as JKB's covering letter, presumably to change some, but not all, of the "Harvey Lee Oswald" references in the Report. (All the references to Oswald in the Durán interview pages have "Lee Harvey Oswald," but subsequent pages dealing with her relatives have "Harvey Lee Oswald.") See Chapter 4.

159 George Munro, a longtime Mexico resident, was an outside liaison officer for both the Mexico City CIA Station and the FBI: and was responsible for overseeing the phone intercept program (Scott, *Deep Politics II*, 5, cf. 120). As we shall see in Chapter 6, on June 23, 1972, after a visit from CIA Deputy Director Vernon Walters, Acting FBI Director Gray ordered that the FBI in Mexico temporarily not interview George Munro, a friend of Howard Hunt's, about Watergate (Senate Watergate Hearings, Vol. 9, 3456; Scott, *Deep Politics*, xvi; cf. FBI memo of 7/21/71 re Hunt, NARA #124-10211-10223).

160 CIA Cable DIR 85758 of November 29, 1963; NARA #104-10015-10229.

161 Oswald visa application; 3 AH 129; 25 WH 814.

162 CIA Cable MEXI 7033 of November 23, 1963; NARA #104-10015-10094.

163 CIA Cable MEXI 6453 of October 9, 1963; NARA #104-10015-10047.

164 Winston Scott, *Foul Foe*, ms. (retrieved for the CIA after Scott's death in 1971 by James Angleton), 268–69, emphasis added; Newman, *Oswald and the CIA*, 415–16; HSCA, Lopez Report, 125.

165 CIA Memo of September 18, 1975 from Chief, CI Staff (Kalaris), NARA #104-10051-10173; Newman, *Oswald and the CIA*, 462; cf. 169.

166 Lopez Report, 82–88. Cf. Newman, *Oswald and the CIA*, 369–77.

167 Ray Rocca deposition of 7/17/78 to HSCA, pp. 82–83. Rocca's remarks may explain why the House Assassinations Committee reported from testimony that the connection between Oswald and the Cuban consulate "had in fact been made in early October 1963" (AR 249n).

168 FBI Memorandum of 22 November from W.A. Branigan to W.C. Sullivan; NARA #124-10027-10395; FBI 62-109060-lst nr 487.

169 Among those who accept the "Phase-Two" version as real are Newman (pp. 356–57), and Russell (pp. 492–94).

170 Philip Shenon, *A Cruel and Shocking Act: The Secret History of the Kennedy Assassination* (New York: Henry Holt and Company, 2013), 496–98, etc.

171 Warren Commission Document 347 of January 31, 1964, p. 10, emphasis added.

172 Lee H. Wigren, C/SR/CI/R[esearch], Memo to File of 4 February 1964; NARA #104-10003-10004.

173 Summers, *Conspiracy*, 194–99; AR, 101-02.

174 Epstein, *Legend*, 16, 237: "The FBI knew through a double agent that Kostikov . . . was a high-level officer of the Thirteenth Department of the KGB, heavily involved in controlling saboteurs. . . . [T]he Thirteenth Department . . . was involved with planning sabotage and other violent acts."

175 *New York Times*, November 23, 1975. In first moving the resolution for a House Select Committee on Assassinations, Congressman Downing, the future HSCA Chairman, supported his case by referring to the Kostin letter, and to the CIA's identification of Kostikov as a member of the KGB's "Liquid Affairs Department, whose responsibilities include assassination and sabotage" (*Congressional Record*, House, September 17, 1976, H10360).

176 *Washington Post*, November 26, 1976; Dick Russell, *The Man Who Knew Too Much* (New York: Carroll & Graf Publishers, 2003). 494; Scott, *Deep Politics II*, 97. Further support for a Cuban conspiracy was dredged from CIA files for David Belin by Raymond Rocca, a former member of the CI Counterintelligence staff under James Angleton (e.g. NARA #157-10011-10072: Memo of 5/20/75 of David Belin on Castro and assassination plots, citing Ray Rocca).

177 Phillips, *Night Watch*, 139.

178 Gus Russo, *Live By the Sword*, (Baltimore: Bancroft Press, 1998), 459.

179 Russo, *Live By the Sword*, 344.

180 CIA Index To HSCA Film, 4; NARA #104-10431-10003.

181 Russo, *Live By the Sword*, 219; cf. Durán, 3 AH 86, 91; LIRING-3, Scott, *Deep Politics II*, 38. The *New York Times Book Review* found Russo's book "compelling, exhaustively researched and evenhanded."

182 Posner, *Case Closed*, 194; Russo, *Live By the Sword*, 345.

183 Posner, *Case Closed*, 191n.

184 Russo, *Live By the Sword*, 219. (Russo does not quote the words, "The fact.")

185 Richard D. Mahoney, *Sons & Brothers: the days of Jack and Bobby Kennedy* (New York: Arcade, 1999), 303.

186 Mahoney, *Sons & Brothers*, 336; citing Schweiker in Gaeton Fonzi, *The Last Investigation* (New York: Thunder's Mouth Press), 31.

187 Russo, *Live By the Sword*, 218.

188 Russo, *Live By the Sword*, 363.

189 Russo, *Live By the Sword*, 218.

190 Scott, *Deep Politics II*, 130–36; Peter Dale Scott, *American War Machine*, 44–57.

191 Church Committee, *Alleged Assassination Plots Involving Foreign Leaders; Interim Report*, Senate, 94th Cong., 1st Sess., Report No 94–465, 182.

192 "Scelso" [Whitten] Deposition to HSCA, 5/16/78, NARA #180-10131-10330, 1–140: "the performance of the Mexico City support apparatus, as we call surveillance, photo-surveillance, phone taps and so forth, was unequalled in the world. There is nothing like it anyplace else in the world."

193 *Deep Politics II*, 117, 130–36.

194 FBI HQ 105-93264-3, NARA #124-90059-10087 SAC Chicago to Director, 2-17-61: "CIA on 2-10-61 advised that subject is not connected with CIA or FRD;" FBI HQ 105-93264-3, NARA #124-90059-10111: FBI SAC Chicago LHM of 11/02/60, 3 ("Army Military Intelligence officer").

195 Scott, *American War Machine*, 49–57.

196 Peter Dale Scott and Jonathan Marshall, *Cocaine Politics: Drugs, Armies, and the CIA in Central* America (Berkeley: University of California Press, 1998), 65 and passim.

197 E.g. Attachment to CIA Cable IN 94192 of 20 June 1967, NARA #104-10408-10436.

198 *Deep Politics II*, 135; *Washington Post*, March 28, 1982 ($30 million).

199 Gary Webb, *Dark Alliance*, 54–56. Cf. CIA Memo to Papich of 12/12/63; NARA #104-10018-10043 (Alvarado-Montiel).

200 "CIA Report on Contras and Cocaine" (Hitz Report), I, para 100; cf. Volume II, 282 353 355 652–4 659; Scott, *Drugs, Contras, and the CIA*, 19.

201 Webb, *Dark Alliance*, 200–05 and passim (Meneses-CIA); Scott and Marshall, *Cocaine Politics*, 36 (Nazar Haro protected).

202 Scott, *Deep Politics*, 105.

203 David Atlee Phillips, *Night Watch*, 113–14.

204 December 1995 Nassau Conference, Proceedings; http://cuban-exile. com/doc_026-050/doc0027-3.htm, http://cuban-exile.com/doc_026-050/doc0027-4.htm. Photo is Warren Commission Bringuier Exhibit No. 1, 19 WH 173.

205 Ray and Mary La Fontaine, *Oswald Talked: The New Evidence in the JFK Assassination* (Gretna, LA: Pelican Publishing, 1996), 288–99, etc. Cf. the DRE arms story in Chapter 5.

206 Ray and Mary La Fontaine, *Oswald Talked,* 277, 283–88, etc.

207 Fonzi, *The Last Investigation*, 232–239, etc.

208 Scott and Marshall, *Cocaine Politics*, 35; Fonzi, *The Last Investigation* 232–39.

209 Noel Twyman, *Bloody Treason* (Rancho Santa Fe, CA: Laurel Pub., 1997), 700–02 (Bernardo de Torres-Morales).

210 Mahoney, *Sons & Brothers*, 135.

211 Fonzi, *The Last Investigation,* 390.

212 Twyman, *Bloody Treason*, 451.

213 Twyman, *Bloody Treason,* 454–57.

214 John Ranelagh, *The Agency: The Rise and Decline of the CIA* (New York: Simon and Schuster, 1986), 515–20. Phillips confirms the assignment in his autobiography (*The Night Watch*, 220–21); he also describes "El Indio" (Morales) as someone whom he met on the Guatemalan operation, "but was to work with in other operations over the years" (p. 49).

215 Twyman, *Bloody Treason*, 438–40 (Harvey-Morales-Rosselli).

216 The CIA Inspector-General's Report on the subject said that "after Harvey took over the Castro [assassination] operation, he ran it as one aspect of ZR/RIFLE (CIA Inspector General's Report, 40–41; Church Committee, Interim Report, 182). Harvey thus took over the CIA contact with Rosselli "as part of Project ZR/RIFLE" (Interim Report, 188).

217 Warren Hinckle and William Turner, *Deadly Secrets* (New York: Thunder's Mouth Press, 1992), 213.

218 Scott, *Deep Politics and the Death of JFK*, 141–45.

219 Mahoney, *Sons & Brothers,* 269.

220 Scott, *Deep Politics*, 141–43. Among the anonymous reports received by the Dallas Police Department after the assassination was one linking Ruby to an international ring smuggling cars and narcotics. (I am grateful to Michael Parks for this information.)

221 Assassination Records Review Board (ARRB), Deposition of Anne Lorene Goodpasture, December 1995, p.67: "we were all advised that he was head of the [Cuban] task force." Task Force W, which directed Operation Mongoose against Castro in 1962, was renamed the Special Affairs Staff in early 1963.

222 Newman, *Oswald and the CIA*, 236–43.

223 CIA Cable DIR 73214 of October 4, 1963: "Mr David Phillips, newly appointed Chief PBRUMEN [Cuba] Ops in MEXI will arrive 7 October EAL FL 655 for two days consultations WAVE" (NARA #104-10046-10003). WAVE was the SAS field station in Miami.

224 Almost certainly there could have been nothing relevant to the October 1 intercept in a pouch the same day in Washington. However there could have been materials pertinent to the alleged but missing intercepts of Oswald in the Cuban Embassy.

225 CIA Cable MEXI 6344 0f October 1, 1963, NARA #104-10092-10212. The full text of the cable is as follows: "Bulk materials under TN 251905, Pouch number 4083, pouched one October to be held in registry until picked up by Michael C. Choaden presently TDY HQS."

226 Scott, *Deep Politics*, 117–18.

227 NARA #104-10015-10045, cover sheet to FBI Hosty Report of 9/10/63; in Newman, *Oswald and the CIA*, 501. William Potocki of CI/OPS initialed this cover sheet on September 25, the day that the Warren Report (WR 413) alleges that "Oswald left [New Orleans] for Mexico City".

228 DIR 74830 of 10 Oct 1963, NARA #104-10015-10048, p. 2. The CIA tried to conceal this trickery from the Warren Commission by giving the September 24 FBI memo a forged FBI transmittal slip, dated "November 8," and burying the memo in the November section of the 201 file (Warren Commission Document 692). But the CIA cover sheet (not seen by the Warren Commission) shows clearly that the FBI memo was received in the CIA on October 3, and seen by Jane Roman on October 4. The forged FBI transmittal slip was re-released by the CIA in May 1992, and was published in the Sckolnick edition of this release (Lewis B, Sckolnick, *Lee Harvey Oswald: CIA Pre-Assassination File, Facsimile Edition* [Leverett, MA: Rector Press, 1993], 112). It has disappeared from the CIA's 1993 release of the same 201 file, but can be seen in Newman's book *Oswald and the CIA* on page 503. The nature of the forgery is this: the CIA took a genuine FBI transmittal slip dated "Nov 8 1963" and added to it the CIA registry number ("DBA-52355") of the 9/24/63 FBI. The cover sheet to the same document (NARA #104-10015-10046; Newman, *Oswald and the CIA*, 502) has a date stamp showing that it was received by CIA on October 3.

229 See Chapter 4.

230 Scott, *Deep Politics*, 206–18, 226–27, 288–90, etc. Gerald Patrick Hemming, an ex-Marine Soldier of fortune involved with anti-Castro Cubans,
has hinted that both Murchison and McLendon were present at a July
1963 meeting in the Dallas Petroleum Club, at which Hemming declined
an alleged proposal to assassinate President Kennedy (Twyman, *Bloody
Treason*, 699, 745). I feel duty-bound to transmit this story, but see no
good reason to believe it.

231 20 WH 39 (Ruby). The information about the McLendon family trip I
owe to Mary Ferrell, a close friend of some of McLendon's children.

232 For William Harvey, see the Rosselli-Meltzer connection noted above.
Angleton spoke at some length about Harvey-Rosselli contacts in his
depositions by the HSCA (p. 87). But John "Scelso" [Whitten], Chief
of the CIA's Western Hemisphere/Mexico Branch, also testified to the
HSCA about Angleton's "ties to organized crime," and specifically about
protection he supplied against RFK's investigation of the skim from Las
Vegas casinos (organized principally by Meltzer's patron Meyer Lansky).
See HSCA, Subcommittee Executive Session, May 16, 1978, Testimony of
John Scelso, NARA #180-10131-10330, 167–69.

233 Warren Report (henceforward WR), 22.

234 Warren Commission Hearings, Vol. V, pp. 12–14 (henceforth 5 WH
12–14). Presumably referring to members of his staff, Warren stated that
"the same people who would demand that we see everything of this kind
would also demand that they be entitled to see it, and if it is security
matters we can't let them see it. It has to go back to the FBI without their
scrutiny" (5 WH 13).

235 Scott, *Deep Politics II* (Ipswich, MA: Mary Ferrell Foundation Press,
2003), reprinted as *Oswald, Mexico, and Deep Politics* (New York: Skyhorse, 2013), 128, 90–91.

236 5 WH 122. Helms made at least one false statement under oath about
Oswald and the CIA: when he told the Warren Commission that no
one in the CIA "even contemplated" contact with Oswald (5 WH 121;
cf. House Select Committee on Assassinations (HSCA), Vol. 4, 210
(henceforth 4 AH 210); Newman, *Oswald and the CIA*, 478; 11 AH
58).

237 A second CIA file was held by the Office of Security (#351-164). A third
was what the HSCA called "a separate Oswald HT/LINGUAL file" (Newman, *Oswald and the CIA*, 285), HT/LINGUAL being the CIA's highly
secret mail opening program.

238 As will be seen, the Counterintelligence Operations officers I am referring

to are Jean Evans, William Potocki of CI/OPS, a [FNU] Hughes of CI/OPS/WH, a D. Lynch of SR/CI/P/OP, and perhaps above all William Hood of WH/COPS.

239 WR 22.

240 Peter Dale Scott, *Deep Politics and the Death of JFK* (Berkeley: University of California Press, 1998), 80–92.

241 Peter Dale Scott, *Deep Politics II*, 18. For the in-house terms "marked card" and "barium test," see e.g. Edward Jay Epstein, *Deception: The Invisible War between the KGB and the CIA* (New York: Simon and Schuster, 1989), 77.

242 Ann Egerter, HSCA interview of May 17, 1978; JFK Classified Document 014731; HSCA Report, 201 (henceforth AR 201) at footnote 40. Although Egerter denied inventing the name, she signed off on a previous document showing his name was Lee Harvey Oswald as recently as November 3, 1960 (NARA #1993.08.14.13:05:31:250056).

243 DIR 74673 of 10 Oct 1963.

244 DIR 74830 of 10 Oct 1963. See discussion in *Deep Politics II*, 26–28; John Newman, *Oswald and the CIA*, 392–405, 511–12.

245 Newman, *Oswald and the CIA*, 405, 511–12. Concerning the untrue sentence in the cable, she speculated, "Well, to me, it's indicative of a keen interest in Oswald, held very closely on a need-to-know basis."

246 John Newman, *Oswald and the CIA*, 327, 351, 394, 513, etc.; Scott, *Deep Politics*, 81–86, 245, 258–66; *Deep Politics II*, 111–12.

247 Cf. William Corson and Susan B. Trento, *Widows* (New York: Crown, 1989), 60.

248 Tim Weiner, David Johnston, and Neil A. Lewis, *Betrayal: The Story of Aldrich Ames, an American Spy* (New York: Random House, 1995), 85.

249 E.g. Newman, *Oswald and the CIA*, 28, where Newman refers to "a very sensitive Agency program, a program imperiled by Oswald's defection;" cf. pp. 34–35.

250 Under this third category one can imagine the molehunt either as the initial covert operation or as the response of others to it. I suggested this second alternative two years ago in my essay on the Lopez Report: see *Deep Politics II*, 18.

251 Birch D. O'Neal's name is on the first incoming State Department despatch on Oswald (Newman, *Oswald and the CIA*, 37). Ann Egerter opened the CIA's 201 file on Oswald, and helped draft the two October cables discussed below (Newman, *Oswald and the CIA*, 176–77, 399, 402). For the alias "Betty Eggeter", see NARA #104-10322-10043 and NARA #104-10015-10043.

252 O'Neal was initially given the post-assassination role of coordinating liaison with the FBI (Warren CD 49, p, 22); in mid-December this role was expanded (11 AH 476–78). O'Neal (as C/CI/SI) was specifically slotted as recipient of MEXI cables re Oswald from as early as MEXI 7069 of 26 Nov 1963 concerning Alvarado (NARA #104-10015-10366).

253 Philip Agee, *Inside the Company: CIA Diary* (Harmondsworth, England: Penguin, 1975), 320 (Diary entry of 2/8/64: "Bill Hood, who has had the newly-created job of Chief of Operations for the past year," cf. p. 610); CIA Cable DIR 74830 of 10/10/63; cf. Scott, *Deep Politics II*, 26–28, 31; Newman, *Oswald and the CIA*, 395–97, 403–05. Newman calls Hood "a WH division deputy" (Newman, 401); but I believe that in October the Deputy Division Chief was John Horton, and that Hood did not receive this promotion until some weeks after the assassination. On November 23 William Hood, WH/COPS (i.e. Chief of Operations) released a misleading cable that covered up the discovery in Dallas that the voice of the "Lee Oswald" on a Soviet Embassy intercept tape was not that of the Lee Harvey Oswald arrested in Dallas. (CIA Cable DIR 84888 of 11/23/63; NARA #104-10015-10015).

254 William Hood, *Mole* (New York: Norton, 1982; Washington: Brassey's, 1993). William Hood may also be the pseudonomic "L.N. Gallary" who authenticated the second CIA Oswald cable 74673 of October 10. If so, then Hood, like Egeter, Roll, and Roman, authenticated two conflicting cables about Oswald on the same day; and his role in the CIA's pre-assassination Oswald deception was greater than the single signature would suggest.

255 CIA Cable DIR 77978 of 10/24/63, NARA #104-10015-10049; Lewis B. Sckolnick (ed.), *Lee Harvey Oswald: CIA Pre-Assassination File* (Leverett, MA: Rector Press, 1993), 123. The six are T. Ward (originator); Hughes, Stephan Roll, Bernard Reichhardt (coordinating), Jane Roman (releasing), and "L.N. Gallary" (possibly William Hood, authenticating). See Appendix.

256 Weiner et al., *Betrayal*, 95.

257 Cf. William Corson and Susan B. Trento, *Widows*, 266–396;

258 American Embassy Moscow Cable 1304 to Secretary of State, October 31, 1959; 18 WH 105, 26 WH 126; Sckolnick, *Lee Harvey Oswald*, 1.

259 Amembassy Moscow Despatch 234 of November 2, 1959, p. 2; 18 WH 98; Sckolnick, *Lee Harvey Oswald*, 5; Newman, *Oswald and the CIA*, 5–6.

260 WR 683; AR 200. Newman noted that "there is not one reference to the U-2 in Donovan's [Oswald's Marine commander's] testimony to the Warren Commission, despite "the public knowledge of the 1960 U-2

shootdown" (Newman, *Oswald and the CIA*, 45). In like manner Robert Blakey's Chapter on "Lee Harvey Oswald: His Role Reconsidered," skips, deadpan, from 1955 to 1962, omitting all of Oswald's service overseas and subsequent defection as if it were irrelevant (G. Robert Blakey and Richard N. Billings, *The Plot to Kill the President* [New York: Times Books, 1981], 340–66). In a House Committee Staff Report, "Analysis of the Support Provided to the Warren Commission by the Central Intelligence Agency (11 AH 471–504), the CIA's initial silence about Oswald's U-2 exposure is not once mentioned. For Oswald's unit and the U-2, cf. e.g. Edward Jay Epstein, *Legend: The Secret World of Lee Harvey Oswald* (New York: Reader's Digest Press, 1978), 54–56, 279–80 (where Donovan reminisces about Oswald and the U-2); Warren CD 631.

261 The Warren Report devoted a full page (WR 693–94), augmented by two pages of another Appendix (WR 747–48), to Oswald's performance on October 31 in the U.S. Embassy. Not once was the offer of information mentioned.

262 CNO Cable 22257 of 4 Nov 59; reprinted in Newman, *Oswald and the CIA*, 446. A copy of this cable was sent to CIA, but was not initially filed in Oswald's 201. This is one of many signs that the CIA has not revealed all of its files on Oswald.

263 Newman, *Oswald and the CIA*, 6; citing Snyder interview with Scott Malone and John Newman, 9/1/93.

264 Richard E. Snyder, "The Soviet Sojourn of Citizen Oswald," *Washington Post* Magazine, April 1, 1979, 29; cited in Philip H. Melanson, *Spy Saga: Lee Harvey Oswald and U.S. Intelligence* (New York: Praeger, 1990), 166.

265 Norman Mailer, *Oswald's Tale: an American Mystery* (New York: Random House, 1995), 405; quoting a composite KGB source, "General Marov:" "He comes out of Botkin Hospital, visits his Embassy, and talks to the American official there in a loud clear voice as if he is also speaking to any instruments, theirs or ours, that might be implanted in the wall. . . . A normal man would never come to such an Embassy and say, 'Okay, I'll give my secrets to the Russians. . . . After this, no KGB man could accept his information. . . . This is an abnormality."

266 Quote from Newman, *Oswald and the CIA*, 42.

267 Oleg Nechiporenko, *Passport to Assassination: The Never-before-told Story of Lee Harvey Oswald by the KGB Colonel Who Knew Him* (New York: Carol Publishing Group, 1993), 39: "[If the KGB had known about Oswald and the U-2]," "more likely than not the KGB's attitude toward him would have been different. But all indications are that our intelligence was unaware of this. It is also clear that Oswald never volunteered such information in any

of his conversations with Soviet officials, but he did use it to blackmail the American embassy in his meeting there on October 31, 1959."

268 Norman Mailer, *Oswald's Tale*, 406. "Marov" suggests that Oswald was instead given programmed interviews by Soviet "journalists" and his Intourist hostess.

269 Newman, *Oswald and the CIA*, 38–39.

270 22 WH 77.

271 18 WH 161; see below.

272 Snyder was a CIA officer in 1949–50, with contact after that (NARA #104-10001-10138).

273 Amembassy Moscow Despatch 234 of November 2, 1959, p. 1; 18 WH 97; Sckolnick, *Lee Harvey Oswald*, 4.

274 WR 687, 688.

275 18 WH 162.

276 18 WH 105 (Moscow 1304 of 10/31/59); 18 WH 161 (passport). As we have seen, in the subsequent despatch (Amembassy Moscow 234) Snyder supplied the Davenport address correctly from a cable received at the Embassy for Oswald. However his failure to report the allotropic "Davanport" address in the passport is even more glaring (in a three-page single-space letter about the alleged defection) than in the cable.

277 Newman, *Oswald and the CIA*, 530 at note 19.

278 State Department Instruction No. A-173, April 13, 1961; 18 WH 136, 368; Sckolnick, *Lee Harvey Oswald*, 33.

279 Amembassy Despatch 29 of July 11, 1961; 18 WH 137, 378; Sckolnick, *Lee Harvey Oswald*, 37.

280 18 WH 140.

281 18 WH 370 (cf. 371–72); Sckolnick, *Lee Harvey Oswald*, 34 (cf. 35–36).

282 18 WH 369; State Department reference slip of 10/5/61 to Miss Geneva Shiflet, CIA Room GH0909.

283 Sckolnick, *Lee Harvey Oswald*, 33. There is at least one other allotropic variant in the retyped version. A reference to the "Embassy's Despatch No. 585 of February 28, 1961," has been retyped as the "Embassy's Dispatch [sic] No. 565 of February 26, 1961."

284 Distribution lists for Despatch 809 ("806") will be found at 18 WH 370 (for State) and Sckolnick, *Lee Harvey Oswald*, 34 (for CIA).

285 CIA SR/CI/P order card appended to 201 File Request for Oswald 201, NARA #104-10015-10002, 18 WH 369 (State Dept. routing slip). Lynch provided information directly to CI/SIG about "Marina Prusakova" in September 1961. NARA #1993.06.16.19:26:57:620000.

286 Routing and Record Sheet for XAAZ-9644 (Amemb Moscow Despatch

"#806"): "WP had originally asked me to pull together all refs on this man [Oswald]." Lynch's initials, "dl," can be seen in the upper left-hand corner of this document (NARA #104-10015-10040; Newman, 495). Both Potocki and Lynch later signed off on the routing sheet for the FBI Fain Report on Oswald of August 1962 (Newman, *Oswald and the CIA*, 499). Cf. Appendix.

287 18 WH 140; 18 WH 370. Only the first page of the File X copy was retyped as "806"; the two remaining pages are still marked "809." The same is true of the copy of the File X copy which reached the CIA as XAAZ 9644 (Sckolnick, *Lee Harvey Oswald*, 34–36).

288 Amembassy Moscow Despatch 29 of 7/11/61; 18 WH 137; cf. 18 WH 378.

289 State Department Instruction W-7, July 11, 1961; 18 WH 143, cf. 18 WH 374.

290 Warren Commission Exhibit (henceforth CE) 938 (18 WH 144); CE 947 (18 WH 174); emphasis added.

291 5 WH 358–60, 282–83; 18 WH 189; WR 755–56.

292 5 WH 359; cf. 375. In his badly mangled description of this anomaly, Posner (*Case Closed*, 68n) similarly refers to a "typing error;" and talks of an "original" and "carbon," where the typed strikeout of the relevant words accidentally missed. But both statements were separately typed by one or more typists as originals; both were signed by Snyder; and the typed strikeouts of the different (and opposing) phrases are of different lengths. There are additional discrepancies (18 WH 144, 174).

293 Warren CE 954, 18 WH 327; 5 WH 359. Compare the very inadequate answer by State to this question on May 8, 1964; CE 948, 18 WH 189. CE 947, the more acceptable version received on June 3, appears (unlike the earlier CE 938) to be a clumsy artefact, in which one part of the usual form is sloppily stapled on to another part (18 WH 173, 174). If CE 947 is in fact a post-assassination forgery, questions about it should be again addressed to Richard Snyder, who apparently signed it.

294 U.S. Cong., Senate, Committee on the Judiciary, Senate Internal Security Subcommittee, *State Department Security 1963–65, Hearing*, p. 429 (Hearing of April 4, 1963).

295 Marguerite Oswald to Secret Service, 11/25/63, 16 WH 728–29 (emphasis added): cf. Newman, *Oswald and the CIA*, 135.

296 Warren Commission CD 1115; State Department File XIII-25.

297 16 WH 594–95, emphasis added.

298 Fain Report of 5/12/60, pp. 1, 3; 17 WH 700, 702. In the Fain Report of 7/3/61 Oswald's father's name is again given as "Edward Lee Oswald" (17

WH 707, 709). In the 7/12/62 Fain Report the father's name is given as "Robert Edward Oswald" (17 WH 731).

299 Fain Report of 7/10/62, p. 14; 17 WH 731.

300 1111 Herring Ave., Waco (17 WH 702, 708, 712); 1612 Hurley, Fort Worth (17 WH 708); 4936 Collingwood (sic), Fort Worth (17 WH 708, 710, 714); 1808 Eagle St., #3, Vernon (17 WH 721). For Marguerite's actual addresses in this period, cf. e.g. 16 WH 629, 631, 531, 615, 619. There can be a defense prepared for the viability of the Waco address on April 26, 1960 (cf. 25 WH 86). But unambiguously Marguerite wrote to Prof. Casparis of Albert Schweitzer College on April 6, giving the address of 1410 Hurley St., Fort Worth (16 WH 629); a reply to this address was not forwarded (16 WH 631); and Marguerite's second letter of June 6 noted no change of address (16 WH 632), yet received a reply (16 WH 636). For more on this mystery, cf. the discussion below of Velma Marlin at 1410 Hurley.

301 Fain Report of 7/10/62, p. 14; 17 WH 731.

302 16 WH 614–45 (Crowell). On July 12, 1962, the day of his report, Fain saw Marina Oswald's INS file (17 WH 733).

303 23 WH 743; cf. WR 715. The Warren Report concluded that the younger Oswalds moved to West Seventh "sometime in July" (WR 715). For conflicting reports, see 16 WH 454, 22 WH 156, 26 WH 28.

304 Newman, *Oswald and the CIA*, 150; cf. 159. Newman refers here to "David Murphy's Soviet Russia division." My understanding is that at the time the Soviet Russia Division Chief was John Maury, with Murphy succeeding him in 1962. Newman reprints the Routing Sheet for the Fain Report at p. 493.

305 Newman, *Oswald and the CIA*, 88, quoting Tom Mangold, *Cold Warrior*, 250.

306 "List of American Defectors;" attachment to letter of 21 Nov 1960 from Richard Bissell, DDP/CIA, to Hugh S. Cumming, Jr., State Department, NARA #104-10087-10040; Newman, *Oswald and the CIA*, 461; Sckolnick, *Lee Harvey Oswald*, 25–31.

307 Letter of October 25, 1960, from Hugh Cumming of State to Richard Bissell, DDP/CIA, NARA #104-10425-10098; Sckolnick, *Lee Harvey Oswald*, 19.

308 Newman, *Oswald and the CIA*, 171–72.

309 Abba Schwartz, *The Open Society* (New York: W. Morrow, 1968), 181; cf. 187.

310 *Chicago Tribune*, November 7, 1963; Peter Dale Scott, *Crime and Cover-Up: The CIA, the Mafia, and the Dallas-Watergate Connection* (Santa Barbara, CA: Open Archive Press, 1993), 8–9.

311 Newman, *Oswald and the CIA*, 152.

312 Newman, *Oswald and the CIA*, e.g. 57, 394–396 (CIA), 140 (State), 152–55, 209–10 (FBI).

313 Newman, *Oswald and the CIA*, 87.

314 17 WH 705. Oswald on his return told Fain "he did not take the birth certificate to Russia. He thinks it is packed in a trunk in his mother's home" (17 WH 738; cf. 729).

315 FBI HQ 105-82555-third after -6; SAC New York to DIR, 5/23/60; reprinted in Newman, *Oswald and the CIA*, 457.

316 Letter of June 3, 1960, from John Edgar Hoover, Director, FBI to Office of Security, Department of State; quoted in Newman, *Oswald and the CIA*, 144. A copy of the letter was sent to the Director of Naval Intelligence. A xerox copy of the letter was later sent to the CIA as well, but not until 1975.

317 FBI Fain Report of 5/12/60, 7; 17 WH 706.

318 26 WH 128–30. Clearly some game was being played, and the FBI was in on it. In response to a request for Oswald's fingerprints, the FBI replied "Unavailable—outside the United States" (26 WH 128). This was not true; the FBI had possessed Oswald's fingerprints since October 1956, shortly after they had been taken by the Marines (17 WH 289, cf. 17 WH 804). Furthermore, the card noted Oswald's measured height (5'8") and weight (135 pounds) when he was fingerprinted in 1956.

319 17 WH 289; cf. 19 WH 615, 656.

320 19 WH 584, 595.

321 22 WH 828.

322 17 WH 308.

323 WR 5, 144; 21 WH 392: "The wanted person in this is a slender white male about thirty five feet ten, one sixty five;" cf. 23 WH 845: "suspect white male, 30, slender build, 5 feet 10 inches, 165 pounds." Cf. Chapter 6.

324 Warren Commission CD 5.13, reprinted in Josiah Thompson, *Six Seconds in Dallas* (New York: B. Geis Associates, 1968), 300.

325 Warren Commission CD 205.16; cf. WR 63, 3 WH 144.

326 WR 5, 145. For further discussion of the unreliability of Brennan's alleged sighting of Oswald, see Bill Simpich, *State Secret*, Chapter 6, https://www.maryferrell.org/mffweb/archive/viewer/showDoc.do?mode=searchResult&docId=146596.

327 Memorandum for the file of 2 November 1959 from J.M. Barron, Op-921D1; in FBI HQ Oswald file, 105-82555-2E. Cf. Newman, *Oswald and the CIA*, 21. Question: was this J.M. Barron of ONI the same as the John Barron who was in ONI in the 1950s, was officially released from the

Navy in 1957, and went on to write a book on the KGB with CIA assistance? The second John Barron was a friend of Mexico CIA Station Chief Win Scott, and had extended conversations with Scott in Mexico City immediately before Scott's mysterious death in April 1971 (Dick Russell, *The Man Who Knew Too Much* [New York: Carroll & Graf Publishers, 2003], 465).

328 Fain Report of 7/3/61, pp. 2, 4, 8, 9; circulated in CIA as DBF 82181 [original CIA copy now missing]; 17 WH 708, 710, 714, 715 [FBI copy]; Sckolnick, *Lee Harvey Oswald*, 42, 44, 48, 49 [CIA duplicate copy]. Newman's handling of the "Collinwood" allotropes is garbled. According to Newman, "Handwriting, now faint, on [an FBI HQ memo of 11/2/59] appears to say '4936 Collinswood St. Fort Worth, Texas,' information not available at the FBI (at that time) except from the Barron ONI memo or from Marine headquarters by telephone" (Newman, *Oswald and the CIA*, 21). This is wrong on two counts: the handwritten address (along with the words "U.S.S.R. Finland") is unambiguously "4936 Collinwood;" just as unambiguously all the handwritten information is taken from Snyder's Cable 1304 of October 31, 1959, which had already reached the FBI.

329 Marine Headquarters Cable of 8 March 1960 to Commander, Marine Air Training Command (19 WH 719, ONI-121). Signed "A. Larson by direction." Reprinted in Newman, *Oswald and the CIA*, 452.

330 Letter of July 25, 1963, from Navy Discharge Review Board to Lee Harvey Oswald, with enclosure of Discharge Certificate: "The service record of petitioner shows that he was discharged as unfit for good and sufficient reasons. This was based on reliable information that he had renounced his U.S. citizenship with the intentions of becoming a permanent citizen of the Union of Soviet Socialist Republics." This important document was not included in the Navy Discharge Review documents published by the Warren Commission, but the same language will be found at 19 WH 690.

331 16 WH 596, 18 WH 121–23, etc. Marguerite wrote again to the State Department on June 18 (16 WH 597), and to Wright in July (18 WH 261), thickening the files still further.

332 19 WH 690.

333 Memo of May 4, 1962, from Robert D. Johnson (Passport Office) to William O. Boswell, (Security Office); 21 WH 403. Cf. Passport Office Memo of 12/28/61; 18 WH 396.

334 18 WH 384; cf. 18 WH 383. It was reportedly for such unauthorized leaks that Otto Otepka of the Security Office, who handled the Oswald file, was fired on November 5, 1963 (*New York Times*, 11/6.63; *Chicago Tribune*, 11/7/63; Scott, *Crime and Cover-Up*, 8–9).

335 It is not clear whether or not the two contradictory Oswald passport renewal applications, both prepared by Embassy typists and signed by Snyder, contributed to this confusion. Cf. WR 756.

336 Secret Service Interview, 16 WH 735 (Captain); Warren Commission Testimony, 1 WH 220 ("letter").

337 19 WH 715; 16 WH 590. On November 22, at about six p.m., the journalist Seth Kantor at the Dallas Police Station transcribed this address phonetically into his notebook, having apparently obtained it from the CIA journalist asset Hal Hendrix (22 WH 362; cf. Summers, *Conspiracy* (1981), 134; Kantor, 378).

338 19 WH 674. As we have seen, his last address on file was 3124 West 5th St., Fort Worth.

339 According to FBI reports, Marguerite told both Fain and her insurance company that on April 26, 1960, the date of the Marine Corps letter, she was working and living in Waco, Texas (17 WH 702; 25 WH 86). These reports, especially the latter, deserve to be read with some suspicion; the dates and the addresses correlate neatly with each other, much less so with other evidence. For example, her insurance company reportedly received the address of 1111 Herring Ave., Waco on April 26, 1960 (25 WH 86). This was two days before Marguerite allegedly gave the same address to John Fain in his interview with her (17 WH 702). April 26, 1960 is also the day of a letter from Albert Schweitzer College addressed to Marguerite at "1410 Hurley, Fort Worth" (16 WH 631), and of a Marine letter addressed to Lee at "3613 Harley, Fort Worth" (16 WH 590).

340 Fain memo of 5/12/60, administrative "Cover Page," B; HSCA copy of Administrative Folder Q10 for Oswald FBI File, NARA #124-10369-10068. p. 35; cf. 44.

341 16 WH 597, 629 (letters), 631 (unforwarded reply).

342 1 WH 322; cf. 26 WH 42–43. Text of Herter cable at 26 WH 89. As far as I know, we do not have the text of the cable sent to Lee, which was read inside the U.S. Embassy but apparently not recorded. Thus we have no way of knowing if it was allotropic. Robert does not mention the two cables in his account of meeting the reporter: see Robert L. Oswald, *Lee: A Portrait of Lee Harvey Oswald* (New York: Coward-McCann, 1967), 98–99.

343 26 WH 42.

344 FBI HQ Oswald file, serial -6B.

345 Warren Commission CD 1114, X-67.

346 Consider the following burst of synchronous events. On March 6 and 7 Marguerite, after speaking to Fain, writes her mutually contradictory

letters to Congressman Wright and Secretary Herter. On March 8 Marine Intelligence tells the Marine Air Training Command to begin processing Oswald for discharge: "Arrangements being made with a federal invest agency to furnish you with rpt which relates to PFC Lee Harvey Oswald." On the same day L.E. Cole of OSI reviews Oswald's Passport file at the State Department. On March 9 the FBI in New York instructs FBI Dallas to conduct interviews to establish reasons for Marguerite's attempted transmittal of funds. (which leads to the Fain report used to justify Oswald's discharge).

347 Newman, *Oswald and the CIA*, 87; citing Mark Riebling, *Wedge: The Secret War Between the FBI and CIA* (New York: A.A. Knopf, 1994), 155.

348 1 WH 137.

349 Biographic data on Amon Carter, Sr., from *National Cyclopedia*, XLIII, 486–87.

350 Scott, *Deep Politics*, 245; *The Dallas Conspiracy* (unpublished manuscript, ca. 1974), III-2, 22. Jerry Rose has discovered that in the 1957 Fort Worth street directory, Marguerite Oswald was listed with two addresses, 4936 Collinwood and 3201 McLean. The crisscross for 3201 McLean listed a John A. Jones (wife Alma), mechanic for Convair. This interesting lead can still hopefully be researched by someone in the Fort Worth area.

351 CIA Memo of 29 January 1964, NARA #104-10109-10432. OSI participated in this investigation (CIA Oswald 201 File, Misc Docs, Set 8, p. 379).

352 *National Cyclopedia*, 486.

353 17 WH 777.

354 9 WH 225–27.

355 Revill to Bob Dorff, 10/2/95; cf. 5 WH 57; *Deep Politics II*, 87.

356 FBI airtel November 22, 1963; FBI HQ 105-82555-6th no. 50; Scott, *Deep Politics II*, 141.

357 Scott, *Deep Politics II*, 70–74.

358 David C. Martin, *Wilderness of Mirrors* (New York: Harper & Row, 1980), 94.

359 Tom Mangold, *Cold Warrior: James Jesus Angleton: The CIA's Master Spy Hunter* (New York: Simon & Schuster, 1991), 414. Other suspects who also handled the Oswald file were Tennant "Pete" Bagley, C/SR/CI, and possibly Paul Garbler, C/SR/10, and Ed Juchniewicz.

360 Letter from DDP, CIA to Dir FBI, Attn Papich, 25 November 1963, NARA #104-10004-10257. The other was a Hughes of CI/OPS/WH (Counterintelligence/ Operations/ Western Hemisphere).

361 Newman, *Oswald and the CIA*, 37.

362 Warren CD 49, 22; Scott, *Crime and Cover-Up*, 12; Paul Hoch in Peter Dale Scott, Paul L. Hoch, and Russell Stetler (eds.), *The Assassinations: Dallas and Beyond: A Guide to Cover-Ups and Investigations* (New York: Random House, 1976), 478; cf. Scott, *Deep Politics II*, 18.

363 DIR 74673, 74830 of 10/10/63, with differing descriptions of Oswald (NARA #104-10015-10052, #104-10015-10048); Sckolnick, *Lee Harvey Oswald*, 116–20). Cf. Appendix.

364 Tom Mangold, *Cold Warrior*, 83–84; cf. Scott, *Deep Politics*, 64.

365 Tom Mangold, *Cold Warrior*, 246.

366 Mark Riebling, *Wedge*, 232; cf. Scott, *Deep Politics*, 64.

367 "Precipitously" is not too strong a word. Oswald was transferred out of his unit for discharge on September 3, 1959 (26 WH 711, 19 WH 658, WR 689). Officially this was in order to support his mother, who had been "unable to work because some boxes [of candy] fell on my face" (19 WH 740). In support of Marguerite's hardship claim, the Marine file contains a letter from Dr. Rex Z. Howard, apparently an oto-laryngologist, dated September 3, and another letter from Dr. Rex J. Howard, an orthopaedist, dated September 4 (19 736–37). The first letter states, deadpan, "I have been treating Mrs. Marguerite Oswald since Sept. 5 [sic], 1959, for Acute Nasopharyngitis." Meanwhile a Texas Industrial Accident Board award of August 4, 1959, given to the Warren Commission but not published by it, had already determined that Marguerite had suffered "no loss of wage earning capacity" from the falling candy boxes.

368 Martin, *Wilderness of Mirrors*, 94. A less likely possibility is that Oswald arrived in Moscow later than we have been officially told. Can we imagine that in fact he arrived a few days later than October 16, in time for his Embassy performance on October 31? The evidence for the October 16 arrival date is thin, and some of it questionable. "Oswald's Historic Diary" begins unambiguously "Oct. 16. Arrive from Helsinki by train" (16 WH 102). But the so-called "Historic Diary" is actually a document Oswald wrote much later, and it is demonstrably wrong with respect to many facts and dates. Harder to refute is Oswald's passport, unambiguously stamped with the date of October 15 for his exit from Finland and entry into the Soviet Union (18 WH 163).

369 Peter Dale Scott, "From Dallas to Watergate," in Scott, Hoch, and Stetler, *The Assassinations*, 366.

370 Mark Riebling, *Wedge*, 162; cf. Burton Hersh, *The Old Boys: The American Elite and the Origins of the CIA* (New York: Scribner's, 1992), 427. The first known CIA documents discussing the assassination of Castro date from December 1959 (Church Committee, *Assassination Report*, 92–93).

371 Burton Hersh, *The Old Boys*, 243, 427–28.

372 *Washington Post*, November 1, 1959 (reprinted in Sckolnick, *Lee Harvey Oswald*, 2; cf. Newman, 18): "[Oswald's] sister-in-law said, 'He said he wanted to travel a lot and talked about going to Cuba.'" The first Fain Report of May 1960 attributed the same general thought to Marguerite: "She stated he had mentioned something about his desire to travel and said something about the fact that he might go to Cuba" (17 WH 703; cf. 17 WH 727). Cuba was the first country mentioned on Oswald's passport application (22 WH 78). The remark attributed by UPI to Robert Oswald's wife Vada Oswald was probably written down by the *Fort Worth Star Telegram* reporter who visited the Robert Oswalds on October 31, 1959.

373 Chief, JMWAVE (Theodore Shackley) to Chief, Special Affairs Staff (Desmond FitzGerald); Dispatch #UFGA-13059 of 13 Dec 63 with attachment, NARA #104-10018-10074.

374 Howard Hunt Fitness Report, 1963–64, NARA #104-10138-10314. The same Report identifies Hunt as in charge of Projects WUHUSTLER and WUBONBON, not hitherto identified.

375 Memo of 9/1/64 to Director, CIA, from J. Edgar Hoover, NARA #124-10369-10063, 51–52.

376 Memorandum of September 30, 1964, from J.H. Gale to Associate FBI Director Clyde Tolson.

377 For identification of Gestetner, see Russell Holmes memo of 17 March 1977, NARA #104-10419-10215.

378 Ibid.

379 CNO Message 22257 of November 4, 1959, to ALUSNA Moscow; Oswald ONI file, NARA #1993.06.18.16:19:23:960000; reprinted in John Newman, *Oswald and the CIA*, (New York: Carroll & Graf, 1995), 446; cf. 14–15.

380 The Warren Commission published the personnel file as the "U.S. Marine Corps record on Lee Harvey Oswald" (19 WH xviii).

381 As a result the record contains a number of duplicate documents (e.g. 19 WH 669 [701], 673 [716], 675 [715], etc.), while it does not contain relevant unclassified Marine records available from the ONI file and elsewhere. Compare the footnote reference below to "Lt. Col. Bill Brewer [of Marine HQ G-2] compiling the Oswald military file for the use of the Warren Commission" (11 AH 542).

382 First Marine Air Wing; Marine Corps Air Station, El Toro; Marine Air Training Command, Glenview. In all, separate files containing Oswald data appear to have been kept by the First Marine Air Wing (1st MAW, 19 WH 683), the Third Marine Air Wing (3rd MAW, 19 WH 724), Marine

Corps Air Station, El Toro (MCAS, 19 WH 724), Marine Air Corps Squadron Nine (MACS-9, 19 WH 724) Marine Wing Headquarters Group (MWHG, 19 WH 724), the Marine Air Reserve Training Command (MARTC, 19 WH 703, etc.), and Commander Marine Corps (CMC), Code CDB (19 WH 721), Code DGK (19 WH 724), Code DK or DKE (19 WH 700; cf. below), Code DMB (19 WH 670). We know now that the so-called Oswald 201 file in CIA, as presented to the Warren Commission, was in fact a post-assassination reconstruction from at least four files: cf. Newman, *Oswald and the CIA,* passim.

383 Letter of 20 July 1960 to Commander, Marine Air Reserve Training, 19 WH 703.

384 In this paper I am deeply indebted to the archival research and analysis of Paul Hoch, as well as to additional research by Larry Haapanen and Mark Allen.

385 The four sources using "Harvey Lee Oswald" are: DIO, 9th Naval District, DIO, 8th Naval District, ONI (NAVCINTSUPPCEN.3) and Army 112th Military Intelligence Group (see Peter Dale Scott, *Deep Politics II,* 144). In response to the request for serial 02049-E, the NIS supplied a record with a serial that was contiguous but slightly different: "DIO, 9th ND confidential report serial 02048-E of 8 Jun 60." The second document, accurately supplied, carried a title different from the first: "Subj: OSWALD, Harvey Lee." We are left to wonder whether serial 02049-E of 8 Jun 60 concerned Harvey Lee Oswald as well.

386 Report in Spanish of November 26, 1963 transmitted by JKB (George Munro) to Mexico City CIA Station "Re: Lee Harvey Oswald and Silvia Tirado de Duran," NARA #104-10068-10084, p. 9. Cf. Chapter 2.

387 For a discussion and incomplete list, see Peter Dale Scott, *Deep Politics II,* 80, 85–89, 118–19, 142–49. The Assassinations Records Review Board acknowledged this phenomenon in their Report (p. 81): "The Mexico City Legal Attache (Legat) opened a file on Lee Harvey Oswald (195-3702) following Oswald's visit to Mexico City. Some of the documents in the Legat's file contain notations for routing records to a file numbered 105–2137, and were captioned "Harvey Lee Oswald." One researcher [i.e. myself] conjectured that this file would predate the Lee Harvey Oswald file, 105–3702, and might lead the Review Board to other FBI documents on Lee Harvey Oswald. In response to the Review Board's request, the FBI searched its Legat's files for a file numbered 105–2137, and captioned "Harvey Lee Oswald," but it did not find such a file."

388 NARA #1993.08.06.17:11:46:400059 p. 14.

389 Scott, *Deep Politics II,* especially pp. 118–19.

390 Memo of 23(?) Nov 63 from ONI Special Agent C.J. Roach, Item 256 in the Oswald ONI file obtained by Paul Hoch (henceforth ONI-256). I have not established how McNaughton was aware of these documents, to which I can find no reference in our version of Oswald's ONI file.

391 Memo of February 25, 1964, from Assistant General Counsel Frank Bartimo for the Director of Naval Intelligence (ONI-299); on line at http://jfk.hood.edu/Collection/Weisberg%20Subject%20Index%20 Files/O%20Disk/Oswald%20Lee%20Harvey%20DoD%20Records/ Item%2004.pdf.

392 In a letter of March 16, 1964 to Counsel J. Lee Rankin of the Warren Commission, Bartimo advised "that all known materials concerning Lee Harvey Oswald under the jurisdiction of the Department of Defense" had already "been furnished to the Commission." Robert McNamara later signed a sworn affidavit certifying that "Lee Harvey Oswald was never an informant or agent of any intelligence agency under the jurisdiction of the Department of Defense" (26 WH 586, 820).

393 CNO [Chief of Naval Operations] Message 22257 of 4 Nov 59 to ALUSNA [Naval Attaché] Moscow; reprinted in Newman, *Oswald and the CIA*, 446; cf. 14–15. Copies of this cable were sent to Air Force and Army Intelligence, whose Headquarters Intelligence files then presumably contained these Oswald records. At least one cable on Oswald from the 112th MIG, Army Intelligence, was once in the Oswald ONI file (cf. below at fn. 77).

394 CIA Cable DIR 74673 of 10/10/63, ONI copy (NARA #104-10010-10103). According to a later NIS report, "The ONI file on Oswald contained a copy of a CNO message with a date/time group of 102012Z October 1963 which readdressed CIA teletype number 74673" (NIS Memo for the General Counsel of the Navy NIS-02F/gdw 5400 Ser U5076 1 May 1978, p. 2). This date/time group 102012Z October 1963 is also that for the transmission of 74673 from CIA (NARA #104-10015-10052). Cf. Naval Attaché Moscow cable 2090 of 3 Nov 59 to CNO; reprinted in Newman, 444. Both cables are slugged "92. . . . ACT"

395 Undated letter from John T. McNaughton (signed by Frank Bartimo). I shall refer in future to the later version of this file, now in the National Archives, as the "file on Oswald," or as "Oswald's ONI file," even though it is clearly a post-assassination artifact, containing for example copies of ONI documents drawn from State Department sources and supplied to the Warren Commission. I shall be citing the originally released "ONI file" obtained and paginated by researcher Paul L. Hoch, which I have not been able to collate with the records cited by John Newman as residing

in "ONI/NIS files NARA, box 1." (Newman actually reproduces copies of important documents from the Hoch-annotated file, e.g. p. 452).

396 Memo to file of 22 November 1963 from Patrick D. Molinari, Duty Officer NAVCINTSUPPCEN (ONI-261, emphasis added). Something analogous may have happened at Marine HQ G-2 as well. A House Select Committee on Assassinations (HSCA) staff report says that the HSCA "contacted Lt. Col. Bill Brewer of the Intelligence Division of Marine Corps Headquarters on August 1, 1977. Brewer had been in charge of *compiling the Oswald military file* [sic, emphasis added] for the use of the Warren Commission" (11 AH 542). This report adds ambiguously that according to Brewer, "his records check had only included local records within the individual commands where Oswald had served and did not include records that were classified secret or top secret" (ibid.). On this and other related matters, see the excellent analysis by Paul Hoch in "Echoes of Conspiracy," 10:2, http://jfkcountercoup.blogspot.com/2011/10/irregularities-relating-to-naval.html.

397 Watch, 23 Nov 1963, USNAVCINTSUPPCEN (ONI-259: "file on Oswald"); Memo to file of 23 Nov.1963 from M. Sherman Bliss, ONI (ONI-254: "General Carroll"); Memo of 23? Nov '63 from Special Agent C.J. Roach to Captain [Robert P.] Jackson[, Jr., Assistant DNI for Security, Op 921] (ONI-256: "Dutton"). One of the topics raised at the all-night emergency meeting may have been the Senate Internal Security Committee and its Counsel, Julien Sourwine (see below). For more on this emergency meeting, see Jerry Rose, "The Feds Spring Into Action," *Fourth Decade*, May 1996, 12; Jerry Rose, "Disinformation Please: J.G. Sourwine in Action," *Fourth Decade*, November 1994, 4.

398 File note, undated [from Capt. Jack O. Johnson, Executive Officer to Asst. DNI for Security] (ONI-266).

399 Note to file [re 23 Nov 1963] (ONI-263).

400 Several pages were quietly withheld from the 1967 ONI file release to Paul Hoch; see discussion by Paul Hoch in "Echoes of Conspiracy," 10:2, http://jfkcountercoup.blogspot.com/2011/10/irregularities-relating-to-naval.html. As stated above, I have not been able to establish what documents are still missing in the current NARA version of this file.

401 ONI-256, Memo of 23? Nov '63 from Special Agent C.J. Roach to Captain [Robert P.] Jackson[, Jr., Assistant DNI for Security, Op 921]. In addition to the two DIO 9th Naval District Records, discussed above, McNaughton requested to see "CNO Ser 015422P92 of 4 Aug 1960" (which, as we shall see below, supplied the "basis" for Oswald's "discharge" from the Marine Reserve). References to the two DIO 9th Naval District records

can no longer be found in the Paul Hoch copy of the Oswald ONI file. Conversely, CNO Ser 015422P92 of 4 Aug 1960 is now *in* the Archives ONI "file on Oswald" (ONI-98).

402 Ibid. The transmitter of this message was CNO Naval Aide Captain Elmo Zumwalt, who seven years later became Nixon's CNO. For the record, each of the two Ninth DIO serials contained a reference to a document missing from the Paul Hoch ONI file.

403 James Carroll, *An American Requiem: God, My Father, and the War that Came between Us* (Boston: Houghton Mifflin 1996).

404 Warren CD 324, p. 3. Apparently the Navy Discharge Review Board did not know that the letter of 4 Aug 1960 had been shown by ONI to Marine G-2, on condition of its swift return (ONI-98).

405 Letter of Alton H. Quanbeck to Thomas K. Latimer, Office of Secretary of Defense, December 3, 1975, 4; forwarded on December 8, 1975, to John Marsh; John Marsh-Richard Cheney Files, NARA #1178-10004-10110, https://www.maryferrell.org/mffweb/archive/viewer/showDoc.do?docId=32065&relPageId=3. For more on Rumsfeld and Cheney, see Chapter 7.

406 Peter Dale Scott, *The Road to 9/11: Wealth, Empire, and the Future of America* (Berkeley: University of California Press, 2007), 52–53.

407 Oswald's personnel file confirms that it was a J. Twitchell, Head Discipline Branch, Personnel Department, who on August 17, 1960 recommended Oswald for discharge (17 WH 699). However this same document (Code DMB) makes it clear that his "basis of recommendation" was an "OP-921D/ck serial 015422P2 of 4 Aug 60," which ONI had loaned to Marine G-2 (Code DK). It is clear that G-2 (Code DK, also coordinating with ONI) was involved in Oswald's discharge at a higher level than the Discipline Branch (Code DMB). It was a Code DK Speedletter that first directed that Oswald be processed for discharge, and the Code DK branch was the final recipient of Oswald's discharge order (17 WH 669).

408 The personnel file shows a continued exchange of correspondence on Oswald with the Headquarters of the U.S. Marine Corps in Washington, under at least five codes (CDB, CDC, DGK, DK or DKE, DMB), each representing a different HQ branch. Although the significant orders came down from HQ in Washington, it would appear that only one or two Washington file copies of these communications are contained in Folsom's official record. One may be the DK-MPV Speedletter of 8 Mar 60, directing that Oswald be processed for discharge (19 WH 719).

409 ONI Messages to ACSI G-2 of 4 Feb 1960 (ONI-122), 4 Aug 60 (ONI-98),

6 Mar 62 (ONI-73); cf. memo of 8 Mar 62 (ONI-68). In general, but not always, it would appear that information received about Oswald at ONI was transmitted to G-2 by OP921D (ONI Investigations; cf. ONI-98), while outgoing Oswald communications were transmitted by Op921E2 (Counterintelligence Programs; cf. ONI-122, ONI-73). The absence of a single file on Oswald might suggest that Oswald was not simply a subject for external investigation, so much as someone with a special relationship to ONI itself.

410 17 WH 719; cf. ONI-121.

411 ONI-98; forwarded to Col. C.E. Dobson of Room 2117, Arlington Annex. This was the address of Marine G-2 (ONI-122). Cf. 17 WH 699 ("basis").

412 Moscow Embassy Cable 1304 of October 31, 1939, 18 WH 105. Compare the Naval Attache's more innocuous report in Cable No. 2090 of 3 November 59: "Oswald stated he . . . has offered to furnish Soviets info he possesses *on US radar*" (reprinted in Newman, *Oswald and the CIA*, 444; emphasis added). See discussion in Newman, 28–46; also Chapter 2.

413 Warren Commission CD 978, 23 WH 795–96; cf. 19 WH 665. Marine G-2 is not identified as the source, except by the code "DK-atv."

414 AR 219; citing 19 WH 665, 23 WH 795–96. See discussion by Hoch, 10 EOC 2.

415 22 WH 77–79 (application, affidavit). See Ray and Mary La Fontaine, *Oswald Talked* (Gretna, LA: Pelican Publishing Company, 1996), 84–85. Researchers should try to obtain an unclassified but referred Marine Corps communication to the State Department of 4 September 1959, which it can locate and review from the State Department copy (NARA #119-10004-10095; State Dept. Copy: Status—Unclassified but referred, 9/24/93). This is possibly Lt. A.G. Ayers' affidavit of the same day (22 WH 79), but apparently it was still unreleased as of 2008.

416 Other missing Marine HQ records suggest that Marine HQ may have had a hand in Oswald's career from as early as 1958. Cf. the reference to an HQ msg 281745Z of 28 Apr 1958 (19 WH 724); note that Oswald's first court martial conviction was ordered executed 29 Apr 1958 (19 WH 663).

417 Oswald ONI file, Item ONI-68, Office memo of 8 Mar 62 from Mr. Jerome Vacek, HQMC (DK), to Mr. Pross Palmer of ONI Counterintelligence (OP-921E). Cf. ONI-72, letter of William Abbott of Op-921E transmitting a copy of ONI-68 to the Office of Security in the State Department, where it was marked, "To SY/E [Office of Security/Evaluations] Otto Otepka" (26 WH 47; cf. 26 WH 46).

418 ONI-69, published at 26 WH 46.

419 Oswald ONI file, Item ONI-68, Office memo of 8 Mar 62 from Mr. Jerome Vacek, HQMC (DK), to Mr. Pross Palmer of ONI Counterintelligence (OP-921E), emphasis added.

420 ONI-50, letter of May 10, 1962 from John Noonan of State to DNI; cf. Warren Commission CD 1114, item XI-7.

421 Annotations to ONI-136, ALUSNA Moscow Cable 5029 of 13 November 1959. The source of the misinformation was apparently V. Buckler of State Passport Office (PT/LL) to Lt. J.G. Evans of ONI OP-921E2 (Counterintelligence Programs): cf. ONI-137, State Dept. buckslip dated 11/13/59.

422 Warren CD 1114, Item X-71(2), supplying the text of an Embassy note. It is hard to imagine how ONI could have believed that an airgram, mailed on November 7 (and in fact only received on November 13), could have been destroyed by November 13.

423 Letter of 6/3/60 from John Edgar Hoover, Director of FBI, to Office of Security, Department of State (ONI-100); Confidential memo of 3/19/62 from William Abbott, Naval Counterintelligence, Office of CNO, to William Boswell, Dir., Office of Security, Department of State (ONI-60, forwarding attachment to Vacek's request of 3/8/60; 26 WH 46; cf. memo of 3/23/62, 26 WH 45); Letter of 4/26/62 from William Abbott, Naval Counterintelligence, Office of CNO, to William Boswell, Dir., Office of Security, Department of State (ONI-53). The last letter cites a record now missing from the Paul Hoch copy of Oswald's ONI file.

424 Letter of 6/3/60 from John Edgar Hoover, Director of FBI, to Office of Security, Department of State (ONI-100). Consider also the unfulfilled requests for information from J. Edgar Hoover on February 27, 1961, and from Emery J. Adams of the State Security Office on March 2, 1961 (Newman, *Oswald and the CIA*, 213–14). As if he had seen military intelligence references to "Harvey Lee Oswald," Adams asked other branches of State to "advise if the FBI is receiving info about Harvey on a continuing basis."

425 16 WH 597; cf. 16 WH 594. On July 16, Marguerite wrote again, astutely raising a potentially embarrassing question: In what city had her son's passport been issued? (16 WH 600). The State Department replied, correctly, "Los Angeles" (16 WH 601). Originally Richard Snyder of the Moscow Embassy had misreported this as "San Francisco" (18 WH 97; cf. above. Marguerite and the State Department continued to correspond vigorously until Oswald's return (16 WH 603–20).

426 16 WH 599 (response of July 7 1960 to Marguerite Oswald); Confidential memo of July 11, 1960, from D.E. Boster of Soviet Division to Emery J. Adams of Security Office (for Hoover).

427 WR 748.

428 For example, the State Department advised the Chiefs of ONI and Marine G-2 on May 10, 1962, that "The Passport Office, with jurisdiction in this matter, has advised . . . that Mr. Oswald . . . has not expatriated himself" (ONI-50). Nevertheless the Navy upheld Oswald's discharge in 1963, finding "proper" an earlier determination "that he had renounced his U.S. citizenship" (19 WH 690).

429 See below.

430 See Chapter 3.

431 ONI-122, letter of 4 Feb 60, transmitting the ONI Confidential case history file on Oswald.

432 See ONI-98, referring to telecon of 2 Aug 60 between MSgt Emerson of G-2 USMC and [Prosser] Parker of ONI; ONI-73, referring to telecon of 5 Mar 62 between Lt. j.g. [P.C.] LeSourd of ONI and Major [G.W.] Houck of G-2 USMC; ONI-31, referring to telecon of 7/20/62 between [P.C.] LeSourd of ONI and Major [G.W.] Houck of G-2 USMC.

433 For some reason the HSCA Committee, after requesting information in April 1978 about the ONI file, apparently never contacted them. One question would have been whether the records pertinent to their discussions were held in a separate file with a classification higher than Confidential.

434 As John Newman wrote, ONI and Marine HQ were together responsible for the sequence of events leading to Oswald's undesirable discharge (Newman, *Oswald and the CIA*, especially 211, 247, 552 at fn. 28).

435 Op921D/ck Ser 015422P92 of 4 Aug 60 (ONI-98), referring to phone conversation between Emerson and Parker. Cf. discussion above. The only other such evidence was from an Air Force OSI report on Oswald's half-brother John Edward Pic. It reported that in November 1959 Pic had turned up at an OSI office in Japan, "and opined [on the basis of a radio broadcast Pic had listened to] that his half brother contemplated renunciation of his citizenship" (OSI Report of 27 Jan 1960, ONI-124).

436 19 WH 716, copy to "CMC (Code DK);" see below. In reality there is no such address as "3613 Hurley, Fort Worth." Yet when the letter was stamped and returned the reason checked for non-delivery was not "No such address," but "Unclaimed" (19 WH 716). The fictitious address was apparently created by combining two earlier addresses for Marguerite in the Marine correspondence, "3613 Harley," and "1410 Hurley" (19 WH 674, 675). Apparently neither Oswald nor his mother had lived at these addresses either. See Chapter 3.

437 Warren Commission General Counsel J. Lee Rankin seems to have

participated consciously in this deception. He described this Mail Arrival
Notice and related documents as "all copies of your papers that you [i.e.
Marguerite] furnished to us" (1 WH 221); yet most are clearly taken from
Marine files (e.g. 16 WH 585, 586, 592, 593). Handwriting experts may
wish to consider whether the handwritten Mail Arrival Notice to "1410
Hurley" (16 WH 587) is not in the hand generally attributed to Marguerite Oswald (e.g. 16 WH 583, 19 WH 685, etc.). If so, the possibility must
be seriously considered that the entire "correspondence" was compiled at
a single center, with Marguerite (or someone writing in her name) playing a role as directed. Marguerite herself told both the Secret Service and
the Warren Commission that she was told what to write on the discharge
matter by a Marine Captain in Fort Worth ("I wrote a letter, and was told
how to write the letter;" 16 WH 735; 1 WH 220). Cf. 19 WH 715, 673.

438 For more extended discussion of this Marguerite-FBI interaction, see
Chapter 3.

439 Curt Gentry, *J. Edgar Hoover: The Man Who Kept the Secrets* (New York:
Norton, 1991), 313. Cf. Athan G. Theoharis and John S. Cox, *The Boss: J.
Edgar Hoover and the Great American Inquisition* (Philadelphia: Temple
University Press, 1988), 210–20.

440 Gentry, *J. Edgar Hoover*, 379; cf. P.D. Scott, *Deep Politics and the Death of
JFK* (Berkeley: University of California Press, 1993), 211–12.

441 Gentry, *J. Edgar Hoover*, 409. McLeod had been an FBI agent from 1942
until hired as a staff assistant by right-wing Senator Styles Bridges in
1949. Senator McCarthy had often consulted McLeod on subversion
matters, and warmly backed his appointment in 1953 to become Admin-
istrator of State's newly-created Bureau of Security and Consular Affairs.

442 18 WH 384–85; cf. 383; 17 WH 707. The relevant correspondence reflects
the tensions between the State Department and its Office of Security,
with Ruth Ulbrich of the latter writing that Oswald "renounced U.S.
citizenship;" and Bernice Waterman of PT/FEA in the Passport Office
responding "incorrect" (18 WH 383).

443 Memo of 8 Mar 1962 (ONI-68).

444 The first Naval Counterintelligence cable of 4 November 1959 (18 WH
116) was assigned for action in the State Department Office of Security to Otepka. By October 1960 the CIA Office of Security knew that
Otepka was collecting information on Oswald and other defectors (Newman, *Oswald and the CIA,* 171–72, 459). As we shall see, material concerning Oswald was in his safe when it was drilled and ransacked in 1963
by his Kennedy-appointed superiors. (SISS, "State Department Security,
1963–1965," *Hearings,* 1235–36).

445 On August 12, 1963, Otepka told the SISS how his Kennedy-appointed superiors had impounded fourteen file cabinets in his outer office, which contained "documented studies on the infiltration of the State Department by Communists and subversives" (SISS, "State Department Security, 1963–1965," *Hearings*, 1781–82).

446 *Dallas Morning News*, June 9, 1962. Otepka himself had been a naval security officer during World War II.

447 Original press accounts reported that Otepka had been dismissed on November 5. After the assassination the State Department issued a clarification that Otepka had not been fired, but charged with conduct unbecoming a State Department officer, and "assigned to special projects" (SISS, "State Department Security, 1963–1965," *Hearings*, 140–42). In the Johnson era both Otepka and his liberal nemesis Abba Schwartz left the State Department. Otepka returned with fanfare under Nixon to a newly created Subversive Activities Control Board, where he received a handsome salary but exercised little real power.

448 SISS, "State Department Security, 1963–1965," *Hearings*, 17 August 1964, 1236.

449 American Security Council memo on Otepka case; reprinted in *Congressional Record*, 1964, 150.

450 Otepka's reasonable and empirical discussion with me must be contrasted with an interview he gave to journalist Joe Trento, in which he allegedly said, "There are no Nazis. That is just the pink, communist method for slandering good Americans" (William W. Turner, *Power on the Right* [Berkeley: Ramparts Press, 1971], 162).

451 SISS, "State Department Security, 1963–1965," *Hearings*, 22 July 1964, 13 August 1964, 1224–27, 1232.

452 Scott, *Deep Politics and the Death of JFK*, 214–15. With acknowledged sources among veterans of army intelligence and the FBI, Revilo Oliver of the John Birch Society argued that Kennedy's murder "was part of a Communist plot engineered with the help of the Central Intelligence Agency" (15 WH 710; Scott, *Deep Politics II*, 34). Some years later Oliver wrote, "It is now clear that the assassination was an operation of the C.I.A., apparently carried out in the spirit of the Jews, who bomb their own synagogues" (Revilo Oliver, *America's Decline: The Education of a Conservative*, [London: Londinium Press, 1981], 164). See Chapter 5.

453 A Marine letter of 29 July 1960 refers to the CMC Speedletter "DK-MDV of 8 Mar 60" (19 WH 703). In fact the Code was "DK-MPV of 8 Mar 1960" (19 WH 719). In the ONI file this becomes "DK-MPV of 9 Mar

1960" (ONI-119, Op921E2/jws ser 0236P92 of 12 April 1960; cf. ONI-120, endorsement of 21 Mar 1960 to Op921E2/kea ser 0628P2 of 4 Feb 1960). It is interesting, but not conclusive, that the relevant ONI documents are from Naval Counterintelligence Programs.

454 Though Oswald defected in October 1959, the CIA 201 file on him was inexplicably not opened until December 9, 1960 (Newman, *Oswald and the CIA*, 168–77, 463). The Fain report of May 1960, reaching ONI the same month, was recorded as sent the same month to the Ninth Naval District, under serial "014167P92 of May 60" (ONI-103). But serial 014167P92 was mysteriously delayed for six months, until November 15, 1960, during which time a simple five-line message was typed and retyped a total of six times (ONI-94). In the end this serial was sent to the Ninth Naval District with no attachments; the May 1960 Fain report was sent, also under serial 014167P92 of November 15, to the Eighth Naval District in New Orleans (ONI-96). DIO 9th ND then shifted its Oswald records to DIO 8th ND on November 30 (ONI-92). DIO 8th ND sent a message to the Dallas FBI on January 11, 1961, causing the opening of a Dallas FBI file on Oswald the same month (Newman, *Oswald and the CIA*, 212). In February the FBI agent in charge of the new Dallas Oswald file wrote to the FBI in New Orleans, which became the first item in a new FBI Oswald file in New Orleans (Newman 213).

455 This comment is written on the New Orleans FBI serial 100-16601-1. It is addressed to FBI Agent John Quigley, the same agent who three years later would interview Oswald in a New Orleans jail. Quigley promptly did make contact with the New Orleans ONI office, whose letter to Dallas six weeks earlier had led to the opening of FBI files on Oswald in Dallas and New Orleans. The Quigley-Oswald interview of August 1963 led to a resumed Quigley-ONI contact, while a second Oswald interview the same day was relayed to the 112th Army Military Intelligence Group (Scott, *Deep Politics and the Death of JFK*, 258).

456 The Warren Commission staff probably considered the State Department the most compliant to their record requests, since by June 4, 1964, State had delivered over 442 Oswald records from thirteen different files (18 WH 327, 329). Yet an important letter of 10/25/60 mentioning Lee Harvey Oswald, from the State Department's Director of Intelligence and Research (suggestive of a fourteenth file with yet more INR records) was not submitted (cf. Newman, *Oswald and the CIA*, 458). This letter, concerning defectors, refers to "informal inquiries . . . from the White House Staff." Otepka told the SISS that data in his safe on Oswald was part of a special defector file which he was later told had been supplied to Mr. Thomas Ehrlich of

the Legal Adviser's Office in State (SISS, "State Department Security, 1963–1965," *Hearings*, 1235–36). Abram Chayes, the Legal Adviser, testified in Ehrlich's presence to the Warren Commission that he thought they now had all of State's Oswald documents (5 WH 345). Yet Otepka's defector file was neither mentioned nor passed on to them.

457 Theoharis and Cox, *The Boss*, 210.

458 *New York Times*, May 21, 1961, 54. After the five-day school, which opened on August 29, 1960, three naval enlisted men from the Great Lakes Naval Training Center went into the community for the next six months, showing the propaganda film "Operation Abolition." An office for the Education for American Security was maintained at the Glenview Naval Air Station, whose commander, Capt. Isaiah Hampton, made clear his support as a "Texas conservative.". See Irwin Suall, *The American Ultras; The Extreme Right and the Military-Industrial Complex* (New York: League for Industrial Democracy, 1962), 7–9, 23.

459 Sara Diamond, *Spiritual Warfare: The Politics of the Christian Right* (Boston, MA: South End Press, 1989), 189–91.

460 "Inventory Of The Jack Mabley Papers, 1937–2003," The Newberry Library, Chicago, http://mms.newberry.org/xml/xml_files/Mabley.xml. The Javk Mabley Papers cover among other matters "the Richard Cain case" (Mabley "defended convicted police and mob figure Richard Cain"). One of the scandals of Chicago in this period was that Cook County Sheriff Richard B. Ogilvie, elected on a reform program, hired Cain to be his chief investigator. In his book *C-1 and the Chicago Mob* ([United States]: Xlibris, 2014), QQ, former FBI agent Vincent Inserra, who knew all three men, speculates that "Mabley may have persuaded Ogilvie to hire Cain."

461 FBI HQ 105-93264-3, NARA #124-90059-10087 SAC Chicago to Director, 2-17-61: "CIA on 2-10-61 advised that subject is not connected with CIA or FRD;" FBI HQ 105-93264-3, NARA #124-90059-10111: SAC Chicago LHM of 11/02/60, 3 ("Army Military Intelligence officer").

462 FBI Teletype of November 1, 1960, NARA #124-90059-10079. Cf. 10 AH 173.

463 *Nation*, June 30, 1962, 571. Skousen was also on the John Birch Society's Speakers Bureau, and the Advisory Board of the American Committee to Free Cuba (for more on which see Scott, *Deep Politics and the Death of JFK*, 265, 373).

464 After Senator Thurmond, a hawk, asked to obtain a copy, Fulbright put the memo into the *Congressional Record*, August 2, 1961. In November 1961 the President publicly attacked those who "object quite rightly

to politics intruding on the military—but . . . are very anxious for the military to engage in their kind of politics" (Arthur Schlesinger, Jr., *Robert Kennedy and His Times*, [New York: Ballantine Books, 1978], 485; cf. Arthur M. Schlesinger, Jr., *A Thousand Days; John F. Kennedy in the White House* [Boston: Houghton Mifflin, 1965], 751–53).

465 Suall, *The American Ultras*, 23.

466 Arthur Schlesinger, Jr., *A Thousand Days*, 754. Before Jackson's appearance, Patrick Frawley of Eversharp Corporation, one of Schwarz's leading backers, obtained an interview with Jackson's employer Henry Luce. Later, so did Schwarz (*Nation*, June 30, 1962, 576). For more on Jackson, *Life*, and the Kennedy assassination, see Peter Dale Scott, *Deep Politics and the Death of JFK*, 55–56, 117.

467 When the Kennedy Justice Department prosecuted Gen. Walker for his role in the Ole Miss riots of 1962, Walker was initially represented by Robert Morris, who described Walker as "The United States' first political prisoner." See Bill Minutaglio and Steven L. Davis, *Dallas 1963: The Road to the Kennedy Assassination* (John Murray, 2013), pp. 160, 176; cf. FBI LHM of October 10, 1962, https://www.maryferrell.org/mffweb/archive/viewer/showDoc.do?mode=searchResult&absPageId=1518261.

468 Turner, *Power on the Right*, 203.

469 Group Research Report of May 25, 1962; quoted by Sara Diamond, *Roads to Dominion: Right-Wing Movements and Political Power in the United States* (New York: Guilford Press, 1995), 322n54.

470 In 1967 Otepka was the hero of a film produced by the Liberty Lobby, "which cast the witch-hunter as himself the victim of a communist-liberal conspiracy" (Turner, *Power on the Right*, 161).

471 Turner, *Power on the Right*, 204. In 1975 Ward teamed up with veteran right-winger Phyllis Schlafly to write a conservative attack on Henry Kissinger, *Kissinger on the Couch* (New York: Arlington House, 1975).

472 In 1961 the John Birch Society had attempted to mount a national protest in support of Senator Thurmond's charge that Senator Fulbright and Defense Secretary McNamara had "muzzled the military" (J. Allen Broyles, *The John Birch Society: anatomy of a protest* [Boston: Beacon Press, 1966], 105).

473 Oliver, *America's Decline*, back cover, 329, 331.

474 Notarized statement of April 10, 1963 to Miami PD Detective Sergeant C.H. Sapp from Detective Lochart F. Gracey, Jr., transmitting his informant's account of COF meeting in New Orleans, April 4–6. See below. Quoted in Dick Russell, *The Man Who Knew Too Much* (New York: Carroll & Graf/ Richard Gallen, 1992), 299; cf. 687 (Oliver as

featured speaker). At this meeting the racist Joseph Milteer renewed his friendship with Willie Somersett; in early November Milteer correctly warned Somersett of a plot to kill the President "from an office building with a high-powered rifle" (Russell, 547–52, 687; Scott, *Deep Politics and the Death of JFK*, 49–51). Milteer was an organizer for the Constitution Party, with links to General Walker, and of the Klan-linked National States Rights Party (Russell, 547–48). On November 15, 1963, the Secret Service heard from FBI Headquarters about an arrested member of the Ku Klux Klan, whose "sources have told him that a militant group of the National States Rights Party plans to assassinate the President and other high-level officials" (17 WH 566; Russell, 551). The Secret Service also heard in October that another former Klan and NSRP member [Norman Lee Elkins] had with his friends "something planned to embarrass President Kennedy during his visit to Dallas" (17 WH 540; cf. 17 WH 821, 25 WH 856).

475 *American Opinion*, March 1964, 1; reprinted at 20 WH 694; cf. 20 WH 731–32.

476 15 WH 724, 718. More candidly articulate than most of his colleagues, Oliver reflected the elite-populist intelligence antagonism in his writings. Having heard from some intelligence source of the Kennedy AMTRUNK operation, Oliver wrote that "Kennedy and Khrushchev were planning to stage . . . a fake revolt' against Castro;" and he predicted that "the *New York Times*, the State Department, the Central Intelligence Agency, and our other domestic enemies could swear once again that the vicious criminal was an 'agrarian reformer'" (20 WH 726).

477 Scott, *Deep Politics and the Death of JFK*, 213–16.

478 For example, Oliver alleged that the Warren Commission would conceal an alleged Ruby trip to Cuba in 1962 to visit someone called "Praskin" (20 WH 734, 747; 26 WH 408). This was a false rumor, circulated by Manuel Salvat and Jose Antonio Gonzalez Lanusa of the CIA-backed Cuban exile group DRE, and brought to the attention of the Secret Service by F.X. Wattersen of the State Department Security Office (26 WH 607–14). Subsequently the DRE brought the story to a Cuban-American investigator, Albert Tarabochia, working in Miami for the Senate Internal Security Subcommittee (9 AH 170). A version of the story was repeated by Frank Sturgis in 1977 (*High Times*, April 1977), before the story was conclusively laid to rest by the HSCA (9 AH 170–72) in 1979. Frank Capell published this rumor on January 15, 1964, nine days before the DRE gave it to Al Tarabochia of the SISS (20 WH 746; 9 AH 170).

479 Oliver also attacked the "bizarre gang" of the CIA (20 WH 732), and "the

unspeakable Yarmolinsky-McNamara gang in the Pentagon," installed by Kennedy "to demoralize and subvert our armed forces and to sabotage our military installations and equipment" (20 WH 724). Deputy Undersecretary Yarmolinsky was the senior DOD civilian at the all-night meeting to which the hastily-prepared ONI "file on Oswald" was delivered, along with Fred Dutton, Abba Schwartz and Abram Chayes from State, and John McNaughton (ONI-256). All three men from State were Kennedy-appointed liberals who had been discussed extensively, and negatively, in Sourwine's SISS Hearings.

480 *Herald of Freedom*, January 17, 1964; reprinted at 20 WH 746. According to Capell, "This was done by order of and under the authority of [Sourwine's target] Abba Schwartz. . . . Within minutes after the word was received of the arrest of Oswald for the assassination of the President, Abba Schwartz was seen hurrying to remove the file on Lee H. Oswald." Quizzed on these points by Sourwine, Schwartz confirmed that he did bring the file to his office on that day, and "immediately took it to [Undersecretary] Ball" (SISS, "State Department Security, 1963–1965," Hearings, 1230). He denied any prior knowledge of Oswald's passport case (1231).

481 *Congressional Record*, December 4, 1963, Vol. 189, No. 197; reprinted at 20 WH 736.

482 *Congressional Record*, December 4, 1963, Vol. 189, No. 197; citing *Washington Post*, December 1, 1963; all reprinted at 20 WH 736.

483 Melvin A. Goodman, *National Insecurity: The Cost of American Militarism* (San Francisco: City Lights Books, 2013), 31.

484 Robert Dallek, *Camelot's Court: Inside the Kennedy White House* (New York: HarperCollins, 2013), 331.

485 Dallek, *Camelot's Court*, 359–60.

486 For the details, see James W. Douglass, *JFK and the Unspeakable: Why He Died and Why It Matters* (Maryknoll, NY: Orbis Books, 2008), 338–50.

487 Arthur M. Schlesinger, Jr., *Robert Kennedy and His Times* (New York: Ballantine Books, 1979), 341–50; cf. Taylor Branch, *At Canaan's Edge: America in the King Years, 1965–68* (New York: Simon & Schuster, 2006).

488 Richard D. Mahoney, *Sons & Brothers: The Days of Jack and Bobby Kennedy* (New York: Arcade, 1999), 186, 188.

489 Cf. Kevin Coogan, "The Defenders of the American Constitution and the League of Empire Loyalists: the First Postwar Anglo-American Revolts Against the 'One World Order," www.iisg.nl/research/coogan.doc.

490 Anthony Summers, *Conspiracy* (New York: McGraw-Hill, 1980), 429.

491 Harold Weisberg, *Frame-Up: The Assassination of Martin Luther King* (New York: Skyhorse, 1913); Peter Dale Scott, *Deep Politics and the Death of JFK* (Berkeley: University of California Press, 1998), 49–52.

492 Somersett report of Milteer interview, 11/23/63, as transcribed by Intelligence Unit of Miami Police Department, 11/26/63; quoted in Dick Russell, *The Man Who Knew Too Much* (New York: Carroll & Graf/ Richard Gallen, 1992), 551.

493 Henry Kissinger in particular was also hated and accused of treason. Meanwhile, "Documents reveal Mr. Kissinger's chilling insight that government budget-crunchers would prefer complete nuclear warfare because it was already planned for and would be cheaper than recasting American capabilities to permit limited strikes. 'They believe in assured destruction because it guarantees the smallest expenditure,' he said in August 1973 at a National Security Council meeting in the White House Situation Room. 'To have the only option that of killing 80 million people is the height of immorality.' The papers show Mr. Kissinger struggling with a reluctant military and intelligence apparatus to sell them on the idea of limited nuclear strikes" (*New York Times*, 11/25/05).

494 Taped conversation between Joseph Milteer and Miami Police informant William Somersett, https://www.maryferrell.org/wiki/index.php/Transcript_of_Milteer-Somersett_Tape. Text in Peter Dale Scott, Paul L. Hoch, and Russell Stetler (eds), *The Assassinations: Dallas and Beyond* (New York: Random House, 1976), 124ss; 3 AH 448. Cf. Russell, *The Man Who Knew Too Much*, 549ss.

495 David Boylan, "A League of Their Own: A Look Inside the Christian Defense League," Cuban Information Archives, http://www.cuban-exile.com/doc_026-050/doc0046.html.

496 Report of Detective Lochart F. Gracey, Jr. to Detect Sergeant C.H. Sapp and State Attorney Richard E. Gerstein (April 10, 1963), available at http://jfk.hood.edu/Collection/Weisberg%20Subject%20Index%20Files/M%20Disk/Milteer%20J%20A/Item%2009.pdf; cf. Scott, *Deep Politics*, 49–50.

497 Stuart Wexler and Larry Hancock, *The Awful Grace of God: Religious terrorism, white supremacy, and the unsolved murder of Martin Luther King Jr.* (Berkeley: Counterpoint, 2012), 79; quoting from Boylan, "A League of Their Own."

498 Scott, Hoch, and Stetler, *The Assassinations*, 127; 3 AH 450; Scott, *Deep Politics*, 51.

499 Somersett report of Milteer interview, 11/23/63, as transcribed by

Intelligence Unit of Miami Police Department, 11/26/63; quoted in Dan Christensen, *Miami Magazine*, September 1976, http://cuban-exile.com/doc_101-125/doc0122.html.

500 Russell, *The Man Who Knew Too Much*, 551–52.

501 "Telephone Conversation between Mr. Colby and Mrs. Clare Boothe Luce," CIA Transcript, NARA #104-10322-10287. The conversation took place in the midst of the potentially explosive Church Committee investigation of the performance of intelligence agencies on the Kennedy assassination. (Six days later, Colby was fired from his post.)

502 18 WH 534. Walthers' source was his mother-in-law, who lived next door on the same street (Larry J Hancock, *Someone Would Have Talked: Documented! The Assassination of John F. Kennedy and the Conspiracy to Mislead History* [Southlake, TX: JFK Lancer Productions & Publications, 2006], 67–68).

503 Dallas FBI AIRTEL of 11/22/75, NARA #124-10370-10030. Cf. Scott, *Deep Politics II* (reprinted as *Oswald, Mexico, and Deep Politics* [New York: Skyhorse, 2013]), 112–15.

504 10 AH 99. Somersett himself reported his understanding from Milteer that "probably in New Orleans or in Miami, maybe N.Y., maybe Chicago that the agreement was reached to infiltrate this [group] unbeknown to them, and to agitate the killing." Wilson and Harber, as it happens, were based in Miami, and Sierra and his cohorts in Chicago.

505 CIA Cable WAVE 8130 of 24 Nov 63; NARA #104-10429-10231, #104-10015-10085; P.D. Scott, *Deep Politics II*, 114. (My copy was almost illegible; and I misread the asset's cryptonym as AMTHOP-2.) AMTAUP-2 is identified by Bill Simpich as JURE Executive Committee member Ernesto Alanis Angulo; see Bill Simpich, *State Secret*, Chapter 3, endnote 17, https://www.maryferrell.org/mffweb/archive/viewer/showDoc.do?mode=searchResult&docId=146590.

506 Cf. Scott, *Deep Politics*, 89–90, 329–30.

507 Somersett report of Milteer interview, 11/23/63, as transcribed by Intelligence Unit of Miami Police Department, 11/26/63; quoted in Russell, *The Man Who Knew Too Much*, 551; Dan Christensen, *Miami Magazine*, September 1976, http://cuban-exile.com/doc_101-125/doc0122.html.

508 *The Thunderbolt*, January 1964, p. 1.

509 26 WH 441; cf. AR 133, 3 AH 372. The story was investigated by the Secret Service until November 30, when the investigation was taken over by the FBI. On that day Chicago FBI agent Walter Rogers reported that according to Echevarria's father, an FBI informant, Homer had stated

that because of the death of JFK, "democracy has lost a great champion" (NARA #124-10027-10044; FBI 62-109060-1581).

510 Anthony Summers, *Not in Your Lifetime* (New York: Marlowe and Co., 1998), 311.

511 House Select Committee on Assassinations, Appendix X, 10 AH 95–101.

512 Somersett report of Milteer interview, 11/23/63, as transcribed by Intelligence Unit of Miami Police Department, 11/26/63, p. 1.

513 Somersett report of Milteer interview, 11/23/63, as transcribed by Intelligence Unit of Miami Police Department, 11/26/63, pp. 10, 2; cf. p. 1.

514 Somersett report of Milteer interview, 11/23/63, as transcribed by Intelligence Unit of Miami Police Department, 11/26/63, pp. 10, 2; cf. p. 1.

515 Scott, *Deep Politics*, 214, 215, 361–62. Among del Valle's associates there were many who became associated with the JFK assassination story, notably Frank Capell, Charles Willoughby, and Herman Kimsey.

516 Ezra Pound, while incarcerated at St. Elizabeth in Washington was in touch with Italian neofascists through his eccentric son-in-law, Boris de Rachewiltz. Immediately upon his release, Pound came to visit del Valle, before his return to Italy. One of Pound's contacts was the mysterious Jean Parvulesco, who was accused, along with the neofascist Guido Giannettini, in the 1969 Piazza Fontana bombing (Fabrizio Calvi and Frédéric Laurent, *Piazza Fontana: La Verità su una Strage* (Milan: Mondadori, 1997], 108–09).

517 Paul Ginsborg, *A History of Contemporary Italy: Society and Politics, 1943–1988* (London: Penguin, 1990), 334; "La relazione di Guido Giannettini sul Golpe Borghese," https://4agosto1974.wordpress.com/2014/05/03/le-relazioni-di-guido-giannettini-sul-golpe-borghese-prima-parte/.

518 Coogan, "The Defenders of the American Constitution."

519 Daniel Levitas, *The Terrorist Next Door: The Militia Movement and the Radical Right* (New York: St. Martin's Press, 2002), 36.

520 Kevin Coogan, "The Defenders of the American Constitution."

521 A personal photograph of a young Borghese appears in del Valle's book, *Roman Eagles over Ethiopia*.

522 Coogan, "The Defenders of the American Constitution."

523 Drew Pearson, *Washington Post*, 11/24/61. In this column Pearson mention del Valle in passing; his main target was Gen. Edwin Walker's "Pro-Blue" program of right-wing propaganda to politicize his troops in Germany. Walker's principal aide in this program, Colonel Arch Roberts, along with Milteer and Col. Gale, "attended the gathering of the Constitution Party in Indianapolis, Indiana during October 18–20, 1963. Also in attendance were notable right wing extremists General Pedro

Del Valle, Curtis Dall of the Liberty Lobby, . . . Richard Cotten, editor of The Conservative Viewpoint, Jack Brown [who figures prominently in the Somersett-Milteer dialogues], Klan leader James Venable, and Kenneth Goff, Constitution Party Committee member and leader of the paramilitary group Soldiers of the Cross, a Minutemen affiliate" (D. Boylan, "A League of Their Own: A Look Inside the Christian Defense League," http://cuban-exile.com/doc_026-050/doc0046.html).

524 Coogan, "The Defenders of the American Constitution."

525 Lt. Gen. Stone succeeded Gen. Claire Chennault as commander of the 14th Air Force in China, and as such was John Birch's commanding officer. He later joined the board of the John Birch Society. His son-in-law, John Hooker, was a Minuteman.

526 Cheri Seymour, *Committee of the States: Inside the Radical Right* (Mariposa, CA: Camden Place Communications, 1991), 229–30. According to Dick Russell, del Valle, Willoughby, and other military officers "put together" the *John Franklin Letters*, but this claim is not borne out by his citation of Seymour. See Russell, *The Man Who Knew Too Much*, 194, cf. 753.

527 A flurry of dubious stories connecting Col. Gale and his associate Clinton Wheat to the Kennedy assassination filled FBI files in 1964, and were later used by Gerry Patrick Hemming to distract the Garrison investigation. See Joan Mellen, *A Farewell to Justice* (Washington: Potomac Books, 2005), 250, 268, 278–79.

528 Alex Houen, *Terrorism and Modern Literature from Joseph Conrad to Ciaran Carson* (New York: Oxford UP, 2002), 13–14. Cf. Joseba Zulaika, "The Self-Fulfilling Prophecies of Counterterrorism," *Radical History Review*, 85, Winter 2003, 191–199. For my skepticism about the official account of McVeigh's guilt, see Peter Dale Scott, "Systemic Destabilization in Recent American History: 9/11, the JFK Assassination, and the Oklahoma City Bombing as a Strategy of Tension," The Asia-Pacific Journal: Japan Focus, September 23, 2012, http://japanfocus. org/-Peter_Dale-Scott/3835.

529 Joseph W. Bendersky, *The "Jewish Threat:" Anti-Semitic Politics of the U.S. Army* (New York: Basic Books, 2000). 417, 420.

530 Russell, *The Man Who Knew Too Much*, 192–93.

531 Bendersky, *The "Jewish Threat,"* 421.

532 Wolfgang Achtner, *Sunday Independent*, 11/11/90.

533 Philip Willan, *Puppetmasters: The Political Use of Terrorism in Italy* (London: Constable and Company, 1991), 91.

534 Willan, *Puppetmasters*, 38; quoting Roberto Faenza and Marco Fini, *Gli Americani in Italia* (Milan; Feltrinelli, 1976), 276.

535 Jeffrey M. Bale, "The 'Black' Terrorist International: Neo-Fascist Paramilitary Networks and the 'Strategy of Tension' in Italy, 1968–1974," (Ph.
D. dissertation, University of California, Berkeley), 260. A personal dis-
claimer: I was the third reader of this excellent dissertation.

536 Bale, "The 'Black' Terrorist International," 270 (Borghese-Sindona);
Luigi DiFonzo, *St. Peter's Banker* (New York: Franklin Watts, 1983), 152
(Sindona-mob); Anthony Summers with Robbyn Swann, *The Arrogance
of Power: The Secret World of Richard Nixon* (New York: Viking, 2000),
512 (Sindona, mob, and Nixon). Borghese became Sindona's successor as
President of the Banco di Credito Commerciale Industriale.

537 Willan, *Puppetmasters*, 40–42, 91.

538 Bale, "The 'Black' Terrorist International," 186.

539 Bale, "The 'Black' Terrorist International," 186.

540 Guido Giannettini, "La varietà delle tecniche nella condotta della guerra
rivoluzionaria," http://www.uonna.it/giannettini.htm.

541 Thomas Sheehan, "Italy: Terror on the Right," *New York Review of
Books,* January 20, 1981, http://www.nybooks.com/articles/7178: "Later
the [Piazza Fontana] massacre was traced to two neofascists, Franco
Freda and Giovanni Ventura, and to an agent of the Secret Services (SID)
named Guido Giannettini. Giannettini fled the country, but continued to
receive checks from SID for a full year. He and three high SID officials
were eventually jailed for conspiracy in the massacre."

542 Calvi and Laurent, *Piazza Fontana: La Verità su una Strage*, 109; Coogan,
"The Defenders of the Constitution," 8n;" Bale, "The 'Black' Terrorist International," 177; Frédéric Laurent, *L'Orchestre noir* (Paris: Stock,
1978), 193. There is confusion both about the lecturer and more importantly the date. Others identify the Ordine Nuovo founder Pino Rauti as
the lecturer, and 1962 as the date. It is possible that there were two sets of
lectures given.

543 Laurent in 1978 claimed that del Valle invited Giannettini to Annapolis
as commandant of the Central Marine College there. But there is no such
college in Annapolis, only the U.S. Naval Academy, and in any case del
Valle had retired from the U.S. Marines in 1948.

544 For example Italian counterespionage chief and P-2 member Gen. Gia-
nadelio Maletti told a newspaper "that the CIA gave its tacit approval
to a series of bombings in Italy in the 1970s to sow instability and keep
communists from taking power. . . . 'The CIA wanted, through the birth
of an extreme nationalism and the contribution of the far right, particularly Ordine Nuovo, to stop (Italy) sliding to the left,' he said" (Reuters,
8/4/00).

545 Warren Report, 298; Summers, *Not in Your Lifetime,* 170.

546 For their views in their words, see "Major General Edwin A. Walker Society," http://www.eoffshore.com/resister.htm (Walker); Prelude: The Republic in Decline from, "The Anatomy Of A Revolution", by Archibald E. Roberts, Lt. Col, AUS, ret. Entered in the *Congressional Record* by Hon. John R. Rarick, MC, 9 October 1968, pp E8766-E8770.

547 John Owen Beaty, *The Iron Curtain over America* (Dallas: Wilkinson Pub. Co., 1951). A sample paragraph: "Thus President Truman, Ambassador Marshall, and the State Department prepared the way for the fall of China to Soviet control. They sacrificed Chiang, who represented the Westernized and Christian element in China, and they destroyed a friendly government, which was potentially our strongest ally in the world government" (116). Beaty claimed that during World War Two "he was one of the two editors of the daily secret 'G-2 Report,' which was issued each noon to give persons in high places, including the White House, the world picture as it existed four hours earlier."

548 William Manchester, *The Death Of A President,* (New York: Harper & Row, 1967), 46. It was mailed from the Dallas suburb of Arlington by "a Texan" to exile leader Tony Cuesta (Warren CD 1107, p. 1058).

549 James K. Galbraith, "Did the U.S. Military Plan a Nuclear First Strike for 1963?" *American Prospect,* September 21, 1994.

550 Gareth Porter, *Perils of Dominance: Imbalance of Power and the Road to War in Vietnam* (Berkeley: University of California Press, 2005), 15.

551 Galbraith, "Did the U.S. Military Plan. . . ." citing Nikita S. Khrushchev, *Khrushchev Remembers* (Boston: Little Brown, 1970), 497.

552 James Bamford, *Body of Secrets* (New York: Doubleday, 2001), 80–81; citing Donald Janson and Bernard Eismann, *The Far Right* (New York: McGraw-Hill, 1963), 197.

553 For the first viewpoint, see Gareth Porter, *Perils of Dominance: Imbalance of Power and the Road to War in Vietnam* (Berkeley: University of California Press, 2005). For the second, see H.R. McMaster, *Dereliction of Duty: Lyndon Johnson, Robert McNamara, the Joint Chiefs of Staff, and the Lies that Led to Vietnam* (New York: HarperCollins, 1997).

554 "Republican mainstream unhappiness with the Birchers intensified after Welch circulated a letter calling President Dwight D. Eisenhower a "conscious, dedicated agent of the Communist Conspiracy." Welch went further in a book titled *The Politician,* written in 1956 and published by the John Birch Society in 1963, which declared that Eisenhower's brother Milton was Ike's superior within the Communist apparatus and alleging that other top government officials were also communist tools, including

"ex president Truman and Roosevelt, and the last Sec. of State John Foster Dulles and former CIA Director Allan W. Dulles" (Wikipedia, http:// en.wikipedia.org/wiki/The_New_American),

555 The two are Frédéric Laurent and Jeffrey Bale, both of whom reproduce parts of Giannettini's documentation verbatim. It is of course conceivable that Giannettini himself invented the story, and quite likely that he exaggerated the circumstances of the visit.

556 Laurent, L'orchestre noir, 103–04. Laurent transmits a report that Giannettini had arranged a meeting in Madrid between representatives of the Italian neo-fascist party M.S.I., and two OAS refugees in Madrid, Antoine Argoud and Pierre Lagaillarde.

557 Alexander Harrison, Challenging De Gaulle: The O.A.S. and the Counterrevolution in Algeria, 1954–1962 (New York: Praeger, 1989), 6, 116, 121, etc.

558 James Reston in the New York Times, April 29, 1961; quoted in William Blum, Killing Hope: U.S. Military and CIA Interventions since World War II (Monroe, ME: Common Courage Press, 1995), 150. Researchers have suggested that the date of the meeting was December 7, 1960, and that Richard Bissell was in attendance (NEW SHAW/ ALLEN FOIA LITIGATION, 31, http://www.maryferrell.org/mffweb/archive/viewer/showDoc.do?docId=6060&relPageId=31).

559 New York Times, 5/2/61; in Blum, Killing Hope, 151.

560 CIA Document AAZ-22592 of 4/1/64, concerning "Jean SOUETRE aka Michel ROUX aka Michael MERTZ." NARA #104-10002-10042; in Russell, The Man Who Knew Too Much, 558–59. Debate continues as to whether the man in Dallas was Souetre or SDECE operative Michel Victor Mertz. See Lamar Waldron and Thom Hartmann, Ultimate Sacrifice (New York: Carroll and Graf, 2005), 491–93, 851.

561 Calvi and Laurent. Piazza Fontana: La Verità su una Strage, 75–76.

562 I am willing to venture that the only groups these could have been are either DRE or, far less likely, the Sierra grouping Alpha 66-SNFE-30th November.

563 Calvi and Laurent. Piazza Fontana, 75–76.

564 Tom Mangold, Cold Warrior—James Jesus Angleton: The CIA's Master Spy Hunter (New York: Touchstone/Simon & Schuster, 1992), 129, 125; P.L. Thyraud de Vosjoli, Lamia (Boston: Little Brown, 1970), 295–97.

565 Chuck Render and Frank M. Brandstetter, Brandy: Portrait of an Intelligence Officer (Oakland, OR: Red Anvil Press, 2007), 181. After Dulles's resignation, de Vosjoli reported in person to the new DCI, John McCone (Ibid., 188).

566 Mangold, Cold Warrior, 129–33.

567 Render and Brandstetter, *Brandy*, 185. When LBJ became president, Brandstetter saw much more of him. Once at LBJ's ranch Brandstetter "made certain President Johnson knew that the politically correct [Kennedy] solution had failed miserably during the Bay of Pigs and the Cuban Missile Crisis" (Ibid., 231).

568 Thyraud de Vosjoli, *Lamia,* 317–19. Brandstetter's own autobiography confirms the visit, but like Mangold's book suppresses the relationship of the flight to the Kennedy assassination (Rodney P. Carlisle and Dominic J. Monetta, *Brandy: Our Man in Acapulco* [Denton, TX: University of North Texas Press, 1999], 218).

569 Carlisle and. Monetta, *Brandy*, 128. Lumpkin's lead car in the 11/22 Kennedy parade made one recorded stop: in front of the Texas School Book Depository. There Lumpkin spoke to one of the policemen who had requested an ambulance for a man who allegedly (but not in fact) had suffered "an epileptic seizure." This led the Dallas police radio to issue a series of commands opening an "emergency" route to Parkland for the ambulance, leaving the Kennedy car no choice but to follow. (Scott, *Deep Politics,* 273–75). Cf. Chapter 6.

570 Carlisle and Monetta, *Brandy*, 225–29.

571 Scott, *Deep Politics*, 275–76, 287–89.

572 Carlisle and Monetta, *Brandy*, 158.

573 Render and Brandstetter, *Brandy*, 182.

574 Carlisle and Monetta, *Brandy*, 127. Jack Ruby described McLendon as one of his six closest friends in Dallas (10 WH 39). Cf. Scott, *Deep Politics,* 127, 227, 233, 234, 358, 363. There has long been speculation that McLendon, on his mysterious visit to Mexico in the summer of 1963, might have visited Phillips, Brandstetter, or both men. Cf. Chapter 1.

575 Carlisle and. Monetta, *Brandy*, 333. Some researchers suspect that a primary purpose of AFIO was to counter accusations of intelligence involvement in the John F. Kennedy assassination, which was undoubtedly the primary focus of Phillips's frequent media appearances (and also of McLendon's lies) in just this period.

576 Bamford, *Body of Secrets*, 82. The documents themselves (NARA #202-10002-10104) are accessible on the Mary Ferrell Foundation website, with an inventory and links at https://www.maryferrell.org/wiki/index.php/Operation_Northwoods. For the chief JCS memo of March 13, 1962, see also the National Security Archive, http://www2.gwu.edu/~nsarchiv/news/20010430/.

577 Bamford, *Body of Secrets*, 82–83; citing White House Top Secret memo of meeting with the president on 1/3/61.

578 Warren Hinckle and William Turner, *Deadly Secrets: The CIA-Mafia War against Castro and the Assassination of J.F.K.* (New York: Thunder's Mouth Press, 1992), 84–85, 89. Cf. Waldron and Hartmann, *Ultimate Sacrifice*, 47–48, 391, 394.

579 Memo of 2/2/62 from Craig to Lansdale, NARA #198-10004-10020, https://www.maryferrell.org/mffweb/archive/viewer/showDoc.do?mode=searchResult&absPageId=49636; summarized in Bamford, *Body of Secrets*, 84, and Gus Russo, *Live by the Sword: The Secret War against Castro and the Death of JFK* (Baltimore: Bancroft Press, 1998), 162, cf. 546. As Russo indicates, the same proposals were revived by the military one year later, in May 1963, for Gen. Taylor.

580 Lemnitzer Memo for SecDef of March 13, 1962, http://www2.gwu.edu/~nsarchiv/news/20010430/.; in Michael C. Ruppert, *Crossing the Rubicon: The Decline of the American Empire at the End of the Age of Oil* (Gabriola Island, BC: New Society Publishers, 2004), 595, cf. 598, 601.

581 Memo of 3/6/62 from Lansdale to Goodwin, in *Foreign Relations of the United States* [henceforward FRUS], 1961–1963, volume X, #310, 766–67.

582 FRUS, 1961–63, X, #304, February 20, 1962, Program Review by the Chief of Operations, Operation Mongoose (Lansdale). The published review ends with these words: "If conditions and assets permitting a revolt are achieved in Cuba, and if U.S. help is required to sustain this condition, will the U.S. respond promptly with military force to aid the Cuban revolt? The contingencies under which such military deployment would be needed, and recommended U.S. responses, are detailed in a memorandum being prepared by the Secretaries of State and of Defense. An early decision is required, prior to deep involvement of the Cubans in this program."

583 FRUS, 1961–63, X, #296, Minutes of Special Group Meeting, 25 January 1962.

584 FRUS, 1961–63, X, #296, Minutes of Special Group Meeting, 25 January 1962

585 See FRUS, 1961–63, X, #307, Memorandum From the [State Dept.] Officer in Charge of Cuban Affairs (Hurwitch) to the Deputy Under Secretary of State for Political Affairs (Johnson), 2/26/62.: "The DOD representative intimated by telephone today that the JCS was unhappy about the draft—apparently feeling that he had conceded too much to State's position."

586 FRUS, 1961–63, X, #309. Program Review, 3/2/62. Bamford attributes this restriction to an outburst by Robert Kennedy, which would have

come at a later meeting of the Special Group (Augmented). Lansdale's own review memo (#309) indicates that the restriction had already been established at the Special Group meeting with McNamara.

587 FRUS, 1961–63, X, #314, Memo of 3/5/62 drafted by Gen. Taylor, italics added. Gus Russo attributes the italicized language to the Lansdale submission of 2/20/62 (Russo, *Live by the Sword*, 42; if so, the language must have been in the attachment to the 2/20 memo, which FRUS did not publish). Russo claims that this early guideline "became the mantra for a reckless new anti-Castro program spearheaded by the Kennedy White House." He does not mention that the military option envisaged by this language was immediately rejected by Kennedy when he first saw it on March 16. See below.

588 FRUS, 1961–63, X, #314: Handwritten covering memorandum by U. Alexis Johnson, dated March 16, 1962.

589 Memo of 5/1/63 to JCS, "Courses of Action Related to Cuba (Case II):" (NARA #202-10002-10018, https://www.maryferrell.org/mffweb/archive/viewer/showDoc.do?mode=searchResult&absPageId=48322).

590 Robert Dallek, *An Unfinished Life: John F. Kennedy, 1917–1963* (Boston: Little Brown, 2003), 568.

591 Northwoods documents, 9–10; *Ruppert, Crossing the Rubicon, 595–608;* quoted in Bamford, *Body of Secrets*, 85.

592 FRUS, 1961–63, XII, #189, "Memorandum From Secretary of State Rusk to President Johnson," November 27, 1963; cf. *New York Times*, 11/4/63; cf. 11/7, 11/29, 11/30, 12/19.

593 Cf. Stephen R. Shalom and Michael Albert, "Conspiracies or Institutions: 9-11 and Beyond," http://indybay.org/news/2002/06/131272_comment.php: "The CIA did fake a shipload of North Vietnamese arms to justify U.S. aggression."

594 Michael Beschloss, *The Crisis Years* (New York: Edward Burlingame, 1991), 666–67.

595 FRUS, 1961–1963, XI, #381, McCone memorandum of 11/29.63 of meeting 11/28/63, http://www.state.gov/www/about_state/history/frusXI/376_390.html. Lamar Waldron has linked the arms cache to his hypothesis of an impending "C-Day" invasion of Cuba on December 1 (Lamar Waldron and Thom Hartmann, *Legacy of Secrecy* [Berkeley: Counterpoint, 2008], 36). But there is no evidence of this. On the contrary there is talk of OAS action, especially after "the renewed Russian pledge [made publicly by Khrushchev on 12/13/63] to aid Cuba by all means if an invasion should be launched" (FRUS, 1961–1963, XI, #387). The arms cache was discussed again at Inter-agency meetings of December 10 (FRUS,

1961–1963, XI, #385) and (with the President) on December 19, NARA #198-10004-100013. For continuing CIA exploitation of the Venezuelan arms cache, see e.g. NARA #104-10413-10034, CIA Memo of 1/21/64, Request for Renewal of the LIENVOY Project, p. 5, http://www.maryferrell.org/mffweb/archive/viewer/showDoc.do?docId=5703&relPageId=1.

596 Michael Beschloss, ed., *Taking Charge: The Johnson White House Tapes, 1963–1964* [New York: Simon & Schuster, 1997], 22. Cf. Chapter 1.

597 In May of 1963, in response to a query from the FBI, James Angleton had replied that the CIA had no information "to indicate that Kostikov was a member of the Thirteenth ['wet affairs'] Department of the First Chief Directorate, KGB" (Memo of 9/1/64 to Director, CIA, from J. Edgar Hoover, NARA #124-10369-10063, 51–52). Thirteen years later, in testimony to the Church Committee, Angleton repeated that the claim had never been confirmed (Testimony of James Angleton to Church Committee, February 6, 1976, NARA #157-10014-10003, pp. 62–63). Cf. Beschloss, ed., *Taking Charge*, 22; Scott, *Deep Politics*, 39–44; *Deep Politics II*, passim; Chapter 1.

598 CIA Memo of November 23, 1963 from Acting Chief, SR Division (Bagley) to Assistant Deputy Director, Plans (Karamessines), NARA #104-10015-10057. Also see FBI memo of 11/23/63 from Brennan to Sullivan, http://www.maryferrell.org/mffweb/archive/viewer/showDoc.do?absPageId=235964, p. 17; Simpich, *State Secret*, Chapter 6, endnote 65, https://www.maryferrell.org/wiki/index.php/State_Secret_Chapter6#body_ftn65.

599 Scott, *Deep Politics*, 275.

600 MEXI 0631 of 4/25/62; NARA #104-10408-10233. See Peter Dale Scott, *Deep Politics II: Essays on Oswald, Mexico, and Cuba. The New Revelations in U.S. Government Files, 1994–1995* (Skokie, IL: Green Archive Publications, 1995), 130–36.

601 10 AH 172. The HSCA listed Cain's employer's name in 1950 as William "Buenz." It is more likely that this was the William J. Burns Detective Agency, the firm for whom he worked at this time in Dallas and Chicago (*Chicago Tribune*, December 21, 1973). Also see NARA #104-10130-10130, where a CIA officer in Chicago discusses both Cain's employment with "William J. Burns" and a tip Cain received from "William Buenz".

602 *Chicago Tribune*, December 28, 1973, p. 16.

603 Scott, *Deep Politics II*, 133; House Select Committee on Assassinations, 10 AH 172–73.

604 CIA Memo of August 20, 1963, "Subject: Request for Assistance from Special Affairs Staff," NARA #104-10110-10359.

605 CIA Memorandum of January 10, 1974, to Chief, Western Hemisphere

Division, NARA #1994.03.04.09:39:04:340005, pp. 2–3, https://www.maryferrell.org/mffweb/archive/viewer/showDoc.do?docId=52099&relPageId=5.

606 CIA Memorandum for the Record of September 25, 1963, NARA #1994.03.04.09:39:04:340005, https://www.maryferrell.org/mffweb/archive/viewer/showDoc.do?mode=searchResult&absPageId=545380.

607 CIA Process Sheet for OO/C Collections, August 9, 1963, NARA #104-10242-10014, https://www.maryferrell.org/mffweb/archive/viewer/show-Doc.do?docId=21799&relPageId=2, covering Report from Richard Cain. Interestingly, the Report was sent to two people discussed above in Chapter 2, Sam Halpern and Jane Roman.

608 For the general tenor of these allegations, see HSCA Staff Report, 10 AH 95–103.

609 CIA Chicago Office Chief Lohmann memo of 11/29/63, NARA #104-10408-10040.

610 In Cain's CIA file is a copy of a Chicago daily newspaper column, Maggie Daly's "Daly Diary," published less than a week after the President's murder. The column prints one false rumor about Oswald which we know originated with Cain, and then adds:

"GUN FOR HIRE? . . . The tip on that Italian 6.5 carbine came from a prominent Chicagoan who recognized the gun and knew that the only place in the country where it was available with the scope and sold as a unit was at Klein's Sporting Goods. The man phoned the Dallas police to save them the trouble of checking thru massive records of gun stores throughout the country. He told us, 'It's a wonder the assassin used such cheap equipment.'"

From a CIA covering memo dated November 29, it appears that Cain may have been the "prominent Chicagoan."

611 Secret Service Report of December 3, 1963 by Richard Tucker and Joseph Noon for File CO-2-34,030, Warren CD 87, p. 7: "[FBI] Agent [Walt] Rogers stated . . . that one Paulino Sierra . . . could possibly be the contact for Tom Mosley. . . . There are allegations that the financial backing of Sierra is hoodlum money, but that Sierra has denied this."

612 There were also damning pre-assassination reports on Sierra in the files of the Bureau of Customs. According to the HSCA Hearings, Bureau of Customs indicate that in Oct. 1963 Jose Cardoso, FNU Sierra and FNU Hernandez went to Willow Run, Michigan, attempting to purchase pistols, sub-machine guns, explosives and ammunition to attempt a Revolution in Cuba. He reportedly purchased $6000 to $7000 worth of weapons to be transported to Miami, with

the assistance of Dennis Lee Harber (3 AH 386, 10 AH 99). But this "Sierra," who was called "Mannie" at the scene, was described as 5'9"; Sierra, whom I interviewed at length, was an imposing 6'1". Professing ignorance of the episode, Sierra speculated that the reference might be to a Manuel Segarra.

613 AR 134.

614 AR 236–37.

615 HSCA, Appendix X, 10 AH 96. This staff report, as printed, says that it was "submitted by" Gaeton Fonzi and Patricia Orr. But Fonzi assured me that he had nothing to do with the preparation of the staff report. Cf. Secret Service Report of December 3, 1963 by Richard Tucker and Joseph Noon for File CO-2-34,030, Warren CD 87, p. 7: "[FBI Agent] Rogers stated . . . that one Paulino Sierra . . . could possibly be the contact for Tom Mosley. . . . There are allegations that the financial backing of Sierra is hoodlum money, but that Sierra has denied this."

616 Lauchli had supplied the dynamite for a DRE arms cache on Lake Pontchartrain that will be discussed in Chapter 6. In addition a Miami police report of 10/22/63 tells how Steve Wilson, a salesman for the Minuteman Rich Lauchli, sold to a Cuban Interpen associate named Manuel Aguilar for $1,000 a "crate of guns" which, when opened contained blocks of cement. Aguilar, predictably, went to the police, who were able to recover and return the money within hours. The episode might seem to be pointless, except insofar as it established a paper trail involving Sierra. For Aguilar was one of the Sierra-supported Cubans, and Loran Eugene Hall (who might almost be called a designated suspect) was staying with him at the time. Sierra denied to me that he had supplied the money for the deal, but confirmed that he had been the attorney who accompanied Aguilar to the police station. The episode was revisited by investigators for Jim Garrison, as a result which we learn that Aguilar was a Naval Intelligence operative. See Joan Mellen, *Farewell to Justice* (Washington: Potomac Books, 2005), 280.

617 HSCA, Appendix X, 97 (10 AH 97).

618 Horace Sutton, "The Curious Intrigues of Cuban Miami," in Peter Dale Scott, Paul Hoch, and Russell Stetler, *The Assassinations: Dallas and Beyond* (New York: Random House, 1976), 399–400.

619 Blakey letter of 5/23/78 to Patrick Carpentier of Office of Legal Counsel, CIA; NARA #104-10406-10353. The Blakey letter also requested the files of the two men fingered by Richard Cain in prospective arms purchase in the Chicago area by the DRE: the DRE's military chief Juan Francisco Blanco Fernandez, and Cardosa.

620 10 AH 99.

621 10 AH 12–13.

622 *New York Times*, 9/16/63, 39; Peter Dale Scott, "From Dallas to Watergate," in Scott. Hoch, and Stetler, *The Assassinations*, 361.

623 AP, 5/10/63; in Russo, *Live by the Sword*, 166.

624 Waldron and Hartmann, *Ultimate Sacrifice*, 139–41, 165–69; citing interview with Ruiz-Williams. February 24, 1992.

625 Waldron and Hartmann, *Ultimate Sacrifice*, 141.

626 10 AH 100.

627 Memorandum of conversation between J.H. Crimmins, Felipe Rivero and Paulino Sierra, August 17, 1963, RFK papers. Cited in Arthur M. Schlesinger, Jr., *Robert Kennedy and His Times* (New York: Ballantine Books, 1978), 1057.

628 Paul Hoch, *Echoes of Conspiracy*, 7/17/86, http://www.skepticfiles.org/weird/eoc8-2.htm.

629 Robert Blakey attended a 2005 Conference on the Kennedy Assassination in Washington. Afterwards I sent him a draft of this essay and asked for a response. He replied that he was unable at this late stage to remember the details.

630 Anthony R. Carrozza, *William D. Pawley: The Extraordinary Life of the Adventurer, Entrepreneur, and Diplomat Who Co-Founded the Flying Tigers* (Washington: Potomac Books, 2012), 255; quoting from letter of Pawley to Nixon, April 15, 1963, Nixon Pre-Presidential Papers).

631 Statement by William Colby in "Telephone Conversation between Mr. Colby and Mrs. Clare Boothe Luce at 4:07 pm Friday, 31 October 1975," NARA #104-10428-10224, concerning tapes of Oswald (discussed in this chapter) whose survival Colby had been alerted to by Luce (fragment of sentence: part of sentence on next page is unavailable). By the end of October 31, Colby had been dismissed as CIA Director.

632 Max Weber, *The Theory of Social and Economic Organization* (New York: Free Press, 1964), 154.

633 Robert D. Novak, *The Prince of Darkness: 50 Years Reporting in Washington*, 210.

634 J. Patrice McSherry, *Predatory States: Operation Condor and Covert War in Latin America* (Lanham, MD: Rowman & Littlefield, 2005), 152–63, etc. The Cuban exiles were also deeply involved in the drug traffic, which may have financed the operation.

635 Guenther Reinhardt, *Crime Without Punishment: the Secret Soviet Terror Against America* (New York, Hermitage House, 1952), 80–83. Cf. Dorothy Gallagher, *All the Right Enemies: The life and murder of Carlo*

Tresca (New Brunswick, NJ: Rutgers University Press, 1988). Galante became a major figure in the Bonanno mafia family's Montreal-New York heroin traffic, and in 1962 was convicted on drug charges.

636 *Life*, September 8 1967, 101. Zicarelli was also involved in the Montreal-New York heroin traffic. According to Douglas Valentine, "Zicarelli's henchmen may even have switched sides and served as the intermediaries in the 30 May 1961 assassination of Trujillo, which relied on guns that were provided to the victim's political opponents by the CIA, as part of Harvey's ZR/RIFLE program" (Douglas Valentine, *The Strength of the Wolf* (New York: Verso, 2004), 255; cf. 185).

637 Discussion in Peter Dale Scott, *The American Deep State: Wall Street, Big Oil, and the Attack on U.S. Democracy* (Lanham, MD: Rowman & Little-field, 2014), 31–42.

638 The mob figures in the three murders just mentioned have also all been accused of their own CIA connections.

639 Anthony Summers, *The Arrogance of Power: The Secret World of Richard Nixon* (New York: Viking, 2000), 50–53, 194–99, 213–15, 240–45.

640 Gus Russo, *Live by the Sword: The Secret War Against Castro and the Death of JFK* (Baltimore: Bancroft Press, 1998), 9.

641 Bruce Cumings, *The Origins of the Korean War* (Princeton: Princeton UP, 1990), II, 133.

642 William Pawley, Memorandum of November 7, 1949 to Secretary of State Acheson; quoted in Carrozza, *William D. Pawley*, 176.

643 Cf. Bruce Cumings, *The Origins of the Korean War*, II (Princeton, NJ: Princeton UP), 133, 511–12, 521–22; Peter Dale Scott, *Drugs, Oil, and War* (Lanham, MD: Rowman & Littlefield, 2010), 109–10; Peter Dale Scott, *American War Machine* (Lanham, MD: Rowman & Littlefield, 2010), 55, 80.

644 Joseph J. Trento, *Prelude to Terror: The Rogue CIA and the Legacy of America's Private Intelligence Network* (New York: Carroll & Graf, 2005), 9.

645 See in general Scott, *American War Machine*, 73–75, 93–95. For the role of CAT President Claire Chennault's widow Anna Chan Chennault in helping to elect Nixon in 1968, see Anthony Summers, *The Arrogance of Power*, 298–306. For the role of Taiwan in subsidizing the 1980 Reagan campaign, see Jonathan Marshall, Peter Dale Scott, and Jane Hunter, *The Iran-Contra Connection* (Boston: South End Press, 1987), 54–57.

646 Many sources document Donovan's involvement in the organized opposition to Acheson's withdrawal of support in 1950 for Chiang Kai-shek (e.g. David Michael Finkelstein, *Washington's Taiwan Dilemma, 1949–1950: From Abandonment to Salvation* [Fairfax, VA: George Mason University

Press, 1993], 257–58). In addition a few, in identifying Commerce International (China) as the firm organized to hire personnel for Pawley's private army on Taiwan, add that the firm was "a subsidiary of [Donovan's] World Commerce Corporation" (David Price Cannon, *More Ruthless Than the Enemy*, http://williampawley.blogspot.com/, Chapter 12). I fear that such sources have been following my own claim that CI(C) was a WCC subsidiary, a claim I no longer believe. Cf. Peter Dale Scott, *The War Conspiracy: JFK, 9/11, and the Deep Politics of War* (Ipswich, MA: Mary Ferrell Foundation, 2008), 42; Scott, *American War Machine*, 291n104.

647 Cumings, *The Origins of the Korean War*, 512–15 (Hunt, Fassoulis, and Donovan), 521–25 (Macarthur and Willoughby). Cf. Scott, *Drugs, Oil, and War*, 63 (Fassoulis). Sometime earlier, Willoughby and C.B. Luce had been lovers.

648 Scott, *American War Machine*, 26–28.

649 John Prados, *Lost Crusader: The Secret Wars of CIA Director William Colby*, 50.

650 Tim Weiner, *Legacy of Ashes: The History of the CIA* (New York: Doubleday, 2007), 102. Pilots were recruited from the CIA's airline CAT by Pawley's old ally Whiting Willauer, another collaborator in the earlier pipeline of aid to General Chennault's Flying Tigers (*loc. cit.*, 94). Cf. Carrozza, *William D. Pawley*, 196, 199–201.

651 Carrozza, *William D. Pawley*, 200.

652 Carrozza, *William D. Pawley*, 198.

653 Ibid. Tim Weiner gives a completely different version of the genesis of the Doolittle Commission in *Legacy of Ashes* (107–08), attributing it to the concerns of the left-leaning CIA officer Jim Kellis. I find Carrozza's account far more persuasive.

654 Among the more prominent liberals to leave the CIA at this time was the future antiwar activist William Sloane Coffin.

655 Athan G. Theoharis and Richard H. Immerman, *The Central Intelligence Agency: Security Under Scrutiny* (Westport, CT: Greenwood Press, 2006), 23.

656 Scott, *American War Machine*, 90–119.

657 Cf. *The Central Intelligence Agency: History and Documents*, ed. William M. Leary (Tuscaloosa: University of Alabama Press, 1984), 64: "Early drafts of instructions to General Doolittle were prepared by the agency. The four members of the committee were well known in the agency. . . . Doolittle himself was a friend of Wisner's; Morris Hadley, a New York lawyer, was an old friend of Allen Dulles . . ."

658 Gaeton Fonzi, *The Last Investigation* (New York: Thunder's Mouth Press, 1993), 56.

659 William Pawley, "A Way Out of Vietnam," *American Security Council Washington Report*," December 1, 1969; quoted in Carrozza, *William D. Pawley*, 320.

660 Paid advertisement by William Pawley, "Have You Ever Faced the Possibility That Your Country Might Cease to Exist?" *Miami Herald*, April 2, 1974; as summarized by Carrozza, *William D. Pawley*, 321.

661 Ray A. Geigle and Peter G. Hartjens, *Representation in the United States Congress, 1973* (Washington: American Political Science Association, 1975), 35; Edward N. Luttwak, *Strategy and Politics: Collected* Essays (New Brunswick, N.J.: Transaction Books, 1980), 157–58; Robert A. Strong, *Working in the world: Jimmy Carter and the making of American foreign policy* (Baton Rouge: Louisiana State University Press, 2000), 25–27; Jerry W. Sanders, *Peddlers of Crisis: The Committee on the Present Danger* (Boston: South End Press, 1983), 226, 279.

662 David Kaiser, *The Road to Dallas: The Assassination of John F. Kennedy* (Cambridge, MA: Belknap Press of Harvard University Press, 2008), 160. Cf. Lamar Waldron, *Watergate: The Hidden History* (Berkeley: Counterpoint, 2012), 217.

663 Carrozza, *William D. Pawley*, 244.

664 Carrozza, *William D. Pawley*, 5; cf. 244, etc.

665 10 AH 84 (House Select Committee on Assassinations, *Hearings*, Vol. 10, p. 84). In the Luce version of the "Fernandez" story, Oswald was taped after "Fernandez" and his friends had "penetrated Oswald's Communist 'cell'"—not, as Carrozza reported, during his interview with "a New Orleans *anti-Communist* group." But there was of course no such "Communist 'cell,'" making the "Fernandez" story sound dubious if not fictitious. On the other hand, no one disputes that Oswald did visit the anti-Communist DRE group in New Orleans, making the Carrozza version the more credible one.

666 "Telephone Conversation [of October 25, 1975] between Mr. Colby and Mrs. Clare Boothe Luce," CIA Transcript, NARA #104-10322-10287, pp. 2–3: "He ["Fernandez"] said, 'We had tape recordings [later handed over to the FBI] of what he [Oswald] was telling his group." See below.

667 FBI Letterhead Memorandum of May 6, 1965, FBI File 105-82555-5414, File Section 226, p. 98; copy to HQ File 174-1-330[?]7. Cf. 10 WH 77, 83.

668 Betty Beale, "Clare Boothe Luce Weaves a Fascinating Tale," *San Francisco Examiner*, November 15, 1975. Cf. 10 AH 83; NARA

#104-10310-10080, p. 7, http://www.maryferrell.org//mffweb/archive/viewer/showDoc.do?absPageId=388203. Luce originally told her story to Vera Glaser of the NANA syndicate, but I have been unable to verify on the Internet whether Glaser ever published the story.

669 My personal belief that Geraci may have transmitted the tape does not imply that I think he made it.

670 10 WH 76–77.

671 10 WH 85; cf. 78. The two young men gave wildly differing accounts of how far they followed Oswald from Bringuier's store at 107 Decatur Street. In Geraci's very confused and self-contradictory account Oswald "he crossed Canal Street and he was—he kept going that way, I think on St. Charles or Claiborne—way down there near the end [of Canal Street]" (10 WH 78). Blalock testified that "we started to [follow him] to the corner [i.e. of Canal Street, a few steps away] and we didn't see him, so we went on our way" (10 WH 85). One or both accounts must be wrong, even though both men agree they did not follow Oswald to his address (which they knew) on Magazine Street. As both deponents were "duly sworn," it would appear that at least one of them may have committed perjury.

672 Beale, "Clare Boothe Luce Weaves a Fascinating Tale."

673 Beale, "Clare Boothe Luce Weaves a Fascinating Tale."

674 Beale, "Clare Boothe Luce Weaves a Fascinating Tale."

675 Washington Post, November 23, 1963; quoted in Scott, Deep Politics, 251.

676 Peter Dale Scott, Deep Politics and the Death of JFK (Berkeley and Los Angeles: University of California Press. 1998), 251; see below.

677 FBI Letterhead Memorandum [LHM] of May 6, 1965, FBI File 105-82555-5414, Section 226, p. 93.

678 FBI LHM of October 11, 1968, FBI file 62-109060, NARA #124-10369-10060, 46–47. The FBI investigation in 1968 was triggered by a report, transmitted to the FBI by Bringuier in October 1968, that researcher Harold Weisberg wished to interrogate Geraci in connection with the Garrison investigation (loc. cit., p. 45). Various accounts allege that by the end of 1968 Philip Geraci was dead, the victim of an "accidental electrocution" (Gerald Posner, Case Closed: Lee Harvey Oswald and the assassination of JFK [New York: Random House, 1993], 496). If Geraci, cited by Garrison as a possible source for a meeting between Oswald and Clay Shaw, did die in 1968, he apparently cannot as alleged have died in August (cf. Craig Roberts and John Armstrong, JFK: The Dead Witnesses [USA]: Createspace, 2014], 54).

679 FBI LHM of May 6, 1965, FBI File 105-82555-5414, File Section 226, p. 105.

680 FBI LHM of May 6, 1965, FBI File 105-82555-5414, File Section 226, p. 100. Cf p. 106: a test of Michoud's "security regulations . . . in order to try and make them more secure."

681 Scott, *Deep Politics and the Death of JFK*, 251. An FBI investigation of an illegal arms cache near the camp led to the arrest on July 31, 1963 (five days before Oswald's visit to the DRE) of two DRE members, along with Minuteman member Richard Lauchli, the source of the dynamite. Two months later Lauchli was reported on by ATF informant Tom Mosley, a source in the false story implicating Paulino Sierra Martinez.

682 Scott, *Deep Politics and the Death of JFK*, 245.

683 23 WH 735 (Branyon); WCD (Warren Commission Document) 75, 45–46 (Claude).

684 Gus Russo, *Live by the Sword*, 312–13.

685 That Pawley knew of a tape of Oswald with Bringuier revives interest in the possibility suggested by FBI Agent James Hosty and John Newman with respect to Oswald's alleged encounter with Dallas Cuban Silvia Odio in September: namely, that "Pawley and his right wing allies were using Oswald and his cohorts to collect information" on Odio's left-wing anti-Castro faction JURE.[56] (In that visit Oswald again allegedly talked of assassination, but, in this case, of assassinating Kennedy rather than Castro). See Fonzi, *The Last Investigation*, 112.

686 Schweiker-Hart Report (Church Committee, Hearings, V), 79.

687 CIA Memo of 1 Feb 1977, NARA #104-10273-10288. According to David Kaiser, no one has established the source of funds for Interpen, "but the most likely suspects seemed to be exiled sugar barons like Julio Lobo, dispossessed mobsters, supporters of [former Cuban Presidents] Prio and Batista, and wealthy Americans like Pawley" (Kaiser, *The Road to Dallas*, 83).

688 Hinckle and Turner, *The Fish Is Red*, 199–200; quoted in Scott, *Deep Politics*, 88–89 (Hemming and Sturgis); Scott, *Deep Politics*, 81 (Bringuier).

689 Warren Hinckle and William Turner, *The Fish Is Red: The Story of the Secret War Against Castro* (New York: Harper & Row, 1981). 161. Cf. Chapter 4.

690 Kaiser, *Road to Dallas*, 163, 165.

691 Carrozza, *William D. Pawley*, 256.

692 Kaiser, *The Road to Dallas*, 160. Kaiser's narrative follows closely what Shackley reported Pawley told him, in a memo of May 22, 1963 (NARA #104-10312-10379). But I believe Pawley was dissembling to conceal his own role. Hinckle and Turner report that John Martino "arranged for two ex-CIA agents on Pawley's payroll to attend"

a planning meeting which was *before* Pawley contacted Shackley on April 16 (Hinckle and Turner, *The Fish Is Red*, 170). In addition Shackley's account treats Nathaniel Weyl as someone presented to Pawley by Senate aide Jay Sourwine in a phone call, whereas in fact Weyl was already collaborating with Pawley on a biography (never published), just as Weyl had collaborated earlier with Martino. Back in 1976, one of the plotters, Loran Hall, also told Warren Hinckle and William Turner that "Pawley was conned" (Hinckle and Turner, *The Fish Is Red*, 349–50). In a similar vein, David Corn writes that "Shackley was conned" when authorizing the TILT operation (David Corn, *Blonde Ghost* [New York: Simon & Schuster, 1994], 100). But Shackley was in contact with Roselli, whom according to Hall was behind the assassination effort. I suspect that Pawley, Weyl, Luce, and perhaps Shackley were on the same page: they all had the same anti-Castro politics, and Pawley was close to them all.

693 Pawley's memoir was never published (Carrozza, *William D. Pawley*, 257). On other political matters Pawley was a Nixon man, while Martino, after the JFK assassination, became a spokesman for the John Birch Society (WCD 561.5). Hall and Hemming also had John Birch contacts (Kaiser, *The Road to Dallas*, 161–62). Weyl also had been associated with the John Birch Society, but had reportedly severed the connection by February 1964 (CIA memo, February 12, 1964, Nara #104-10161-10026).

694 Gus Russo, *Live by the Sword*, 186, 187.

695 CIA Memo of May 12, 1964, 11 AH 65.

696 Hinckle and Turner, *The Fish Is Red*, 167.

697 Arthur M. Schlesinger, *Robert Kennedy*, 582; Gaetan Fonzi, *The Last Investigation*, 121–22; Hinckle and Turner, *The Fish Is Red*, 135, 155–56. Behind the Kennedy decision to curb the exile raids may have been the desire to bolster Khrushchev's waning status in Moscow against the rising hardliners, headed by Frol Kozlov, who sought reconciliation with Beijing at the expense of U.S.-Soviet reconciliation (Beschloss, *The Crisis Years*, 583–84).

698 Hinckle and Turner, *The Fish Is Red*, 156–57.

699 Hinckle and Turner, *The Fish Is Red*, 167. *Life* magazine dispatched a correspondent, Andrew St. George, to take part in the March 27 attack on the Soviet freighter *Baku*. (Such arrangements meant that *Life* helped underwrite the costs of the raid.)

700 U.S. Department of State, *Bulletin*, April 22, 1963; Richard P. Stebbins, *The United States in World Affairs, 1963* (New York: Harper and Row, for the Council on Foreign Relations, 1964), 279–80; and sources therein cited.

Although the *New York Times* did not immediately carry this announcement, it reported on April 1 that fifteen exiles had been curbed by the
Justice Department.

701 U.S. Department of State, *Foreign Relations of the United States, 1961–
1963*, XI, *Cuban Missile Crisis and Aftermath* (available on line at http://
www.state.gov/www/about_state/history/frusXI/index.html; henceforward cited as FRUS), #303-04; 740, 746. On March 28, Secretary of State
Rusk had written to the President that such hit and run raids could work
"to the disadvantage of our national interest" (FRUS, #302; 738).

702 Carrozza, *William D. Pawley*, 258. Cf. Kaiser, *The Road to Dallas*, 161:
"Pawley . . . said that he had to continue to use [Martino]."

703 Hinckle and Turner, *The Fish Is Red*, 350.

704 Carrozza, *William D. Pawley*, 264; cf. Hinckle and Turner, *The Fish Is Red*,
349–50; Scott. *Deep Politics*, 116; Kaiser, *Road to Dallas*, 161–63,

705 Carrozza, *William D. Pawley*, 265; citing Dick Russell, "Loran Hall," *Village Voice*, October 3, 1977, 23. Cf. Jack Anderson (from Roselli), *San
Francisco Chronicle*, March 3, 1967; Richard D. Mahoney, *Sons and
Brothers*, 273: "the *Bayo-Pawley* mission fit nicely with Rosselli's later
claim that President Kennedy was assassinated by an anti-Castro sniper
team sent in to murder Castro, captured by the Cubans, tortured, and
redeployed in Dallas."

706 Anderson, *San Francisco Chronicle*, March 3, 1967; http://www.google.
com/url?sa=t&rct=j&q=&esrc=s&source=web&cd=3&sqi=2&ved=
0CCkQFjAC&url=http%3A%2F%2Fjfk.hood.edu%2FCollection%2
FWhite%2520Materials%2FWhite%2520Assassination%2520Clipp
ings%2520Folders%2FKennedy%2520Family%2520Folders%2FKe
nnedy%2520Robert%2520F%2FRFK%25200063.pdf&ei=7Q6DUI_
aKuni0gGMm4H4Cw&usg=AFQjCNHDLCr6j4JRSxXaPA
kId-3pMSI8Xw&sig2=uKJS-RaISi8NyvTjBzsRCQ.

707 Scott, *Deep Politics*, 112–13; citing Warren Commission Memo of April 1,
1964 from W, David Slawson to J. Lee Rankin, 11 AH 439: "The substance
of Mr. Martino's assertions is that the death of the President resulted
from a Castro plot, which itself resulted from a plot by President Kennedy to overthrow Castro" (citing Warren Commission documents 657
and 662); cf. WCD 657.1-2 "Mr. Martino . . . said he was quoted correctly
in the statement that his sources informed him that President Kennedy
was engaged in a plot to overthrow the Castro regime. . . . Martino . . .
said it was the opinion of his sources, as well as his personal opinion, that
President Kennedy was assassinated because Castro had learned of this
preparation for a new invasion of Cuba." See also Peter Dale Scott, *Crime*

and Cover-Up, 19–30, on the John Roselli story in the *San Francisco Chronicle*, May 3, 1967, as "political blackmail."

708 McCone to William Manchester, conversation, April 14, 1964, NARA #104-10306-10017, p. 4; David Talbot, *Brothers: The Hidden History of the Kennedy Years* (New York: Free Press, 2007), 6.).

709 Talbot, *Brothers*, 10, 212, quoting Haynes Johnson in *Washington Post*, April 17. 1981. Cf. Jefferson Morley, *Our Man in Mexico: Winston Scott and the Hidden History of the CIA*, 330.

710 Scott, *Deep Politics II*, 44–57, 61–66, 114.

711 According to journalist Leo Janos in 1973, Johnson had told him that on taking office in November 1963 he discovered that "we had been operating a damned Murder Inc. in the Caribbean;" he noted that a CIA-backed assassination team had been picked up in Havana, and he reportedly speculated to Janos that Dallas had been a retaliation for this "thwarted attempt" (Leo Janos, "The Last Days of the President," *Atlantic Monthly*, July 1973, 39); reprinted in Peter Dale Scott, Paul L. Hoch, and Russell Stetler (eds.), *The Assassinations: Dallas and Beyond: A Guide to Cover-ups and Investigations* (New York: Random House, 1976), 302–03). We know that in McCone's briefing of the incoming president on November 25, 1963, McCone covered "a number of topics, including ongoing efforts via the CIA to overthrow Fidel Castro's dictatorial regime" (Max Holland, *The Kennedy Assassination Tapes* [New York: Knopf, 2004], 82).

712 Joseph A. Califano Jr., *Inside: A Public and Private Life* (New York: Public Affairs, 2004), 126.

713 Scott, *Deep Politics*, 117; cf. Peter Dale Scott, "The CIA-Mafia Plot as Political Blackmail," in Peter Dale Scott, *Crime and Cover-Up: The CIA, the Mafia, and the Dallas-Watergate Connection* (Santa Barbara, CA: Open Archive Press, 1993), 23–27.

714 Robert K. Brown and Miguel Acoca, "The Bayo-Pawley Affair," *Soldier of Fortune*, February 1976, 13.

715 CIA Cable WAVE 9342 of June 5, 1963 to DCI, NARA #104-10312-10361, 7.

716 According to author Larry Hancock, the two CIA officers from JM/WAVE on the mission were William "Rip" Robertson (a controversial "cowboy" who when briefly furloughed from the CIA was involved in business with Pawley's friends the Somoza brothers), and Mickey Kappes (perhaps the future CIA senior officer Mickey Kappes); while a third participant was CIA agent Eugenio Martinez (a future Watergate burglar along with fellow TILT plotter Frank Sturgis (Larry J Hancock, *Someone Would Have Talked: Documented! The Assassination of John F. Kennedy*

and the Conspiracy to Mislead History [Southlake, TX: JFK Lancer Productions & Publications, 2006], 8–9). Bill Simpich suspects that "Fortson" may have been the controversial CIA officer Tony Sforza, who once allegedly said that the CIA "was behind the Dallas plot" (Talbot, *Brothers*, 400).

717 Brown and Acoca, "The Bayo-Pawley Affair," 19. Cf. Hancock, *Someone Would Have Talked*, 7.

718 Talbot, *Brothers*, 348. Cf. Scott, *Crime and Cover-Up*, 23; Scott, *Deep Politics*, 66–67.

719 *Miami Herald*, January 19, 1971; reprinted in Peter Dale Scott et al., *The Assassinations: Dallas and Beyond* (New York: Random House, 1976), 379.

720 Scott et al., *The Assassinations*, 375; quoting from memo from former New York policeman Jack Caulfield to John Dean, Senate Watergate Hearings, Volume 21, 9755. Cf. Scott, *Crime and Cover-Up*, 23–34, etc. The Anderson columns produced a reaction inside the CIA as well, see Memo of 15 February 1972 on John Roselli, CIA "Family Jewels," June 25, 2007 Release, 39, https://www.maryferrell.org/mffweb/archive/viewer/showDoc.do?docId=60409&relPageId=39.

721 Summers, *The Arrogance of Power*, 197: "Meanwhile, Assistant Attorney General Will Wilson was quickly assigned to review whatever the Justice Department might hold on the CIA-Mafia contacts. The Nixon White House, he would later tell Watergate investigators, was hoping to turn up proof that it was the Kennedy brothers who tried to kill Castro."

722 Undated memo from Terry Lenzner and Mark Lackritz to Senator Ervin; reprinted in Waldron, *Watergate*, 731–32. Roselli was subsequently interviewed in February 1974 by Mark Lackritz and two other committee investigators. At the interview Roselli's attorney explained that Roselli "would rather go to jail than be compelled to testify" about his Cuban activities, but the investigators persisted anyway (undated memo from Bob Muse to Terry Lenzner, 734; reprinted in Waldron, *Watergate*, 734; cf. 702–03). Leslie Scherr, one of Roselli's attorneys, later said that, "judging from the questions posed to Roselli . . . the prosecutors felt that the reason why the break-in occurred . . . was because Nixon or somebody in the Republican Party suspected that the Democrats had information as to Nixon's involvement with the CIA's original contract with Roselli" (Charles *Rappleye* and Ed Becker, *All American Mafioso* [New York: Barricade, 1995], 307; quoted in Waldron, *Watergate*, 703).

723 Summers, *The Arrogance of Power*, 198. Watergate burglar Frank Sturgis later told Andrew St. George that one of the motives for the Plumbers'

burglaries was to obtain "a thick secret memorandum from the Castro government" on the topic of plots to assassinate Castro (Summers, *The Arrogance of Power*, 413). Leslie Scherr concluded from the questions posed to her client Roselli that the White House believed that a "document existed showing Nixon was involved with or knew what was going on with the CIA and the assassination of Castro" (Sally Denton and Roger Morris, *The Money and the Power: The Making of Las Vegas and Its Hold on America, 1947–2000* [New York: Alfred A. Knopf, 2001], 307). Massive evidence to corroborate this allegation has recently been presented by Lamar Waldron in his book *Watergate: The Hidden History* (Berkeley: Counterpoint Press, 2013).

724 Summers, *The Arrogance of Power*, 198.

725 Summers, *The Arrogance of Power*, 198.

726 Fred Emery, *Watergate: The Corruption of American Politics and the Fall of Richard Nixon* (New York: Random House/ Times Books, 1994), 191.

727 H.R. Haldeman, with Joseph DiMona, *The Ends of Power* (New York: Times Books, 19789), 68; quoted in Summers, *The Arrogance of Power*, 198; cf. Len Colodny and Tom Schachtman, *The Forty Years War: The Rise and Fall of the Neocons, from Nixon to Obama* (New York: Harper, 2010), 142; Waldron, *Watergate*, 632.

728 Senate Watergate Hearings, Vol. 9, 3456; Scott, *Deep Politics*, xvi; cf. FBI memo of 7/21/71 re Hunt, NARA #124-10211-10223

729 Carrozza, *William D. Pawley*, 255; quoting from letter of Pawley to Nixon, April 15, 1963, Nixon Pre-Presidential Papers).

730 Carrozza, *William D. Pawley*, 235; cf. 229.

731 Carrozza, *William D. Pawley*, 315.

732 David Price Cannon, *More Ruthless than the Enemy: The Dark Diplomacy of Ambassador William Douglas Pawley*, web-published, http://william-pawley.blogspot.com/2009/12/chapter-57-detente-betrayal.html. Cf. Carrozza, *William D. Pawley*, 266.

733 William P. Hoar, "Henry Kissinger: This Man Is On The Other Side," *American Opinion*, June 1975, http://www.freerepublic.com/focus/news/797596/posts.

734 Carrozza, *William D. Pawley*, 267.

735 Carrozza, *William D. Pawley*, 315.

736 Jerry W. Sanders, *Peddlers of Crisis: The Committee on the Present Danger* (Boston: South End Press, 1983), 226. See also Peter Dale Scott, *The Road to 9/11: Wealth, Empire, and the Future of America* (Berkeley: University of California Press, 2007), 58–61, etc. Although not one of the self-denominated neocons, Luce could have claimed the title: in the

1930s she had been close to leftists like the San Francisco waterfront leader Harry Bridges.

737 Carrozza, *William D. Pawley*, 313.

738 A relevant example of a right-wing attack on both the Kennedy brothers and a cabal in the CIA was Paul D. Bethel, *The Losers: The Definitive Report, by an Eyewitness, of the Communist Conquest of Cuba and the Soviet Penetration in Latin America* (New Rochelle, NY: Arlington House, 1969). In 1963 Bethel had organized and directed an anti-Castro coalition called the Citizens Committee for a Free Cuba (CCFC). Clare Boothe Luce was a member of this committee, and according to Gaeton Fonzi one of its major backers was William Pawley (Fonzi, *The Last Investigation*, 321–23).

739 Gus Russo, *Live by the Sword*, 438–39.

740 Morley, *Our Man in Mexico*, 176–77. Cf. also Jefferson Morley, "The George Joannides Coverup," JFKLancer, May 19, 2005, http://www.jfklancer.com/morley.html.

741 Fonzi, *The Last Investigation*, 429.

742 Fonzi, *The Last Investigation*, 53. Russo adds that, at Schweiker's request, "Luce herself contacted 'Fernandez'" (Russo, *Live by the Sword*, 313).

743 "Telephone Conversation Between Mr. Colby and Mrs. Clare Boothe Luce at 12:40 on Saturday, 25 October 1975," NARA #1993.08.11.11:24:15:960060.

744 "Telephone Conversation between Mr. Colby and Mrs. Clare Boothe Luce at 4:07 pm Friday, 31 October 1975" (transcribed from steno notes December 22, 1976), NARA #104-10428-10224, concerning tapes of Oswald that Colby had been alerted to by Clare Boothe Luce.

745 For discussion of this important event see Scott, *Road to 9/11*, 50–92; also Chapter 8. There is no evidence linking Colby's dismissal to the issue of the tapes. However the date of the transcription of the second phone call (from another secretary's steno notes) catches our eye. The date was December 22, 1976, or after Colby's successor as DCI, George H.W. Bush, had learned that he would soon be replaced by Carter's choice for DCI, Adm. Stansfield Carter.

746 Ford was the only Commission member with the poor sense to defend its findings in a book: *Portrait of the Assassin*, by Gerald R. Ford and John R. Stiles (New York: Simon & Schuster, 1965).

747 Scott, *Deep Politics II*, 58–69.

748 CIA Inspector-General's Report, 129, NARA #1993.06.30.17:15:56:650140, 1137; section title cited also in 10 AH 194n227. Cf. HSCA Record, "Background," NARA #180-10145-10205.

749 Fonzi, *The Last Investigation*, 429.

750 Larry Hancock, *Someone Would Have Talked*, 15–18: "John Martino had pre-knowledge of the plan to kill John Kennedy in Texas. John Martino 'talked' in a very believable and credible fashion. At first, he talked only to his immediate family, nervously, hesitantly, and excitedly. Shortly before his death, he talked with two long time friends—part confession and part simply recollection. He made no grand claims, downplayed his own role and limited his statements to things he would have personally come in contact with in playing the role he described with the Cuban exiles whose cause he was demonstrably devoted to at the time. His story is certainly consistent and totally in context with his documented activities and personal associations in 1963."

751 Fonzi, *The Last Investigation*, 430, 432–33.

752 David Martin, *Wilderness of Mirrors*, 219–22. In 1967, after the publication of the Anderson story, Harvey (by then retired) saw Roselli in a series of meetings that aroused concern in both James Angleton and the CIA's Security Director Howard Osborn; see Memo of 11 December, 1967 on "Meetings Between William K. Harvey and Johnny Roselli," NARA #19 93.07.01.10:53:07:500800, https://www.maryferrell.org/mffweb/archive/viewer/showDoc.do?docId=110951&relPageId=2.

753 Robert D. Novak, The Prince of Darkness: 50 Years Reporting in Washington, 210.

754 Talbot, Brothers, 399; Fonzi, The Last Investigation, 385n ("Kappes . . . was very close to Morales"). For what it is worth, Howard Hunt also told his son St. John Hunt that he, along with David Morales and others, had been involved in the killing of JFK (Erik Hedegaard, "The Last Confessions of E. Howard Hunt," Rolling Stone, April 7, 2007).

755 Fonzi, The Last Investigation, 57.

756 Peter Dale Scott, *The American Deep State: Wall Street, Big Oil, and the Attack on U.S. Democracy* (Lanham, MD: Rowman & Littlefield, 2014), 1.

757 For a partial list of anomalies between the JFK assassination and 9/11, see Peter Dale Scott, *The War Conspiracy: JFK, 9/11, and the Deep Politics of War* (New York: Skyhorse, 2013), 341–96.

758 Scott, *The American Deep State*, 31–42.

759 Tim Shorrock, *Spies for Hire* (New York: Simon & Schuster, 2008), 6.

760 Alfonso Chardy, "Reagan Aides and the Secret Government," *Miami Herald*, July 5, 1987, http://bellaciao.org/en/article.php3?id_article=9877: "Some of President Reagan's top advisers have operated a virtual parallel government outside the traditional Cabinet departments and agencies almost from the day Reagan took office, congressional investigators and administration officials have concluded." Iran-Contra

Committee Counsel Arthur Liman, questioning Oliver North, "had North repeat his testimony that the diversion was Casey's idea" (Arthur Liman, *Lawyer: a Life of Counsel and Controversy* [New York: Public Affairs, 1998], 341).

761 Scott, *The American Deep State*, 117–18.

762 James Bamford, *A Pretext for War: 9/11, Iraq, and the Abuse of America's Intelligence Agencies* (New York: Doubleday, 2004), 72.

763 Peter Dale Scott, "North, Iran-Contra, and the Doomsday Project: The Original Congressional Cover Up of Continuity-of-Government Planning," Asia-Pacific Journal: Japan Focus, February 21, 2011, http://japan-focus.org/-Peter_Dale-Scott/3491.

764 Peter Dale Scott, *The Road to 9/11: Wealth, Empire, and the Future of America* (Berkeley: University of California Press, 2007), 213–14, 219–29.

765 Bamford, *A Pretext for War*, 71–81. That COG plans were implemented on 9/11 is confirmed by the 9/11 Commission Report, 38, 326. Cf. p. 555n9 (emphasis added): "The 9/11 crisis tested the U.S. Government's plans and capabilities to ensure the continuity of constitutional government and the continuity of government operations. *We did not investigate this topic,*except as needed in order to understand the activities and communications of key officials on 9/11. The Chair, Vice Chair, and senior staff were briefed on the general nature and implementation of these continuity plans." This constraint on the Commission's investigation explains their failure to find records of key decisions on that day (cf. Scott, *The Road to 9/11*, 212–14, 220–29).

766 John Dean, *Worse Than Watergate: The Secret Presidency of George W. Bush* (New York: Little Brown, 2004), 120. In addition Howard Baker, in 1973 the ranking Republican member of the Senate Committee that investigated Watergate, was later part of the COG secret leadership (CNN Special Assignment, November 17, 1991).

767 Bob Woodward and Carl Bernstein, *All the President's Men* (New York: Simon and Schuster, 1974), 23.

768 Jim Hougan, *Secret Agenda* (New York: Random House, 1984), 16. For more on WISP, see David Wise, *The Politics of Lying: Government Deception, Secrecy, and Power* (New York: Random House, 1973), 134–37.

769 Hougan, *Secret Agenda*, 237.

770 James Mann, *Rise of the Vulcans: The History of Bush's War Cabinet* (New York: Viking, 2004), 142. The NPO was established by a secret executive order (National Security Decision Directive 55) signed on 14 September 1982 by President Reagan.

771 Warren Commission Hearings, Vol. 9, 106 (henceforward 9 WH 106); Peter Dale Scott, *Deep Politics and the Death of JFK* (Berkeley and Los Angeles: University of California Press. 1998), 275–76; Russ Baker, *Family of Secrets: The Bush Dynasty, the Powerful Forces That Put It in the White House, and What Their Influence Means for America* (New York: Bloomsbury Press, 2009), 119–22.

772 This vulnerability was heightened due to the failure of the Secret Service to deploy agents on the running boards of the limousine. See discussion in Vincent Palamara, "The Good, the Bad, and the Ugly," CTKA, http://www.ctka.net/reviews/kennedydetailreview.html.

773 "White House Communications Agency," Signal Corps Regimental History, http://signal150.army.mil/white_house_communications_agency.html.

774 In the 1990s the WHCA supplied statements to the ARRB concerning communications between Dallas and Washington on November 22 (NARA #172-10001-10002 to NARA #172-10000-10008). The Assassination Records Review Board also attempted to obtain from the WHCA the unedited original tapes of conversations from Air Force One on the return trip from Dallas, November 22, 1963. (Edited and condensed versions of these tapes had been available since the 1970s from the Lyndon Baines Johnson Library in Austin, Texas.) The attempt was unsuccessful: "The Review Board's repeated written and oral inquiries of the White House Communications Agency did not bear fruit. The WHCA could not produce any records that illuminated the provenance of the edited tapes." See *Assassinations Records Review Board: Final Report*, chapter 6, Part 1, 116, http://www.archives.gov/research/jfk/review-board/report/chapter-06-part1.pdf.; Douglas Horne, "Inside the Assassination Records Review Board," 1099, https://www.maryferrell.org/mffweb/archive/viewer/showDoc.do?docId=145509&relPageId=1286.

775 17 WH 394–95, 23 WH 841; 17 WH 368, 395. As I note in *Deep Politics* (p. 773) Lumpkin's car made an unexplained stop at the same site, three minutes before the President would be shot there. The alleged epileptic walked away from the ambulance after it arrived at Parkland (Warren Commission Document [WCD] 1245, 6–10).

776 Statement of Special Agent Winston E. Lawson [to Secret Service]," 17 WH 632; Scott, *Deep Politics and the Death of JFK*, 278.

777 Richard Pollock, "The Mysterious Mountain," *The Progressive*, March, 1976; cf. "Mount Weather's 'Government-in-Waiting,'" http://www.serendipity.li/jsmill/mt_weather.htm.

778 Russ Baker, *Family of Secrets*, 121.

779 Dee Garrison, *Bracing for Armageddon: Why Civil Defense Never Worked* (New York: Oxford University Press, 2006), 46.

780 In the 1950s Frank Brandstetter was also attached to "the 488th Strategic Intelligence Team in Dallas, where he collaborated with "oil and mining engineer Colonel Jack Crichton" on "a study of the capability of Soviet oil fields;" Crichton "was later to explore the oil and gas reserves in the former Soviet Union in the 1990s" (Rodney P. Carlisle and Dominic J. Monetta, *Brandy: Our Man in Acapulco* [Denton, TX: University of North Texas Press, 1999], 158). Cf. Chapter 4.

781 Warren Commission Exhibit 1778, 23 WH 383–84; emphasis added.

782 Edward Coyle Deposition. ARRB, 3: All DPD intelligence section officers "were in army intelligence."

783 Scott, *Deep Politics*, 275, emphasis added.

784 Scott, *Deep Politics*, 275.

785 Revill Memo of November 22, 1963, 21 WH 307. Revill reported, and later swore, that his source was FBI Agent James Hosty; Hosty, also under oath, denied this.

786 Scott, *Deep Politics II*, citing "Lee Harvey Oswald" visa application form (25 WH 214–25), also testimony from Cuban Consul Alfredo Mirabal (3 AH 176).

787 Edward Coyle Deposition. ARRB, 3: All DPD intelligence section officers "were in army intelligence." Col. Robert E. Jones, Deposition: "Gannaway . . . could have been a reserve." Lumpkin and an active Army Intelligence officer, James Powell, were in the Texas School Book Depository when a search organized by Revill discovered the disputed "sniper's nest" from which Oswald is supposed to have shot the president (Scott, *Deep Politics*, 374–75, etc.)

788 Hoover memo of conversation with Attorney General of 4:01pm, November 22, 1963, FBI File 60-109060-59, http://www.maryferrell.org/mffweb/archive/viewer/showDoc.do?absPageId=753904.

789 Benjamin R. Epstein and Arnold Forster. *The Radical Right; Report on the John Birch Society and its allies* (New York: Vintage Books, 1967), 208. Cf. Chapters 4.

790 Commission Document 344 - SS [Mike] Howard Tape Copy of 01 Dec 1963, p. 23.

791 Lee Harvey Oswald fingerprint card, 17 WH 308. The heaviest Oswald was ever actually weighed at was 150 pounds, when he joined the Marine Reserves in 1959 (19 WH 584, 595).

792 FBI report by Special Agent Fain, dated May 12, 1960, 17 WH 706. In the same report Marguerite reportedly named Oswald's father as "Edward

Lee Oswald." His actual name was Robert Edward Lee Oswald (WR 669–70). Cf. Chapter 3.

793 Testimony of Inspector Herbert Sawyer, 6 WH 321–22: "I remember that he was a white man and that he wasn't young and he wasn't old." Cf. Dallas Police Channel Two Tape at 12:25 PM (23 WH 916).

794 For a summary, see Anthony Summers, *Conspiracy* (New York: McGraw-Hill, 1980), 109–10. In addition Ian Griggs has made a case that Brennan never saw Oswald in a line-up that evening (Ian Griggs, "Did Howard Leslie Brennan Really Attend an Identification Lineup?" http://spot.acorn.net/jfk-place/09/fp.back_issues/28th_Issue/id_draft.html; cf. Ian Griggs, *No Case to Answer* [Southlake, TX: JFK Lancer Productions & Publications, 2005], 92).

795 Statement of Secret Service Winston Lawson, 17 WH 630: "I checked with Chief Curry as to location of Lead Car [at Love Field] and had WHCA portable radio put in and checked."

796 "The lead car was in radio contact with the pilot car by police radio, and with the Presidential limousine by Secret Service portable radios" (Pamela McElwain-Brown, "The Presidential Lincoln Continental SS-100-X," Dealey Plaza Echo, Volume 3, Issue 2, 23, http://www.maryferrell.org/mffweb/archive/viewer/showDoc.do?docId=16241&relPageId=27). Cf. Scott, *Deep Politics and the Death of JFK*, 272–75 (Lumpkin).

797 David Talbot, *Brothers: The hidden history of the Kennedy years* (New York: Free Press, 2007), 148.

798 http://en.wikipedia.org/wiki/Seven_Days_in_May.

799 Jonathan M. Schoenwald, *A Time for Choosing: The rise of modern American conservatism* (New York: Oxford University Press, 2001), 100–02.

800 Hope Yen, "Eisenhower Letters Reveal Doomsday Plan: Citizens Tapped to Take Over in Case of Attack," AP, *Deseret News*, March 21, 2004, http://www.deseretnews.com/article/595050502/Eisenhower-letters-reveal-doomsday-plan.html?pg=all.

801 E.g. James Mann, *The Rise of the Vulcans: The History of Bush's War Cabinet* [New York: Viking, 2004], 138–40 (Cheney and Rumsfeld); CNN Special Assignment, November 17, 1991 (Helms).

802 Alfonso Chardy, "Reagan Aides and the Secret Government," *Miami Herald*, July 5, 1987, http://bellaciao.org/en/article.php3?id_article=9877: "Some of President Reagan's top advisers have operated a virtual parallel government outside the traditional Cabinet departments and agencies almost from the day Reagan took office, congressional investigators and administration officials have concluded."

Iran-Contra Committee Counsel Arthur Liman, questioning Oliver North, "had North repeat his testimony that the diversion was Casey's idea"

(Arthur Liman, *Lawyer: a Life of Counsel and Controversy* [New York: Public Affairs, 1998], 341). Cf. "The 'October Surprise' allegations and the circumstances surrounding the release of the American hostages held in Iran," Report of the Special Counsel to Senator Terry Sanford and Senator James M. Jeffords of the Committee on Foreign Relations, United States Senate, Volume 4, p. 33 (October Surprise Group).

803 Scott, *The American Deep State*, 31–32.

804 CNN Special Assignment, November 17, 1991.

805 James Mann, *Rise of the Vulcans*, 145.

806 Andrew Cockburn, *Rumsfeld: His Rise, Fall, and Catastrophic Legacy* (New York: Scribner, 2007), 88.

807 Joseph J. Trento, *Prelude to Terror: The Rogue CIA and the Legacy of America's Private Intelligence Network* (New York: Carroll & Graf, 2005), 61. Discussion in Scott, *The American Deep State*, 25–29, 107–09.

808 Piero Gleijeses, *Visions of Freedom: Havana, Washington, Pretoria and the Struggle for Southern Africa, 1976–1991* (Chapel Hill: The University of North Carolina Press, [2013]), 66–68; Elaine Windrich, "The Laboratory of Hate: The Role of Clandestine Radio in the Angolan War," *International Journal of Cultural Studies* 3(2), 2000.

809 Alfonso Chardy, "Reagan Aides and the Secret Government," *Miami Herald*, July 5, 1987, http://bellaciao.org/en/article.php3?id_article=9877: "The group, led by campaign foreign policy adviser Richard Allen, was founded out of concern Carter might pull off an 'October surprise' such as a last-minute deal for the release of the hostages before the Nov. 4 election. One of the group's first acts was a meeting with a man claiming to represent Iran who offered to release the hostages to Reagan.

Allen—Reagan's first national security adviser—and another campaign aide, Laurence Silberman, told The Herald in April of the meeting. They said McFarlane, then a Senate Armed Services Committee aide, arranged and attended it. McFarlane later became Reagan's national security adviser and played a key role in the Iran-contra affair. Allen and Silberman said they rejected the offer to release the hostages to Reagan." [The Iranian was Houshang Lavi, and after Lavi's death Robert Parry confirmed from Lavi's diary that the meeting did take place]. Discussion in Scott, *The American Deep State*, 27–29, 103–06.

810 Chardy, "Reagan Aides and the Secret Government," *Miami Herald*, July 5, 1987.

811 "America's False History Allows the Powerful to Commit Crimes Without Consequence," Mark Karlin Interview of Robert Parry, January 15,

2013, Truthout Interview, http://www.truth-out.org/progressivepicks/item/13904-americas-false-history-allows-the-powerful-to-commit-crimes-without-consequence.

812 Robert Parry, *Trick or Treason*, 175.

813 Peter Dale Scott, *The Road to 9/11: Wealth, Empire, and the Future of America* Berkeley: University of California Press, 2007), 81–83, 88. A key figure was CIA veteran and Copeland friend Archibald Roosevelt, in 1980 a Carter foe and also an employee of the Chase Manhattan Bank. The recently created Federal Emergency Management Agency (FEMA), a successor agency to the Office of Emergency Preparedness, was also involved in the Alpha project (Scott, *The Road to 9/11*, 70).

814 Mann, *Rise of the Vulcans*, 145.

815 Aleksandr Fursenko and Timothy Naftali, *One Hell of a Gamble: Khrushchev, Castro, and Kennedy, 1958–1964* (New York: W.W. Norton, 1997), 343.

816 Ibid. 344–45. Cf. David Talbot, *Brothers: The Hidden History of the Kennedy Years* (New York: Free Press, 2007), 25–33; James W. Douglass, *JFK and the Unspeakable: Why He Died and Why It Matters* (Maryknoll, NY: Orbis Books, 2008), 379–81.

817 Johnson proved more faithful to Kennedy's policy of détente than Bobby feared. LBJ "sent a private message to Khrushchev through Mikoyan just after Kennedy's funeral. . . . "I should like you to know," Johnson wrote, "that I have kept in close touch with the development of relations between the United States and the Soviet Union and that I have been in full accord with the policies of President Kennedy" (Fursenko, *One Hell of a Gamble*, 347).

818 Scott, *American War Machine: Deep Politics, the CIA Global Drug Connection, and the Road to Afghanistan*. (Lanham, MD: Rowman & Littlefield, 2010), 31–34, 175–76, 209–11.

819 Rachel Bronson, *Thicker than Oil: America's Uneasy Partnership with Saudi Arabia* (Oxford: Oxford University Press, 2006), 168: "Afrding of his voice. These Special Agents are of the opinion that the above-referred-to individual was not Lee Harvey Oswaldter a decade of détente, a policy Saudi Arabia never supported, King Fahd welcomed Reagan's determination to confront Soviet pressure more directly."

820 Robert Dallek, *An Unfinished Life: John F. Kennedy, 1917–1963* (Boston: Little Brown, 2003), 570–71; citing Michael Beschloss, *The Crisis Years: Kennedy and Khrushchev, 1960–1963* (New York: Edward Burlingame Books, 1991), 544.

821 Dallek, *An Unfinished Life*, 554–55.

822 Talbot, *Brothers*, 172–73; quoted in Andrew Gavin Marshall, "The

National Security State and the Assassination of JFK," Global Research, November 23, 2010, http://www.globalresearch.ca/index. php?context=va&aid=22071.

823 Peter Dale Scott, *The War Conspiracy: JFK, 9/11 and the Deep Politics of War* (New York: Skyhorse, 2013), 149–77.

824 Peter Dale Scott, *The Road to 9/11: Wealth, Empire, and the Future of America* (Berkeley: University of California Press, 2007), 52–53. One consequence of the shake-up was the appointment of George H.W. Bush to be CIA Chief, where he agreed (as his predecessor William Colby had not) to the appointment of an outside anti-Soviet Team B to reassess (and inevitably exaggerate) CIA estimates of the Soviet threat (Scott, *The Road to 9/11*, 60–61, 66–67).

825 Stanley I. Kutler, *The Wars of Watergate: The Last Crisis of Richard Nixon* (New York: Knopf, 1990), 117, cf. 457–58. Cf. Zumwalt in Chapter 4.

826 See Phyllis Schlafly and Chester Ward, *Kissinger on the Couch* (New Rochelle, N.Y.: Arlington House, 1975).

827 William Arkin, *American Coup: How a Terrified Government Is Destroying the Constitution* (New York: Little Brown, 2013), 34–35.

828 See the discussions of the personnel changes in the so-called Halloween Massacre of October 1975 under Ford, and the contest between Brzezinski and Vance under Carter (Scott, *Road to 9/11*, 50–92).

829 In 2007 I wrote that they "had a precedent: Nixon's secret deals with Vietnamese president Nguyen van Thieu in 1968" (*Road to 9/11*, 100).

830 Robert Parry, "The CIA/Likud Sinking of Jimmy Carter," Consortiumnews, June 24, 2010, http://www.consortiumnews.com/2010/062410. html: "Inside the CIA, Carter and his CIA Director Stansfield Turner were blamed for firing many of the free-wheeling covert operatives from the Vietnam era, for ousting legendary spymaster Ted Shackley, and for failing to protect longtime U.S. allies (and friends of the CIA), such as Iran's Shah and Nicaragua's dictator Anastasio Somoza."

831 Tom Wicker et al., "C.I.A.: Maker of Policy, or Tool?" *New York Times*, April 25, 1966; quoted in Douglass, *JFK and the Unspeakable*, 15.

832 Tim Weiner, *Legacy of Ashes: The History of the CIA* (New York: Doubleday, 2007), 374.

833 Weiner, *Legacy of Ashes*, 376.

834 Hugh Wilford, *America's Great Game: The CIA's Secret Arabists and the Shaping of the Modern Middle East* (New York: Basic Books, 2013), 295.

835 Scott, *Road to 9/11*, 62–63. See Chapter 7.

836 Ibrahim Warde, *The Price of Fear: The Truth behind the Financial War on Terror* (Berkeley: University of California Press, 2007), 133.

837 American Chargé d'Affaires Bruce Laingen had warned from Tehran that the Shah should not be admitted until the Embassy had been provided with a protective force, as "the danger of hostages being taken in Iran will persist" (Barry M. Rubin, *Paved with Good Intentions: The American Experience and Iran* [New York: Oxford University Press, 1980], 296–97).

838 Details in Scott, *Road to 9/11*, 80–92.

839 *New York Times*, 11/18/79; Pierre Salinger, *America Held Hostage: The Secret Negotiations* (New York: Doubleday, 1981), 25. Hamilton Jordan, who was one of those present and advising for the Shah's admission, later gave a more hypothetical version: "What are you guys going to advise me to do if they overrun our embassy and take our people hostages?" (Hamilton Jordan, *Crisis: The Last Year of the Carter Presidency* [New York: Putnam, 1982], 32). Earlier, on July 27, 1979, Carter had commented that "he did not wish the Shah to be here playing tennis while Americans in Tehran were being kidnapped or even killed" (Zbigniew Brzezinski, *Power and Principle: Memoirs of the National Security Advisor, 1977–1981* [New York: Farrar, Straus, Giroux, 1983], 474).

840 See Robert Sherrill, *The Oil Follies of 1970–1980: How the Petroleum Industry Stole the Show (and Much More Besides)* (Garden City, NY: Anchor Press/Doubleday, 1983), 470–80; Peter Dale Scott, *The American Deep State: Wall Street, Big Oil, and the Attack on U.S. Democracy* (Lanham, MD: Rowman & Littlefield, 2014), 27–29.

841 Trento, *Prelude to Terror*, 61.

842 Trento, *Prelude to terror*, 104–05.

843 Trento, *Prelude to terror*, 113–14.

844 "In 1980, Shackley was set on putting his former boss, George Bush, in the White House and possibly securing the CIA directorship for himself. Shackley volunteered his prodigious skills to Bush in early 1980. Though that fact has come out before, Shackley's involvement in the Iran hostage issue, the so-called October Surprise controversy, has been a closely held secret, until now" (Robert Parry, "Bush & a CIA Power Play —The Consortium," Consortiumnews, http://www.consortiumnews.com/archive/xfile7.html. Cf. "The CIA/Likud Sinking of Jimmy Carter," Consortiumnews, June 24, 2010, http://www.consortiumnews.com/2010/062410.html: "Inside the CIA, Carter and his CIA Director Stansfield Turner were blamed for firing many of the freewheeling covert operatives from the Vietnam era, for ousting legendary spymaster Ted Shackley, and for failing to protect longtime U.S. allies (and friends of the CIA), such as Iran's Shah and Nicaragua's dictator Anastasio Somoza."

845 Robert Parry, *Trick or Treason: The October Surprise Mystery* (New York: Sheridan Square Press, 1993), 154–55.

846 David Teacher, "The Pinay Circle and Destabilisation in Europe," *Lobster*, 18, October 1989, http://wikispooks.com/wiki/Document: The_Pinay_Circle.

847 David Rockefeller, *Memoirs* (New York: Random House, 2002), 412–13.

848 W. Carl Biven, *Jimmy Carter's Economy: Policy in an Age of Limits* (Chapel Hill: University of North Carolina Press, 2002), 1: "There were more practical consequences of the Iranian crisis that tested the temper of the public; perhaps the most visible were a gasoline shortage and long lines of cars at gas stations caused by the cutoff of Iranian oil." Cf. Daniel Yergin, *The Quest: Energy, Security and the Remaking of the Modern World* (New York: Penguin Press, 2011), 531: "The Iranian Revolution led to chaos in the oil market, rapid increases in prices, new gas lines, and a second oil shock, and the Carter administration started to come unwound." In 2007 I myself wrote that "By effectively restricting the access of Iran to the global oil market, the Iranian assets freeze became a factor in the huge oil price increases of 1979–81 (and thus an indirect cause of Carter's electoral defeat in 1980)" (Scott, *The Road to 9/11*, 88). It was indeed a factor. But in the context I was arguing that the Iranian assets freeze attributed to Carter in 1979 was in fact part of a complex strategy arranged by the Alpha Group advisers to the Chase Manhattan Bank. Prominent among these was Archibald Roosevelt, a former CIA officer and colleague of Copeland, whom Parry also accuses of involvement in the Republican October Surprise (Scott, *The Road to 9/11*, 91; Parry, *Trick or Treason*, 49, 51, 257).

849 Robert Sherrill, *The Oil Follies of 1970–1980*, 435–37. In like manner, William Engdahl has attributed the European oil crisis in 1979 to the market behavior of BP (F. William Engdahl, *A Century of War: Anglo-American Oil Politics and the New World Order* [London: Pluto Press, 2004], 173).

850 David B. Ottaway, *The King's Messenger: Prince Bandar bin Sultan and America's Tangled Relationship with Saudi Arabia* (New York: Walker & Company, 2008), 41.

851 Robert Lacey, *The Kingdom: Arabia & the House of Sa'ud* (New York: Avon, 1981), 452–55: "Crown Prince Fahad decided he must distance himself from Washington. In February 1979 he cancelled a trip he had scheduled to meet President Carter in the following month" (452). In ensuing months of negotiations, Saudis first increased production in late 1979 and then increased their oil price in 1980. At issue also was

the Saudi desire to acquire AWACS (airborne warning and control system) aircraft, which were not supplied to them until under Reagan (Ottaway, *The King's Messenger*, 42–47).

852 Peter Schweizer, *Victory: The Reagan Administration's Secret Strategy That Hastened the Collapse of the Soviet Union* (New York: Atlantic Monthly Press, 1994), 121.

853 NSDD-32, "U.S. National Security Strategy." NSDD-32 of May 20, 1982, http://fas.org/irp/offdocs/nsdd/23-1618t.gif.

854 William E. Pemberton, *Exit with Honor: The Life and Presidency of Ronald Reagan* (Armonk, NY: M.E. Sharpe, 1997), 156.

855 Paul Kengor, *The Judge: William P. Clark, Ronald Reagan's Top Hand* (San Francisco: Ignatius Press. 2007), 378.

856 Schweizer, *Victory*, 218, 242–43, etc.

857 Ahmed Rashid, *Taliban: Militant Islam, Oil, and Fundamentalism in Central Asia* (New Haven, CT: Yale University Press, 2001), 145.

858 Rodney P. Carlisle and Dominic J. Monetta, *Brandy: Our Man in Acapulco* (Denton, TX: University of North Texas Press, 1999), 158.

859 Milt Bearden and James Risen, *The Main Enemy: The Inside Story of the CIA's Final Showdown with the KGB* (New York: Random House, 2003). 381. Cf. John Prados: "As for Poland, the CIA assisted the underground and Solidarity, but it was not the determinator" (John Prados, *How the Cold War Ended: Debating and Doing History* [Washington, DC: Potomac Books, 2011], 162).

860 Scott, *American Deep State*, 168–71.

861 In the follow-up to that confrontation, "The US vice-president, Dick Cheney, . . . issued a direct challenge to Moscow's sway over Georgia, pledging Washington's support for its eventual membership of Nato, while denouncing Russia's "illegitimate" invasion. 'Georgia will be in our alliance,' Cheney said after talks with President Mikheil Saakashvili" (Julian Borger, "Defiant Cheney vows Georgia will join Nato," *Guardian*, September 4, 2008, http://www.theguardian.com/world/2008/sep/05/georgia.nato).

862 I would like to repeat here my comment in *The American Deep State* on "how foolish, international crises could be initially provoked by very small, uncontrolled, bureaucratic cabals. The Fashoda incident in South Sudan involved a small troupe of 132 French officers and soldiers who had trekked for 14 months, in vain hopes of establishing a west-to-east French presence across Africa (thus breaching Rhodes's vision of a north-to-south British presence). The 1911 provocative arrival (in the so-called "*Panzersprung*") of the German gunboat Panzer at Agadir

in Morocco was the foolish brainchild of a Deputy Secretary of Foreign Affairs; its chief result was the cementing of the Anglo-French Entente Cordiale, thus contributing significantly to Germany's defeat in World War I" (*American Deep State*, 171).

INDEX

ABOUT THE AUTHOR

Peter Dale Scott, a former Canadian diplomat and professor of English at the University of California, Berkeley, is a poet, writer, and researcher. His diplomatic service from 1957 to 1961 included two years of work at UN conferences and the UN General Assembly, as well as two years in Poland. In addition to teaching poetry and medieval literature at Berkeley, he was a cofounder of the university's Peace & Conflict Studies (PACS) program.

Scott's most recent political books are The Road to 9/11: Wealth, Empire, and the Future of America (2007); The War Conspiracy: JFK, 9/11, and the Deep Politics of War (2008); American War Machine: Deep Politics, the CIA Global Drug Connection, and the Road to Afghanistan (2010); and The American Deep State: Wall Street, Big Oil, and the Attack on U.S. Democracy (2014).

Scott's books have been translated into six languages, and his articles and poems have been translated into twenty. The former US poet laureate Robert Hass has written that, "Coming to Jakarta is the most important political poem to appear in the English language in a very long time." In 2002, Dale Scott received the Lannan Literary Award for Poetry.

Scott's website is www.peterdalescott.net and his Facebook page is www.facebook.com/peter.d.scott.9.

PETER DALE SCOTT

FROM OPEN ROAD MEDIA

INTEGRATED MEDIA

INTEGRATED MEDIA

Find a full list of our authors and
titles at www.openroadmedia.com

FOLLOW US
@OpenRoadMedia

CPSIA information can be obtained
at www.ICGtesting.com
Printed in the USA
BVHW070739290420
578625BV00001B/82